The Minqar-i Musiqar

Inayat Khan, Hyderabad

The Minqar-i Musiqar

Hazrat Inayat Khan's classic 1912 work
on Indian musical theory and practice

Translation and introduction by Allyn Miner
with Pir Zia Inayat-Khan

Sulūk Press
Richmond Virginia

Published by Sulūk Press
an imprint of Omega Publications, Inc.
Richmond VA
www.omegapub.com

Originally published as *Minqār-i Mūsīqār* by Professor Inayat Khan R. Pathan Sahab 1912 Indian Press, Allahabad

Cover image adopted from Indian miniature painting of Tansen.
Marbled cover background from Shutterstock.com.
Cover design by Sandra Lillydahl

This edition is printed on acid-free paper
that meets ANSI standad X39-48.

Inayat Khan (1882–1927)
The Minqār-i Mūsīqār:
Hazrat Inayat Khan's classic 1912 work
on Indian musical theory and practice

Translation and introduction by Allyn Miner with Pir Zia Inayat-Khan
Includes preface, notes on translation, introduction,
appendices, bibliography, glossary, index, notes on translators
1. Music—India—Instruction and study
2. Sitar—Instruction and study
3. Harmonium—Instruction and study
4. Tabla—Instruction and study
4. Dance—India—Instruction and study
I. Inayat Khan II. Miner, Allyn III Inayat-Khan, Zia IV. Title

Library of Congress Control Number: 2016914551

Printed and bound in the United States of America

ISBN 978-1-941810-187

Contents

List of Photographs ix
Foreword *by Pir Zia Inayat-Khan* xi
Preface xiii
Acknowledgments xv
Notes on the Translation xvii
Introduction xix
The Topics of the *Minqār*: Part One xxvii
The Topics of the *Minqār*: Part Two xxxvi
Preliminaries 1
- Extract from the Testimonials of Prof. Inayat Khan, R. Pathan 3
- The *Mūsīqār* 8

The *Minqār-i Mūsīqār* 9
In Praise of Mir Mahbub Ali Khan 11
Part One: The Theory of Music *(Sangīt vidyā)*
- Prefatory Verses 15
- In Praise of the Pīr-o Murshid Hazrat Sayyid Muhammad Abu Hashim Madani 17
- Invocation 19
- The Reason for the Composition of the Book and a Personal Statement 21
- Chapter One: Fundamentals of the Science of Music 25
- Chapter Two: Sound (*āvāz*) 30
    - Bodily Sound 31
    - Hearing 33
- Chapter Three: Musical Sound (*sur*) 35
    - Ascent and Descent (*ārohī, avarohī*) 35
    - The Properties of the *surs* 37
    - Chart of the Properties of the *surs* 37

Saptak 38
Chart of the *saptak*s 39
English Chart of the Seven *saptak*s 39
Varieties of *sur* 40
Chart of the Twenty-one *mūrchanā*s 42
Sruti 42
Chart of Twelve *sruti*s 42
Chart of Sixteen *sruti*s 43
Chart of Twenty-two *sruti*s 43
Grām 43
Chart of Three *grām*s 43
Vādī— vivādī sur 43
Chapter Four: *Rāg* 45
Chart of Six *rāg*s and Their *rāginī*s, *putra*s and *bhārjā*s 47
List of Current *rāg*s 49
Chapter Five: *Tāl* 78
Divisions of Timings 81
Chart of the Divisions of Timings 82
Chart of the Divisions of One *kāgpad* 82
Tāl ang 83
Chart of *ang*s 84
Chart of Combinations of *ang*s 84
Tāl jāt 85
List of Current *tāl*s 87
Chapter Six: Tempo (*lay*) 104
Time Measure (*kāl*) 104
Chart of *kāl* 105
Grah 105
Yatī 106
Chapter Seven: The Notation of Music 108
The Current Method of Musical Notation 109
Verse in praise of Maula Bakhsh Sahab 119

Part Two: The Practice of Music (*Sangīt kalā*)
Verse in praise of Sir Kishen Pershad 123

Preface	125
Chapter One: Vocal Music (*gāyan*)	128
Defects of a Vocalist	130
Virtues of a Vocalist	130
The Sixteen Adornments of the Vocalist	131
Types of Current Vocal Compositions	132
Chapter Two: Systematic Notations of Vocal Compositions	137
*G͟hazal*s in Various Styles	181
Chapter Three: Instrumental Music (*vādan*)	301
Detailed List of Contemporary Instruments	302
List of English Musical Instruments	309
Chapter Four: Rules for Playing the *sitār*	310
Drawing of the *sitār*	310
Tuning the *sitār*	311
Positioning the frets	311
Sitting position for a *sitār* player (The Author's Father, the late Rahmat Khan Sahab)	313
Chart of the Twelve *ṭhāṭ*s	314
Ten Types of *gamak*	314
Chart of Ten *gamak*s	315
*Gat*s to Play on the *sitār*	317
Chapter Five: Rules for Playing the Harmonium	326
Sitting Position for a Harmonium Player	326
Drawing of the Keyboard	327
Sargams to Play on the Harmonium	327
Chapter Six: Rules for Playing the *tabla*	339
Sitting Position for *tabla* Playing	339
Drawing of the *tabla*	340
The Syllables of *tabla*	340
Method for Playing the *bols* of *Cautālā*	342
*Tabla ṭhekā*s for Common *tāl*s	343
Chapter Seven: Dance	348
Drawing of a Dancer	348

Tāṇḍav 350
Lās 350
Sukumār 350
Paristān kā nāc 351
The Syllables of Dance 351
"Limbs" *(ang)* of Dance 352
"Filling the movements" *(gat bharnā)* 352
Bhāv 353
The Structure of a Dance 354
Descriptions of *gats* 355
Toṛās for Dance 364
Commonly Used Patterns for the *manjīrā* 367
Final Verse Set of the Book with the Date by the Author 369
Verse Set Pertaining to Date 371
Appendix A: List of Ragas *notated by Hidayat Inayat-Khan* 375
Appendix B: List of Tabla Rhythms *notated by Hidayat Inayat-Khan* 394
Appendix C: Poets in the *Minqār-i Mūsīqār* 403
Appendix D: *Toṛās* and *Parmalūs* from the *Sarmāya-i ishrat* 405
Glossary of Names and Terms 409
Bibliography 417
Notes on the translators
Allyn Miner 425
Pir Zia Inayat-Khan 427
Index 429

List of Photographs

Inayat Khan, Hyderabad ii
Mir Mahbub Ali Khan Bahadur, Nizam of Hyderabad 10
Professor Inayat Khan R. Pathan (the author) 14
The Late Professor Maula Bakhsh Sahab 118
Maharaj Sir Kishen Pershad Bahadur, Prime Minister of Hyderabad 122
The Author's Father, the Late Rahmat Khan Sahab 313

Foreword

As a young man, Hazrat Inayat Khan spent four years in the southern Indian city of Hyderabad. During these years he immersed himself in the teachings of his Sufi guide, Sayyid Abu Hashim Madani, whose spiritual heir he became in the end. At the same time, as a Hindustani vocalist he attained the pinnacle of success, winning the title "Tansen az-Zaman" from the Nizam. It was during this eventful period of his life that Hazrat Inayat Khan wrote his principal musicological work, *Minqār-i Mūsiqār*.

A number of years ago, the eminent scholar of Indian music, Allyn Miner, told me of her project to translate the *Minqār*, and invited my collaboration. Of course, I enthusiastically accepted. My contribution was small, but working with Dr. Miner was an enormous pleasure.

One of the wonderful features of the *Minqar* is the presence in it of seventy-eight Persian and Urdu *g͟hazals* put to music by the author. The Persian series includes poems by Hafiz, Rumi, Sa'di, Jami, Nizami, Amir Khusrau, Bidil, and others. The Urdu series includes works by Mir, Sauda, Mu'min, Dagh, Zafar, and Amir Mina'i. A number of minor Urdu poets are also represented, including such prominent Hyderabadis as the reigning Nizam (Asif) and the sitting Prime Minister (Shad).

Hazrat Inayat Khan's selection reflects his mystical focus. The *g͟hazals* in the *Minqār* are concerned largely with spiritual rather than secular themes. The *g͟hazal* by Hashimi is possibly a composition by Sayyid Abu Hashim Madani. The last Urdu *g͟hazal* in the collection is by Hazrat Inayat Khan himself. It gives eloquent testimony to the author's love of the Prophet Muhammad and his devotion to his teacher.

I am sorry that Dr. R.C. Mehta, the founder of the Indian Musicological Society and a stalwart champion of the music of Hazrat Inayat Khan, did not live to see this publication of the *Minqār* in English. Dr. Mehta always asked me about the project and continuously expressed his strong encouragement. In the annual concerts that Dr. Mehta organized for the Sangitratna Mawlabakhsh and Hazrat Inayat Khan Trust in Baroda, Hazrat Inayat Khan's compositions from the *Minqār* were sometimes performed. My hope is that the present translation of *Minqār-i Mūsiqār* will motivate more musicians, in India and elsewhere, to take up this extraordinary music.

Pir Zia Inayat-Khan

Preface

I first read the *Minqār-i Mūsiqār* at the Raza Library in Rampur when I was working toward my doctorate from Banaras Hindu University. My advisor, Dr. Prem Lata Sharma, proposed to the Sangeet Natak Akademi that this important book be translated, and I was provided a photocopy of it. It was not until some years later that the project got underway after I proposed a collaboration to Pir Zia Inayat-Khan, who immediately agreed to translate the poetry in the book. Over the next few years Pir Zia finished his beautiful translations, and I translated the text and notations. When I again approached publishers it turned out that the editorial costs for laying out the charts and notations were prohibitive. I put the project aside and corresponded periodically about it. Over the years I wrote some articles about the work and received messages of interest and support from all over the world. A couple of years ago Omega Publications offered to publish the translation if I would lay out the notations and text. This gave me the opportunity to go over the text again and to use the sources and references that had since become available. The project has taken a long time to complete, but I trust it will prove worth the wait.

Allyn Miner

Acknowledgments

I wish to acknowledge the late Professor Prem Lata Sharma of Varanasi, who inspired and guided me along with so many others in our historical and theoretical studies of Indian music. I thank the Sangeet Natak Akademi, New Delhi, for initiating the project, providing a photocopy of the text, and continuing to encourage the work over the years. The project would not have happened without the collaboration of Pir Zia Inayat-Khan, the author's grandson and teacher of Sufism in his lineage. His translations of the more than sixty Persian and Urdu poems are treasures at the center of this book. His warm, quiet encouragement throughout was essential to the entire undertaking.

I am deeply grateful to Shaikh al-Mashaik Mahmood Khan, Inayat Khan's nephew, who delighted me with his observations and penetrating insights about the Maula Bakhsh family. I cherish the memory of my time in his and Harunnisa's welcoming home. Many thanks to Hamida Verlinden of the International Headquarters of the Sufi Movement in the Netherlands, who kept up with the work's progress over the years and provided the excellent photocopy of the *Minqār* from which the charts are reproduced. She also provided Appendices A and B, notations of the *rāg* and *tāl* list handwritten by the author's son, Hidayat Inayat-Khan. The photographs that enliven the book were also made available by her request. They were provided by Hassan Suhrawardi Gebel and Cathy Cone.

Many people who have long and deep associations with the teachings of Hazrat Inayat Khan have corresponded with me, expressed their interest, and shared ideas. I appreciate every communication. The Department of South Asia Studies at the University of Pennsylvania has always provided the ideal supportive environment. Warm thanks to Omega Publications and especially Sandra Lillydahl, whose patient labor has resulted in this book. Gratitude to my husband, family, and friends, who have listened to my updates with enthusiasm.

Notes on the Translation

The language of the *Minqār-i Mūsiqār* is the standard Urdu of early twentieth century north India. The author's language ranges from formal to conversational, which I have tried to reflect in the translation. Many Urdu words appear in transliteration, following the Library of Congress rules for Urdu Romanization. Readers may wish to consult audio sources for precise guides to the pronunciation, but a few notes are appropriate here. Long and short vowels are clearly differentiated, especially "a," "i," and "u." They are pronounced as follows: "a" as in "above;" "ā" as in "father;" "i" as in "in;" "ī" as in "piece;" "u" as in "put;" "ū" as in "rude." Most consonants can be sounded as they would be in English. "c," however, is pronounced "ch." The "r" of Urdu is rolled. Consonants with a dot or two dots below them are retroflex or other special sounds. Consonants with an "h" following, such as "bh, dh, ph, th" are aspirated consonants, pronounced with a quick exhalation of air. South Asian languages all share vocabulary, and the same words may be pronounced differently in different languages. In general I have transliterated the words to reflect the colloquial presumably used by Inayat Khan and his readers at the time the book was written. In some cases this differs slightly from modern Hindi, which favors Sanskrit pronunciation over colloquial. See the glossary for notes about the sources, spellings, and pronunciations of important technical terms. Proper names and places in this translation are written without diacritics and are spelled as they usually appear in print.

Inayat Khan notated the songs that make up much of Part Two of the *Minqār-i Mūsiqār* in a notational system designed by his grandfather, Maula Bakhsh. It is described in Part One, Chapter Seven. For the translation I use the notation standard to north Indian music today based on that of V.N. Bhatkhande. Guidelines to reading it are to be found in the introductory sections describing Part Two.

Introduction

The *Minqār-i Mūsīqār* is of rare interest both for its contents and for its distinguished author. Its sections on theory are based on the teachings of the author's grandfather and other late nineteenth century sources. The songs at the center of the book are the author's own compositions, some of which he recorded and are available to us. The poetry collection includes more than sixty choice Urdu and Persian *g͟hazals*. Overall the book communicates the musical learning and enthusiasms of the twenty-five-year-old Inayat Khan, whose personal drive, ambition to engage with the wider world, and longing for the divine are palpable throughout the book.

Orientation to Hindustani Music

The formal music of the courts and temples of the Indian subcontinent, which later came to be known as Indian classical music, carries a long history of changing contexts and theory. In practical terms, it is based on formal melodies and rhythmic cycles called *rāga* and *tāla* (Urdu *rāg, tāl*). Hindustani and Karnatak (also spelled "Carnatic") music are the systems of north and south India, which developed in separate styles after about the fourteenth century. Performance practices are transmitted orally, but a large body of written theory is preserved in Sanskrit, Persian, and vernacular texts. Practitioners and scholars typically draw on both oral and text-based sources of knowledge.

A *rāg* is a set of melodic motifs used for performing composed and improvised material. Each *rāg* uses specific pitches in particular phrasings and contours. Some pitches are resting tones on which the melody often lingers. Phrases are often characterized by delicate slides and tonal nuance. And just as fundamental to a *rāg* as its scale and phrases are its expressive qualities and imaginative associations. Each is thought to express a personality, a mood, and a relationship with the natural environment. In Hindustani music each is associated with a particular time of day and is performed at its proper time.

A *rāg* is typically performed by a main vocalist or instrumentalist accompanied by a small ensemble. The main musician sits in the center. A drum accompanist, in Hindustani music usually a *tabla*, sits to the musician's right. An accompanying harmonium or *sārangī* player often sits to the left. Behind the musicians, on one or both sides will be players of the *tambura* (or *tānpūra*) drone. The musician performs a *rāg* in a sequence of composed and improvised sections whose order and style are determined by the genre. The composed sections and variations are set to a rhythmic cycle (*tāl*) kept by the drummer. Audiences savor the mood of the *rāg* as they respond to the poetry of the song, the beautiful compositions and the extempore interplay between the main musician and the drummer.

In the *Minqār-i Mūsīqār* Inayat Khan has given us a compilation of theory and practice current during his time and taught in his family line. Readers familiar with present-day Hindustani music will find many recognizable terms and some that are no longer in use. The sections below, entitled "The Topics of the *Minqār*," provide summaries of each chapter, observations about Inayat Khan's likely sources, and comments on current practice.

As valuable as it is for its musical content, the *Minqār* is equally fascinating for what it tells us about the writer and the times in which it was written. Substantial changes in music were taking place in the late nineteenth and early twentieth centuries. Public audiences and urban venues were replacing royal patrons and elite settings. Music theory was being formulated for classroom teaching, while hereditary professionals transmitted their own lineages orally. Various urban classes were participating in music. Hereditary and non-hereditary music professionals mingled with amateur enthusiasts. Early twentieth century trends in education and fashion pervaded urban life. Inayat Khan's family background reflects many of the social and musical dynamics of the time. The sections below overview the background on which Inayat Khan wrote the *Minqār-i Mūsīqār*. It was a background of family traditions and expectations, to which Inayat Khan brought his own ideals and formidable drive.

Maula Bakhsh and Inayat Khan

Inayat Khan (1882–1927) was born to Rahmat Khan (1843–1910), a musician from Punjab, and Khadija Bibi, one of the three daughters of Maula Bakhsh (1833–96). Maula Bakhsh, a prominent figure in music education, was a dominant model for Inayat Khan's early career in music. Born as Chole or Shole Khan to a land-owning family in modern Haryana state, Maula Bakhsh is said to have been encouraged to pursue music by a Sufi ascetic who gave him his name: "God-given."[1] After initial training with his grandfather, Maula Bakhsh left home and studied with a prominent musician Ghasit Khan. He then travelled widely, pursuing musical expertise and making a serious study of the music of south India. In the 1860s he spent a year or more as a court musician in Mysore, where he received royal honors and married a descendant of the royal lineage of Tipu Sultan, the eighteenth century "Tiger of Mysore."

Maula Bakhsh settled in Vadodara (formerly Baroda), in India's present-day Gujarat, as the chief court musician of the ruler Khanderao II Gaekwar (1828–70). He had two sons and three daughters and built a thriving household in the city. In the 1870s Maula Bakhsh traveled and lived for about a year in Kolkata (formerly Calcutta), the epicenter of social and educational reform at the time. An essay by him appears in a late nineteenth century compilation published by the prominent music scholar S.M. Tagore. His summary of music theory and endorsement of a notational system designed by scholar Ksetra Mohun

1 Khan, Shaikh, 12.

Goswami was signed by thirty-four performers.[2] Upon his return to Vadodara, Maula Bakhsh created a notational system of his own and founded a school, which soon received sponsorship from the State. Later known as the Gayanshala, "House of Singing," it was the first and most prominent school of its type in western India. Maula Bakhsh devoted the rest of his life to the school. His sons Murtaza and Alauddin, his son-in-law Rahmat Khan, and his grandsons Inayat Khan and his brothers all held positions as teachers and administrators.

Maula Bakhsh was a brilliant and controversial figure. Eclectic, progressive, and innovative, his new methods and his background as a non-lineage musician made him something of an outsider among music professionals. There are anecdotes about rivalries, traded insults, and musicians refusing to acknowledge his notational system.[3] Later, Maula Bakhsh's work would be overshadowed by that of other performers and theorists, some of whom were clearly influenced by him.

Royal connections, erudite music training, and public distinction characterized the Maula Bakhsh household in which Inayat Khan was raised. Musicians, poets, and spiritual figures passed through the home. In the 1890s Inayat Khan traveled with his father and spent a year in Nepal. He was exposed to Western music and style in Vadodara. His uncle, Alauddin Khan, studied in London for five years under State sponsorship. When he returned in 1897, A.M. Pathan, as he became known, affected Western manners and brought ideas of European style to the Bakhsh household, along with a brother and sister who also married into the family household.

In 1900–02 Inayat Khan undertook his own first solo tours. Surely motivated by his grandfather's earlier successes in south India, he traveled to Chennai (formerly Madras) and Mysore. A testimonial written in Madras describes the qualities for which

2 Tagore, 389–97.

3 Bor, 1994.

he was recognized: a distinguished family, education, skills in performance and teaching, and an engaging personality.

> 16th June 1902
> Belmont House Coonor
>
> Mr. Inayat Khan was a teacher of music to my children when I was employed in Baroda as the Dewan of the state. He comes of a family of distinguished musicians, his grandfather being the famous professor of Hindu music and inventor of a system of notation for it as well as the Author of a series of graduated text books in music which are in use in the music schools of the Baroda State. He is the nephew of Dr. A. M. Pathan L.R.A.M., who was educated in England in the European system of music and passed his examinations with high distinction. Mr. Inayat Khan has studied both the Hindu and European systems scientifically and has already acquired great proficiency especially in the former. He has winning manners and the art of rousing the interest and intelligence of his pupils, and my children remember with pleasure the days they passed under his tuition. I shall be glad always to hear of his success and advancement in life.
>
> (Sg) Sreenivasa Raghavaiyengar,
> Inspector General of Registration, Madras
> and late Dewan Baroda State.[4]

Back in Vadodara, Inayat Khan wrote instructional books on harmonium and violin for the Gayanshala along with a collection of seventy-five songs, all of which were published in 1903.[5] With other family members occupying the teaching positions in the Gayanshala, however, he must have seen little career potential for himself in Vadodara. In 1903 he set out for Hyderabad, the largest of the Indian princely states,

4 *Biography*, 280.
5 Khan, Inayatkhan, 1903 a,b.

Stopping in Mumbai (formerly Bombay) on the way to Hyderabad he was reportedly disappointed to see that audiences preferred light music over *rāgs*, and that even people who considered themselves connoisseurs did not appreciate serious music. And music scholars, he is said to have remarked, were hardly better. They challenged performing musicians just in order to prove their own superiority. V. N. Bhatkhande (1860–1936), the music educator whose notational system would later supplant that of Maula Bakhsh, is said to have questioned Inayat Khan about the authenticity of his *rāgs.*[6]

Arriving in Hyderabad, Inayat Khan settled with a Parsi family on the outskirts of Hyderabad city. Known for its courtly and literary culture, Hyderabad is recalled as peaceful and prosperous under the rule of Nizam Mir Mahbub Ali Khan (1866–1911). The Nizam was a beloved figure who is still remembered for his intelligence, dignity and generosity. Socially liberal, he cherished traditional learning and protected Hyderabad's courtly heritage.[7] The Nizam's Prime Minister, Sir Kishen Pershad, was a well-known poet, learned in languages and fine arts. Inayat Khan would dedicate the *Minqār* to the Nizam and to Sir Kishen Pershad, and include poems by them in the book.

Inayat Khan spent four years in Hyderabad and seems to have been comfortable there. He wrote about the city's musical environment in a 1909 article for "The Hindu." In it he named prominent dancers, singers, and instrumentalists. He reported that he performed for the Nizam more than once, spoke with him about music, and found him kind and receptive. He noted, however, that while the Prime Minister and other court dignitaries were appreciative of serious music, the general public was less so. The people of Hyderabad, he wrote, were "musically inclined," but more interested in it as an amusement than as a "science and art." He did find, however, a thriving interest in Sufism and its music in the city.

6 *Biography*, 67.

7 Ahmed, 140–2.

> The *kanwālī* (the philosophical music) is performed more generally than the classical music, the former being performed on the Darghās (tombs of holy men), on the *urs* ceremonies and also in the assembly of the soofys (the people are generally interested in soofism and I have a luck of seeing greatly advanced people) [Sic].[8]

In Hyderabad, Inayat Khan was introduced to Sayyid Muhammad Abu Hashim Madani, who became his Sufi master (*murshid*).[9] He began an intense engagement in Sufi spiritual practices under his guidance. The inspiration that he felt at this time is evident throughout the *Minqār*, and is most explicit in the introductory sections. Inayat Khan completed writing the *Minqār* in 1906. After his murshid's death in 1907 he would leave Hyderabad.

Inayat Khan left Hyderabad and traveled through central and south India, visiting shrine and court centers, and giving music presentations. He spent some time in Yangon (formerly Rangoon) before settling in Kolkata in 1909, where he gave lectures and concerts, and recorded the tracks preserved in *Inayat Khan: The Complete Recordings of 1909*. It is likely that while in Kolkata he made the connections that resulted in the publication of the *Minqār*. He spent some time in Murshidabad and in Sylhet (present-day Bangladesh) before returning to Baroda and leaving for the United States in 1910.[10]

The *Minqār* was published by the well-regarded Indian Press of Allahabad in 1912. The printer was Apurva Krishna Bose, whose prolific work in various scripts is still to be found in many libraries. The *Minqār* must have been attractive to the proprietor of the Indian Press. Music instructional books were being published by most leading publishers at this time, and

8 *Biography*, 342.

9 For summaries and analyses relating to Sayyid Madani see *Pearl in Wine* (Khan , Z. 2001, 106–14 and 317–19).

10 Khan, Shaikh, 84–7.

the author was surely recommended by respected Calcutta sources. We do not know the print run of the *Minqār*. Like most music instructional books of the time, it soon became relatively scarce.

The Topics of the *Minqār*: Part One

Much of the *Minqār* reflects the teachings of Maula Bakhsh, whose *Sangitanubhav* of 1888 contains most of the technical terms found in the book. Inayat Khan, however, drew material from other published sources as well. The *Ghuncha-i rāg* and the *Sarmāya-i ishrat*, well-known music instructional books of the late nineteenth century, were sources for his coverage of *rāg* classification and dance. The *Tāl Paddhatī* of 1888 by Usmankhan Sultankhan, *tabla* master in Maula Baksh's school, provided material for the *tāl* chapter in Part Two. The author used English sources for English terms and likely published sources from south India for the *rāg* list. The songs notated in Part Two were Inayat Khan's own musical settings. He performed them himself, as we know from the recordings of 1909. The book is the author's effort to produce a thorough compilation of musical knowledge.

The layout of the *Minqār* has traditional and modern characteristics. It is divided overall into two parts covering theory and practice, or as the author terms it, the science and art of music. Each part has seven chapters, a nod to musicological traditional modeled on the thirteenth-century *Sangītaratnākara*. Each part begins with tributes to God, patrons, and teachers, as is traditional in Persian and Urdu literature. Personal statements by the author follow in the colloquial Urdu of the time. The sequence of topics is similar to that in other instructional books. Discussions of sound, scales, *rāg*, and *tāl* are followed by descriptions of vocal, instrumental music and dance. An outstanding feature of the *Minqār* is its collection of notated songs. The Maula Bakhsh notational system was innovative, accessible, and very successful during its time.

Preliminary Sections

Extracts from English-language testimonials about Inayat Khan's music performances are affixed inside the cover of the *Minqār*. They are a fascinating record of the places Inayat Khan performed after he left Hyderabad. Here are notes about performances for royal and distinguished patrons in Karnataka, Tamil Nadu, Kerala, and Sri Lanka, and in music societies, clubs, and colleges in south India and in Vadodara, Kolkata, and Myanmar. Admiring remarks are made of Inayat Khan's musical proficiency. His education in English and in European music theory, and his scientific approach are mentioned in several notes. Several writers wish him success in bringing reforms to north and south Indian music. The points mentioned in the testimonials surely express Inayat Khan's own aims as well: to be a versatile and expressive performer, to educate listeners about Indian music, and to be a messenger of the spirituality behind the music. The Theosophical Society of Madurai indeed, notes "He is a man of broad sympathies and philosophic side of Islam soofism."

The colorful *Musiqār* bird graces the frontispiece. This magical bird produced all the musical tones through the holes in its beak. Its beak represents the two parts of the book and the two sides of music, namely theory and performance, or science and art.

The Nizam of Hyderabad, Mir Mahbub Ali Khan (1866–1911) is the book's dedicatee. The photograph shows the Nizam, regal and relaxed, his arm resting on the back of a Victorian chair. Inayat Khan's verses of tribute are in Persian befitting the elite legacy that he represented.

A photograph of the author in European suit and vest shows him displaying medals awarded for his performances. The text begins in accord with Urdu and Persian literary convention, with verses to God and the Prophet. The Urdu verses feature musical terms in inspired double meanings. A tribute to the author's *murshid*, Sayyid Muhammad Abu Hashim Madani, follows. Expressions of longing and spiritual awe feature in these moving Urdu stanzas.

In the "Invocation" the author describes the enlightened state of modern Hyderabad where science and spirituality thrive together. He presents his theme that music is equally scientific and spiritual, and tells of his own ecstatic relationship to it. He devotes a long paragraph to his grandfather, Maula Bakhsh, the source for his inspiration and training. He details some of Maula Bakhsh's accomplishments including his creation of a music notation and the founding of the College of Music in Vadodara.

In the "The Reason for the Composition of the Book and a Personal Statement," Inayat Khan introduces himself to readers and formally honors his patrons, the Prime Minister and the Nizam of Hyderabad. Their pen names appear here: "Shad" for Minister Kishen Pershad and "Asif" for Nizam Mahbub Ali. In the paragraph that ends the section Inayat Khan states his motive for writing the book. He has observed that many who call themselves experts *(ustād)* do not know its principles and finer points. He does not elaborate here, but notes that music requires intellect, discipline, zeal, and kindness. He offers his book with the hope that readers will find in it easy access to theory and practice.

Chapter One: Fundamentals of Music

The chapter begins with the origin of music as told in Arabic sources. The story is found in the *G͟huncha-i rāg*, from where Inayat Khan likely got it.[1] For him the main point, however, is that music has divine origins. Following Maula Bakhsh's teaching, he moves on to the Sanskrit term for music, *sangīt*, which includes song, instrumental music, and dance. He adds his own comments that the three practices are universal to human experience, and that theory and art are equally essential and thus make up the two parts of his book.

1 Khan, M. 14–15.

In the rest of Chapter One Inayat Khan gives us an inspired essay on the fundamental qualities of music. Beginning with the idea that sound and rhythm pervade the world, he touches on Sufi ecstatic ideals, the celebration of music in Christianity, and its acceptability in Islam. He then turns to the quality of contemporary musicians and listeners, which he finds problematic. Here he articulates some grievances about lineage professionals, saying they are low-natured and that, while they may know how to perform, they cannot explain technicalities. And listeners who are likewise unsophisticated will praise and admire them. The higher levels of music on the other hand, he writes, require refinement of spirit and temperament.

Chapters Two and Three: Sound, Musical Sound

In Chapter Two Inayat Khan explains the scientific definition of sound and its production in the human body. He will tackle both physics and anatomy. Vibration, waves, the speed of sound through different media, the parts of the throat, and the parts of the ear are all described here. The singing voice is touched on. These subjects were not standard in other instructional books of the time. He must have used English textbooks on physics and anatomy available at the time.[2] We are reminded that he was writing for an Urdu-reading public who was interested in up-to-date knowledge as well as in traditional learning.

Chapter Three covers some basic theoretical concepts concerning musical tone *(sur)* and scale. Extramusical associations for pitches are found in various language sources, and Inayat Khan's chart seems to be a compilation. Sanskrit texts link each tone with an animal, lineage, caste, color, region, deity, and sentiment.[3] Arabic and Persian texts include associations with the elements, cardinal directions, body fluids, animal sounds, performance times,

2 Hastings, Martin.

3 *Sangita-Ratnakara*, 147–58.

therapeutic effects and planets.[4] The last three categories in the *Minqār* chart appear in the *Sangītanubhav*.[5]

Technical terms introduced here include ascent and descent (*ārohī, avarohī*), octave (*saptak*), immoveable and moveable pitches (*sthāī, sancārī*), shifting scales (*mūrchanā*), micro-intervals (*sruti*), ancient scale configurations (*grām*), and consonant and dissonant pitches (*vādī, samvādī, vivādī, anuvadī*). These technical terms, of Sanskrit origin, are all known today but are explained differently in various oral and written traditions. Inayat Khan drew on Maula Bakhsh's teaching, but he was also likely inspired by the *G͟huncha-i rāg* and the *Sarmāya-i ishrat*, both of which include extensive explanations and charts related to these topics. Inayat Khan explains the terms in commonsense language. He adds a modern touch by giving equivalent terms in English along with a few examples of Western notation. In this chapter he also introduces some aspects of his grandfather's notation.

Chapter Four: *Rāg*

The chapter begins with the common and most practical definition of *rāg* as found in Sanskrit and oral sources, which was taught in the Maula Bakhsh school. *Rāgs* are of five types defined by the order in which their tones are played (*auṛav, sāḍav, sankīrn, sampūrn, vakra sampūrn*). The author gives examples using some well-known *rāgs*. He continues with the mention of an archaic categorization of *rāgs* as pan-regional or regional (*mārg, desī*).

He then explains four past traditions (*mat*), which classified six main *rāgs* as male and linked each with derivative female *rāginīs*, sons (*putra*), and wives (*bhārjā*). The tradition of visualizing *rāgs* as male and female characters, describing them in verse and listing them in family configurations spread across north India beginning in the sixteenth century. Poetry and painting and music all came together in this appealing expression of

4 Pacholczyk, 1996.
5 Bakhsh, 6–7.

courtly aesthetics. *Rāg-rāginī* sets and *rāgamālā* paintings are the subjects of an extensive literature in the fields of music and art history. Maula Bakhsh does not touch on *rāg-rāginīs* in his *Sangītanubhav*. Inayat Khan appears to have drawn on the *G͟huncha-i rāg* for this section. A chart showing a list nearly identical to the *Minqār's rāg-rāginī-putra-bhāryā* chart appears there.[6] The *Sarmāya-i ishrat* also contains an extensive fifteen-page section on *rāg-rāginī* sets and the four traditions.[7] By the early twentieth century the idea of *rāgs* as male and female was dying out, but the poetic echoes of the *rāg-rāginī* tradition linger in listeners' imaginations even today.

In the rest of Chapter Four Inayat Khan gives us a list of four hundred and eighty-four *rāgs* with their ascending and descending scales. This comprehensive list includes old and current *rāgs* from both the Hindustani and Karnatak repertoires, though the author has not marked them as such. He has indicated a time of day for some (*pahar*), which serves to flag the Hindustani *rāgs*. He likely drew on the Urdu works mentioned above for names and scales of arcane north Indian *rāgs* and on his own knowledge for current *rāgs*. The Karnatak sources he used are not known, but modern lists include all of the *rāgs* listed here and comparable sources must have been available during his time. The intention here seems to have been to gather as many *rāgs* as possible. I have added a column to the translation noting where a *rāg* name appears elsewhere in the *Minqār*.

Appendix A, "List of Ragas," is marvelous addition to this translation by the author's own son and a gift of the International Headquarters of the Sufi Movement. It is Hidayat Inayat-Khan's meticulously handwritten transcription of the scales of all 484 *rāgs* in the *Minqār*. Readers will find it easy to match the numbered transcriptions with the *rāg* names in the translation.

---

6 Khan, M. 1863, ff.44, 1879 ff.26.

7 Khan, Sadiq, 1869, 31–46.

Chapter Five: *Tāl*

Chapter Five begins with an essay on the delights of rhythm in sacred and ritual music. Terms used here include *samā'* (Sufi ritual music), and *mehfil-i qavālī* (the musical gathering). A commonsense explanation of *tāl* cycles in Indian classical music follows. A description of *Tīntāl*, (here called *Tetālā*) describes its sounds on the *tabla* drum. Terms in this section include the names of various drums and percussion instruments (*ḍhol, jhānjh, mridang, naqāra, naubat khāna, raushan caukī, tāsh, tabla, pakhāvaj*), Hindu ritual genres *(bhajan, kirtan)* and the technical terms related to *tāl* cycles *(sam, āvart, khālī, tāl, bol).*

The next part of the chapter deals with rhythmic timings. Maula Bakhsh and Inayat Khan adopted the concepts used by Karnatak music educators, which were derived from Sanskrit usage. They are still in use in Karnatak music but did not remain standard in Hindustani theory. Terms include *kāgpad, devguru, guru, laghu, bisrām, drut, anādrut, trivaṛī, karā, nimesh, chan, tāl ang, surūp, vīrām, tāl jāt, catūsra jāt, tīsra jāt, misra jāt, sankīrn jāt, dīvyasankīrn jāt.* This section will stand as a record of the Maula Bakhsh school of thinking about *tāl* and its notation.

The chapter continues with a list of two hundred *tāls* showing the groupings of their beats and their pattern of hand actions. The *tāl* list is similar to the *rāg* list in style and function: it is a comprehensive collection of all the *tāls* the author could collect. The names are given in Urdu alphabetical order. There is no indication of whether a *tāl* belongs to the Hindustani or Karnatak repertoire. In the Urdu, the number of beats in the subsections of each *tāl* is indicated by the durational symbols described earlier in the chapter. Hand actions for the subsections are written just below in Maula Bakhsh notation. In the translation, I have added below the initials of the durations (*l, d,* etc.) the number of beats they represent. I have translated the hand actions into standard modern notation. "x" indicates a clap on the first beat of the *tāl* cycle (*sam*). "0" indicates a silent wave (*khālī*). A number indicates a sounded clap.

Appendix B, "List of Tabla Rhythms," is the author's son's handwritten transcription of the full *tāl* list into Western notation. Hidayat Inayat-Khan has noted the handclaps on *sam* with an accent mark and other claps with a dot. The silent waves have no mark. We get the additional gift here of Hidayat Inayat-Khan's interpretation of a Western time signature for each *tāl*.

Chapter Six: Tempo

Chapter Six covers more concepts related to timing, and introduces notation for melisma and ornaments. The levels of tempo (*vilamb kāl, ṭhā lay, made kāl, barābar āy, drut kāl, dugun lay, tigun kī lay, caugun kī lay*) described here are still in use in north India as are the terms denoting complex rhythms (*āṛ, kuāṛ*). The terms involving "place" (*grah*) denote where a sung phrase begins or ends in relation to the *tāl* cycle. These terms are from Sanskrit and are used in Karnatak music but are not standard in Hindustani music. *Yatī*, "pause," in Maula Bakhsh's tradition is similar to the slur, tie, or phrase of Western music. As a notational mark it denotes a syllable to be held over a number of notes, various ornaments, or changes in volume. The *yatī* slur is not found in other Indian notations and appears to have been inspired by Western notation. Overall, this section gives us some rhythmic concepts from the Maula Bakhsh school, including some that are commonly used in Hindustani practice.

Chapter Seven: The Maula Bakhsh Notational System

This chapter is a guide to the notation created by Maula Bakhsh, which Inayat Khan has used for the compositions in Part Two. He begins the chapter with an essay on the merits of notation. Notation communicates music, he says, as a letter communicates thoughts and a photo portrays objects.

Like most other modern systems, the Maula Bakhsh notation is adaptable to different language scripts. It is used in the Hindi and Gujarati books by those of his school. Scale tones *Sā Re Ga Ma Pa Dha Ni* are notated by their initial syllables. Specific marks denote octaves (*mandra, mada, tār saptak*) and the natural, flat, and sharp versions of tones (*shuddh, komal, tīvra*). Vertical bar lines divide the sections of the *tāl* cycle. The rhythmic terms of the Maula Bakhsh system and their notations are as described in Chapter Five. *Kāgpad, devgurū, gurū, laghu, drut, anādrut, bisrām* appear as symbols beneath each tone indicating their durations. Maula Bakhsh's *yatī* marks and his signs for beginning, end, and repeats, are unique and were probably inspired by Western notation.The Maula Bakhsh notation is fairly intuitive to read. Except for the rhythmic markings, it resembles the Bhatkhande notation that would later become standard across north India. Indeed, it was a likely model for Bhatkhande's and other later notations.

The Topics of the *Minqār*: Part Two

Part Two on performance contains chapters on vocal music, *sitār*, harmonium, and *tabla*, and an overview of dance. Its central feature is a collection of more than sixty songs in notation.

A photograph of Maula Bakhsh in courtly dress and a warmly inspired Urdu verse mark the beginning of the section. A photograph of the Prime Minister, Sir Kishen Pershad and Persian verses in tribute to him preface the text. In a touching opening verse Inayat Khan expresses his yearning appeal to God. As in previous introductory sections he expresses his regret that music has lost its venerable status and has come to be thought of as a mere sport or sensual pleasure. He gives a summary history of the noble position that music held among the world's Muslims and wishes for the restoration of its proper status in India. He mentions ill-intentioned people as being responsible for what he sees as the poor state of music. He had brought up a similar theme in the introduction to Part One. Inayat Khan evokes here his central concerns: dignity, learning, spiritual uplift, and the benefits of music to modern society.

Chapter One: Vocal Music

The author reiterates the universally held view in India that song is the primary form of music. He introduces the song genres that he will describe in more detail. He names the four historical styles (*bānī*) of the *dhrupad* genre and discusses several traditional categories of musicians. His use of the category "self-taught" (*a'tāī*) is interesting here, highlighting the fact that public performance by non-hereditary musicians was relatively new at this time. Also interesting is his use of the terms *mirās* and *dhād* as additional categories of *bānī*. In most accounts of this time the *mirāsī* and *ḍhāḍī* hereditary musician castes were placed low in the musical hierarchy.

The four ancient musician categories *gāyak, gunī, gandharv, nāyak,* the author notes, have recently been replaced with designations for separate "households" (*ghar*). The rise of *gharānās* "household styles" was a significant development in twentieth century *khayāl* vocal music. Interestingly Inayat Khan expresses a low opinion of this development. He admires the degree systems used in Western educational institutions. A three-fold ranking of excellent, middling, and low is generally used in India, he seems to say, and is acceptable.

Defects and virtues in singers is a traditional subject of Indian musicological texts. Inayat Khan draws on these traditions and presents them in his own words, offering advice to aspiring singers and his own opinions on style and quality. He is disapproving of trends for males to sing in high voices and employ feminine gestures, and for women to sing in low voices. One cannot help but think that he was referring to Abdul Karim Khan (1872–1937), who was noted for his sweet high-pitched voice. Abdul Karim lived in Vadodara for a time and became one of the leading *ṭhumrī* singers of his period. Except for the passing remark above on women singers, Inayat Khan does not touch on the subject of women professionals or the salon environments in which *ṭhumrīs* and *g̲h̲azals* were sung for male patrons. In a final paragraph of this section he gives his opinion about the pros and cons of singing with a *tānpūra* or other string instrument.

The remainder of Chapter One consists of informative descriptions of twenty-three song genres. The descriptions are still applicable and serve as a nice introduction to north Indian classical and semi-classical vocal genres. Ten of them will be represented in the notations in Chapter Two.

Chapter Two: Systematic Notations of Vocal Compositions

This chapter is a centerpiece of the *Minqār*. Sixty-one notations in ten of the genres mentioned in the previous chapter give us a treasury of Inayat Khan's compositions. Five of the songs notated here can be heard on *Inayat Khan: the Complete Recordings of 1909*. The book and the recordings in combination provide a rare resource indeed.

Guide to Reading the Notation

The notation used for the translation is that typically used in Hindustani music today. The paragraphs below are a guide to reading it. It is designed to be intuitive, and is fairly simple to read once one has memorized the *sargam* scale tones.

Scale tones are denoted by the syllables *S R G M P D N* pronounced "Sā Re Ga Ma Pa Dha Nī." As in the Western solfege, the tonic pitch (*Sā*) can be chosen to suit the singer's range or the instrument's tone. The Hindustani natural scale is equivalent to the Western major scale, such as the C scale with no sharps or flats. The notated scale tones are natural (*shuddh*) if they are not marked otherwise. The second, third, sixth, and seventh (*R, G, D, N*) can be flat *(komal)* in which case they are notated with an underline ($\underline{R}$, $\underline{G}$, $\underline{D}$, $\underline{N}$). The fourth (*M*) can be sharp *(tīvra)*, in which case it is notated with a vertical line above ($\overset{|}{M}$). The twelve tones that form the Hindustani scale tones thus are *S* $\underline{R}$ *R* $\underline{G}$ *G M* $\overset{|}{M}$ *P* $\underline{D}$ *D* $\underline{N}$ *N*. They correspond roughly to the twelve-tone Western chromatic scale.

A dot below a tone indicates a note in the lower octave. A dot above indicates the higher octave. A curved line beneath joining two or more notes indicates that they are to be sung in one beat ($\underset{\smile}{GM}$).

Vertical bar lines mark the conventional subdivisions of the *tāl* cycle. Numbers above the bar lines designate how the divisions are marked by hand actions. "x" is a clap marking the first beat of the cycle (*sam*). Numbers indicate a handclap (*tālī*). "0" indicates a silent wave of the hand (*khālī*).

Subtleties of slides and ornaments are to be learned through oral training, but Maula Bakhsh's *yatī* marks provide some indications. A curved line above indicates that a sung syllable is carried over more than one musical tone. The placement of the lyrics beneath the tones carries the same information, but the marks are visually helpful and are a feature of the Maula Bakhsh notation.

The Songs

Each song genre of the north Indian classical repertoire is characterized by specific poetic content, musical structure and style, and social and aesthetic history.

The first three genres, *dhrupad*, *āstāī* (now called *khayāl*) and *ṭhumrī*, comprise the top of the musical hierarchy. Five songs are given for each in the *Minqār*. The language is poetic Hindi. The next six genres (*horī-dhamār, horī cāncar kī, ṭappa, tarānā, tirvaṭ chok varnam*) are represented by one song each. The *ṭappa* is in Panjabi (also spelled "Punjabi") and the *tarānā* includes Persian words. The language of the others is Hindi. As in most South Asian poetry, the poet's pen name may appear in the final verse. "Inayat" is the composer of several of the poems. A few are by other known poets (Madan Piya, Sadarang, Achpal). Other lyrics have no attribution and may be assumed to be traditional. The range of genres used here is typical of the song repertoire of Hindustani performing musicians.

G͟hazals, the beloved poetry of India's Urdu and Persian-knowing population, dominate the chapter with forty notations. Hyderabad, known for its Urdu literary culture, must have been an inspiring place for Inayat Khan to build his repertoire. He would later collaborate on two translated collections published in London.[1] Seven *g͟hazals* from among those in the *Minqār* appear there. A passage from the foreword of one of the books nicely conveys Inayat Khan's message about Urdu poetry:

> The poetry is very varied and of great interest. It includes moral verses and counsels..heroic poems..elegies,.. devotional poems in praise of Muhammad and the

1 Khan 1915, 1996.

> Imams,..eulogies,..satires upon men and institutions,.. Above all there is a great wealth of love poetry, both secular and mystic, where, in impassioned *ghazals* or odes, the union of man with God is celebrated under various allegories.
>
> Most of the poets represented in this book write as Sufis, or Muslim mystics, and scoff at the unenlightened orthodox. For them God is in all and through all, to be worshipped equally in the Ka'ba and in the Temple of the Idols, or too great to be adored adequately through the ritual of any creed. He is symbolized as the beautiful and cruel Beloved, difficult to find, withdrawn behind the veil, inspiring and demanding all worship and devotion. The Lover is the Madman, derided by the unsympathetic crowd, but happy in his ecstatic despair.[2]

In the *Minqār* we are given one *ghazal* poem in Urdu and one in Persian for each musical notation. The first two couplets of the Urdu are given in the notation. Forty-seven poets are represented. The poets' full names and dates, where traceable, are given in Appendix C. Seven *ghazals*, the most in the collection, are by Amir Minai (1828–1900). Inayat Khan prepared short biographical notes on some of the poets for the later books. In *Hindustani Lyrics* he introduces Amir Minai, making special note of his mystical as well as literary achievements:

> Amir Minai of Rampur, one of the best poets of the latest period: a great mystic poet: his Qasidas for Muhammad are sung by devotees: Court poet of Rampur: travelled to Mecca and Medina, and, after the death of his patron, Kalbe Ali Khan, came to Hyderabad on hearing of the Nizam's fame and interest in poetry: rival of Dagh, by whose side he lies buried in Hyderabad.[3]

2 Khan, 1996, 1–3.

3 Khan, 1996, 5.

Five *ghazals* by the Nizam of Hyderabad and both Urdu and Persian *ghazals* by the Prime Minister Kishen Pershad are included in the collection.

Rāg and *tāl* in the Songs

Inayat Khan has employed thirty-five different *rāgs* for the notated songs. We can assume that they were among the most well known of the time. Many are familiar today but the scales and phrasings of some differ from present-day practice. Footnotes in the translation record some specific points of difference, but interested readers will want to look to other sources to compare the melodies with current *rāg* practice. The *rāgs* that appear most frequently in the *Minqār* are *Bhairavī, Kāfī* and *Ẓila'*, with four or more songs each. *Bihāg, Bihārī,* and *Jhinjhoṭī* are used for three or four songs each. Two songs each are composed in *Khamāj, Pīlū, Shahāna,* and *Sindhūra.*

The most frequently used *tāl* in the notations is *Qavālī*, an eight-beat cycle. Second is *Dādrā*, a six-beat *tāl.* Third in frequency is the sixteen-beat *Tetālā*, known today as *Tīntāl.* The notations include designations of tempo, slow, medium or fast. The terms *Catūsra, Tisra* and *Misra Jātī* denoting the internal rhythms of a *tāl* were used in Maula Bakhsh's teachings, but are used only in Karnatak music now.

The notations in Chapter Two are valuable records indeed. It is exciting that these "photos" of Inayat Khan's compositions exist and that the songs can be recreated according to his own specifications.

Chapter Three: Instrumental Music

Musical instruments, the author begins, fulfill the need to augment the voice. He describes the ancient fourfold categorization *(tat, vitat, sushir, ghan)* and gives examples. He expresses admiration for Europeans' attention to improving musical instruments and bemoans the lack of similar efforts in India. The rest of the chapter consists of descriptions of more than thirty-six instruments. The section is useful for its accounts of instruments that have since become obsolete, including varieties of *bīn* and *sitār*. The author's comments add a touch of color to the descriptions. The sound of the *bīn*, for example, is soulful and pleasant, and playing it requires discipline. A list of "English Musical Instruments" at the end of the chapter gives us a sense of the European instruments that might have been seen in India at the time.

Chapter Four: Rules for Playing the *sitār*

A line drawing of a seven-string *sitār* prefaces the chapter. The *sitār* was, as Inayat Khan writes, much loved in India and was played by professionals and amateurs alike. Solo music based on *rāg* consisted of a short composition (*gat*) set to a *tāl* cycle followed by variations (*toṛā*). Inayat Khan will give fifteen examples in this chapter. The *Sarmāya-i ishrat*, mentioned above was one of the several Urdu instructional books for the *sitār* published beginning in the later nineteenth century. The content and layout here is similar to those in the earlier books. We might assume that Inayat Khan consulted the *Sarmāya-i ishrat* and other sources but that the material in this chapter was largely based on what he had learned from his father, who played the *sitār*, and from his other teachers.

The positioning of the frets, the basic hand positions, and the two main styles (*bāj*) of *sitār* playing (*Musīdkhvānī, Firozkhvānī*) are described in brief. A rare photograph of the author's father provides an illustration of the sitting position for a *sitār* player. Rahmat Khan in courtly garb sits with the right knee upright supporting the *sitār* neck.

A list of twelve *thāṭ* "arrangements" for the moveable *sitār* frets are given. Each *thāṭ* is named after a prominent *rāg* that uses that scale. *Thāṭ* charts were found in all the *sitār* instructional books of this period and had been used to describe scales on fretted instruments since at least the seventeenth century in north India (Brown). Inayat Khan's chart is similar to those in other Urdu instructional books but does not exactly match any one that I have identified. Different *thāṭ* systems were circulating at the time and this set may have been used in the Maula Bakhsh circles. V. N. Bhatkhande would later popularize a system of ten *thāṭs* for grouping *rāgs* overall.

Next, Inayat Khan gives us a chart of ten techniques or ornaments (*gamak*) used in *sitār* playing. The ten *gamaks* here are from Sanskrit and Karnatak tradition but Inayat Khan has added a colloquial north Indian term for each, providing a valuable set of contemporaneous terminology. He has given descriptions of the techniques along with notation in the Maula Bakhsh system.

Fourteen *sitār* compositions give us a sample of the middle-speed and fast-speed styles. The *rāgs* span times of day, seasons and moods. These *gats* can still be enjoyed on their own or used to build longer pieces with extemporized variations, which the author calls *fiqrā*. The phrasings and scales of some of the *rāgs* differ from modern practice, as they do in the song notations.

Chapter Five: Rules for Playing the Harmonium

An illustration of a harmonium player sets up the chapter. The author's prose describes a full-sized harmonium with bellows controlled by the feet. The "portable" harmonium such as that in the illustration would soon become ubiquitous across India, used by professionals and amateurs for every genre of music.

In this chapter Inayat Khan gives readers exercises called *sargam* with which to learn to read notation and build musical skills. He recommends that beginners practice them before attempting the songs and *gats* of the previous chapters. They are taken from his book, *Ināyat Hārmoniam Śikṣak*, written in Hindi and published in Baroda in 1903. The *Minqār* chapter contains the first thirty-two exercises of the book. The others in the book, totaling forty-seven, include songs in various *rāgs*. *Shankarabharan*, a predominantly Karnatak *rāg*, was used frequently in the Maula Bakhsh school. It uses the natural *(shuddh)* scale.

Chapter Six: Rules for Playing the *tabla*

This chapter is a basic guide to the *tabla*, north India's versatile two-piece drum. The parts of the *tabla* (*chānt, lav, thāp, syāhī, bāyān*), hand actions for producing the strokes and their spoken syllables *(bol)* are given in the chapter. We also get a list of eighteen *ṭhekās*, the sequence of strokes that define a *tāl* in performance.

The contents of this chapter come directly from the *Tāl Paddhati*, a work by Usmankhan Sultankhan, a *tabla* player and teacher at the Gayanshala. The book was published in 1888 with the assistance of Maula Bakhsh. It contains a novel notational system and substantially more material, including variations and compositions. The book is the subject of a thorough study by James Kippen.

In the *Minqār*, underlined syllables apparently derive from the *Tāl Paddhati's* notations of left and right hand strokes on the *tabla* (Kippen). The underlining is inconsistent, however, and I have omitted them in the translation.

Chapter Seven: Dance

Inayat Khan follows Indian musicological tradition in devoting the seventh and last chapter of his work to dance. Most of the chapter describes the dance currently called *kathak*. As in other sources of the time, the term is used here to denote a hereditary caste and not a dance genre. Inayat Khan surely saw dance in Hyderabad and in other places he lived and visited, and he uses his own language, but the technical material in this chapter is a condensation of the dance sections in the *Sarmāya-i ishrat*, where the same terms and topics are covered in more than twenty pages.[4]

4 Khan, Sadiq,152–75.

The chapter opens with drawing of a female dancer and a paragraph about the marvelous and universal nature of dance. The author recalls the ecstatic dancers that he saw while he was in Nepal and notes that in Europe people of all classes dance together, enjoying themselves immensely. It continues with mention of the masculine and feminine categories of dance (*tāndav, lās*), a brief description of typical dress, gestures, and instrumentation, mention of a few lesser-known dance genres (*sukumār, paristān kā nāc, mardānī nrit*) and some basic terminology (*nrit, nrittam, nāṭyā*).

Substantial sections describe the syllables (*bol*) recited in dance, some typical moves called "limbs" (*ang*), and movements and positions called *gat*. The central feature of the chapter is illustrations with descriptions of nineteen *gats*. All the material of the chapter has been taken from the *Sarmāya-i ishrat*, but the author's visually descriptive language and the illustrator's stylish drawings are informative and appealing.

He concludes the chapter with notations of dance syllable recitations called *toṛā* and *parmalū*. These are taken from the *Sarmāya-i ishrat* and notated in the Maula Bakhsh system. Inayat Khan's interpretations differ from the original enough to warrant a short appendix. Appendix D contains my readings of the nine *toṛā* and *parmalū* notations in the *Sarmāya-i ishrat* that were the basis of those in the *Minqār*.

Final Verses

In a lovely set of final verses Inayat Khan expresses gratitude to God and tributes to his patrons in Hyderabad. The date of the book's completion, communicated through a chronogram, is 1324 Hijri (1906 CE). Indeed, if the *Minqār* was successful in communicating to readers something of the beauty and divine nature of music which is so elusive, the author's thought in the final verse is entirely apt:

"What 'gift' *('ināyat)* is there in Inayat's book? —it's all magic!"

The Minqar-i Musiqar

EXTRACT FROM THE TESTIMONIALS OF

Prof. INAYAT KHAN, R. PATHAN

FAMOUS MUSICIAN (INDIA)

GOLD MEDALIST

Highly patronised by H.H. the Nizam, Gaikwar, H.H. The Maharaja of Mysore, &c.

Gives public and private performances in Vocal and Instrumental music (on Veena and Jaltarang, etc.) at the Durbars, Exhibitions, Social, Religious and Matrimonial gatherings.

Gives systematic training in music to both sexes professionals and amateurs

—— —— ——

H. H. the Nizam of Hyderabad — Prof. Inayat Khan performed his music to the satisfaction of H.H. the Nizam and the premier nobles and was awarded with 100 ashrafees and one emerald ring valued Rs. 14,000; since this day he has been granted the honour of performing music several times before His Highness.

(Sd.) LAKMAN UL-DOWLAH,
Surgeon, H.H. the Nizam's Staff.

H.H. the Maharaja of Mysore — H.H. the Maharaja was pleased with Prof. Inayat Khan's perfomance.

(Sd) P. RAGHAVENDRA RAO,
Asst. Private Secy. To H.H. the Maharaja of Mysore.

H.E. Maharaja Kishan Pershad, Bahadur, Prime Minister of Hyderabad. — Prof. Inayat Khan's music every time used to give a fresh pleasure to the heart and unliited peace to the soul. There is no question about his high qualities in his profession.

H.H. the Prince of Arcot. —Prof. Inayat Khan performed his music to the satisfaction of His Highness and his family and was amply rewarded. His Jaltarang was simply marvellous and everyone felt highly delighted. He is a master of the science and art of music.

(Sd.) AGUM HUSSAIN
Private Secy. To H.H. the Prince of Arcot

Prince Shivaji Rao, Raja Saheb of Tanjore. — Raja Saheb was highly pleased with your performance of music. He hopes that you will be the pioneer of a uniform scientific system of Indian music.

(Sd.) U.P. SUBRAMANI INGAR, Tutor.

Mr. T. Kair Hardie, M.P. – I admired and enjoyed the performance.

The Hon'ble Resident, Mysore. – The Resident was very pleased with your performance which appears to have been admired by the leading gentlemen of Bangalore present at the Residency.
(Sd.) U.S. TIRMALAI IYANGAR, Registrar.

The Dewan Bahadur Srinivas Raghava Ingar of Baroda. — Prof Inayat Khan has studied both the Hindu and European systems scientifically and already acquired great proficiency, especially in the former. He has winning manners and the art of rousing the interest and intelligence of his pupils. My children remember the days they have passed under his tuition.

Sir Solomon Dias Bandara Naike, Mahamudaliar and A.-D.-C. to the Governor, Colombo. —Your entertainment was unique and unlike anything that has ever been heard before in Ceylon and I thoroughly enjoyed it.

The Hon'ble Nawab Saiyed Mahmood Bahadur, Madras. — I have much pleasure to say that Prof. Inayat Khan is thoroughly proficient in Indian music.

The Hon'ble Mr. Ananda Charlu, Madras. — Professor's rare merit lies in uniting in himself what is best in the Carnatic and Hindustani system of music in each of which he is quite proficient. I am really proud of him as a lover of music. Professor has excelled his grandfather Maula Bux by his versatile powers.

The Diwan Bahadur Raja Gopalachar, Prime Minister, Travancore. — Professor's music was much appreciated. A gold medal was presented to him as a mark of appreciation by the citizens of Trivandrum.

The Diwan Bahadur Patta Bhiram Rao, Prime Minister, Cochin. — Professor has a very sweet voice and his singing is quite scientific.

Hon'ble Mr. S.P. Sinha, Law Member, Imperial Council, Calcutta. — I was quite charmed with the music. It has never been my good fortune to listen to such Jultarang and the vocal music was of a very superior order.

The Hon'ble Justice Gooroodass Banerjee, Calcutta.— I consider Professor's performance to be of a superior order of merit.

Dr. A.M. Pathan, L.R.A.M., L.L.C.M., &c., &c., Baroda. — Prof. Inayat Khan possesses a very good knowledge of the science of Indian music and has studied the theory of European music. He is proficient in the art of Indian singing. It is of the utmost importance to have an Indian knowing both European and Indian music.

The Public of Madras. — It is highly gratifying to us that you have made it your life-work to improve the music of India and to introduce a uniform system for the whole of India.

The Public of Mysore. — Permit us to say that the opinion that we have formed about your music is no ordinary one. You have not only afforded us pleasure by your sweet music but you have taught us the true import by your short discourse on music. It is, indeed, a matter for congratulation that you have made it your life-work to advance the cause of Hindustani and Karnatic music.

The Public of Bangalore. — It is gratifying to us to know that even now when the fine arts are fast disappearing there are to be found men possessing such rare talents as you do. We note with pride your explanations of the theory of Indian music which is in some respects even superior to that of the English music.

The Public of Tanjore.— The Prof. has an excellent voice very carefully trained. His knowledge of music appears to be great.

The Public of Cochin, Malabar.— The numerous certificates and medals possessed by the Prof. testify to his great abilities in the art and they hardly require further amplifications. We wish only to add with great pleasure that his reputation will be a piece of valuable asset to the credit of Hindustani music.

The Muhammedan Public of Coimbatore. — Your marvelous performance, we are proud to say, was the living example of the ancient Muhammedan fames in the fine arts.

The Public of Rangoon. — We have been, to say, enraptured by his {Professor's} excellent attainments and as a recognition thereof, we are happy to present to him this certificate and a gold medal.

Sayaji Mowla Music Society, Baroda. — It is highly gratifying to us that you have put your heart and soul for the improvement of the science of music in India and are endeavoring to introduce a uniform system of notation for the whole of India for which you have published many books.

Bhawanipur Sangit Sammilani, Calcutta. — We find in you the ardent student of music and the most original exponent of the Indian Notation system devised by your renowned ancestor Prof. Mowla Bux. We have learnt to look upon you as the Morning Star of the Indian Music Revival.

Theosophical Society, Madura.—The audience were highly pleased with the Professor's performance and with his intimate acquaintance with different schools of music. He is a man of broad sympathies and philosophic side of Islam soofism.

Cosmopolitan Club, Madras. — Professor's melodious voice and scientific singing fully confirmed the high reputation he bears in the art of music.

Maharaja College, Trivandrum. — Professor's performance exhibited his remarkable talents and careful training.

E. Maconochie, Esq. I.C.S., Private Sec'y to the H.H. the Maharaja of Mysore.— The Professor seems to have considerable mastery over Veena and Jaltarang. His music is ingenious and effective.

Mr. A. Hydari, Hyderabad. — What has pleased me is the manliness of his voice accompanied with greatest subtlety in its variations. I have derived more benefit in a few minutes than in hours' conversation with others.

Haji Mahamed Mucan, Turkish Consul, Colombo.— I appreciated exceedingly the performance which apart from its merits recommends itself as something quite uncommon.

The Indian Patriot of 8–9–1908. — Beyond and above what the Professor has inherited from distinguished musicians with whom he is connected by ties internal and paternal, he had the benefit of systematic course of training in the theory and practice of Indian music for over 12 years under Prof. Mowla Bux himself. He has made a critical study of the standard works on Sangit and is also the author of some good books in Hindi on the same subject.

The Hindu of 23–3–1908. — He kept the audience spell-bound. His sweet melodious voice, his grasp of both the Hindustani and Carnatic science of music, his complete mastery over Swarams, the effective modulations of his voice touched the hearts of everyone whether he had a taste for music or not.

The Daily Post of 20–1–1908. — He is one of the best musicians that we have in Southern India. His performances on the Jaltarang and other instruments have been greatly appreciated by Indians and Europeans alike. He has been honoured by invitations to give performances before Lord Elgin, Lord Curzon and Lord Ampthill, who expressed their admiration and appreciation.

The Mysore Herald of 4–11–1907, — The young man is in one way an improvement over his grandfather. He is not only a musician but he knows English also. The English song that he sang on the occasion was so captivating that it pleased the audience extremely. His vocal music was simply splendid. His performance on Jaltarang was equally good. He promises to become a great expert in music.

The Independent of 18–11–1908. — His handling of Veena is spoken of very highly by all there who saw it, while his playing at Jaltarang (an arrangement of water bowls) has been pronounced to be simply marvelous.

The Bangalee of 16–3–1909. — Some fine Dhrupada and Khiyal songs were gone through and were highly appreciated by the assembly and these kept the audience spell-bound.

Head Office: — MAULA BOX HOUSE Baroda (India)

Mūsīqār

The Minqar-i Musiqar

The Beak of the Musical Bird

A Rare Illustrated Book on the Art of Music

by

Professor Inayat Khan R. Pathan Sahab

1912

Printed and published by
Indian Press, Allahabad
with
Apurva Krishna Bose, Printer

Various goods have I brought
in tribute to Shah Mahbub Ali Khan Bahadur.
Should the smallest detail meet with his eye's approval,
Inayat would rise to the heights of pride.

In praise of

His Exalted Highness who embodies all the power of
the Sublime One's servants, Mir Mahbub Ali Khan Bahadur,
GCB, GCSI, ruler of the kingdom of the Deccan
(may Allah preserve it from strife).[1]

Kingship suits the stature of Mahbub Ali:
behold this image of eternal splendor!
Happy King, most sublime among the earth's creatures,
In all of creation, who but he is irreplaceable?
Among his forefathers, none equals him
in grandeur and magnificence—this resplendent grace!
May his sword be held above the heads of his enemies,
in God-given triumph, for Prophet and saint.
By the grace of this pure King, Inayat, behold,
in the lap of happiness, the rose which the heart seeks.

1 Mir Mahbub Ali Khan, Nizam of Hyderabad, ruled 1869–1911. GCB "Knight or Dame Grand Cross of the Order of the Bath," bestowed on the Nizam in 1902 (Lynton 46–7). GCSI "Knight Grand Commander of the Order of the Star of India." (http://www.burkes-peerage.net). For titles of address, and a genealogy of the rulers of Hyderabad, see Buyers.

Part One

The Theory of Music

(*Sangīt vidyā*)

Professor Inayat Khan R. Pathan
(the author of this book)

In the Name of the Merciful, the Compassionate

The melody (*tarāna*) of praise befits the Divine Musician, who by the prelude (*ālāp*) of "*kun*," ("Be!") enraptured the gathering (*mehfil*) of "*fayakūn*," ("and it was)" and by the sound of "*alastu*," ("am I not...") intoxicated the subtle-bodied instrumentalists (*gatkār*) with the rhyme of "*balā*," ("indeed").[1]

Verse

They say sharp and flat:
  But it is the Lord, it is the Lord, it is the Lord,
  the Lord.
Sā rī gā mā pā dhā nī
  you, me, we, he, she, they, all
In the daytime, *Pilū* and *Bhīmpalās*,
  at night, *Yaman* and *Shahānā*:
He is everything, everything is He, *har har har*!
  Like this, like that, now, when, then;
in the musical string, in the body, in the soul, indeed
  He alone is in all; He himself is all.

And the fanfare of the bounty of singing "I am *ahmad* without the *mīm*" (*ahad*, the One) and "I am *'arab* without the *'ayn*" (*rab*, the Lord) is fitting for him, whose inferiors in ardor

1 Music terms are worked into two passages from the Qur'ān: "Our word for a thing when We intend it, is only that We say to it, Be, and it is" (16.40); "And when your Lord brought forth from the children of Adam, from their backs, their descendants, and made them bear witness against their own souls: Am I not your Lord? They said: Yes! we bear witness" (7.172) (Koran) University of Michigan Digital Library, 2000. http://quod.lib.umich.edu/k/koran/

even are quenched of their thirst, those parched-lipped ones of the desert of meditation. I speak of Muhammad, Allah's mercy, upon whom and whose family is His peace; in whose ear of certainty are the notes of eternal sound, as his peace is upon his companions; whose eager intentions are filled with the voice of service. Blessings be upon the best of created beings, our master Muhammad, and upon his family and companions, one and all.

Verse

In sweet tones, the ages have proclaimed
 Muhammad's countenance to be the image of truth.
Kindle the melodies of *rāg Dīpak* with inner burning;
 if this my whole being should burn, it is for the best.
Sweet Muhammad, loved by the Beloved
 as Surayyā Sahānā, is our esteemed Prophet.
Let the tunes of the drunken ones flow in the passion of oblivion;
 now neither "yours" nor "mine" remains.
Among the *yogis*, the burning is one of detachment:
 right there dwells the force of life, my *yogi*.
Oh Inayat, let the melodies sound in the melodious tones of the Arabs;
 come, leave behind all this vain display.

In Praise of Pir-o Murshid Hazrat Sayyid Muhammad Abu Hashim Madani

Inayat, look about you; proceed with caution;
this is a place for propriety, take care, take care!
In hope we will set out for the dwelling of the Lord,
we will abide in love and in longing for the Beloved.
How can the unactualized know divine charity?
What does non-being know of our living Lord?
Without shape, independent, formless, the giver of all things
manifesting color and form in whatever there is.
He became the gardener of the garden and orchard of Chisht.
He became the greenness of the leaf and the redness of the rose.
Sayyid Muhammad was the rose in the garden of creation.
Yes, Sayyid Muhammad was the full figure of guidance.
How will a call enliven those whose hearts have died?
But his kindness is for the perfected ones, one and all.
Citizen of Medina, elegant in form,
Pure Abu Hashim, cryptic in formlessness.
Whatever canopy shelters me is his spiritual bounty,
thus divinity wholly protects me.
Longing for servitude is the gift (*ʿināyat*) of that king of the faith;
to have it is ample return.
Oh God, shower the resting place of the king of the faith
with the roses of your kindness and mercy.

Invocation

Truly these days divine grace enfolds us. The present ruler is vigilant, natures are affectionate, the star of baseness is setting, and the ornaments of prosperity are in view. If you take art, for example, it is springtime in the world's garden. And consider science, which is the sun in the sky of perfection. In all cases, be it art or science, it is formal when done for the sake of the brilliance of structure; and it is spiritual when done for freshness of spirit. The virtue of every art and science lies in its being recognized and appreciated on the basis of its content and its fundamental principles. In this regard, the science of music has especially spiritual properties. Indeed, *rāg* is in reality the soul of the soul, and those who know things as they really are consider it to belong to the realm of worship. And why not? If one's fortunate destiny in listening to music (*samaʿ*) is divine purity, then detachment transpires and absorption in God is attained. Truly, the status of *rāg* is that of interlocutor between man and God, and in it are hidden secrets. How well some wise one has expressed it:

> They say that the soul entered the body through music.
> In private, they have said that the music was itself the soul.

If you ask me the truth, this absolute harmony, this ecstasy of my whole being, that is to say the boldness or aspiration which provokes my words, is a vision for those with eyes to see. Due entirely to the generous and beneficent glance of favor from one whose essence was one of lofty attributes, my upbringing was in the shade of protection, and I was brought up with both physical discipline and spiritual refinement. It is by his countenance that today this lowly wretch is brought before the elect of the divine court and before them who enjoy the approval of the Eternal Presence. He of whom I speak is my maternal grandfather, my prayer-niche, the luminous lamp of the night of wealth and prosperity, the ornament of the palace of sound and voice, Janāb Maula Bakhsh Sahab, upon whom be God's mercy and forgiveness. Oh Allah, bring him into the abode of happiness. He contributed greatly to the science of music, and by his presence added glory to his era, to such an extent that he was honored by the British government with the titles "Professor of Music" and "Founder of Indian Musical Notation." And he was given the insignia of distinction—the parasol, fly-whisk, jeweled crest, pearled coronet, and torch—and was looked on with honor and respect in the greater number of India's princely states. The coin of his expertise is still current, since his College of Music in Baroda exists under the protective shadow of Maharaja Sir Sayaji Rao Gaekwar, where the children of both the elite and the common achieve a certain level of perfection. By the grace of God, it is as if the branches and blossoms of this College are always finding the spring season and enjoying brilliance. The College has seven levels. Each class must complete a textbook in which songs are transcribed. This technique, the writing of music, is called "notation" in English. The textbooks contain instruction on melody and rhythm, and the yearly examinations of each class are based on them. My maternal uncle, Doctor Alauddin Khan Sahab, L.R.A.M., L.L.C.M. etc. (Royal Academy of Music, London), is now in this Department.[1]

1 LRAM: Licentiate of the Royal Academy of Music, a diploma administered to performers, teachers, and composers. LLCM: Licentiate of the Liberty College of Music (Rosse, 141).

The Reason for the Composition of the Book and a Personal Statement

As I write this book, this insignificant and negligible one has, by divine grace, reached the age of twenty-five. After learning the greater part of the science of music, I spent my life traveling, since my nature is inclined to travel. During that time I witnessed the wonders and marvels of many regions of God's creation. I offer thanks and gratitude to Him that through every beloved kingdom this humble one has passed, those in charge have granted me the eye of solicitude and the glance of kindness. Likewise, by the grace of God, in the bounty-laden land of the Deccan this same favor prevails in the person of His Excellency of high descent, the right hand of authority, the pillar of dominion, the most glorious of noblemen, the most dignified of leaders, the rājā of rājās, Maharaja Kishen Pershad Bahadur. May his dignity and prosperity endure.

Kishen Pershad, revered Prime Minister;
under his charge, creation flourishes.
Oh Allah, keep the realm of governance happy (*shād*),[1]
for when the realm is happy, so too is the world.

His Excellency, the Prime Minister above celebrated (may his dignity and prosperity endure), is obliging in his solicitude and kindness. By the glance of his special consideration, this insignificant one has been solemnly honored and granted the royal grace and the robe of ennoblement from the Shadow of God himself, His Majesty Mir Mahbub Ali Khan, in the magnificent court of the Perpetual Lord of Mighty Grandeur and Empowered Dominion. Ruler of the land of the Deccan (may Allah preserve it from strife), he is abundant in mercy and

1 Shād is also the pen name of Kishen Pershad.

modest in wrath, beyond beyonds, majesty to many servants, and sublime orderer of the age. He is like Asif in wisdom, like Sikandar in combat, the most excellent in the world, the beloved of God, majesty to many servants, sublime and elevated. May Allah immortalize his kingship and authority.

Asif of governance, orderer of the world,
most excellent among created beings, Sikandar of combat,
ruler of the kingdom of the Deccan, the shadow of God,
is His Majesty Mir Mahbub Ali Khan.
In his munificence an ocean of bounty, a rain cloud of generosity;
in his forgiveness and mildness a phenomenon of power.
Sword-swinging, enemy-smiting, fortress-besieging,
in times of valor he becomes the very awe of God.
In his service the poor and the rich
are roses in his lap, as befits their aspiration.
Oh Lord, Shadow of God, King of the Deccan,
may you always flourish with magnificence.

Praise be to Allah if today, in the land of India, Muslims take pride in the fact that we too are possessed of throne and crown, and collect tax and tribute. The source of that pride is none other than this pleasant and joyous kingdom, the splendor of Muslims and of Islam, Hyderabad, Deccan (may Allah enhance the magnificence of its ruler throughout the age). Oh Allah, your slave, ashamed of his sins, with utter humility and sincerity beseeches at your court:

Oh divinely favored one, may you remain alert;
may your dominion always be your friend.
With the rose of your prosperity always in bloom,
may a thorn pierce the eye of your enemy.

In the blessed service of the respected readers of this book, I submit that it is completely by divine grace and through the bounty of my teacher (may mercy be upon him) that this insignificant one has attained the satisfaction of attaining some understanding of the art of music. It is clear that because of the lack of attention given to it by people these days, this art is becoming uprooted. For, what can I say, people who call themselves masters (*ustād*) and experts in this art are revealed upon critical examination to be completely without a foot to stand on. And why? As the cultured know, this art is of noble pedigree and is more difficult than all the others, since all of the fine points, subtleties and movements of this science depend on the mind and the intellect, and through it the masters control even desire itself. Thus, the complete attainment of this phenomenon depends on tranquility, zeal, peace of mind, and an affectionate, kind, and able teacher, and all of these things must come together at once, without contingencies except as Allah may wish. And so, in accordance with my heritage, in memory of my dear maternal grandfather (may mercy be upon him) this insignificant one offers the gift of this book to the readers of this blessed art. May its easy language prove understandable upon considered thought and reflection, and may difficult explanations prove easy during the course of practice. Since I have divided this book into two parts, I have entitled it "The Beak of the *Mūsīqār* bird." I ask the readers for their prayers and hope that they will correct the author's errors.

Chapter One
Fundamentals of the Science of Music

It is appropriate that a discussion of the fundamentals of music begin with an account of the origin and derivation of the musical art. Various accounts of its source are given and are generally well known. Some say that the art originated from the beak of a bird called the *mūsīqār*. This bird had a number of holes in its beak from which it produced assorted high and low sounds. Some say that the art was revealed to Hazrat Sulaiman (peace be upon him) or Da'ud (peace be upon him). One story is that Hakim Pythagoras was its inventor. Others say that it was named after Hazrat Musa (Moses) (peace be upon him). Once while he was in the wilderness, he was passing by a stream whose gentle flow was washing over the pebbles and producing soft and loud sounds. He received the revelation "*yā Mūsā qe*!" that is, "Oh Musa, wait!" The word *taharnā* "wait" means to concentrate, think, or understand. So, under the guidance of that heavenly or divine communication, Hazrat Musa drew forth *rāg* from those sounds. If this is indeed true, then by the grace of God this science is divine. How wonderful it is that it is the very life of the soul. Given that in this world spiritual, bodily, material, imaginary, and mental phenomena are all manifest on the outer plane, nevertheless they surely obtain power from the inner treasury. Thus, in every outer form is the disclosure of something inner. Having pointed this out, I begin a discussion of the principles of music.

This science is built on three foundations: melody (*rāg*), instrumental music, (*bāj*), and dance (*nāc*). In Sanskrit the first is called *gāyan*, the second *vādan*, and the third *nart*. Before expanding on this, I should point out that there is no place on earth, and no people of desert, wilderness, or village, which is excluded from this excellent knowledge. These three things are thoroughly cultivated in every human society, and every culture has the canon and practices for this science. Thus, in Latin the science is called "music," in English "meusic" [sic], and in Sanskrit *sangīt*; and it is *sangīt* which contains the three categories mentioned above.

The three fundamentals are interrelated, and they are not only used in playing and singing, but are connected with every activity. In speaking, for example, the sound that emerges from the throat is singing. That produced by the tip of the pen is instrumental playing, and the actions of the tongue, lips, and teeth, and the face, forehead, eyes, eyebrows, head, neck, and hands when one strikes a pose appropriate for the words, is dance. These facts prove that nothing is empty of *sangīt*. The science has two branches: *sangīt vidyā*, the theory of music, and *sangīt kalā*, the practice of music. *Sangīt vidyā* includes the principles of melody, rhythm, *rāg*, tempo and the like, as well as the theoretical canon. *Sangīt kalā* refers to the artistic practices of singing and playing. In English, *sangīt vidyā* is called "Theoretical Music,"[1] and *sangīt kalā* is called "Practical Music."

This science has two fundamentals: *sur*, that is, sound, and *tāl*, the limit of sustain. The two fundamentals are as close to each other as skirt and blouse. In speech, one can observe that emphasis is necessary, and emphasis is essentially a delimitation of delay, that is, a pause. Without a pause between one word and the next, the intended meaning would be obscure. In truth, rhythm is the soul of sound. *Tāl* and *sur* are the substance of the musical science and they are manifest and present in everything. Evidence for this is, for example, when two pieces of wood or stone are held in each hand. They cannot produce a sound unless they are struck together. Sound becomes manifest when they are struck together, proving that sound is concealed in them. This also indicates that nothing is empty of *sur* and *tāl*.

1 The text reads "Theatrical Music," which I interpret to be a typographical error.

And *tāl* cannot be manifest without *sur*, but is perceived only through *sur*. Now, consider that in your own body the movement of the pulse, the beating of the heart, the passing in and out of the breath, and the sensation and movement of all the limbs are never empty of *sur* and *tāl*. Indeed, creation's every activity confirms the validity of my claim. If we cast our eyes upward, there is above all the beguiling charm of the lovely wink of eternity. The original manifestation was that of sound, which is "*kun*" ("Be!"). All things and beings are its manifestation.

Its virtue is by nature ambrosial;
  the whole *ālāp* of "*kun*" is the essence of sweetness.
All this is the beloved of that "*kun*:"
  the earth, the universe, space, the stars.
Sur and *tāl* are a gift (*ʿināyat*) from eternity itself;
  the Lord is pleased with them to the utmost.
If something has since all preeternity been,
  then certainly it will forever more be.
This world is not without the sun of preeternal being;
  the keeper of its secret is Adam.
"*Kun*" having been pronounced, within this universe
  beauty has become reflected as in a mirror.

The noble Sufis are the swimmers in this ocean of truth. The sound "*kun*" still echoes in their ears. They thrash their arms and legs in deep waters, plunge into annihilation, and safely wash up on the shore of immortality.

Marvelous is the state of one intoxicated by the sound of preeternity:
  his milieu is neither land nor sea.
He has meditated on that sound since the day of preeternity,
  and is fallen at the foot of the Beloved.
By practicing godliness, it manifests in the soul,
  whether I find myself in an idol's temple or the Kaʿaba's precincts.

Inayat has sacrificed his whole being to the divine sound,
   and is prostrate since preeternity at the Beloved's door.
Whatever should be His is exactly how it should be;
   the phenomenal and the real are inseparably linked.
Inayat, enough of you and this matter,
   this talk of reality and these circumstances of yours.
Of God's kindness the sun is just a speck.
   Where there is kindness, hope blossoms forth.

The Christians call this art the "divine art," that is, *fan-i haqīqī*. In any case, as for the merits of this refined art and its proper appreciation, I will explain as much as the scope of explanation allows, for explanation's range is limited. And if I may say so, the pages of the mind are themselves insufficient. In every community in every land, the adornment of feasts and the bluster of battles depend on music. Even in the religion of Islam (where the mullah is there to guard against improprieties) it is allowed for feasts and battles. In wedding ceremonies, for example, the marriage announcement requires the beating of a drum (*daf*). To rally warriors in holy war for the cause of Allah, the use of *daf*, *naqāra*, and belligerent, manly, rhythmic poetry is not only allowed, but manditory. Such is the ancient Arab custom. And in other countries as well, this art is promoted to the utmost. It is we who are stuck in a corner with the cheap and low-natured. Those few who want to learn attach themselves, for the sake of company, to those who have even the least understanding. It is a pity that if anything at all is learned from them it is simply the genealogy of their ancestors or the story of their lineage. Some wise man said: "Be a son of art, not a son of the father." Now, it is astounding that those who can to some extent use a particular *rāg* or *tāl* cannot necessarily explain what "*tīvra*" and "*komal*" mean, and what measure of "*tāl*" and "*mātrā*" are being used. To sing something one does not need to be conversant with its principles. When artists are of this standard, then what is there to say about their listeners and admirers? Facts and principles are eclipsed by pleasure and delight, and pleasure and delight are contingent upon temperament. Thus the pleasure of a listener will depend on his temperament, and accordingly, his exclamations of "*āh, vāh*" may be appropriately timed or misplaced. The whole problem is ignorance about the art. Unfortunately, temperament is intertwined with the spiritual, and because of ignorance or indiscrimination *rāg* has become meaningless. But such people are still our respected companions. It is not for us to make faces at them out of superiority and to receive threatening glances in return. I offer a small example of the difference between temperaments in the experiences of pleasure and delight. If several pictures of mixed quality are set up on a single level, viewers, distinguishing the beautiful from the ugly differently according to their temperaments, will be impressed by different pictures. It is the same with eloquence and the perception of it. One person is ardent about Hafiz of Shiraz, while another thinks the world of Jan Sahab Lakhnavi. The intention in my wordiness here is to arouse interest, but one needs something beyond that to reach the summit of perfection. When confronted with a veil of concealment, good fortune, ardor, and effort are required.

Chapter Two
Sound (*āvāz*)

The scope and extent of sound and its presence in every place and situation were mentioned in the first chapter. I now describe its origin and its source of production. Sound is produced through the vibration of an object. When a person takes a piece of wood in hand, for example, and vibrates it, as many waves as it produces are carried in the air. When the waves pass by the ear a sound is heard. Evidence of the waves becomes visible when one partially fills a thin glass with water, holds it firmly in the hand and rubs a finger on it so as to produce a sound. If one observes the water closely one can see it shaking. When one touches a metal or gut string of an instrument one can clearly feel the vibrations. If one strikes the skin of a *ḍhol* or *naqāra* and immediately puts one's hand on it, or puts a hand on the case of a piano or harmonium while it is being played, one will know for sure that it is the vibration of the object that is producing the sound.

Sound cannot be produced from a space without air. A specific vibration is produced in the air when one strikes a sound-producing object. A sound is heard when the vibrating air touches the eardrum. The intensity of the sound depends on the air in the space in which the sound is produced. For example, sound produced at the top of a mountain cannot be heard as clearly as the same sound produced and carried at the bottom of the mountain, because no matter how strongly it is made there is only thin air. As one descends, the air is thicker. Aside from air, water, metal, wood, earth, and the like also carry sound. In water, for example, the sound of splashing carries to the shore and alerts the people there. And if one puts a small clock on one side of a wooden table and puts one's ear to the other side and listens, one can hear the ticking through the wood. Putting one's ear on a train rail, one can hear the train approaching from a distance. Similarly, during an earthquake, horses grazing in pastures hear sounds from the earth, become startled, and immediately begin to run. Such occurrences are evidence that these are all sound-carrying materials.

Sound carries faster in water than in air, and sound carries faster in a solid than in water. When the air is cold and icy, the speed of sound is 1,090 feet per second, and the speed of sound increases correspondingly as the air becomes warmer. In water, the speed of sound can reach 4,708 feet per second. In an open pond of about 4,708 feet, when a sound is made on one side it will first reach people standing in the water, and after three seconds it will be audible to people standing on the shore. Of the four metals, iron, copper, silver, and gold, sound is carried the fastest in iron. The speed of sound is fifteen times faster in iron than in air. Sound is like the ocean in that its level depends on its waves. A sound has the same succession of waves as the waves at the source of the sound. A sound with more waves per second is perceived as loud, and one with fewer waves as soft. If one produces sixteen waves per second, it is perceived as soft, and if one produces a thousand waves per second, it will seem to be the loudest of loud sounds. These particulars apply to the human voice, and the degrees of musical sound (*sur*) are fixed according to this sort of calculation.

Bodily Sound

Sound produced from the mouth relies on four organs of the body. The first is the lung, which performs the job of a bellows. The second is what in English is called the "larynx." This is the space in the body where air passes and is turned into waves. The third is the organ in which the sound is strengthened, which is called the "pharynx." The fourth is the mouth, including the lips, teeth, tongue and palate. The sacks of the lungs are on both sides of the chest. In each sack, air passes through small tubes and collects in one large tube. The tube where the other tubes meet is the trachea, the organ of the utterance of sound, which is near the pharynx. When air enters the lungs, the sacks fill like balloons, and when it is empty of air they shrink. In the space below the lungs and the ribs and above the stomach there is a divider. In English this is called the "diaphragm."[1] Air enters and leaves the lungs through its movement. When it is stretched with the entering air, the chest and ribs expand, and when air is expended the ribs contract. The pharynx is a part of the larynx, which produces the sound. The larynx is an organ like a small rubber tube, of which the upper portion is called the "pharynx" and the lower portion is the trachea. The larynx is made of three soft bones, which are bound together by a skin in such a way that a movement of one affects them all equally. The names of the three bones are "thyroid," "cricoid," and "arytenoid." On both sides of the arytenoid, two pieces of flesh are joined by skin. The portion between the two pieces of flesh is called the "glottis," which is like lips.[2] Sound is produced from the movement of these pieces of flesh. When you take a breath, the glottis separates, and when you speak, the two pieces touch each other.

All four things are necessary to produce a vocal sound. First, the two pieces of flesh as described above; second, their touching each other; third their tightening to the same degree, because without the tautness, sound production is impossible; and fourth, the movement of air, because the air enters and touches the two pieces of flesh and moves them. The pharynx is a tube, which makes up the upper portion of the larynx. The stream of air emerging from the glottis gives the pharynx force. If one should compare these three organs with a harmonium, the lungs would be comparable to the bellows, the two pieces of flesh of the larynx to the reeds, and the pharynx to the sounding board. In fact, the larynx does not do the work of just one reed; it can easily do the job of twenty reeds with more

1 The text reads "Diapharym."
2 The text reads "Glothis."

or less tension on the two pieces of flesh. Just as the pitch of a *tampura* is made higher or lower by increasing the tension or loosening the strings, the two pieces of flesh mentioned above become more or less taut due to the movement of the tubes and the bones, creating the high or low voice. Furthermore, the sounds can be made loud or soft by actions of the tongue and the throat. In other words, the voice is produced high or low according to the desire of the singer. The lower the larynx is in the throat, the lower the tone. A man's larynx is comparatively lower in the throat than a woman's. But the range or extent of the voice depends on the strength of the singer's organs. Usually a male voice can reach two octaves. A person who has specifically practiced singing a great deal can have a voice that reaches three *saptak*s, that is, three groups of seven notes. Compared to the male voice, the female voice is naturally strong in one *saptak*. The limit of the male voice in music is said to be four *saptak*s. There are two types of male voice: bass and tenor. There are also two types of female voice: contralto, and soprano. A third type of male voice is sometimes mentioned, which is baritone. Similarly, a third type of female voice is mezzo-soprano.[3] The last two types are not very common.

Hearing

The ear has three levels: outer, middle, and inner. The outermost level is shaped like a shell. Its job is to collect airwaves, introduce them to the ear, and signal the direction from which the sound has come. The outer level is called the "ear canal." Its outside mouth is open, and the adjacent part is connected by a thin membrane, which in English is called the "tympanum."[4] The middle ear takes the sound toward the brain. It is a small hole made of bone enclosed on one side by the aforementioned membrane. The second hole is called the "finestriavoali." When the sound strikes the tympanum, the tympanum itself begins

3 The text reads "Suprano" and "Mazo-Suprano."
4 The text reads "Tempanum."

to vibrate and the waves are carried to the finestriavoali via the mentioned bone, and shake the covering. Three bones are called the "hammer," "anvil" and "stirrup."[5] The third level of the ear is very twisted. In English it is called the "labyrinth" because it is crooked like a maze. So the waves carried by the finestriavoali arrive at the inner ear where there are bones inside the snake-like coils. The bones are filled with a sort of marrow in which there is also a type of outer layer of fibers that vibrate. This layer of fibers is called the "coritia fibres" in English. The bones are connected to the brain by the fibers.

Now you can understand how sound is heard: the waves are collected by the outer ear, move through the channel of the outer ear and strike the tympanum, at which point the outermost bones of the tympanum vibrate and set the wall to the middle ear into motion. Then the marrow inside it begins to vibrate, and the fibers of the coritia fibres carry the waves to the brain. The human ear has about three thousand coritia fibres. The ear can perceive about seven *saptak*s. From the example of the ear it is clear that the merciful Lord gave everyone hearing of the same sort. But proficiency in understanding musical sound in the end depends on the training one has received.

---

5 The text reads "Haminer."

Chapter Three
Musical Sound (*sur*)

The essence of singing and playing is musical sound and rhythm (*sur* and *tāl*), but *tāl* is impossible without *sur* because *tāl* is perceived through it. *Sur* is the term for the degrees of higher and lower sounds as determined by the expert practitioners (*ustād*). There are seven *surs*. Just as the seven days have different designations in various regions, the seven *surs* have been given different names in various countries. The names of the seven *surs* are *Kharaj, Rikhab, Gandhār, Madham, Pancam, Dhaivat,* and *Nīkhād.* For ease in singing, they have been given the following names: *Sā, Re, Gā, Mā, Pā, Dhā, Nī,* which are also used in written notations of music. In English they are called the "seven notes" and in English notation they are C, D, E, F, G, A, B. In singing, the syllables *do re mi fa sol la ti* are used.

Ascent and Descent (*ārohī, avarohī*)

The seven *surs* have been fixed at positions, each higher than the one before. Their climb is called *ārohī* and their descent is called *avarohī*, and this is illustrated below.

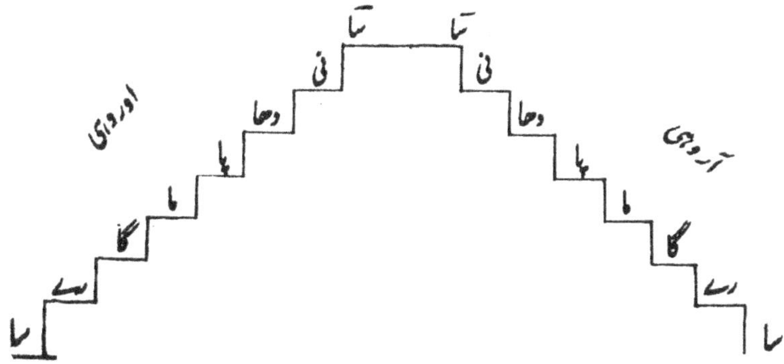

In English, the term for *ārohī* is "ascending" and that for *avarohī* is "descending." In notation they are written as shown below.

In Western music, the five horizontal lines on which the notation is written are called the "staff." On one side of the staff is the sign (𝄞). This is the G clef or treble clef, from which one knows which notes are intended. If the sign for G clef is on the staff, for example, the note on the second line will be G. Similarly, (𝄢) this sign designates F clef or bass clef." Here, notes lower than in the G clef are used, in other words the *kharaj* notes. If the sign appears on the side of the staff, it indicates that F is on the fourth line of the staff. This is shown in the illustration below.

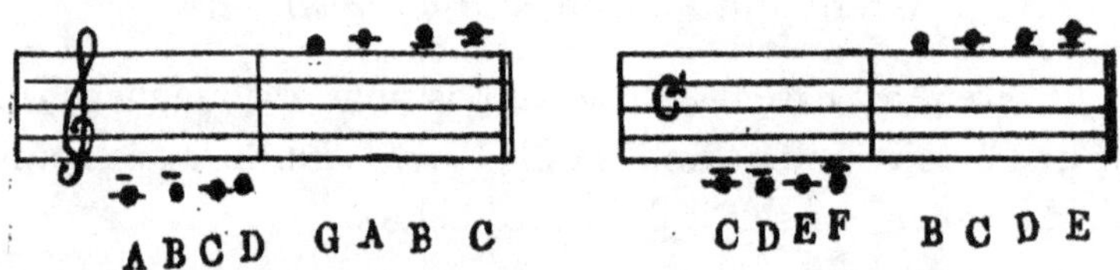

To notate the range beyond the notes on the five lines and the four spaces of the staff, one makes small lines above and below the staff and writes the notes there.

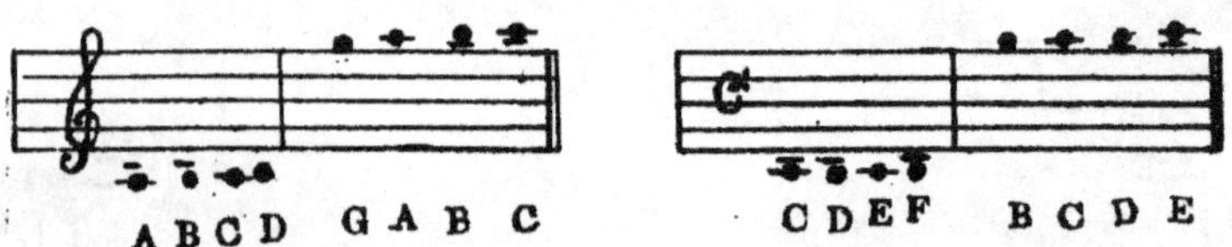

The Properties of the *surs*

In *sangīt*, attributes such as color, dress, effects, and season have been assigned to the seven *surs*. In addition, which *sur* is appropriate to a person's voice at what age, which *sur* is produced from what organ of the human body, and which *sur* is found in what animal's voice, all this is indicated in the chart below.

Chart of the Properties of the *surs*

No	1	2	3	4	5	6	7
Name	*Sa*	*Re*	*Ga*	*Ma*	*Pa*	*Dha*	*Ni*
Color	pink	light green	orange	pearly	red	yellow	black
Dress	white	red	red	white	yellow	red	black
Planet	Moon	Mercury	Venus	Zodiac (*rās*)	Mars	Jupiter	Saturn
Season	all	spring	summer	rainy	cold	winter (*hemant*)	winter (*sisir*)
Effects	cool, moist	cool, dry	cool, moist	warm, dry	warm, dry	cool, warm	cool, dry
Emotional impact (*tāsīr*)	happiness, love	love, happiness	happiness, despair	happiness, love, agitation	lust, despair, anger	happiness, love, anger	happiness, love, lust
Organ of production	navel	heart	middle chest	throat	mouth	head	nose
Singer's age	70	60	50	40	30	20	10
Animal	peacock	cow	sheep	crane	cuckoo	horse	elephant

Saptak

A group of seven notes, *Sā Re Gā Mā Pā Dhā Nī*, is called the *saptak*. However many *saptak*s there may be, the human voice can usually cover three. The first is the *mandra saptak*, which is the low or *kharaj* range. Its notes are notated with a mark beneath the letter: (پا) (*Pā*). Because of the mark below it, one should recognize this *Pā* to be in the *mandra saptak*. The second is *madh*, the middle *saptak*, which is the most commonly used range in vocal and instrumental music. A human sings naturally in this *saptak*. There is no notational mark used to denote it, so a note written without a mark should be recognized as being in the *madh saptak*: (رے) (*Re*). The third is the *tār saptak*, the range above the *madh*, which is also commonly called *tīp*. A line is drawn above the notes of this *saptak*, for example: (سا) (*Sā*). One should understand from the mark above it that it is in the *tār* range.

Aside from the three *saptak*s, an additional two can commonly be produced on instruments. The *mandratar saptak* is the range below the *kharaj* or *mandra*. Those notes have a mark like this: (پا) (*Pā*). Below the *Pā* is a line with a dot above and below it. The *tārtar* is the range above the *tīp* or the *tār saptak*. Such notes will have this mark on them: (ما) (*Mā*). There is a line above the *Mā* with a dot above it. This *saptak* is not very common. Several instruments can reach even above the *tārtar saptak* and below the *mandratar saptak*, but only rarely is it necessary to play them, so no specific names have been assigned to the ranges above and below the five *saptak*s.

Chart of the *saptaks*

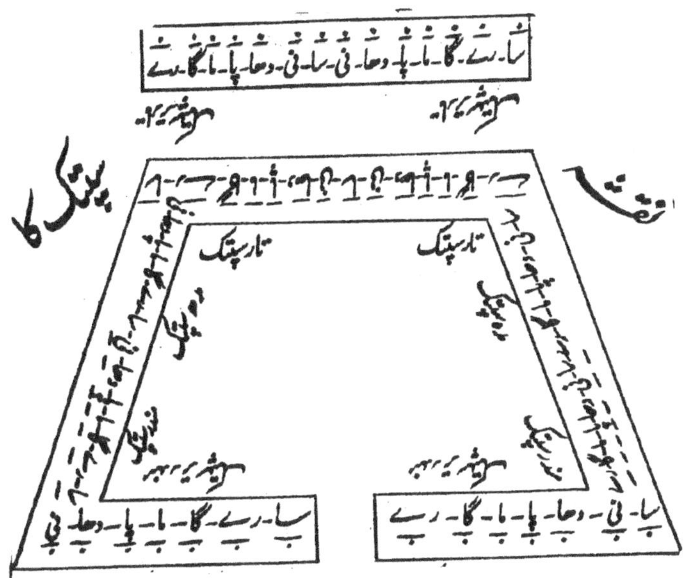

The Low, Middle, High, and Highest Octaves

The English word for *saptak* is "octave." Seven octaves are standard. In Western notation the octaves are as shown below.

English Chart of the Seven *saptaks*

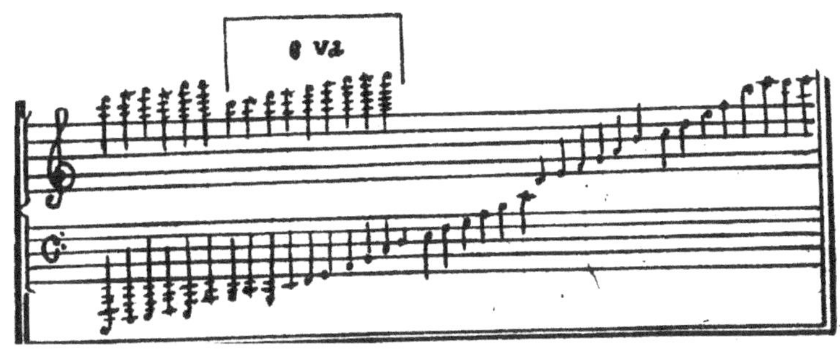

The intervals between the seven *surs* are illustrated in the diagram below:

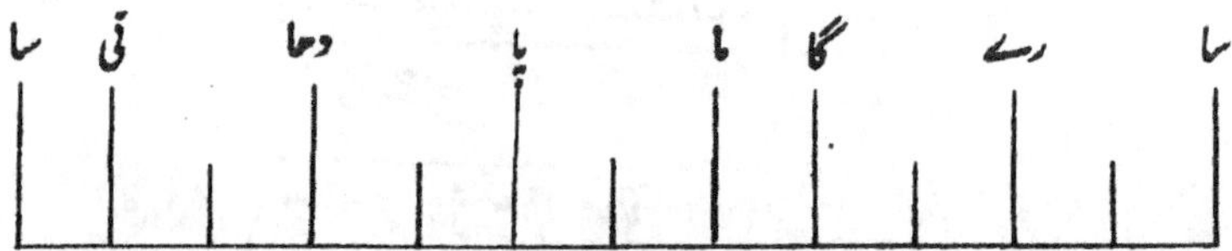

In the diagram above, each division is a half interval. Two half divisions make a full-tone interval. Between *Sā* and *Re*, for example, are divisions of two half intervals, so the interval from *Sā* to *Re* is that of one full tone. From *Re* to *Gā* there is also one full tone. *Gā* to *Mā* has the interval of a half tone. *Mā* to *Pā* is a full tone. *Pā* to *Dhā* is a full tone. *Dhā* to *Nī* is a full tone, and *Nī* to *Sā* is a half-tone interval.

Varieties of *sur*

Surs are of two types: fixed (*sthāī*) and moving (*sancārī*). *Sthāī* is the type that always remains in its original position. Of all the notes, the two of this type are *Sā* and *Pā*. *Sancārī* notes are those that can move from their true positions to a higher or lower position. There are five of them: *Re, Gā, Mā, Dhā, Nī*. The original positions of the seven notes are shown in the chart above. They are called "pure" (*shudh*). In written music, a *shudh* note is notated without any mark. In the case when a notational mark is necessary, however, the following mark will be attached to the note: (ں) . A note with this mark will become *shudh*, as in the example: (ساں-ماں-پاں-) . A raised note is called *tīvra*, and a lowered note is called *komal*. In common language these are also called *caṛhī* and *ūtarī* (raised and lowered). Only one note, *Mā*, can be raised a half tone from its original place and become *tīvra*. Its notation is: (۱) . The other four *Re, Gā, Dhā, Nī*, can be lowered a half tone from their original positions and become *komal*. The notation for komal is (V). One should read a note with a mark like this as *komal.* In all, there are twelve tones, including the *surs* with notational marks, and these are illustrated in the chart below.

Halfway between *Sā* and *Re* is the position of *komal Re.* Between *Re* and *Gā* is *komal Gā. Gā* to *Mā* is an interval of a half tone, so there is no lowered or raised note there. Between *Mā* and *Pā* is *tīvra Mā.* Between *Pā* and *Dhā* is *komal Dhā*, and between *Dhā* and *Nī* is *komal Nī.* Since the interval between *Nī* and *Sā* is a half tone, there is no raised or lowered note here. The half tone intervals together with all the original positions total twelve.

In English, the term for a *shudh sur* is "natural." Its notational sign is (♮). The term for *komal* is "flat." Its notational sign is (♭). The term for *tīvra* is "sharp," and its notational sign is (#). Sometimes a *rāg* requires the use of *atīkomal* and *atītīvra surs. Atīkomal* means lower than *komal* and the notational sign for it is (w). *Atītīvra* means higher than *tīvra* and its sign is (\\). In Western music, *atīkomal* is called "double flat" and its sign is like this: (♭♭). *Atītīvra* is called "double sharp" and its sign is like this: (##). The diagram below shows how these sorts of notes appear in staff notation.

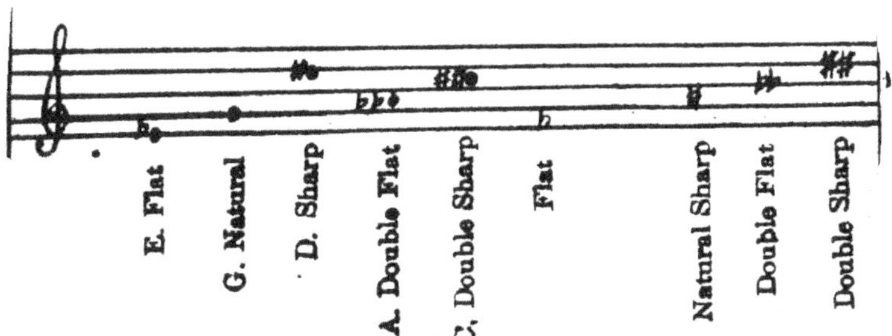

In Western music there are no restrictions about *sthāī* and *sancārī*, so all the notes can be raised and lowered as though they were *sancārī*. We have a method as well in which each of the seven notes takes each of the three positions *shudh*, *komal*, and *tīvra*, making altogether twenty-one. This is called the twenty-one *mūrchanā*s. A diagram is given below.

Chart of the Twenty-one *mūrchanā*s

Sā	*Re*	*Gā*	*Mā*	*Pā*	*Dhā*	*Nī*
Sā komal	*Re komal*	*Gā komal*	*Mā komal*	*Pā komal*	*Dhā komal*	*Nī komal*
Sā tīvra	*Re tīvra*	*Gā tīvra*	*Mā tīvra*	*Pā tīvra*	*Dhā tīvra*	*Nī tīvra*

Sruti

Sruti originates from *sur*. It is a position in the interval between the *sur*s. In the northern part of India, twelve notes consisting of the seven *sur*s with the *komal* and the *tīvra* are called the "twelve *sruti*s," and these are in general use. In the southern area of India they say there are sixteen *sruti*s. Ancient theory texts told of twenty-two *sruti*s. These days a few authorities are considering the possibility of employing twenty-four *sruti*s, each measured as one quarter of each *sur*. To recognize and determine *sruti*s is very difficult indeed, which is why they are not extant. They do, however, come into use spontaneously in singing and playing.

Chart of Twelve *sruti*s

Sā shudh	*Re komal*	*Gā komal*	*Mā shudh*	*Pā shudh*	*Dhā komal*	*Nī komal*
	Re tīvra	*Gā tīvra*	*Mā tīvra*		*Dhā tīvra*	*Nī tīvra*

Chart of Sixteen *srutis*

Sā	*Re* *Re* *Re*	*Gā* *Gā* *Gā*	*Mā* *Mā*	*Pā*	*Dhā* *Dhā* *Dhā*	*Nī* *Nī* *Nī*
shudh	*shudh* *catūsruti* *shatsruti*	*shudh* *sadhāran* *antar*	*shudh* *pratī*	*shudh*	*shudh* *catūsruti* *shatsruti*	*shudh* *kaisikī* *kākilī*

Chart of Twenty-two *srutis*

Sā	*Re*	*Gā*	*Mā*	*Pā*	*Dhā*	*Nī*
tīvrā *kaumudatī* *mandā* *chandavatī*	*dayāvatī* *ranjanī* *ratīkā*	*raudrī* *krodhā*	*vajrīkā* *prasārinī* *prītī* *mārjanī*	*kshitī* *raktā* *sandīpinī* *alāpinī*	*mandatī* *rohinī* *ramyā*	*ugrā* *kshobhīnī*

Grām

In non-technical usage the term *grām* means "village," and here in the art of music, it means the positions of the notes. There are three *grāms*. Masters of the art have various opinions about it, but *kharaj grām, madham grām* and *nikhād grām* are the generally accepted ones.

Chart of Three *grāms*

	Sā Re Gā Mā Pā Dhā Nī	*nikhād grām*
	Sā Re Gā Mā Pā Dhā Nī	*madham grām*
Sā Re Gā Mā Pā Dhā Nī		*kharaj grām*

Vādī— vivādī sur

The principal *sur* that illuminates the *rāg* is called the *vādī*. This note is to the *rāg* as the chief minister (*vazīr*) is to the empire. Along with the *vādī*, the *sur* that illuminates the *rāg* and gives it its character is the *samvādī*, and it is like a nobleman (*amīr*) in the *rāg* empire. The *sur* which is a companion to the *vādī* and the *samvādi* in illuminating the *rāg* is called the *anūvādī*. This is the loyal friend of the empire. The *sur* that obscures the *rāg* is called the *vivādī*, and this note is the enemy of the empire. In *rāg Darbārī Kānarā* for example, the *gandhār* is used frequently and the *rāg* is illuminated through it. Therefore *gandhār* is the *vādī sur*. *Dhaivat* is the *samvādī* and *pancam* is the *anūvādī*. If *shudh gandhār* should sound, it would be a *vivādī sur*. In Western music the *vādī, samvādī* and *anuvādī* are termed "consonant" and the *vivādī* is termed "dissonant."[1]

1 The text reads "Desonant."

Chapter Four
Rāg

Rāg is an appealing arrangement of different notes. There are five types. The first, the *auṛav rāg* has only five notes in ascent and descent, and the rest are *varjit*, that is they are not permitted to sound. In *rāg Bībhās*, for example, the ascending scale is *Sā - Re - Gā - Pā - Dhā* and the descent is *Sā - Dhā - Pā - Gā - Re* -. These are the only notes used, and the others, *Mā* and *Nī*, are *varjit*. The second type is the *shāṛav rāg*, which has six notes. In *rāg Kaunsī Kānharā*, for example, the ascent is *Sā - Re - komal Gā - Mā - Dhā - komal Nī* - and the descent is *Sā - komal Nī - Dhā - Mā - komal Gā - Re* -. The *Pā* is *varjit*. The third type is the *sankīrn rāg* which is different in ascent and descent. *Āsāvarī*, for example, has five notes in ascent and seven notes in descent. The ascent is *Sā - komal Re - Mā - Pā - komal Dhā* - and the descent is *Sā - komal Nī - komal Dhā - Pā - Mā - komal Gā - komal Re* -. *Gā* and *Nī* are *varjit* in the ascent, and all seven notes are used in the descent. The fourth type, the *sampūrn rāg*, uses all seven notes. In *rāg Bhairavīn*, for example, the ascent is *Sā - komal Re - komal Gā - Mā - Pā - komal Dhā - komal Nī* -, and the descent is *Sā - komal Nī - komal Dhā - Pā - Mā - komal Gā - komal Re* -. The fifth type is the *vakra sampūrn rāg* in which the sharp and flat notes are not all the same in ascent and descent and it proceeds in a winding way. *Rāg Gauṛ Sārang*, for example, is like this: *Nī - Sā - Gā - Re - Mā - Gā - - Pā tīvra Mā Dhā Pā - Gā Mā Re Mā Gā - Gā Re Mā Gā - Pā tīvra Mā Dhā Pā - Sā Nī Dhā Pā - Gā Mā Re Mā Gā - - Gā Mā Re Sā* -. Each of these types includes many *rāgs*, of which some are currently practiced and some are rare, and so all *rāgs* exist as permutations (*rāg prastār*). There are some *rāgs* that are known by the same name in every region. These are called *mārg rāgs*. Some *rāgs* have names and manners of singing that differ from region to region. These are called *desī rāgs*.

The ancient experts on *rāg* considered their temperaments and grouped them into divisions of male and female. In their theory some were *rāgs*, that is, fathers, and some were *rāginīs*, mothers, and a few were *putras*, sons, and a very few were *bhārjās*, daughters. Seasons and times were established for *rāgs* as well, which is followed to this day. The ancient stories of the marvelous effects of *rāgs* are well known. There are four different ways of grouping the *rāgs*. The first is *Shīvmat*, which is the lord Shiva's method. The second is *Kishanmat* and it is lord Krishna's method. The third is *Bharatmat* which is the sage Bharat's method. The fourth is *Hanumatmat*, which is Hanuman's method. Each *rāg* has five *rāginīs* and eight *putras*, and each *putra* has one *bhārjā*.

English music does not have the restrictions of *rāg*, but three scales are used for singing and playing: the major scale, the minor scale and the chromatic scale. Their notes are shown in the chart below.

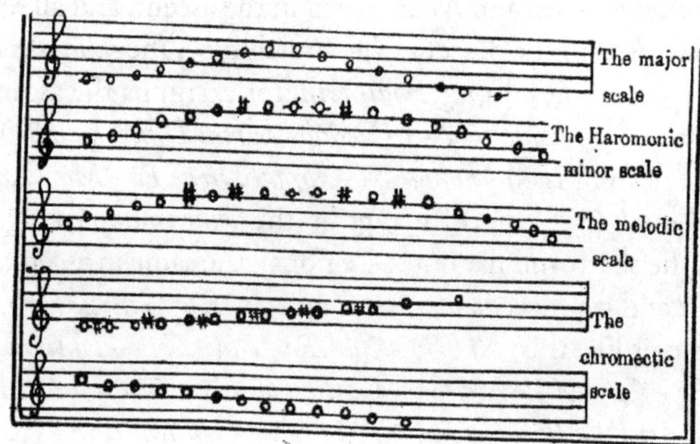

Chart of Six *rāgs* and Their *rāginīs*, *putras* and *bhārjās*[1]

Pancam (66)	*Khokhar*	*Bībhās* (28)	*Hamāl*	*Behāgṛā* (38)	*Shāhānā* (255)

Six *rāgs*

Bhairav (19)	*Mālkaus* (389)	*Hinḍol* (465)	*Dīpak* (156)	*Srī* (200)	*Megh* (383)

Five *rāginīs*

Bhairavī (20)	*Toṛī* (92)	*Rāmkalī* (166)	*Desī*	Mālasrī (378)	*Ṭank*
Barārī (22)	*Gaurī* (340)	*Devsākh* (163)	*Kāmod* (286)	*Āsāvarī* (7)	*Malhār* (384)
Madmād-avī (*Madmā-vat Sārang* 385)	*Gunkalī*	*Lalit* (370)	*Naṭ* (421)	*Dhanāsrī* (138)	*Gujarī* (343)
Sindhavī (232)	*Khambā-vatī* (290)	*Bilāval*	*Kedārā* (288)	*Basant* (32)	*Bhūpālī* (30)
Bangālī	*Kūkab* (292)	*Paṭman-jarī* (62)	*Kānarā* (307)	*Mārvā* (382)	*Deskār* (137)

Eight *putras*

Harak	*Mārū* (375)	*Candra-bhans*	*Kuntal*	*Sindhū* (230)	*Jalandhar*
Thalak	*Mevāṛ*	*Mangal*	*Kanaul*	*Mālva*	*Sārang*
Din kī pūriyā (134)	*Baṛhans* (25)	*Shoba*	*Kaling*	*Gauṛ* (see 341, 342)	*Naṭ nārāyan* (416)
Mādhava	*Prabal*	*Ānand*	*Campak*	*Gunsāgar*	*Shan-karā-bharan*
Sūhū	*Candrik*	*Vīnod*	*Kusum*	*Gumbar*	*Kalyān* (*Shudh Kalyān* 256)
Balnhe	*Nand*	*Pradhān*	*Rām*	*Gambhīr* (355, 361)	*Gajdhar*
Madhva	*Bhanūr*	*Gaurā*	*Jhīl*	*Shankar*	*Gundhār*

1 The numbers in parentheses are my added references to their positions in the complete *rāg* list that follows below.

Eight *bhārjās*

Sūhā	*Dhanāsrī* (138)	*Līlāvatī*	*Mangal Gujarī*	*Vijayā*	*Kinaṛ nāṭ*
Bilāval	*Mālasrī* (378)	*Kīrvī*	*Jaijai-vantī* (97)	*Dayāvatī*	*Gāvadī*
Soraṭī (199)	*Jaitsrī* (95)	*Jaitī* (96)	*Mālgajrī*	*Kanjar*	*Kadam nāṭ*
Kham-bhārī	*Sugarāī* (198)	*Pūrvī* (59)	*Bhūpālī* (30)	*Sohinī*	*Bihārī* (23)
Andāhī	*Durgā*	*Pārvatī*	*Manoharī* (377)	*Sarvā*	*Mānjh (Mānjhī 386)*
Bhal Gujarī	*Gan-dhārī* (345)	*Trivenī*	*Ahīrī* (6)	*Kshīmā*	*Paraj* (60)
Paṭman-jarī (62)	*Bhīm-palāsī* (26)	*Devgirī* (139)	*Iman* (484)	*Shashī-rekhā*	*Naṭ manjarī*
Sīrdī	*Kāmodī* (287)	*Sursatī* (201)	*Hamīr*	*Sarāsatī*	*Shudh nāṭ* (265)

List of Current *rāgs*[1]

	Rāg Name	*Sur*	Time	References
1	*Ālaiyā Bilāval*	*S R G P D N Ṡ* *Ṡ N D P M G R S*	2nd *pahar*, day	*gat* 68
2	*Aṛānā Kānaṛā*	*S R G̲ G M P N̲ N Ṡ* *Ṡ N N̲ P M G G̲ R S*	night	
3	*Irkal Kāmodī*	*S R G M P D N̲ N* *Ṡ N N̲ D P M G R S*		
4	*Ānand Bhairavī*	*S R G̲ M P D N̲ Ṡ* *Ṡ N̲ D P M G̲ R S*		
5	*Ārabhī*	*S R M P D Ṡ* *Ṡ N D P M G R S*		
6	*Āhīrī*	*S R M P D Ṡ* *Ṡ N̲ D P M G̲ R S*	midnight	*bhārjā*
7	*Āsāvarī*	*S R̲ M P D̲ Ṡ* *Ṡ N̲ D̲ P M G̲ R̲ S*	1st *pahar*, day	*rāginī*
8	*Urnakāntā*	*S R M P M D N̲ Ṡ* *Ṡ N̲ D P M D M G* *R S*		
9	*Amritvāhinī*	*S G̲ M P D N̲ Ṡ* *Ṡ N̲ D̲ M G̲ R S*		
10	*Abhīrī*	*S G̲ R G̲ M N̲ Ṡ* *Ṡ N̲ D̲ P M G̲ R S*		
11	*Abhogī*	*S R G̲ M D̲ Ṡ* *Ṡ D̲ M G̲ R S*		
12	*Ādī Bhairavī*	*S G̲ R G̲ M P D̲ Ṡ* *Ṡ D̲ P M P G̲ R S*		
13	*Udaycandrīkā*	*S R G̲ M P D̲ N̲ Ṡ* *Ṡ D̲ P M R S*		
14	*Urnacandrīkā*	*S G̲ M P N̲ Ṡ* *Ṡ N̲ P D P M G̲ S*		
15	*Udayravīcandrikā*	*S R̍ G M D̍ N Ṡ* *Ṡ N D̍ M G R̍ S*		
16	*Ānandlīlā*	*S R̍ G M P N Ṡ* *Ṡ N D̲ P M G R̍ S*		
17	*Urnajvalit*	*S R G̲ M̍ D N Ṡ* *Ṡ N D P M̍ G̲ R S*		

1 The reference column is my addition, noting where else in the *Minqār* the *rāg* appears.

18	*Utarī*	$S\ G\ \overset{'}{M}\ P\ D\ \underline{N}\ \dot{S}$ $\dot{S}\ \underline{N}\ D\ \overset{'}{M}\ G\ S$		
19	*Bhairav*	$S\ \underline{R}\ G\ M\ P\ \underline{D}\ N\ \dot{S}$ $\dot{S}\ N\ \underline{D}\ P\ M\ G\ \underline{R}\ S$	end of night	*rāg*
20	*Bhairavī*	$S\ \underline{R}\ \underline{G}\ M\ \overset{'}{M}\ P\ \underline{D}\ \underline{N}\ \dot{S}$ $\dot{S}\ \underline{N}\ \underline{D}\ P\ \overset{'}{M}\ \underline{G}\ \underline{R}\ S$	1st *pahar*, day	*rāginī* songs 18, 31, 44, 61 *gat* 73 *sargam* 106
21	*Bhavapriyā*	$S\ \underline{R}\ \underline{G}\ \overset{'}{M}\ P\ \underline{D}\ \underline{N}\ \dot{S}$ $\dot{S}\ \underline{N}\ \underline{D}\ P\ \overset{'}{M}\ \underline{G}\ \underline{R}\ S$		
22	*Barārī*	$S\ \underline{R}\ G\ M\ P\ \underline{D}\ N\ \dot{S}$ $\dot{S}\ N\ \underline{D}\ P\ M\ G\ \underline{R}\ S$	4th *pahar*, day	*rāginī*
23	*Bīhārī*	$S\ R\ M\ P\ D\ \underline{N}\ N\ \dot{S}$ $\dot{S}\ N\ \underline{N}\ D\ P\ M\ G\ R\ S$		*bhārjā songs* 13, 36, 39
24	*Bilāval*	$S\ R\ G\ P\ D\ \dot{S}$ $\dot{S}\ N\ \underline{N}\ D\ P\ M\ G\ R\ S$		*rāginī*
25	*Baṛhans*	$S\ R\ G\ M\ P\ D\ N\ \dot{S}$ $\dot{S}\ N\ \underline{N}\ D\ P\ M\ G\ R\ S$	night	*putra*
26	*Bhīmpalās*	$S\ R\ \underline{G}\ M\ P\ D\ \underline{N}\ \dot{S}$ $\dot{S}\ \underline{N}\ \underline{D}\ P\ M\ \underline{G}\ R\ S$	3rd *pahar*, day	*bhārjā* song 3
27	*Bilāval Surparda*	$S\ R\ G\ M\ P\ D\ \underline{N}\ N\ \dot{S}$ $\dot{S}\ N\ \underline{N}\ D\ P\ M\ G\ R\ S$	1st *pahar*, day	
28	*Bībhās*	$S\ R\ G\ P\ D\ \dot{S}$ $\dot{S}\ D\ P\ G\ R\ S$	1st *pahar*, day	*putra*
29	*Bāgesrī Kānaṛā*	$S\ R\ \underline{G}\ M\ P\ D\ \underline{N}\ \dot{S}$ $\dot{S}\ \underline{N}\ D\ P\ M\ \underline{G}\ R\ S$	night	
30	*Bhūpālī*	$S\ R\ G\ \overset{'}{M}\ P\ D\ N\ \dot{S}$ $\dot{S}\ N\ D\ P\ \overset{'}{M}\ G\ R\ S$	1st *pahar*, day	*rāginī*, *bhārjā*
31	*Bhūdevkriyā*	$S\ R\ M\ P\ D\ \dot{S}$ $\dot{S}\ D\ P\ M\ R\ S$		
32	*Basant*	$S\ \underline{R}\ G\ M\ \overset{'}{M}\ \underline{D}\ D\ N\ \dot{S}$ $\dot{S}\ N\ D\ \underline{D}\ P\ M\ \underline{G}\ R\ S$	spring season	*rāginī* song 7
33	*Bindrabanī Sārang*	$S\ R\ \underline{G}\ M\ P\ D\ \underline{N}\ \dot{S}$ $\dot{S}\ \underline{N}\ D\ P\ M\ \underline{G}\ R\ S$	2nd *pahar*, day	

34	*Bahār*	*S R G̲ M P D N̲ N Ṡ* *Ṡ N N̲ D P M G̲ R S*	1st *pahar*, night	song 5
35	*Barvā*	*S R G̲ G M P D N̲* *N Ṡ* *Ṡ N N̲ D P M G G̲* *R S*	3rd *pahar*, day	*gat* 72
36	*Basvāṛā*	*S R G M P D N Ṡ* *Ṡ N D P M G R S*	monsoon season	
37	*Bihāg*	*S R G M M̍ P D N Ṡ* *Ṡ N D P M̍ M G R S*	midnight	songs 10, 19, 38, 51
38	*Bihāgṛā*	*S R G M P D N Ṡ* *Ṡ N D P M G R S*	1st *pahar* night	*putra*
39	*Bilāval Devgirī*	*S R G M P D N Ṡ* *Ṡ N D P M G R S*		
40	*Bilhārī*	*S R G P D Ṡ* *Ṡ N D P M G R S*	1st *pahar*, day	
41	*Bhabanvikram*	*S R G M P D Ṡ* *Ṡ N D P R S*	3rd *pahar*, night	
42	*Bahāvalī*	*S R̲ G P D̲ Ṡ* *Ṡ N D̲ P G R̲ S*		
43	*Bogī*	*S R̲ M P D̲ Ṡ* *Ṡ D̲ N D̲ P M R̲ M* *G R̲ S*		
44	*Bhālayatī*	*S R̲ G M P D N̲ Ṡ* *Ṡ N̲ M P R̲ G*	2nd *pahar*, day	
45	*Balāngī*	*S G R̲ G M P D̲ P Ṡ* *Ṡ N D̲ P M G R̲ S*		
46	*Bhujang*	*S R̲ S M G M N̲ D* *N̲ Ṡ* *Ṡ N̲ D M G R̲ S*		
47	*Balhas*	*S R M P D Ṡ* *Ṡ N̲ D P M R M G S*		
48	*Bhanglā*	*S R G M P Ṡ* *Ṡ N̲ D P M R G R S*	2nd *pahar*, night	
49	*Bhoglīlā*	*S R G P D̲ N Ṡ* *Ṡ N D̲ M G R S*		
50	*Bhūpālpancī*	*S G̳ R̲ G̳ P M D̲ Ṡ* *Ṡ P D̲ M̍ G̳ R̲ S*		

51	*Bhavalāmukhī*	*S R̲ G̲ M̍ P N Ṡ* *Ṡ N D̲ P M̍ G̲ R̲ S*		
52	*Bhūsāvalī*	*S R G M̍ P D Ṡ* *Ṡ N̲ D P M̍ G R S*		
53	*Barbar*	*S G M̍ R G M̍ R G* *M̍ D N̲ D Ṡ* *Ṡ N̲ D M̍ G R S*		
54	*Bhūp Kalyān*	*S R M̍ P D Ṡ* *Ṡ N D P M̍ G R S*		
55	*Bharranjanī*	*S R G P D N Ṡ* *Ṡ N D M̍ G R S*		
56	*Bhānumatī*	*S R G̳ R̲ M P Ṡ* *Ṡ D P M G̳ R̲ S*	last *pahar* night	
57	*Bhogcintāman*	*S R̲ M P D̲ Ṡ* *Ṡ N̳ D̲ P M G̲ R̲ S*		
58	*Bhogayī*	*S G̲ M P D̲ P D N̳ Ṡ* *Ṡ N̲ D̲ P M D̲ P M* *G̲ R̲ S*		
59	*Pūrvī*	*S R̲ G M M̍ P D̲ D* *N Ṡ* *Ṡ N D D̲ P M̍ M G* *R̲ S*	3rd *pahar* day	*bhārjā gat* 76
60	*Paraj*	*S R̲ G M M̍ P D̲ D* *N Ṡ* *Ṡ N D D̲ P M̍ M G* *R̲ S*	midnight	*bhārjā*
61	*Prabhāvatī*	*S R̲ G P D̲ N Ṡ* *Ṡ N D̲ P G R̲ S*		
62	*Paṭmanjarī*	*S R̲ G̲ M M̍ P D̲ N̲* *N Ṡ* *Ṡ N N̲ D̲ P M̍ M G̲* *R̲ S*	1st *pahar* night	*rāginī, bhārjā*
63	*Panthuvarālī*	*S R̲ G̲ M̍ P D̲ N Ṡ* *Ṡ N D̲ P M̍ D̲ M̍ G̲* *R̲ S*		
64	*Pāvanī*	*S R̲ G̳ M̍ P D N Ṡ* *Ṡ N D P M̍ G̳ R̲ S*		
65	*Pradīpak*	*S G M M̍ P N Ṡ* *Ṡ N P M̍ M G R S*		

66	*Pancham*	S R̲ G M P D̲ N Ṡ Ṡ N D̲ P M G R̲ S	2nd *pahar* day	*putra*
67	*Pahāṛī*	S R G̲ G M P D N̲ N Ṡ S N N̲ D P M G G̲ R Ṡ		
68	*Pahāṛī Kāmodī*	S R G M P D N̲ Ṡ Ṡ N̲ D P M G R S		
69	*Pahāṛī Jhinjhoṭī*	S R G M P D N̲ N Ṡ Ṡ N N̲ D P M G R S	3rd *pahar* day	see songs 23, 28, 57
70	*Pīlū*	S R̲ R G̲ G M P D̲ N Ṡ Ṡ N D̲ P M G G̲ R R̲ S	3rd *pahar* day	songs 32, 47 *gat* 72
71	*Pīlāsī*	S R G̲ G M P D̲ N̲ N Ṡ Ṡ N N̲ D D̲ P M G G̲ R S		
72	*Punnāgvarālī*	S R G̲ M P D̲ N̲ Ṡ Ṡ N̲ D̲ P M G̲ R S		
73	*Panādavatī*	S R̲ M P D̲ N Ṡ Ṡ N̲ D̲ P M G̳ R̲ S		
74	*Phanagarav*	S M̍ G M̍ P N D̲ N Ṡ Ṡ N P M̍ G R̲ S		
75	*Pushpālalit*	S G M̍ D̲ N Ṡ Ṡ D̲ P M̍ R̲ S		
76	*Pārvatīrav*	S M G M P D N Ṡ Ṡ N D P M G M G R S		
77	*Purvakālailī*	S R̲ G M̍ P D N P D N P Ṡ Ṡ N D P M̍ G R̲ S		
78	*Pūrnacandrīkā*	S R G M P D N Ṡ Ṡ N P D P M G M R S		
79	*Pūrnasādham*	S R̲ G M P D̲ P M G R̲ S N D̲ N S		
80	*Phanāg Toṛī*	Ṇ̲ Ḍ̲ Ṇ̲ S R̲ G̲ M P D̲ N D̲ P M G̲ R̲ S N̲ D̲ N̲ S		

81	*Palmanjarī*	*S G̲ M D Ṡ* *Ṡ N̲ D P M G̲ R S*		
82	*Pūrna Kāmbodī*	*S R G M P N̲ Ṡ* *Ṡ D P M G R S*		
83	*Pratāpvarālī*	*S R M P D N̲ D P D* *N̲ Ṡ* *Ṡ N̲ D P M G R S*	4th *pahar* day	
84	*Pūranodaye*	*S R M P D Ṡ* *Ṡ N P M R G R S*		
85	*Pratīravā*	*S R̲ G M̍ P D N Ṡ* *Ṡ N D N P M D P M̍* *G R M̍ G R S*		
86	*Pūrvahūtīkā*	*S M P D N Ṡ* *Ṡ N D P M S*		
87	*Pūrvī*	*S R̲ G M P D̲ N P Ṡ* *Ṡ N D̲ P M G R̲ S*		
88	*Trivan*	*S R̲ G M̍ D N Ṡ* *Ṡ N D M̍ G R̲ S*	4th *pahar* day	time of day misplaced for *Pūrvī* above?
89	*Tilang*	*S R G M P N̲ N Ṡ* *Ṡ N N̲ P M G R S*	2nd *pahar* day	song 34
90	*Tilak Kāmod*	*S R G M P D N̲ N Ṡ* *Ṡ N N̲ D P M G R S*	night	song 33 *gat* 70
91	*Tānrūpī*	*S R̲ G̲ M P D̲ N Ṡ* *Ṡ N D̲ P M G̲ R̲ S*		
92	*Toṛī*	*S R G̲ M̍ P D̲ N Ṡ* *Ṡ N D̲ P M̍ G̲ R̲ S*	1st *pahar* day	*rāginī sargam* 108
93	*Tān Vasant*	*S G̲ M P N̲ Ṡ* *Ṡ N̲ D P M G̲ R S*		
94	*Trishūlī*	*S G M P N Ṡ* *Ṡ N D P M Ṙ S*		
95	*Jaitsīrī*	*S R̲ G M̍ P D̲ N Ṡ* *Ṡ N D̲ P M̍ G R̲ S*	4th *pahar* day	*bhārjā* (*Jaitshrī*)
96	*Jait*	*S R̲ G M̍ P D̲ N Ṡ* *Ṡ N D̲ P M̍ M G R̲ S*	4th *pahar* day	*bhārjā* (*Jaitī*)
97	*Jaijaivantī*	*S R G̲ G M P D N̲* *N Ṡ* *Ṡ N N̲ D P M G G̲* *R S*	midnight	*bhārjā* song 26 *gat* 97

98	*Jogī Āsāvarī*	*S R̲ M P D̲ Ṡ* *Ṡ N D̲ P M G R̲ S*	1st *pahar* day	song 48 see *gat* 75
99	*Jaunpūrī Toṛī*	*S R M P D̲ Ṡ* *Ṡ N̲ D̲ P M G̲ R S*	1st *pahar* day	song 50
100	*Jhinjhoṭī*	*S R G M P D N̲ N Ṡ* *Ṡ N N̲ D P M G R S*	3rd *pahar* day	songs 23, 28, 57
101	*Janglā*	*S R G̲ G M P D N̲ Ṡ* *Ṡ N̲ D P M G G̲ R S*	3rd *pahar* day	song 52
102	*Jīlaf*	*S R̲ G M P D̲ N Ṡ* *Ṡ N D̲ P M G R̲ S*	last *pahar* night	
103	*Jog*	*S R̲ G M M̍ P D̲ N Ṡ* *Ṡ N D̲ P M̍ G R̲ S*		
104	*Jalāvarnam*	*S R̲ G̲ M̍ P D̲ N Ṡ* *Ṡ N̲ D̲ P M̍ G̲ R̲ S*		
105	*Jhālvarālī*	*S R̲ G̲ M̍ P D̲ N Ṡ* *Ṡ N D̲ P M̍ G̲ R̲ S*		
106	*Jotīsvarūpinī*	*S R̍ G M̍ P D̲ N̲ Ṡ* *Ṡ N̲ D̲ P M̍ G R̍ S*		
107	*Jogī Vasant*	*S R G M P D N Ṡ* *D N D P M G R S*		
108	*Jhanīkār*	*S R G M D N S* *S N D M G R S*		
109	*Jhankār Dhanī*	*S R R G̲ M P D N̲ Ṡ* *Ṡ N̲ D̲ P M R S*		
110	*Jaganmohinī*	*S G M P N Ṡ* *Ṡ N P M G R̲ S*	3rd *pahar* night	
111	*Jog Bhairavī*	*S R G̲ M P D̲ Ṡ* *Ṡ N̲ D̲ P R S*		
112	*Jaimanoharī*	*S R G̲ M D Ṡ* *Ṡ N̲ P M G̲ R S*		
113	*Jairamā*	*S R G M P D N̲ Ṡ* *Ṡ N D P M G S*		
114	*Jalshekhar*	*S R G M P N̲ D N̲ Ṡ* *Ṡ D P M R G R S*		
115	*Jogī Bhairavī*	*S R G M P D N̲ Ṡ* *Ṡ N D P M N̲ D M G* *R M G S*		
116	*Jaimunhav*	*S G M P D Ṡ* *Ṡ N D P M̍ G R̲ S*		

117	*Janranjanī*	$S R G M P D N \dot{S}$ $\dot{S} D P M R S$		
118	*Jhankārdhvanī*	$S R \underline{G} M P \underline{D} \underline{\underline{N}} \dot{S}$ $\dot{S} \underline{\underline{N}} \underline{D} P M \underline{G} R S$		
119	*Chāyā*	$S R \underline{G} G M P D \underline{N}$ $N \dot{S}$ $\dot{S} N \underline{N} D P M G \underline{G}$ $R S$		
120	*Chāyānaṭ*	$S R G M P D \underline{N} N \dot{S}$ $\dot{S} N \underline{N} D P M G R S$	2nd *pahar* night	
121	*Cakrāvak*	$S \underline{R} G M P D \underline{N} \dot{S}$ $\dot{S} \underline{N} D P M G \underline{R} S$		
122	*Cārūkesī*	$S R G M P \underline{D} \underline{N} \dot{S}$ $\dot{S} \underline{N} \underline{D} P M G R S$		
123	*Cal Nāṭ*	$S \overset{|}{R} G M P \underline{D} N \dot{S}$ $\dot{S} N \underline{D} P M G \overset{|}{R} S$		
124	*Catamīrī*	$S R G \overset{|}{M} P \overset{|}{D} N \dot{S}$ $\dot{S} N \overset{|}{D} P \overset{|}{M} G R S$		
125	*Caranvarālī*	$S R \underline{G} M \underline{D} \underline{N} \underline{D} \dot{S}$ $\dot{S} \underline{N} \underline{D} M \underline{G} R S$		
126	*Candrīkā Bhairavī*	$S \underline{G} R \underline{G} M \underline{D} \underline{N} \dot{S}$ $\dot{S} \underline{N} \underline{D} M \underline{G} R S$	midnight	
127	*Caitanjanī*	$S R G R G M P D \underline{N}$ $D \underline{N} \dot{S}$ $\dot{S} \underline{N} D \underline{N} M G M R$ $G R S$		
128	*Citraman*	$S \underline{R} M P D N \dot{S}$ $\dot{S} N D P M \underline{G} \underline{R} S$		
129	*Candrajot*	$S \underline{R} \underline{\underline{G}} \overset{|}{M} P D P \underline{N} \dot{S}$ $\dot{S} N P D P \overset{|}{M} \underline{\underline{G}} \underline{R} S$		
130	*Candrārekha*	$S R \underline{G} \overset{|}{M} P D \dot{S}$ $\dot{S} \underline{N} D \overset{|}{M} \underline{G} R S$		
131	*Cakūrdhvanī*	$S R \underline{G} \overset{|}{M} P D \underline{N} \dot{S}$ $\dot{S} \underline{N} \overset{|}{M} \underline{G} R S$		
132	*Catāvatī*	$S R \overset{|}{M} P D N \dot{S}$ $\dot{S} N D P \overset{|}{M} G R S$		
133	*Cāturranjanī*	$S \overset{|}{M} G \overset{|}{M} P \underline{\underline{N}} \dot{S}$ $\dot{S} \underline{\underline{N}} \underline{\underline{D}} \underline{\underline{N}} P G \overset{|}{M} \overset{|}{R} S$		

134	*Din kī Pūriyā*	*S R̲ G M̍ P D̲ N Ṡ* *Ṡ N D̲ P M̍ G R̲ S*	4th *pahar* day	*putra*
135	*Des*	*S R G M P D N̲ N Ṡ* *Ṡ N N̲ D P M G R S*	1st *pahar* night	song 46
136	*Desāk*	*S R G̲ M P D N̲ N Ṡ* *Ṡ N N̲ D P M G̲ R S*	1st *pahar* day	
137	*Deskār*	*S R G P D N Ṡ* *Ṡ N D P G R S*	1st *pahar* night	*rāginī*
138	*Dhanāsrī*	*S R G̲ M P D̲ N̲ N Ṡ* *Ṡ N N̲ D̲ P M G̲ R S*	3rd *pahar* night	*rāginī* *bhārjā*
139	*Devgirī*	*S R̲ M̍ P D̲ Ṡ* *Ṡ N D̲ P M̍ G S*	4th *pahar* day	*bhārjā* song 37
140	*Devgandhār*	*S R̲ R G̲ M P D̲ D* *N̲ Ṡ* *Ṡ N̲ D D̲ P M G̲ R* *R̲ S*	last *pahar* night	song 9
141	*Darbārī Kānaṛā*	*S R G̲ M P D̲ N̲ Ṡ* *Ṡ N̲ D̲ P M G̲ R S*	night	songs 6, 16
142	*Dhānī*	*S R G̲ M P D N̲ Ṡ* *Ṡ N̲ D P M G̲ R S*	3rd *pahar* day	
143	*Dhavalsīrī*	*S R G̲ M P D N̲ Ṡ* *Ṡ N̲ D P M G̲ R S*	2nd *pahar* day	
144	*Dhanevakā*	*S R̲ G̲ M M D̲ N Ṡ* *Ṡ N D̲ P M G̲ R̲ S*		
145	*Dhīr Shankarābharan*	*S R G M P D N Ṡ* *Ṡ N D P M G R S*		
146	*Dholāmbarī*	*S R̲ G M̍ P D̲ N̲ Ṡ* *Ṡ N̲ D̲ P M̍ G R̲ S*		
147	*Dhātuvarohinī*	*S R̍ G M̍ P D̲ N Ṡ* *Ṡ N D̲ P M̍ G R̍ S*		
148	*Desgaul*	*S R̲ S P D̲ N Ṡ* *Ṡ N D̲ P R̲ S*		
149	*Devkriyā*	*S G̲ R G̲ M P D N̲* *D Ṡ* *Ṡ N̲ D P M G̲ R S*	last *pahar* night	
150	*Devmukhārī*	*S R G̲ M P D N̲ Ṡ* *Ṡ N̲ D M P M R G̲* *M R S*		

151	*Darbār*	*S R M P D N̲ Ṡ* *Ṡ N̲ D P M P D P* *G̲ R S*		
152	*Devmanoharī*	*S R M P N̲ D N̲ Ṡ* *Ṡ N̲ D P M G̲ R S*		
153	*Darajransatī*	*S R G M P M D P N̲* *D N̲ Ṡ* *Ṡ D P D N̲ D P M G* *M G R S*		
154	*Divratāvardān*	*S R G M P̍ D Ṡ* *Ṡ N D P M R G R S*		
155	*Dīvyākuntal*	*S R̲ G̲ M P D̲ Ṡ* *Ṡ N D̲ P M G̲ R̲ S*		
156	*Dīpak*	*S G M P Ḋ̲ P Ṡ* *Ṡ N D̲ N Ṡ G P M* *G R̲ S*		*rāg*
157	*Darpmanjarī*	*S G R̲ G M̍ P N Ṡ* *Ṡ N D P M G S*		
158	*Dīye*	*S R G̲ M P̍ D Ṡ* *Ṡ N D P M G̲ R S*		
159	*Dīrgdarshī*	*S R M P Ḋ N Ḋ Ṡ* *Ṡ N D P M G M S*		
160	*Dīmavarāshtra*	*S R M P Ṅ Ṡ* *Ṡ N D̲ P M G R S*		
161	*Dhātūpancamī*	*S R G M̍ P N P Ṡ* *Ṡ N D̲ P M̍ R G M* *R S*		
162	*Dharmavatī*	*S R G̲ M P D N Ṡ* *Ṡ N D P M G̲ R S*		
163	*Devsāksh*	*S R M P Ḋ N Ṡ* *Ṡ N D P M G R S*	last *pahar* night	*rāginī*
164	*Dīvaman*	*S R̲ G̲ M̍ P D P N̲ Ṡ* *Ṡ N̲ D P M G̲ R̲ S*		
165	*Davīmkipriyā*	*S G R M P N Ṡ* *Ṡ N D M G R S*		
166	*Rāmkalī*	*S R̲ G M P D N Ṡ* *Ṡ N D P M G R̲ S*	1st *pahar* day	*rāginī* *gat* 74 *sargams* 82, 95, 102

167	*Rāmsākh*	*S R G̲ G̍ M P D N̲ N Ṡ* *S N N̲ D P̍ M G G̲ R Ṡ*		
168	*Rāmpriyā*	*S R̲ G M P D N̲ Ṡ* *Ṡ N̲ D P M G R̲ S*		
169	*Rītgaul*	*S R G̲ M P D N̲ Ṡ* *Ṡ N̲ D P M G̲ R S*		
170	*Rūsīcandrīkā*	*S R G M̍ D N̲ D Ṡ* *Ṡ N D M G̍ R S*		
171	*Rāt kī Pūriyā*	*S R̲ G M P D N Ṡ* *Ṡ N D P M G R̲ S*		
172	*Ratarangī*	*S R̲ G̳ M P D̲̍ N̲ Ṡ* *Ṡ N̲ D̲̍ P M G̳ R S*		
173	*Rūpavatī*	*S R̲ G̲ M P D N Ṡ* *Ṡ N D P M G̲ R̲̍ S*		
174	*Rāgvardhanī*	*S R̲ G M̍ P D̲̍ N̲ Ṡ* *Ṡ N̲ D̲̍ P M̍ G R S*		
175	*Raghūpriyā*	*S R̲ G̳ M̍ P D N Ṡ* *Ṡ N D P M̍ G̳ R̲ S*		
176	*Rīshabpriyā*	*S Ṙ G M̍ P D̲̍ N̲ Ṡ* *Ṡ N̲ D̲̍ P M̍ G R̍ S*		
177	*Rasikpriyā*	*S R G M P D N Ṡ* *Ṡ N D P M G R S*		
178	*Rāmlalit*	*S R̲ G M P N P Ṡ* *Ṡ N D̲ M P M G S*		
179	*Rūdragandhār*	*S R G̲ R M P M D̲* *N̲ Ṡ* *Ṡ N̲ D̲ M G̲ S*		
180	*Rūdrapancam*	*S G M N̲ D Ṡ* *Ṡ N̲ D M G R̲ S*		
181	*Rāgmālin*	*S R̲ G M P D Ṡ* *Ṡ D R̲ D P M G R̲ S*		
182	*Ratnajotī*	*S G M P N Ṡ* *Ṡ N̲ D G R S*		
183	*Raghūpatī*	*S R G P D Ṡ* *Ṡ D P M G R S*	1st *pahar* day	
184	*Rasāvalī*	*S R̲ G̳ M D N̲ Ṡ* *Ṡ N̲ D P M G̳ R̲ S*		
185	*Ratnaman*	*S R̲ G̲ M P D N Ṡ* *Ṡ N D P G̲ R̲ S*		

186	*Rāmmanoharī*	S G M P N Ṡ Ṡ N D̲ P M̍ G S		
187	*Rūdramanjarī*	S R̲ G̲̍ P N D̲ Ṡ Ṡ N D̲ P̍ M G̲ R̲ S		
188	*Rūshabhavāhinī*	S R̲ M̍ P D̍ N Ṡ Ṡ N D M̍ G̲ R̲ S		
189	*Ratnamatī*	S G̲ M P M D N Ṡ Ṡ D P M P G̲ R̲ S		
190	*Rāmkriyā*	S R̲ G M̍ P M D̲ N Ṡ Ṡ N D̲ P̍ M G M S		
191	*Ranjanī*	S R G̲̍ M D Ṡ Ṡ N D M̍ G̲ S R S		
192	*Rāj Kalyān*	S G M D N̍ Ṡ Ṡ N D M G̍ R S		
193	*Ratī*	S G̲ R̲ G̲̍ M P D N Ṡ Ṡ N D P M̍ G̲ R̲̍ S		
194	*Ramākhpriyā*	S R̲ G M P D̲ N Ṡ Ṡ N D̲ P M R̲ M G R̲ S		
195	*Surāvalī*	S R G M P D N̲ N Ṡ Ṡ N N̲ D P M G R S		
196	*Sindh Bhairavī*	S R G̲ M P D̲ N̲ Ṡ Ṡ N̲ D̲ P M G̲ R S	1st *pahar* day	
197	*Sūhā*	S R G̲ M P D N̲ Ṡ Ṡ N̲ D P M G̲ R S	2nd *pahar* day	
198	*Sugharāī*	S R G̲ M P N̲ Ṡ Ṡ N P M G̲ R S	4th *pahar* day	*bhārjā*
199	*Soraṭ*	S R G M̍ P D N̲ Ṡ Ṡ N̲ D P M̍ G R S	1st *pahar* night	*bhārjā* song 29
200	*Srīrāg*	S R̲ G̍ M P D̲ N Ṡ Ṡ N D̲ P M̍ G R̲ S	4th *pahar* day	*rāg*
201	*Sarsvatī*	S R M P D N̲ Ṡ Ṡ N̲ D P M R S		*bhārjā* (*Sarāsatī*)
202	*Sindhaṛā*	S R G̲ M P D N̲ Ṡ Ṡ N̲ D P M G̲ R S	4th *pahar* day	
203	*Sindhūrā*	S R G̲ M̍ P D N̲ N Ṡ Ṡ N N̲ M̍ P D N̲ N S		songs 4, 17 gat 71
204	*Suhanī*	S R̲ G M D N Ṡ Ṡ N D M G R̲ S	3rd *pahar* night	song 49

205	*Soraṭ Malhār*	*S R G M P D N̲ N Ṡ* *Ṡ N N̲ D P M G R S*		
206	*Srīranjanī*	*S R G̲ M D N̲ Ṡ* *Ṡ N̲ D M G̲ R S*		
207	*Surparda Bilāval*	*S R G M P D N̲ N Ṡ* *Ṡ N N̲ D P M G R S*		
208	*Srīrāgam*	*S R M P N̲ Ṡ* *Ṡ N̲ P D N̲ P M G̲ R S*	3rd *pahar* night	
209	*Sūhā Kānaṛā*	*S R G̲ M P D N̲ N Ṡ* *Ṡ N N̲ D P M G̲ R S*	2nd *pahar* day	
210	*Sāvanī*	*S R G̲ M P D N̲ N Ṡ* *Ṡ N N̲ D P M G̲ R S*		
211	*Sugarāī Kānaṛā*	*S R G̲ M P D N Ṡ* *Ṡ N̲ D P M G̲ R S*	2nd *pahar* day	
212	*Sāmīrī*	*S R M P N̲ Ṡ* *Ṡ N̲ D̲ P M G̲ R S*	1st *pahar* night	
213	*Sāmīrī Malhār*	*S R M P N Ṡ* *Ṡ N D P M G R S*		
214	*Sīnāvatī*	*S R̲ G̲ M P D̲ N̲ Ṡ* *Ṡ N̲ D̲ P M G̲ R̲ S*		
215	*Sūrnaye kā Nat*	*S R̲ G M P D N Ṡ* *Ṡ N D P M G R̲ S*		
216	*Sarsāngayī*	*S R̍ G M P D̲ N Ṡ* *Ṡ N D̲ P M G R̍ S*		
217	*Sīvlīnī*	*S R G M̍ P D N Ṡ* *Ṡ N D P M̍ G R S*		
218	*Sālagmū*	*S R G̲ M P D N̲ Ṡ* *Ṡ N̲ D P M̍ G̲ R S*		
219	*Sūrnāmganī*	*S R̲ G̲ M̍ P D N Ṡ* *Ṡ N D P M̍ G̲ R̲ S*		
220	*Syāmalāngī*	*S R G̲ M̍ P D̲ N̲ Ṡ* *Ṡ N̲ D̲ P M̍ G R S*		
221	*Sīmhendramadham*	*S R̍ G̲ M̍ P D̲ N Ṡ* *Ṡ N D̲ P M̍ G̲ R̍ S*		
222	*Sucaritra*	*S R G M P D̲ N̲ Ṡ* *Ṡ N̲ D̲ P M G R S*		
223	*Sindutāranjanī*	*S R̲ G M D̲ N Ṡ* *Ṡ N P D̲ M G R̲ S*		

224	*Sārang Nāṭ*	*S R̲ M P D̲ Ṡ* *Ṡ N D̲ P M R̲ M G* *R̲ S*		
225	*Sindhū Rāmkriyā*	*S R̲ M P D̲ N D̲ Ṡ* *Ṡ N P M R̲ G R̲ S*		
226	*Sāranggam*	*S R̲ G M G P N D̲ M* *P D̲ N Ṡ* *Ṡ D̲ M P M G R̲ S*		
227	*Sarasmangal*	*S G M N D̲ Ṡ* *Ṡ D̲ P M G R̲ S*		
228	*Saurāshṭra*	*S R̲ M G M D N Ṡ* *Ṡ D P M G S*	4th *pahar* day	
229	*Sāhūlī*	*S G M P N Ṡ* *Ṡ N D P G R̲ S*	3rd *pahar* day	
230	*Sindhū*	*S G R̲ M P D N Ṡ* *Ṡ D P M G R̲ G S*		*putra*
231	*Sindh Dhanāsrī*	*S R̲ G M P N̲ D Ṡ* *Ṡ N̲ D P M G̲ R S*		
232	*Sindhavī*	*Ṇ̲ Ḍ̲ Ṇ S R G̲ M P* *D N̲* *N̲ D P M G̲ R S Ṇ̲* *Ḍ̲ Ṇ̲*		*rāginī*
233	*Sudhanpāl*	*S R G̲ M P D Ṡ* *Ṡ N D M G̲ R G̲ S*		
234	*Sārangrām*	*S R M D N̲ P Ṡ* *Ṡ N̲ D G̲ R S*		
235	*Sarasvatīmanoharī*	*S R G M D S* *S N̲ D N̲ P M G R S*		
236	*Suratī*	*S R M P N̲ Ṡ* *Ṡ N̲ D P M G P M* *R S*	3rd *pahar* night	
237	*Sūrvilambī*	*S G M P N̲ Ṡ* *Ṡ N̲ D P M G R S*		
238	*Surabpriyā*	*S R G P N̲ Ṡ* *Ṡ N̲ D P M G R S*		
239	*Sarangī*	*S R M P D N̲ Ṡ* *Ṡ P M G R S*		
240	*Saukalmanjarī*	*S R̲ G̲ P D̲ N̲ Ṡ* *Ṡ N̲ D̲ M G̲ R̲ S*		

241	*Sanjīvanī*	*S G̲ R G̲ M P D̲ N Ṡ* *Ṡ N D̲ P M G R̲ S*		
242	*Sarasvāhinī*	*S R G R M P D̲ N Ṡ* *Ṡ D̲ P M G̲ R S*		
243	*Sārasānan*	*S R G M D̲ N Ṡ* *Ṡ N D̲ M G R S*		
244	*Sadākshīrī*	*S G̲ R̲ G̲ M̍ P D̲ N Ṡ* *Ṡ N D̲ M̍ G̲ R̲ S*		
245	*Sūnāmbahūvahanī*	*S R̲ G M̍ P Ṡ* *Ṡ N D̲ P M̍ G R̲ S*		
246	*Srīlalit*	*S R̲ G R̲ M̍ P N D P Ṡ* *Ṡ N D P M̍ G R̲ S*		
247	*Syāmalā*	*S G̲ R G̲ M̍ P D̲ N* *D̲ Ṡ* *Ṡ N D̲ P M̍ G̲ S R*		
248	*Sumandhanī*	*S R G̲ M̍ P D̲ N Ṡ* *Ṡ P M̍ G̲ R S R S*		
249	*Sīnhārav*	*S R M̍ P N̲ Ṡ* *Ṡ N̲ P M̍ R G̲ R S*		
250	*Sindhūnī*	*S R S G̲ M̍ P D N̲ Ṡ* *Ṡ N̲ D P M̍ G̲ S*		
251	*Sārangā*	*S R G M̍ P D N Ṡ* *Ṡ D P M̍ R G M̍ R S*	2nd *pahar* day	
252	*Saras Kalyān*	*S R G M̍ P D N Ṡ* *Ṡ N D P M̍ G M̍ R S*		
253	*Suhānā*	*S R G M P D N Ṡ* *Ṡ N D P M G M G R S*		
254	*Shankarā*	*S R G P D N Ṡ* *Ṡ N D P G R S*		
255	*Shāhāna Kānaṛā*	*S R G̲ M P D N S N Ṡ* *Ṡ N N̲ D P M G̲ R S*	night	*putra* songs 24, 54
256	*Shudh Kalyān*	*S R G M̍ P D N Ṡ* *Ṡ N D P M̍ G R S*	1st *pahar* night	*putra* (*Kalyān*)
257	*Shām Kalyān*	*S R G M M̍ P D N Ṡ* *Ṡ N D P M̍ M G R S*	1st *pahar* night	

258	*Shankarābharan*	*S R G M P D N Ṡ* *Ṡ N D P M G R S*	midnight	*putra* song 45 *sargams* 77, 78, 79, 80, 81, 87, 89, 90, 91, 92, 93, 94
259	*Shām*	*S R M P D Ṡ* *Ṡ D P M G R S*		
260	*Shokvarālī*	*S R̲ M G̲ M P M D R* *Ṡ M P D N D Ṡ* *Ṡ N̲ D M G̲ R̲ S*		
261	*Shobhāpantvarālī*	*S R̲ G̲ M̍ P D̲ N Ṡ* *Ṡ N D̲ P M̍ G̲ R̲ S*		
262	*Shadbadmārganī*	*S R̲ G̲ M̍ P D N̲ Ṡ* *Ṡ N̲ D P M̍ G̲ R̲ S*		
263	*Shankhapriyā*	*S R G̲ M̍ P D̲ N̲ Ṡ* *Ṡ N̲ D̲ P M̍ G̲ R̲ S*		
264	*Shadmukhī*	*S G̳ R̲ G̳ M P N̳ D̲ Ṡ* *Ṡ N̳ D̲ M G̳ R̲ S*		
265	*Shud Nāṭ*	*S G M P N D̍ N Ṡ* *Ṡ N D̍ P M R̍ S*		*bhārjā*
266	*Shud Sāverī*	*S R M P D Ṡ* *Ṡ D P M R S*		
267	*Shudhkriyā*	*S R̲ M P D̲ P N Ṡ* *Ṡ N D̲ P M R̲ G M* *R̲ S*		
268	*Shudh Desī*	*S R M P D̲ N̲ Ṡ* *Ṡ N̲ D̲ P M G̲ R S*		
269	*Shudsanam Nat*	*S R̲ G̲ M P N̲ D̲ Ṡ* *Ṡ D̲ N̲ P D̲ M G̲ R̲ S*		
270	*Shudh Dhanāsrī*	*S G̲ M P N̲ Ṡ* *Ṡ N̲ P M G̲ S*		
271	*Shāṛvalārav*	*S R̲ M P D̲ Ṡ* *Ṡ N̲ D̲ N̲ P M G̲ R̲ S*		
272	*Shud Gandharvī*	*S R̲ G M P D N Ṡ* *Ṡ D P M R̲ S*		
273	*Shudh Banglā*	*S R M P D Ṡ* *Ṡ N̲ D P M G̲ R̲ S*		

274	*Shud Bhairavī*	*S G̲ R M P N̲ D N̲ Ṡ* *Ṡ N̲ D P M R G̲ M* *R S*		
275	*Shām Mukhārī*	*S R G̲ M P D N̲ Ṡ* *Ṡ D N̲ D̲ P M G̲ S*		
276	*Shīv Kāmbodī*	*S R G M N̲ Ṡ* *Ṡ N̲ P M G R S*		
277	*Shud Sārang*	*S R G M P D N D Ṡ* *Ṡ D P M R G R S*	2nd *pahar* day	
278	*Shambhūkriyā*	*S G R M P N M G R* *M P N Ṡ* *Ṡ N P N M G R S*		
279	*Shudh*	*S R G̲ M̍ P N Ṡ* *Ṡ N P M̍ G̲ S*		
280	*Shankhārav*	*S G̲ R G̲ M̍ D N Ṡ* *Ṡ N̲ P M̍ G̲ R S*		
281	*Shunyāmadham*	*S R M̍ P N̲ D Ṡ* *Ṡ N̲ D P M̍ G R S*		
282	*Sharāranav*	*S R G M̍ P D Ṡ* *Ṡ N D P M̍ G S*		
283	*Shiromatī*	*S R M̍ P D N Ṡ* *Ṡ N P M̍ G R S*		
284	*Shāmbharantak*	*S G M̍ P D Ṡ* *Ṡ N D P M̍ G R S*		
285	*Z̤ila‘*	*S R G̲ G M P D N̲* *N Ṡ* *Ṡ N N̲ D P M G G̲* *R S*	3rd *pahar* day	songs 11, 40, 41, 42, 43, 53, 56, 57
286	*Kāmod*	*S R G M M̍ P D N Ṡ* *Ṡ N D P M̍ M G R S*	1st *pahar* night	*rāginī*
287	*Kāmodī*	*S R G M P D N̲ N Ṡ* *Ṡ N N̲ D P M G R S*	1st *pahar* night	*bhārjā*
288	*Kedārā*	*S R G M M̍ P D N Ṡ* *Ṡ N D P M̍ M G R S*	night	*rāginī* song 20
289	*Kedārāgaul*	*S R G̲ G M P N̲ N Ṡ* *Ṡ N N̲ D P M G R S*		
290	*Khambāvatī*	*S R G M P D N̲ N Ṡ* *Ṡ N N̲ D P M G R S*	3rd *pahar* night	*rāginī*

291	*Kāmākshī*	*S G M P N Ṡ* *Ṡ N D P M G R S*		
292	*Kūkab*	*S R G M P D N Ṡ* *Ṡ N D P M G R S*	1st *pahar* day	*rāginī*
293	*Kaunsī Kānaṛā*	*S R G̲ M D N̲ Ṡ* *Ṡ N̲ D M G̲ R S*		song 8
294	*Khamāj*	*S R G̲ G M P D N̲ N Ṡ* *Ṡ N N̲ D P M G G̲ R S*		songs 1, 12
295	*Khaṭ*	*S R̲ G̲ M P D̲ N̲ Ṡ* *Ṡ N̲ D̲ P M G̲ R̲ S*	1st *pahar* day	
296	*Kāfī*	*S R G̲ M P D N̲ Ṡ* *Ṡ N̲ D P M G̲ R S*	3rd *pahar* day	songs 14, 30, 35, 41, 55, 56, 60 *gat* 67 *sargams* 83, 98, 105
297	*Kālingrā*	*S R̲ G M P D̲ N Ṡ* *Ṡ N D̲ P M G R̲ S*	midnight	*gat* 62
298	*Kīrvānī*	*S R G̲ M P D̲ N Ṡ* *Ṡ N D̲ P M G̲ R S*		
299	*Kedār*	*S M G̲ P N Ṡ* *Ṡ N P M G R S*		
300	*Karnāṭī*	*S R̲ G̲ M P D̲ N̲ Ṡ* *Ṡ N̳ D̲ P M G̳ R̲ S*	3rd *pahar* night	
301	*Kangāngī*	*S R̲ G̳ M P D̲ N̳ Ṡ* *Ṡ N̳ D̲ P M G̳ R̲ S*		
302	*Kokalīlpriyā*	*S R̲ G̲ M P D N Ṡ* *Ṡ N D P M G̲ R̲ S*		
303	*Kharharpriyā*	*S R G̲ M P D N̲ Ṡ* *Ṡ N̲ D P M G̲ R S*		song 21
304	*Kāmvardhanī*	*S R̲ G M̍ P D̲ N Ṡ* *Ṡ N D̲ P M̍ G R̲ S*		
305	*Kāntāmanī*	*S R G M̍ P D̲ N̳ Ṡ* *Ṡ N̳ D̲ P M̍ G R S*		
306	*Kosal*	*S R̍ G M̍ P D N Ṡ* *Ṡ N D P M̍ G R̍ S*		
307	*Kānarā*	*S G M D N Ṡ* *Ṡ D P M G M R S*		*rāginī*

308	*Kānaṛā*	S R G M P M D N Ṡ Ṡ N D N P M P G R S		
309	*Kalābharan*	S R G M P D N̲ Ṡ Ṡ D P G R S		
310	*Kāntalvarālī*	S M P D N̲ D Ṡ Ṡ N̲ D P M S		
311	*Kokīlāvarvānī*	S M G P D̲ N Ṡ Ṡ N D̲ M G R S		
312	*Kanaka Vasant*	S R M P N̲ Ṡ Ṡ N̲ P M G̲ R M G̲ S		
313	*Karāyātī*	S R G̲ P D̲ Ṡ Ṡ N̲ D̲ P D̲ M G̲ R S		
314	*Kanaṛgaul*	S G̲ R G̲ M P D̲ N̲ Ṡ Ṡ N̲ D̲ P M G̲ R S		
315	*Kalāvatī*	S R̲ G M P D N̲ P Ṡ Ṡ N̲ D N̲ P M G R̲ S		
316	*Karnakvarālī*	S R M P N̲ Ṡ Ṡ N̲ D N̲ P M G R S		
317	*Kapī*	S R G̲ M P D N̲ Ṡ Ṡ D P M R G̲ M R S	3rd *pahar* day	
318	*Kokaldhvanī*	S R G M D N̲ D Ṡ Ṡ N̲ D N̲ P M G R G M G R S		
319	*Kolāhal*	S R G M P N D N Ṡ Ṡ N P D M G R S		
320	*Kanaranjī*	S Ṇ S G R G M P D P M G R S Ṇ S	1st *pahar* day	
321	*Kandaramā*	S G M D M N Ṡ Ṡ N M G R S		
322	*Kākambhīrī*	S R̲ G̲ M P D̲ Ṡ Ṡ N̲ D̲ P M G̲ R̲ S		
323	*Kokilārav*	S R̲ G̲ M P D Ṡ Ṡ N D P M G̲ R̲ S		
324	*Kalākāntī*	S R̲ G M P N̲ D̲ N̲ Ṡ Ṡ N̲ D̲ M G R̲ S		
325	*Kālgārav*	S R̲ M G R̲ G M P D̲ N̲ Ṡ Ṡ N̲ P D̲ N̲ D̲ P M G R̲ S		

326	*Karnāvalī*	S R M P D̲ N Ṡ Ṡ N D̲ P M G̲ R S		
327	*Kalyān Vasant*	S M G̲ P D̲ N Ṡ Ṡ N D̲ P M G̲ R S		
328	*Kalhambas*	S R̍ G M P D̲ Ṡ Ṡ N̲ D̲ P M G R S		
329	*Kokilāpancamī*	S R̲ G̳ P D̲ N Ṡ Ṡ N D̲ P M̍ G̳ R̲ S		
330	*Kusumranjanī*	S R̲ M̍ P D̲ N Ṡ Ṡ N D N̲ P M̍ G̲ R̲ S		
331	*Kālmūrat*	S G̲ R̲ G̲ M̍ P Ṡ Ṡ N̲ D̲ P M̍ G̲ R̲ S		
332	*Kāmranjanī*	S R̲ G̲ R M̍ P D̲ N Ṡ Ṡ N D̲ M̍ G̲ R̲ G̲ S		
333	*Kumudprabhā*	S R̲ G D̲ N Ṡ Ṡ P M̍ G Ṇ S		
334	*Kumrūkī*	S R G M̍ N Ṡ Ṡ N M̍ G R S		
335	*Kalyānkesrī*	S R G P D Ṡ Ṡ D M̍ P M̍ G R S		
336	*Kriyābharan*	S R G M̍ P N D Ṡ Ṡ N D M̍ G R S		
337	*Kāmaksh*	S M G M P D N Ṡ Ṡ N̲ D P M G M S		
338	*Kahalāmanoharī*	S G M P N̲ Ṡ Ṡ N̲ D̲ P M G S		
339	*Gārā Kānaṛā*	S R G̲ G M P D N̲ N Ṡ Ṡ N N̲ D P M G G̲ R S	2nd *pahar* night	
340	*Gaurī*	S R̲ G M D N Ṡ Ṡ N D M G̲ R S	4th *pahar* day	*rāginī*
341	*Gauṛ Malhār*	S R G M P D N̲ N Ṡ Ṡ N N̲ D P M G R S	rainy season	song 15 *gat* 63
342	*Gauṛ Sārang*	S R G M M̍ P D N̲ N Ṡ N N̲ D P M̍ M G R S	2nd *pahar* day	
343	*Gūjarī*	S R̲ G̲ M M̍ P D̲ N Ṡ Ṡ N D̲ P M̍ M G̲ R̲ S	1st *pahar* day	*rāginī*

344	*Gārā*	*S R G M P D N̲ N Ṡ* *Ṡ N N̲ D P M G R S*	3rd *pahar* day	*gat* 69
345	*Gandhārī*	*S R G̲ M P D̲ N Ṡ* *Ṡ N̲ D̲ P M G̲ R S*	1st *pahar* day	*bhārjā*
346	*Gandhārī Toṛī*	*S R̲ R G̲ M M̍ P D̲ N̲ Ṡ* *Ṡ N̲ D̲ P M̍ M G̲ R R̲ S*	1st *pahar* day	
347	*Gānmurtī*	*S R̲ G̲ M P D̲ N Ṡ* *Ṡ N D̲ P M G̲ R̲ S*		
348	*Gāyakpriyā*	*S R̲ G M P D̲ N̲ Ṡ* *Ṡ N̲ D̲ P M G R̲ S*		
349	*Gaurīmanoharī*	*S R G̲ M P D N Ṡ* *Ṡ N D P M G̲ R S*		
350	*Gāngebhūshanī*	*S R G M P D̲ N Ṡ* *Ṡ N D̲ P M G Ṙ S*		
351	*Gavāmbodī*	*S R̲ G̲ M̍ P D̲ N̲ Ṡ* *Ṡ N̲ D̲ P M̍ G̲ R̲ S*		
352	*Gamansharmā*	*S R̲ G M̍ P D N Ṡ* *Ṡ N D P M̍ G R̲ S*		
353	*Gandhkriyā*	*S R̲ G R̲ M P N D̲ N Ṡ* *Ṡ N D̲ P M G R̲ S*		
354	*Gaulīpant*	*S R M P N Ṡ* *Ṡ N D P M D M G R S*		
355	*Gambhīr Vasant*	*S M G̲ M R̲ G̲ M P N̲ D̲ N̲ P Ṡ* *Ṡ D̲ P M R S*		
356	*Gajvardhan*	*S G M D N Ṡ* *Ṡ D P M G R̲ S*		
357	*Gaṛūṛdhūtī*	*S R G M P D N Ṡ* *Ṡ D P G R S*		
358	*Girvānpriyā*	*S Ṇ G M D Ṡ* *Ṡ N D M G R S*		
359	*Gamanbhāskar*	*S R G P D P N Ṡ* *Ṡ D P M G S*		
360	*Garjanām Bhairavī*	*S R G M P D N Ṡ* *Ṡ N R P M D S*		
361	*Gambhīr Nāṭ*	*S G M P N Ṡ* *Ṡ N P M G S*		

362	*Gandharva*	*S Ṇ̲ S G̲ R̲ G̲ M P N̲ Ṡ* *Ṡ N̲ D̲ P M G̲ R̲ S*		
363	*Ghomatī*	*Ṇ S R̲ G̲ Ṁ P Ḋ N* *P Ṁ G̲ R̲ S Ṇ S*		
364	*Govardhan*	*G̲ R̲ G̲ P D̲ Ṡ* *Ṡ N D̲ N Ṁ G̲ R̲ S*		
365	*Gamakkriyā*	*S R̲ G Ṁ P N Ṡ* *Ṡ N P Ṁ G R̲ S*		
366	*Gaurīkriyā*	*S G̲ Ṁ P Ḋ N Ṡ* *Ṡ N Ḋ N P Ṁ G̲ S*		
367	*Gaul*	*S R̲ M P N Ṡ* *Ṡ N P M G M R̲ G* *M R̲ S*		
368	*Gandharvā*	*P Ḋ N P R̲ G̲ R̲ S N P* *Ṁ P Ḋ N S N P*		
369	*Lācārī Ṭoṛī*	*S R̲ R G̲ M P D̲ N̲ N Ṡ* *Ṡ N N̲ D̲ P M G̲ R R̲ S*	1st *pahar* day	
370	*Lalit*	*S R̲ G M Ṁ D̲ N Ṡ* *Ṡ N D̲ P Ṁ M G R̲ S*	1st *pahar* day	*rāginī*
371	*Lankadahan*	*S R G̲ G M P D N̲* *N Ṡ* *Ṡ N N̲ D P M G G̲* *R S*		
372	*Latāngī*	*S R G Ṁ P D̲ N Ṡ* *Ṡ N D̲ P Ṁ G R S*		
373	*Latāmatī*	*S R̲ G̲ P Ṁ P D̲ P Ṡ* *Ṡ N D̲ P Ṁ D̲ Ṁ G̲* *R̲ S*		
374	*Multānī*	*S R̲ G̲ Ṁ P D̲ N Ṡ* *Ṡ N D̲ P Ṁ G̲ R̲ S*	3rd *pahar* day	
375	*Mārū*	*S R̲ G M Ṁ P D̲ N Ṡ* *Ṡ N D̲ P Ṁ M G R̲ S*	2nd *pahar* night	*putra*
376	*Māṛa*	*S R G M P D N̲ N Ṡ* *Ṡ N N̲ D P M G R S*	night	
377	*Manoharī*	*S G̲ R G̲ M P D Ṡ* *Ṡ D P M G̲ R G̲ S*		*bhārjā*

378	*Mālasrī*	*S G P D̲ N Ṡ* *Ṡ N D̲ P G S*	4th *pahar* day	*rāginī, bhārjā*
379	*Mālīgaura*	*S R̲ G M̍ P D̲ N Ṡ* *Ṡ N D̲ P M̍ G R̲ S*	4th pahar day	
380	*Miyān kā Kānaṛā*	*S R G̲ M P D N̲ Ṡ* *Ṡ N̲ D P M G̲ R S*	night	
381	*Miyān kī Malhār*	*S R G̲ M P D N̲ N Ṡ* *Ṡ N N̲ D P M G̲ R S*		*gat* 65
382	*Mārvā*	*S R̲ G M̍ D̲ N Ṡ* *Ṡ N D̲ M̍ G R̲ S*	4th *pahar* day	*rāginī*
383	*Meg*	*S R G M P D N̲ N Ṡ* *Ṡ N N̲ D P M G R S*	rainy season	*rāg*
384	*Malhār*	*S R G M P D N̲ N Ṡ* *Ṡ N N̲ D P M G R S*	rainy season	*rāginī*
385	*Madmāvat Sārang*	*S R G̲ M P N̲ N Ṡ* *Ṡ N N̲ P M G̲ R S*	2nd *pahar* day	*rāginī* (*Mad-mādavī*)
386	*Mānjhī*	*S R G̲ M P D̲ D N̲ N Ṡ* *Ṡ N N̲ D D̲ P M G̲ R S*	1st *pahar* night	*bhārjā* (*Mānjh*)
387	*Manjarī*	*S R G̲ G M P D N̲ N Ṡ* *S N N̲ D P M G G̲ R Ṡ*	midnight	
388	*Mūkhārī*	*S R P M D N̲ Ṡ* *Ṡ N̲ D P M G̲ R S*		
389	*Mālkauns*	*S G̲ M D̲ N̲ Ṡ* *Ṡ N̲ D̲ M G̲ S*	2nd *pahar* night	*rāg*
390	*Mānvatī*	*S R̲ G̳ M P D N Ṡ* *Ṡ N D P M G̳ R S*		
391	*Māyāmālavagaul*	*S R̲ G M P D̲ N Ṡ* *Ṡ N D̲ P M G R̲ S*		
392	*Mārranjanī*	*S R G M P D̲ N̳ Ṡ* *Ṡ N̳ D̲ P M G R S*		
393	*Mejkalayanī*	*S R G M̍ P D N Ṡ* *Ṡ N D P M̍ G R S*		
394	*Māgada Srīrāg*	*S R̲ G̲ M P D Ṡ* *Ṡ N̲ P G̲ S*		

395	*Matsabhāvalī*	*S R̲ G P D̲ N Ṡ* *Ṡ N D̲ P M G R̲ S*	end of night	
396	*Manarang*	*S R M P N̲ Ṡ* *Ṡ N P M G̲ R S*		
397	*Mātakokila*	*S R P D N̲ Ṡ* *Ṡ D N̲ D P R S*		
398	*Mohan*	*S R G P D Ṡ* *Ṡ D P R G P R S*	3rd *pahar* day	
399	*Mālav*	*S R G M P N̲ M D* *N̲ Ṡ* *Ṡ N̲ D N̲ P M G M* *R S*	4th *pahar* day	
400	*Megjayanī*	*S R M G P D N̲ Ṡ* *Ṡ P M G R S*		
401	*Mārū kī Nat*	*S M G̩ M P D̍ P Ṡ* *Ṡ N D̍ P M G R S*		
402	*Mālinī*	*S R̲ G̲ M P Ṡ* *Ṡ N̳ D̲ M G̲ R̲ S*		
403	*Mādhavī*	*S R G̲ M D̲ N D̲ M P* *D̲ N Ṡ* *Ṡ N P G̲ R̍ S*		
404	*Māpech Srī*	*S R̲ G̲ M̍ P N Ṡ* *Ṡ N D P M̍ G̲ M̍ R̲ S*		
405	*Manmatalāṭ*	*S Ṇ S R̲ G M̍ P D̲ N Ṡ* *Ṡ D̲ P M̍ G R̲ S Ṇ S*		
406	*Mevar Vasant*	*S R̲ G M̍ P D N Ṡ* *Ṡ N P D N D P M̍ R̲* *M̍ G R̲ G S*		
407	*Mādhavīmanoharī*	*S G̲ R G̲ M̍ P N D̲* *N Ṡ* *Ṡ N D̲ M̍ G̲ M̍ G̲ R S*		
408	*Mārjanayatī*	*S R M̍ P D̲ N Ṡ* *Ṡ N D̲ P M̍ G̲ R S*		
409	*Mohan Kalyān*	*S R G P D Ṡ* *Ṡ N D P M̍ G R S*		
410	*Mrigānandan*	*S R G D N Ṡ* *Ṡ N D M̍ D G R S*		
411	*Megharanjanī*	*S R̲ G P D̲ N Ṡ* *Ṡ D̲ P M G R̲ S*		

412	*Māhurī*	*S M G M R G M P D N Ṡ* *Ṡ D P M R G M S*		
413	*Manjarī*	*S R G̲ M P N̲ Ṡ* *Ṡ N̲ D M G̲ R S*		
414	*Mātāsarasvatī*	*S G M̍ P D Ṡ* *Ṡ N D P M R S*		
415	*Naṭ Malhārī*	*S R G M P D N̲ N Ṡ* *Ṡ N N̲ D P M G R S*	2nd *pahar* day	
416	*Naṭ Nārāyan*	*S R G M P D N̲ N Ṡ* *Ṡ N N̲ D P M G R S*		*putra*
417	*Nārāyanī*	*S R G P D N Ṡ* *Ṡ N D P M G R S*	4th *pahar* day	
418	*Nāṭkūranjī*	*S R G M D N̲ P D N̲ Ṡ* *Ṡ N D M G S*		
419	*Nāyakī Kānaṛā*	*S R G̲ G M P D N̲ Ṡ* *Ṡ N̲ D P M G G̲ R S*	night	
420	*Navaroz*	*S R G M P D N Ṡ* *Ṡ N D P M G R S*		
421	*Naṭ*	*S R̍ G M P̣ D N P N Ṡ* *Ṡ N P M R̍ S*	4th *pahar* day	*rāginī*
422	*Nāṭpriyā*	*S R̲ G̲ M P D N̲ Ṡ* *Ṡ N D P M G̲ R̲ S*		
423	*Naṭ Bhairavī*	*S R G̲ M P D̲ N̲ Ṡ* *Ṡ N̲ D P M G̲ R S*		
424	*Nāgnandanī*	*S R G M P D̍ N Ṡ* *Ṡ N D̍ P M G R S*		
425	*Navanīt*	*S R̲ G̳ M̍ P D N̲ Ṡ* *Ṡ N̲ D P M̍ G̳ R̲ S*		
426	*Nāmnārāyanī*	*S R̲ G M̍ P D̲ N̲ Ṡ* *Ṡ N̲ D̲ P M̍ G R̲ S*		
427	*Nītīmatī*	*S R G̲ M̍ P D̍ N Ṡ* *Ṡ N D̍ P M̍ G̲ R S*		
428	*Nāsīkābhūshanī*	*S R̍ G M̍ P D N̲ Ṡ* *Ṡ N̲ D P M̍ G R̍ S*		
429	*Nāgsvarāvalī*	*S G M P D Ṡ* *Ṡ D P M G S*		

430	*Navaras Kānaṛā*	*S G M P D P Ṡ* *Ṡ N̲ M G R S*		
431	*Naibavaranjanī*	*S R̲ G R̲ M P D̲ N Ṡ* *Ṡ N D̲ M G S*		
432	*Nādnāmkriyā*	*S R̲ M G M P D̲ Ṡ* *Ṡ N D̲ P M G R̲ S*		
433	*Nāṭmangal*	*S G̲ G̲ M P D̲ N̲ Ṡ* *Ṡ N̲ D̲ P M R G̲ R S*		
434	*Navamanoharī*	*S R M D̲ N̲ Ṡ* *Ṡ N̲ P M R S*		
435	*Nāgvarālī*	*S Ṇ̲ S R̲ M P D̲* *P Ṃ G̲ R̲ S Ṇ S*		
436	*Nāyakī*	*S R M P D N̲ P Ṡ* *Ṡ N̲ D P M G̲ R S*		
437	*Nādatāranjanī*	*S R M P D P N Ṡ* *Ṡ D N̲ P D M G̲ R* *G̲ S*		
438	*Nārayangaul*	*S R M P N̲ D N̲ Ṡ* *Ṡ N̲ D P M G R S*		
439	*Nīmparī*	*S R G M S D M P N Ṡ* *Ṡ N̲ P D N̲ P M G M* *R G R M G S*		
440	*Navaroz*	*Ṃ Ḍ Ṇ S R G M P* *M G R S N Ḍ S*		
441	*Nāgdhūtī*	*S G R G M G M P D* *N D P N P D N Ṡ* *Ṡ N D N D P M D P* *M R G M G R G S*		
442	*Nepāl*	*S R M G̲ M P N Ṡ* *Ṡ N D̲ P M R S*		
443	*Nābavaman*	*S R̲ G̲ R̲ M̍ P Ṡ* *Ṡ N D P M̍ G̲ R̲ S*		
444	*Nāgāvagī*	*S R G M̍ P Ṡ* *Ṡ N D P M̍ G R S*		
445	*Vegvāhanī*	*S R̲ G M P D N̲ Ṡ* *Ṡ N̲ D P M G R̲ S*		
446	*Vanaspatī*	*S R̲ G̲ M P D N̲ Ṡ* *Ṡ N̲ D P M G̲ R̲ S*		
447	*Vakulābharan*	*S R̲ G M P D̲ N S* *S N̲ D̲ P M G R̲ S*		

448	*Varūnpriyā*	*S R G̲ M P D̍ N Ṡ* *Ṡ N D̍ P M G̲ R S*		
449	*Vāgadhī Srī*	*S R̍ G M P D N̲ Ṡ* *Ṡ N̲ D P M G R̍ S*		
450	*Vasūmbharī*	*S R̲ G M̍ P D̍ N Ṡ* *Ṡ N D̍ P M̍ G R̲ S*		
451	*Vacāspatī*	*S R G M̍ P D N̲ Ṡ* *Ṡ N̲ D P M̍ G R S*		
452	*Vasantvarālī*	*S G̲ M P D̲ N̲* *Ṡ D̲ P G̲ R S*		
453	*Vasantlīlā*	*S R̲ M P D N̲ Ṡ* *Ṡ N̲ D P G R̲ S*		
454	*Vāsanī*	*S R G̲ M P N̲ D N̲ Ṡ* *Ṡ N D M P M G̲ R S*		
455	*Van Kāmbodī*	*S M G R S M P D N̲ Ṡ* *Ṡ N̲ P N̲ M G R S*		
456	*Vīvardhanī*	*S M P Ṡ* *Ṡ N D P M G R S*		
457	*Vedānganī*	*S G M P D N Ṡ* *Ṡ N D P D M G R S*		
458	*Vīrpratāp*	*S G M P D N* *Ṡ N D P M G R S*		
459	*Vasant Mukhārī*	*S G R̲ G M P N̲ D̲* *N̲ Ṡ* *Ṡ N̲ D̲ P M R̲ S*		
460	*Varālī*	*S G̲ R̲ G̲ M̍ P D̲ N Ṡ* *Ṡ N D̲ P M̍ G̲ R̲ S*	4th *pahar* day	
461	*Vījaykokilā*	*S R̲ G̲ M̍ P D̲ Ṡ* *Ṡ N D̲ P M̍ G̲ R̲ S*		
462	*Vilambinī*	*S M̍ G M̍ P N D̲ N Ṡ* *Ṡ N̲ D̲ N P M̍ G S*		
463	*Vīpramandar*	*S R̲ M̍ P D̲ N Ṡ* *Ṡ D̲ P M̍ G R̲ S*		
464	*Vyāghranandan*	*S R G P D̲ Ṡ* *Ṡ N D̲ N D̲ P M̍ G* *R̲ S*		
465	*Hiṇḍol*	*S G M̍ D N Ṡ* *Ṡ N D M̍ G S*	4th *pahar* day	*rāg*

466	*Hamīr Kalyān*	*S R G M M̍ P D N Ṡ* *Ṡ N D P M̍ M G R S*	1st *pahar* night	
467	*Harscandrīkā*	*S R G P D Ṡ* *Ṡ N̲ D P M G R S*		
468	*Hemam Kalyān*	*S R G M P D N Ṡ* *Ṡ N D P M G R S*	1st *pahar* night	
469	*Hansdhanī*	*S R G P N Ṡ* *Ṡ N P G R S*		
470	*Hanmāvatī*	*S R G̲ M̍ P D N̲ Ṡ* *Ṡ N̲ D P M̍ G̲ R S*		
471	*Hanam Toṛī*	*S R̲ G̲ M P D̲ N̲ Ṡ* *Ṡ N̲ D̲ P M G̲ R̲ S*		
472	*Haṭkāmbīrī*	*S R̲ G M P D̍ N Ṡ* *Ṡ N D̍ P M G R̲ S*		
473	*Harī Kāmbodī*	*S R G M P D N̲ Ṡ* *Ṡ N̲ D P M G R S*		
474	*Hinḍol Basant*	*S R M P D̲ N̲ D Ṡ* *Ṡ N̲ D̲ P M D̲ M G̲* *R S*		song 58
475	*Hemkriyā*	*S R G̲ M P D̲ N̲ Ṡ* *Ṡ D̲ P M R G̲ M R S*		
476	*Hemvardhanī*	*S R̲ M P N̲ Ṡ* *Ṡ N̲ D̲ P M D̲ M G̲* *R S*		
477	*Harī Nāṭ*	*S M G M P D N Ṡ* *Ṡ N P D N P M G S*		
478	*Hamsnād*	*S R̲ G M̍ N Ṡ* *Ṡ N P M̍ R̍ S*		
479	*Hamsnandā*	*S R M̍ P D̍ N Ṡ* *Ṡ N D̍ N P M̍ R S*		
480	*Yadūkal Kāmbodī*	*S R M P D Ṡ* *Ṡ N̲ D P M G R S*		
481	*Yāgpriyā*	*S R̍ G M P D̲ N̲ Ṡ* *Ṡ N̲ D̲ P M G R̍ S*		
482	*Yashpriyā*	*S R M̍ P N̲ Ṡ* *Ṡ N̲ D P M̍ G̲ R S*		
483	*Yogjot*	*S R M̍ P N D Ṡ* *Ṡ N D P M̍ G R S*		
484	*Yaman Kalyān*	*S R G M M̍ P D N Ṡ* *Ṡ N D P M̍ M G R S*		*bhārjā* song 25 *sargam* 107

It is clear from the list above that *rāg*s are often similar. In fact, the notes of some are not just similar, but precisely the same as those of others. There is always a difference, however, in the ascent and descent and the movement of each. To know the *sur*s of the *rāg*s as notated above is not sufficient for one to recognize the *rāg*. A *rāg* becomes clear only after one has gained experience by listening and learning, and after the ear has become completely familiar with *sur*. To recognize a *rāg* from its song is difficult, and after recognizing a *rāg*, to know its notes, or rather to know its essence, is even more difficult.

Chapter Five
Tāl

Tāl is the sustain of sound or the lifespan of sound. *Sur* without *tāl* is absolutely meaningless, since *sur* and *tāl* are inseparable. The excellence of the art of Indian music, *sangīt*, lies in *tāl*. *Tāl* dwells in and is a very great part of every natural thing. *Tāl* is present in every event and action. In the *sama*ʿ gathering, for example, which is often held for the *urs* at the tombs of the great saints, the gathering is usually graced with noblemen, holy persons, learned men and mendicants, and the common and the most elite all participate as well. This gathering is called the *meḥfil-i qavālī*. As soon as a *qavāl* begins to sing a *g͟hazal* of a mystical type or an amorous type, or one in praise of the Prophet, the *ḍhol* player gives a slap and gradually begins to play the *tāl*. When its speed reaches a certain stage, the *tāl* intensifies the feelings as the beautiful meaning of the verses stirs the heart. The *tāl*, called *qavālī ṭheka*, creates such an effect that the hearts of all, both great and humble, begin to tremble in a state of ecstasy. As the pace of the *tāl* grows faster the heart is even more stirred, and each stroke of the *tāl* gives more impetus to the ecstasy and intoxication. And the motions that are displayed in this state of ecstasy are themselves not devoid of *tāl*. Likewise, the Hindus in their temples often sing *bhajan*s or *kirtan*s. It is well known that when Guru Nanak or Guru Tukaram sang *bhajan*s, the *tāl* was supplied by the *jhānjh* and *mridang*, which had the effect of bringing on a state of tranquility, not only in their disciples but in ordinary listeners as well. It is true that *bhajan*s and *kirtan*s are a part of Hindu religious worship, but the *tāl* creates such a special effect that even those who do not have a *jhānjh* in their hands clap to the beat of the *ḍhol* so forcefully that the sound produced is even louder than that of the *jhānjh* and *mridang*, and they achieve a state of reverie. This practice is current among the Hindus to the present day. Another example is the sound of the *naqāra* in the field of battle, the sound of the *naubat k͟hāna* and the *raushan caukī* ensembles in the royal palaces, and the playing of the *ḍhol* and the *tāsh* at weddings. *Tāl* is something that helps the music achieve its full impact on every heart. This is true to such an extent that during a wedding, if after the distribution of sweets and snacks the music is delayed, the relatives and guests just cannot be inspired to joy. The sound of just one *ḍhol*, on the other hand, can bring the full delight of a wedding to one's heart. Skin-covered instruments such as the *tabla* or *pak͟hāvaj* are used to manifest the *tāl* in every song or instrumental performance. The full effect of the music cannot be achieved without these instruments.

In everyday language, *tāl* means the regulation of timing. Hundreds of *tāls* are described in Indian music. The stations (*maqām*) of the *tāl* are shown by claps of the hands. There are three of these, the first of which is *sam*. *Sam* is where the *tāl* begins, and it occurs again after one *āvart*, that is after one cycle. The significance of the arrival of *sam* is that the *tāl* and *sur* begin again as if anew. If we say, as an analogy, that *sam* is the sound of one o'clock striking, then after the clock passes two, three, and so on to beyond twelve, *sam* will arrive again. Another would be a woodcutter cutting wood. When he strikes the wood with an axe, that is *sam*. When he raises the axe to strike it a second time, that is the station called empty or *k͟hālī*. The sounds emanating from the wood and associated with the *sam* and *k͟hālī* give comfort to the woodcutter. In fact, because he is enjoying the sounds he will continue to chop over and over again. The task would feel very tedious without the *tāl* and *sur*. Similarly, when a bearer lifts a palanquin or when the porter lifts his load, he walks along using a *tāl* and a few words to ease his effort. So also with the goldsmith and the ironsmith, whose hammers mark the junctures of *sam* and *k͟hālī*. The movement of all living things is through *tāl*. I have explained *sam* and *khālī*. The third station is called the *tāl*, which is a place between *sam* and *khālī*. The *tāl* of *sam* is denoted with a clap of the hands, at which point the heads of the listeners spontaneously move and the sound "āh" emanates from the mouths of those who know music. The notation for *sam* is (+) . *Khālī* is marked by a wave of the hands without clapping. Its notation is (7). And the other *tāl* sections are marked by a clap of the hands. The notation is (–) The three locations of *tāl* are shown below, along with the syllables (*bol*) of the *tabla*. The *bols* of *Tetāla* on the *tabla* are as follows — *nā dhī dhī nā nā dhī dhī nā nā tī tī nā nā dhī dhī nā*.

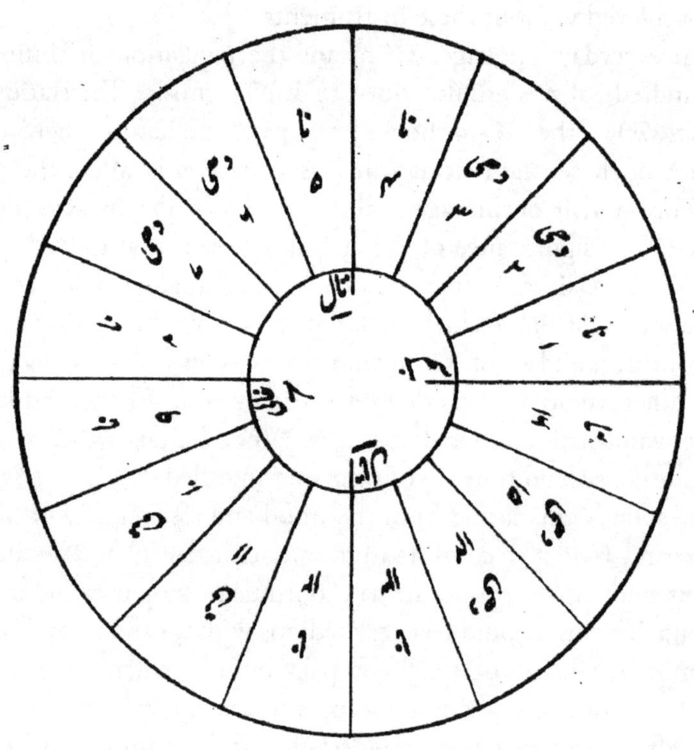

Divisions of Timings
(*taqsīm-i avaqāt*)

In the art of music, timings have been established for pauses of sound. In the Arabic language, for example, a rest on any sound produces an emphasis. Even in the dashing and surging of the waves of the sea there is the measure of the ebb and tide, and that is its God-given melody. Especially in Quranic Arabic, there is emphasis, pause, and silence; and a reading is defective if it has an improper sound. In the art of poetry, the subject, object, and the like are emphasized. Likewise, texts on music describe six timings, and they are categorized according to their pauses.

The first is *kāgpad*, "crow's foot," whose notation is like this: (⅄). A sound on which this sign appears should be held for eight *mātrās*, in other words as long as a count of 1-2-3-4-5-6-7-8. The second is *dvīguru* whose notation is (8). It should be held for a count of four *mātrās*. The third is *guru*, whose notation is (ع). One should hold it for a count of two *mātrās*. The fourth is *laghu*, (Γ), which one should hold for a count of one *mātrā*. In written music, if no notation is given with the *sur* one should assume that the *sur* is *laghu*. To signify a rest, called *bisrām*, however, a sign will definitely appear. The fifth is *drut* (ر). When this sign appears one should hold the *sur* for a half *mātrā*, that is, a half duration. The sixth is *anādrut*: (رر). When this appears one should hold the *sur* for a quarter *mātrā*. This is the smallest division. *Bisrām* is the name for an interval during which a singer or instrumentalist takes a breath and then begins again to sing or play along with the *tāl*. A *bisrām* is empty of *sur*, that is, it is when one pauses in the song for a little while during singing or playing. There are designations and marks for *bisrām* which are given instead of the *sur* in the notation. Western music has a name and notations for *bisrām* as well. In English it is called "rest." The notations are shown below.

Chart of the Divisions of Timings

Name	Notation with *sur*	Notation of rest	*Mātrās*	English notation of rest	English notation as *sur*	Remarks
kāgpad			8			8 *laghus*
dvīguru			4			4 *laghus*
guru			2			2 *laghus*
laghu			1			1 *laghu*
drut			1/2			1/2 *laghu*
anādrut			1/4			1/4 *laghu*

Of the above-mentioned main divisions, the *kāgpad* is the largest. Its duration can consist of two *dvīgurus*, four *gurus*, eight *laghus*, sixteen *druts* or thirty-two *anādruts*. Their measures will be clear from the chart below.

Chart of the Divisions of One *kāgpad*

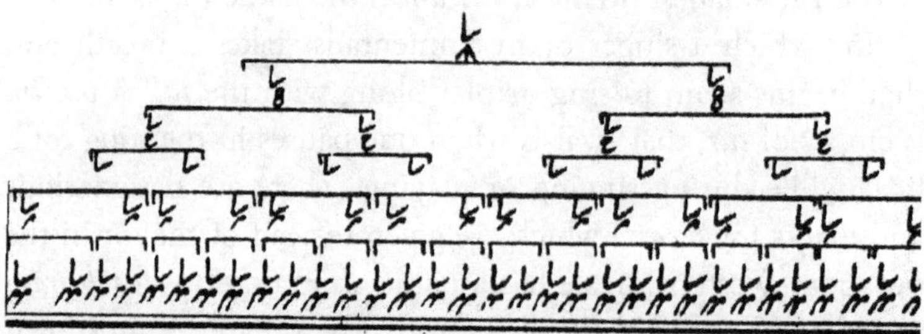

Sā rhythmically divided six times

Besides these six divisions there is one smaller than *anādrut,* which is called *trivaṛī*; one smaller called *kaṛā*; one smaller than this called *nimesh*; and the smallest, which is *chan.* An example of the duration of a *chan* is when a needle is passed through a stack of one hundred lotus leaves. As much time as it takes to pierce one leaf is the duration of a *chan.*

If a dot is added to the notation of a time division, the duration is increased by half, that is, it becomes one-and-a-half in size. A *guru* is two *mātrās*, for example, but if a dot is added, (·ऽ) it will have a count of three *mātrās*. Similarly a *dvīdrut* will become three-quarters of a *mātrā,* (ʸ·). If two dots are added, the duration will increase by two-thirds. If two dots are added to a *guru* like this (··ऽ), there will be two counts for the *guru*, one for the first dot, and half for the second dot. Altogether this adds up to two plus one-and-a-half, which is three-and a-half. This method is also used in Western music.

Tāl ang

In *sangīt*, several *angs* have been fixed to define the style (*ang*), or the pattern (*shakal*) of the *tāl.* For each *tāl* a structure or *surūp*, "form," has also been created. There are six *angs* by themselves and ten *angs* in combinations, altogether making sixteen *angs*. They have the same names and almost the same notations as the time divisions. When the notations for the *angs* are written to show the character of the *tāl*, however, their *mātras* are four times as long. This will be clear from the chart below.

Chart of *angs*

Name	Notation	*Mātrās*
kāgpad	[illegible]	16
plut	8	12
guru	[illegible]	8
laghu	|	4
drut	o	2
vīrām	∪	1

In order to show the structure or form (*surūp*) of a *tāl*, *angs* are sometimes written in combination with each other. Their names, notations, and *mātrās* are given in the chart below. In the musical notations in Part Two, the *surūp* of the *tāl* is given at the beginning of each composition and it will clarify the measure of each time division.

Chart of Combinations of *angs*

Name	Notation	*Mātrās*
drut vīrām	[illegible]	3
laghu vīrām	[illegible]	5
laghu drut	[illegible]	6
laghu drut vīrām	[illegible]	7

guru vīrām		9
guru drut		10
guru drut vīrām		11
plut vīrām		13
plut drut		14
plut drut vīrām		15

The *surūp* structures are written out as above. For *Tetālā*, make a chart with spaces for sixteen *mātrās*. There are four divisions in one cycle, namely *sam*, *tāl*, *k̲h̲ālī*, and another *tāl*. Each of the divisions has four *mātrās*, so the structure of the *tāl* will be written as:

Other *tāls* will be written out similarly.

Tāl jāt

There are five classes of *tāls*, which in the terminology of *sangīt* are called *jāt*. First, *catūsra jāt*. A *tāl* that is counted in four, eight or sixteen *mātrās* is called *catūsra jāt*. For example, *Tetāla* has sixteen *mātrās*, and within each division one counts four *mātrās*, so it will be considered *catūsra jāt*. The second is *tīsra jāt*, which are *tāls* in which three *mātrās* are counted, for example in *Tīvrā tāl*. The third is *misra jāt*, which are *tāls* that have a count of seven *mātrās*, for example, *Dharūpanc*. The fourth is *khanḍ jāt* in which there is a count of five *mātrās*, as in *Dhamār*. The fifth is *sankirn jāt*, in which there is a count of nine *mātrās*, as in *Hansnād*. All the *tāls* belong to one or another of these five *jāts*. Besides the five, there is one other called *dīvyasankirn jāt*, in which there is a count of three *mātrās*, as in *Shashṭī tāl.*

Also, each *tāl* can be made in every *jāt*. The *surūp* of *Tetāla*, for example, will be different in different *jāts*. In *catūsra jāt* it will be like this

and have a count of sixteen *mātrās*. In *tīsra* it will be

and have a count of twelve *mātrās*. In *khanḍ jāt* the *surūp* will be

and will have twenty *mātrās*. In *misra jāt* its *surūp* will look like this

and it will have twenty-eight *mātrās*. In *sankirn jāt* the *surūp* will be

and it will have thirty-six *mātrās*. In a similar manner, all the *tāls* can be made in all the *jāts*. There is a convention to note the *tāl jāt* along with the names of the *rāg* and the *tāl.*

The list below contains *tāls* in current usage as well as rare ones belonging to the various *jāts*. They appear along with their *surūp* structures and *mātrās*.

List of Current *tāl*s

Number	Name	*Surūp*	*Mātrās*
1	*Ektāl*	*l* (*ang*) 4 (*ang* counts) x (hand actions)	4
2	*Ektālā*	*l l l* 4 4 4 x 0 2 0 3 0	12
3	*Achav*	*l d d d* 4 2 2 2 x 2 3 4	10
4	*Āṛācautālā*	*d l l l* 2 4 4 4 x 2 3 4	14
5	*Aiṛavān*	*d l d d l* 2 4 2 2 4 x 2 3 4 5	14
6	*Abhang*	*l ld ld* 4 6 6 x 2 0	16
7	*Ashṭ*	*d d d dv d d d dv* 2 2 2 3 2 2 2 3 x 2 3 4 5 6 7 8	18
8	*Adrī*	*l l d d l l* 4 4 2 2 4 4 x 2 3 4 5 6	20
9	*Abhīnandan*	*l l d d l l* 4 4 2 2 4 4 x 2 3 4 5 0	20
10	*Anang*	*l ld ld l l l l* 4 6 6 4 4 4 4 x 2 0 3 4 5 0	32
11	*Aṭ*	*l l d d* 4 4 2 2 x 2 3 4	12
12	*Ughashṭā*	*g g g* 8 8 8 x 2 3	24
13	*Adhī*	*l* 4 x	4

مروج تالون کی فہرست

تال کے ما	تال کے سروپ	تال کے نام	عدد
۴	[illegible]	ایک تال	۱
۱۲	[illegible]	ایک تالا	۲
۱۰	[illegible]	اچھو	۳
۱۴	[illegible]	آڑا چوتالا	۴
۱۴	[illegible]	ایڑوان	۵
۱۶	[illegible]	ابھنگ	۶
۱۸	[illegible]	اشٹ	۷
۲۰	[illegible]	ادری	۸
۲۰	[illegible]	ابھی نندن	۹
۳۲	[illegible]	اننگ	۱۰
۱۲	[illegible]	اٹ	۱۱
۲۴	[illegible]	اُوگھشتا	۱۲
۴	[illegible]	ادھی	۱۳
۳۶	[illegible]	ابھنگ لیلا	۱۴
۲۴	[illegible]	بھدر مالی	۱۵
۲۵	[illegible]	بھگن	۱۶
۲۸	[illegible]	برم	۱۷

List of Current *Tāls*, first page

14	*Anglīlā*	*l k l l g* 4 16 4 4 8 x 2 3 4 5	36
15	*Bhadramālī*	*l l d d d d l l* 4 4 2 2 2 2 4 4 x 2 3 4 5 6 7 8	24
16	*Bhagan*	*l l d d d d dv dv dv* 4 4 2 2 2 2 3 3 3 x 2 3 4 5 6 7 8 9	25
17	*Bram*	*l l d l d d l d d d* 4 4 2 4 2 2 4 2 2 2 x 2 3 4 5 6 7 8 9 10	28
18	*Bramajog*	*l d l d d l d d d l* 4 2 4 2 2 4 2 2 2 4 x 2 3 4 5 6 7 8 9 10	28
19	*Bindumālinī*	*g d d d d g* 8 2 2 2 2 8 x 2 3 4 5 6	24
20	*Pashto*	*dv d d* 3 2 2 0 2 3	7
21	*Pratimaṭṭa*	*l l d* 4 4 2 x 2 3	10
22	*Pratībhānmatī*	*l d v l* 4 2 1 4 x 2 3 4	11
23	*Panjābī*	*l l l l* 4 4 4 4 x 2 0 3	16
24	*Pradhān*	*d d ld ld* 2 2 6 6 x 2 3 0	16
25	*Pratīvardhan*	*l lv l l* 4 5 4 4 x 2 3 4	17
26	*Pratāpshekar*	*ld ld d dv* 6 6 2 3 x 2 0 3	17
27	*Pradhan*	*d dv d ldv lv* 2 3 2 7 5 x 2 3 4 0	19

28	*Pūranmahākāl*	*d d d d l l l* 2 2 2 2 4 4 4 x 2 3 4 5 0 6	20
29	*Pancak*	*l l l l v l l l l* 4 4 4 4 1 4 4 4 4 x 0 2 0 3 4 0 5 0	33
30	*Pārvatīrocan*	*l l l l l l l ld ld l l l l d d d* 4 4 4 4 4 4 4 6 6 4 4 4 4 2 2 2 x 0 2 0 3 0 4 5 6 7 8 0 9 10 11 12	62
31	*Pratīdharav*	*l l d d d* 4 4 2 2 2 x 2 3 4 5	14
32	*Parīkram*	*l l l g g* 4 4 4 8 8 x 2 3 4 5	28
33	*Paktīng*	*g g g l l* 8 8 8 4 4 x 2 3 4 5	32
34	*Pratī*	*l d d* 4 2 2 x 2 3	8
35	*Prabhang*	*l g l g* 4 8 4 8 x 2 3 4	24
36	*Pratīmaṭ*	*l l g g l l* 4 4 8 8 4 4 x 2 3 4 5 6	32
37	*Tetālā*	*l l l l* 4 4 4 4 x 2 3 4	16
38	*Tīvrā*	*dv d d* 3 2 2 x 2 3	7
39	*Talkāmod*	*l l d d d d* 4 4 2 2 2 2 x 2 3 4 5 6	16
40	*Tīlvāṛā*	*l l l l* 4 4 4 4 x 2 0 3	16
41	*Trikhaṇḍvajar*	*lv lv d d lv* 5 5 2 2 5 x 2 3 4 5	19

42	*Tathī*	*l l l d d d ld ld dv dv dv l l d d d* 4 4 4 2 2 2 6 6 3 3 3 4 4 2 2 2 x 0 2 3 4 5 6 7 8 9 10 11 12 13 14 15	53
43	*Trupaṭ*	*l d d* 4 2 2 x 2 3	8
44	*Tribhin*	*l g k* 4 8 16 x 2 3	28
45	*Tīsravaran*	*l d d l g* 4 2 2 4 8 x 2 3 4 5	20
46	*Turanglīlā*	*d d l* 2 2 4 x 2 3	8
47	*Trutī*	*d d d v* 2 2 2 1 x 2 3 4	7
48	*Jaitmān*	*l lv lv* 4 5 5 x 2 3	14
49	*Jhaptālā*	*d dv d dv* 2 3 2 3 x 2 0 3	10
50	*Jhampak*	*v l d dv* 1 4 2 3 x 2 3 4	10
51	*Jagpāl*	*lv d d d* 5 2 2 2 x 2 3 4	11
52	*Jhūmrā*	*dv l dv l* 3 4 3 4 x 2 0 3	14
53	*Jhīmpā*	*l l d d dv* 4 4 2 2 3 x 0 2 3 4	15
54	*Jaimukh*	*l l l l l l l l* 4 4 4 4 4 4 4 4 x 2 3 0 4 5 6 0	32

55	*Jaisirī*	*l l l l l l l l* 4 4 4 4 4 4 4 4 x 0 2 3 0 4 5 0	32
56	*Jhampā*	*l v d* 4 1 2 x 2 3	7
57	*Jaimangal*	*l l g l l g* 4 4 8 4 4 8 x 2 3 4 5 6	32
58	*Jai*	*l g l l d k* 4 8 4 4 2 16 x 2 3 4 5 6	38
59	*Jakjhamp*	*g l l v* 8 4 4 1 x 2 3 4	17
60	*Jhap*	*d d l d* 2 2 4 2 x 2 3 4	9
61	*Jank*	*l l l l g g g g l g* 4 4 4 4 8 8 8 8 4 8 x 2 3 4 5 6 7 8 9 10	60
62	*Catur*	*d d d l* 2 2 2 4 x 2 3 4	10
63	*Cand*	*l l d d* 4 4 2 2 x 2 3 4	12
64	*Cautālā*	*l l d d* 4 4 2 2 x 2 3 0 4 0	12
65	*Chakkā*	*ld d l d d l* 6 2 4 2 2 4 x 2 3 4 5 6	20
66	*Caturmukh*	*l l l l ld ld* 4 4 4 4 6 6 x 2 3 4 5 0	28
67	*Candrakāntā*	*l l l l l l dv dv* 4 4 4 4 4 4 3 3 x 0 2 0 3 0 4 0	30

68	*Cakor*	*dv dv dv d d dv dv dv l l l d d* 3 3 3 2 2 3 3 3 4 4 4 2 2 x 2 3 4 5 6 7 8 9 10 11 12 13	38
69	*Cang*	*l l l l l l l l l l* 4 4 4 4 4 4 4 4 4 4 x 2 3 4 5 0 6 0 7 8	40
70	*Candakalā*	*l d d l d d l l l l l l l l l d d* 4 2 2 4 2 2 4 4 4 4 4 4 4 4 4 2 2 x 2 3 4 5 6 7 8 0 9 10 11 0 12 13 14 15 16	60
71	*Cascaspuṭ*	*g g l k* 8 8 4 16 x 2 3 4	36
72	*Cācāpuṭ*	*g l l g* 8 4 4 8 x 2 3 4	24
73	*Carcarī*	*d dv l d dv l d dv l d dv l d dv l d dv l d dv l d dv l* 2 3 4 2 3 4 2 3 4 2 3 4 2 3 4 2 3 4 2 3 4 2 3 4 x 2 3 4 5 6 7 8 9 10 11 12 13 14 15 16 17 18 19 20 21 22 23 24	72
74	*Catursharavan*	*g l l d d g* 8 4 4 2 2 8 x 2 3 4 5 6	28
75	*Chast*	*g d d d* 8 2 2 2 x 2 3 4	14
76	*Dādrā*	*dv dv* 3 3 x 0	6
77	*Dīpcandī*	*dv l dv l* 3 4 3 4 x 2 0 3	14
78	*Dāvānal*	*ld ld* 6 6 x 2	12

79	*Dharav*	*l l d d d* 4 4 2 2 2 x 2 3 4 5	14
80	*Dīvyāman*	*l l l d v* 4 4 4 2 1 x 2 3 4 5	15
81	*Dashāngī*	*l l l l l* 4 4 4 4 4 x 0 2 3 0	20
82	*Dhammār*	*lv lv l* 5 5 4 x 2 3	14
83	*Dharūpancak*	*dv l dv l dv l d d* 3 4 3 4 3 4 2 2 x 0 2 0 3 0 4 5	25
84	*Dīpakdhar*	*d d l l l l l l* 2 2 4 4 4 4 4 4 x 2 3 4 5 0 6 0	28
85	*Dharmavtāl*	*l l d l* 4 4 2 4 x 2 3 4	14
86	*Darpan*	*d d g* 2 2 8 x 2 3	12
87	*Daurīkshanā*	*l d v v* 4 2 1 1 x 2 3 4	8
88	*Dīpak*	*d d l l g g* 2 2 4 4 8 8 x 2 3 4 5 6	28
89	*Ḍankī*	*g l g* 8 4 8 x 2 3	20
90	*Ḍamelī*	*l l v* 4 4 1 x 2 3	9
91	*Rūpak*	*d l* 2 4 x 2	6
92	*Ratī*	*l l l* 4 4 4 x 0 2	12

93	*Rājmāṛmanḍ*	*l l l d* 4 4 4 2 x 2 3 4	14
94	*Rājmargāng*	*d d l l l* 2 2 4 4 4 x 2 3 0 4	16
95	*Rājbidhyādhar*	*l l l l d d* 4 4 4 4 2 2 x 2 3 0 4 5	20
96	*Rājnarāyan*	*d d l l l l l l* 2 2 4 4 4 4 4 4 x 2 3 4 0 5 6 0	28
97	*Rūdra*	*l l d d d d d d d d d d d d* 4 4 2 2 2 2 2 2 2 2 2 2 2 2 x 0 2 3 4 0 5 6 7 0 8 9 10 11	32
98	*Ratīlīlā*	*l l g g* 4 4 8 8 x 2 3 4	24
99	*Rang*	*d d d d g* 2 2 2 2 8 x 2 3 4 5	16
100	*Rājcūṛāman*	*d d l l l d d l g g* 2 2 4 4 4 2 2 4 8 8 x 2 3 4 5 6 7 8 9 10	40
101	*Rangdhaivatan*	*g g g l k* 8 8 8 4 16 x 2 3 4 5	44
102	*Rāj*	*g k k d d g l l k* 8 16 16 2 2 8 4 4 16 x 2 3 4 5 6 7 8 9	76
103	*Rājbidhyādhār*	*l g d d* 4 8 2 2 x 2 3 4	16
104	*Rangpradīpak*	*g g l l k* 8 8 4 4 16 x 2 3 4 5	40
105	*Rājbanksūl*	*g l g d d* 8 4 8 2 2 x 2 3 4 5	24
106	*Rāgvardhan*	*l l k l v* 4 4 16 4 1 x 2 3 4 5	29

<table>
<tr><td>107</td><td>Sirī</td><td>v v
1 1
x 0</td><td>2</td></tr>
<tr><td>108</td><td>Sam</td><td>l d dv
4 2 3
x 2 3</td><td>9</td></tr>
<tr><td>109</td><td>Sanmuktharā</td><td>l l dv d
4 4 3 2
x 2 3 4</td><td>13</td></tr>
<tr><td>110</td><td>Savārī</td><td>l l l d d
4 4 4 2 2
x 2 3 4 5</td><td>16</td></tr>
<tr><td>111</td><td>Savārī</td><td>dv l l l
3 4 4 4
x 2 3 4</td><td>15</td></tr>
<tr><td>112</td><td>Sarasvatī</td><td>l d l l l
4 2 4 4 4
x 2 3 4 5</td><td>18</td></tr>
<tr><td>113</td><td>Sāras</td><td>l d d d l l
4 2 2 2 4 4
x 2 3 4 5 6</td><td>18</td></tr>
<tr><td>114</td><td>Sammahākāl</td><td>l l l l l
4 4 4 4 4
x 0 2 0 3</td><td>20</td></tr>
<tr><td>115</td><td>Srīkritī</td><td>l l l l l l
4 4 4 4 4 4
x 0 2 0 3 4</td><td>24</td></tr>
<tr><td>116</td><td>Sarsavatyābharan</td><td>l l l l l l d d
4 4 4 4 4 4 2 2
x 0 2 0 3 4 5 6</td><td>28</td></tr>
<tr><td>117</td><td>Srīvand</td><td>l l l l l ld ld
4 4 4 4 4 6 6
x 0 2 0 3 4 0</td><td>32</td></tr>
<tr><td>118</td><td>Sītāsīnā</td><td>lv lv lv lv lv lv lv d
5 5 5 5 5 5 5 2
x 2 3 4 5 6 7 8</td><td>37</td></tr>
<tr><td>119</td><td>Srīkhanaṛ</td><td>l l l l l d d l l l l
4 4 4 4 4 2 2 4 4 4 4
x 0 2 3 0 4 5 6 0 7 0</td><td>40</td></tr>
<tr><td>120</td><td>Sārangdev</td><td>d d l ld ld l l l l l
2 2 4 6 6 4 4 4 4 4
x 2 3 4 0 5 0 6 0 7</td><td>40</td></tr>
</table>

121	*Shabtaṛashī*	*l d d l d d l l l l d d d* *l d d d* 4 2 2 4 2 2 4 4 4 4 2 2 2 4 2 2 2 x 2 3 4 5 6 7 8 9 10 11 12 13 14 15 16 17	48
122	*Sūrajtāl*	*l l l l l l l l d d l d d l* 4 4 4 4 4 4 4 4 2 2 4 2 2 4 x 2 0 3 0 4 5 6 7 8 9 10 11 12	48
123	*Samapdevshaṭīkā*	*k g g g k* 16 8 8 8 16 x 2 3 4 5	56
124	*Sīhvanlīlā*	*l d d d l* 4 2 2 2 4 x 2 3 4 5	14
125	*Sīhvanvikram*	*g g g l k l g k k* 8 8 8 4 16 4 8 16 16 x 2 3 4 x 5 6 7 8	88
126	*Srīrang*	*l l g l k* 4 4 8 4 16 x 2 3 4 5	36
127	*Sīhvanvakṛadīt*	*l l k g l k l k k* 4 4 16 8 4 16 4 16 16 x 2 3 4 x 5 6 7 8	88
128	*Sīhvanād*	*l g l l g* 4 8 4 4 8 x 2 3 4 5	28
129	*Sīhvanandan*	*g g l k l g d d g g l k l* *k g l l* 8 8 4 16 4 8 2 2 8 8 4 16 4 16 8 4 4 x 2 3 4 5 6 7 8 9 10 11 12 13 14 15 16 17	124
130	*Samā*	*l l d d v* 4 4 2 2 1 x 2 3 4 5	13
131	*Srīnandan*	*g l l k* 8 4 4 16 x 2 3 4	32
132	*Sārvatīlocan*	*l l d d g g l l l l g l l* 4 4 2 2 8 8 4 4 4 4 8 4 4 x 2 3 4 5 6 7 8 9 10 11 12 13	60

133	*Sūlfā<u>kh</u>ta*	*l d l* 4 2 4 x 2 3	10
134	*Shanka*	*l d* 4 2 x 2	6
135	*Shishṭitāputrak*	*l l d v* 4 4 2 1 x 2 3	11
136	*Sharabalīlā*	*l d d d d l l* 4 2 2 2 2 4 4 x 2 3 4 5 6 7	20
137	*Shaṭ*	*d d d d d d* 2 2 2 2 2 2 x 2 3 4 5 6	12
138	*Farodast*	*d d d dv* l 2 2 2 3 4 x 2 3 4 5	13
139	*Qavālī*	*d d d d* 2 2 2 2 x 2 0 3	8
140	*Karan*	*d d d d* 2 2 2 2 x 2 3 4	8
141	*Kārvalīcitrapuṭ*	*dv d d d* 3 2 2 2 x 2 3 4	9
142	*Khaṭ*	*d d d d d d* 2 2 2 2 2 2 x 2 3 4 5 6	12
143	*Kokilā*	*l d l dv dv* 4 2 4 3 3 x 2 3 4 5	16
144	*Khanḍmahākāl*	*d d l l l l* 2 2 4 4 4 4 x 2 3 0 4 0	20
145	*Kavīd*	*l l d d l l ld ld* 4 4 2 2 4 4 6 6 x 2 3 4 5 0 6 0	32
146	*Kritī*	*l ld ld l l l ld ld* 4 6 6 4 4 4 6 6 x 2 0 3 0 4 5 0	40

147	*Khanḍshashṭī*	*lv lv d d d d* 5 5 2 2 2 2 x 2 3 4 5 -6	18
148	*Kandarp*	*d d l g g* 2 2 4 8 8 x 2 3 4 5	24
149	*Kirīṛā*	*d d v* 2 2 1 x 2 3	5
150	*Kokilpriyā*	*g l k* 8 4 16 x 2 3	28
151	*Kandūk*	*l l g g* 4 4 8 8 x 2 3 4	24
152	*Karūnā*	*l l* 4 4 x 0	8
153	*Gaj*	*l l ld* 4 4 6 x 2 3	14
154	*Gajlīlā*	*ldv ldv v d* 7 7 1 2 x 2 3 4	17
155	*Gaurī*	*l l l l l* 4 4 4 4 4 x 2 3 4 5	20
156	*Ganesh*	*l d d l l v v v v* 4 2 2 4 4 1 1 1 1 x 2 3 4 5 6 7 8 9	20
157	*Gauṛ*	*l l d d l l l* 4 4 2 2 4 4 4 x 2 3 4 5 6 0	24
158	*Gaṛūr*	*d d d dv* 2 2 2 3 x 2 3 4	9
159	*Labdhā*	*l dv* 4 3 x 2	7
160	*Lalit*	*d d l l l* 2 2 4 4 4 x 2 3 4 0	16

161	*Līlā*	*d l ld ld* 2 4 6 6 x 2 3 0	18
162	*Lacharī*	*l l l l v d d* 4 4 4 4 1 2 2 x 2 3 4 5 6 7	21
163	*Lalitpriyā*	*l l l l l l l* 4 4 4 4 4 4 4 x 2 3 0 4 5 0	28
164	*Lakshvamī*	*l d d dv d d d d d dv dv d d d dv d d d* 4 2 2 3 2 2 2 2 2 3 3 2 2 2 3 2 2 2 x 2 3 4 5 6 7 8 9 10 11 12 13 14 15 16 17 18	42
165	*Laghūshekhar*	*v l* 1 4 x 2	5
166	*Madan*	*l l l* 4 4 4 x 2 0	12
167	*Mukund*	*l d d d d l l* 4 2 2 2 2 4 4 x 2 3 4 5 6 0	20
168	*Mal*	*l l l l dv d* 4 4 4 4 3 2 x 2 3 4 5 6	21
169	*Mathkā*	*l l d ld ld* 4 4 2 6 6 x 0 2 3 0	22
170	*Mohan*	*l l d d l l l l* 4 4 2 2 4 4 4 4 x 2 3 4 5 6 7 0	28
171	*Misrgārgīpancak*	*ldv d d d d* 7 2 2 2 2 x 2 3 4 5	15
172	*Misrgajlīlā*	*ldv ldv dv* 7 7 3 x 2 3	17
173	*Maṭ*	*l l g l l l l* 4 4 8 4 4 4 4 1 2 3 4 5 6 7	32

174	*Makarand*	*d d l l l g* 2 2 4 4 4 8 x 2 3 4 5 6	24
175	*Maṭhiā*	*l d l* 4 2 4 x 2 3	10
176	*Miṣr*	*d d d dv d d d dv d d d dv* 2 2 2 3 2 2 2 3 2 2 2 3 x 2 3 4 5 6 7 8 9 10 11 12	27
177	*Malīkāmod*	*l l d d d d* 4 4 2 2 2 2 x 2 3 4 5 6	16
178	*Maṭhīkā*	*g v k* 8 1 16 x 2 3	25
179	*Mal*	*l l l l d d v* 4 4 4 4 2 2 1 x 2 3 4 5 6 7	21
180	*Nandan*	*l d d ld ld* 4 2 2 6 6 x 2 3 4 0	20
181	*Nandī*	*l l d d l l l l l l* 4 4 2 2 4 4 4 4 4 4 x 2 3 4 5 6 7 8 9 10	36
182	*Nainaglīlā*	*k g k l* 16 8 16 4 x 2 3 4	44
183	*Nainag*	*l l l ld ld l l l l l l l* 4 4 4 6 6 4 4 4 4 4 4 4 x 2 0 3 4 5 0 6 0 7 8 0	52
184	*Varanjat*	*d d l l* 2 2 4 4 x 2 3 4	12
185	*Vijayānand*	*l l l l l l l l* 4 4 4 4 4 4 4 4 x 2 3 0 4 0 5 0	11
186	*Vipravikram*	*l d d g* 4 2 2 8 x 2 3 4	16
187	*Varanbhān*	*d d l g* 2 2 4 8 x 2 3 4	16

188	*Vanmālī*	*d d d d l l d d g* 2 2 2 2 4 4 2 2 8 x 2 3 4 5 6 7 8 9	28
189	*Vijay*	*k g k g* 16 8 16 8 x 2 3 4	48
190	*Vijaynandan*	*l l g g g* 4 4 8 8 8 1 2 3 4 5	32
191	*Vīshammahākāl*	*l l l l* 1 4 4 4 4 4 x 2 0 3 0	20
192	*Vīshamkankāl*	*l g g* 4 8 8 x 2 3	20
193	*Vasant*	*l l l l l l l l l* 4 4 4 4 4 4 4 4 4 x 2 3 4 0 5 6 0 7	36
194	*Varthīn*	*d d l g* 2 2 4 8 x 2 3 4	16
195	*Vīnāyak*	*g g g l l k g l l k* 8 8 8 4 4 16 8 4 4 16 x 2 3 4 5 6 7 8 9 10	80
196	*Varanītī*	*l l k k* 4 4 16 16 x 2 3 4	40
197	*Harmukh*	*l d d d d* 4 2 2 2 2 x 2 3 4 5	12
198	*Hans*	*dv dv dv dv* 3 3 3 3 x 0 2 0	
199	*Hansnād*	*gv gv d d d d gv* 9 9 2 2 2 2 9 x 2 3 4 5 6 7	35
200	*Hanslīlā*	*v l l* 1 4 4 x 2 3	9

The *tāls* listed above were used by the ancients. Some of them were inspired by the movements and voices of beasts and birds, for example *Hansnād* (sound of the swan), *Cakor* (partridge), and *Gajlīlā* (play of the elephant). These days, attention to this aspect of the art has decreased and interest in the compositions of *ṭhumrī*, *g͟hazal* and theater (*nāṭak*) has increased so that difficult rhythmic work (*laykārī*) and challenging *tāls* have disappeared. Some of these *tāls* remain in use among the people of south India. The control of difficult *tāls* is considered a great achievement for musicians.

In Western music there are three classes of *tāl*: "duple," "triple" and "quadruple," and all the *tāls* belong to one or another of the three classes. The current *tāls* of Western music are shown in the chart below.

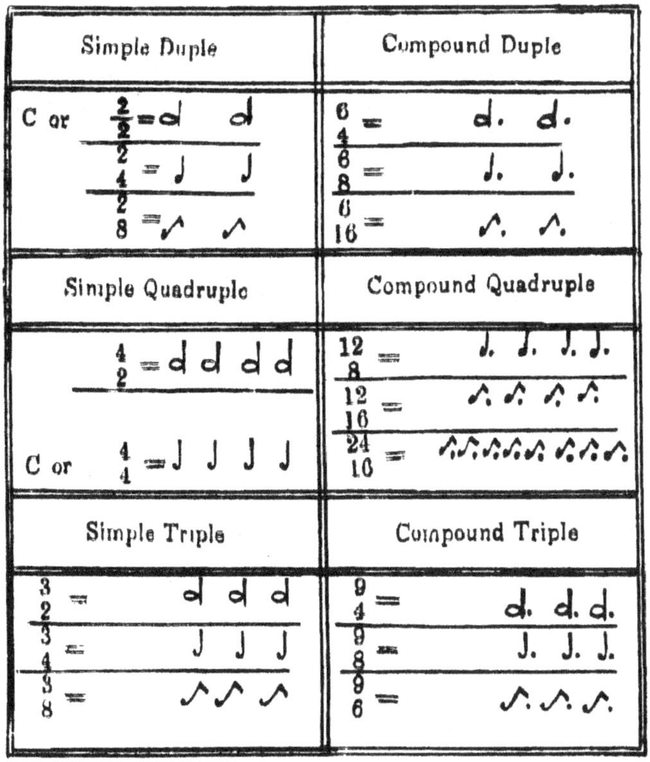

Simple Duple	Compound Duple
C or 2/2 = 𝅗𝅥 𝅗𝅥	6/4 = 𝅗𝅥. 𝅗𝅥.
2/4 = ♩ ♩	6/8 = ♩. ♩.
2/8 = ♪ ♪	6/16 = ♪. ♪.
Simple Quadruple	**Compound Quadruple**
4/2 = 𝅗𝅥 𝅗𝅥 𝅗𝅥 𝅗𝅥	12/8 = ♩. ♩. ♩. ♩.
C or 4/4 = ♩ ♩ ♩ ♩	12/16 = ♪. ♪. ♪. ♪.
	24/16 = ♪. ♪. ♪. ♪. ♪. ♪. ♪. ♪.
Simple Triple	**Compound Triple**
3/2 = 𝅗𝅥 𝅗𝅥 𝅗𝅥	9/4 = 𝅗𝅥. 𝅗𝅥. 𝅗𝅥.
3/4 = ♩ ♩ ♩	9/8 = ♩. ♩. ♩.
3/8 = ♪ ♪ ♪	9/6 = ♪. ♪. ♪.

Chapter Six
Tempo (*lay*)

In technical terminology *lay* is the tempo and timing in the performance of a *rāg*, or the hesitation in the movement of the *sur* and the *tāl*. If a *rāg* is recognized by its *sur*, *lay* is manifested by the clapped measures (*tāl*). One sings or plays according to the *lay* that is established, so if the *lay* is slow, one will sing slowly and if it is fast, one will sing quickly.

Time Measure (*kāl*)

Lay is of three main types. The first is *vīlamb kāl*, which in common language is called *ṭhā lay*, when the pace of the music is very slow. In the sixteen *mātrā*s of *Tetāla*, for example, when the speed of each cycle is so slow that the completion of one cycle lasts for a count of thirty-two *mātrā*s, it is *vīlamb kāl*. The second is *made kāl*, which is commonly called *barābar kī lay* (equal tempo). In this tempo the pace should not seem too slow or too fast, so that a cycle of *Tetāla* is complete in a count of sixteen *mātrā*s. The third is *drut kāl* which is commonly called *dugun lay* (double tempo). Here the music is fast, so that one cycle of *Tetāla* is completed in a count of half, that is, eight *mātrā*s. A *lay* faster than this is commonly called *tigun kī lay* (triple tempo), and a lay faster than this is called *caugun kī lay* (quadruple tempo). The relationship of the three tempos is shown in the chart below.

Chart of *kāl*

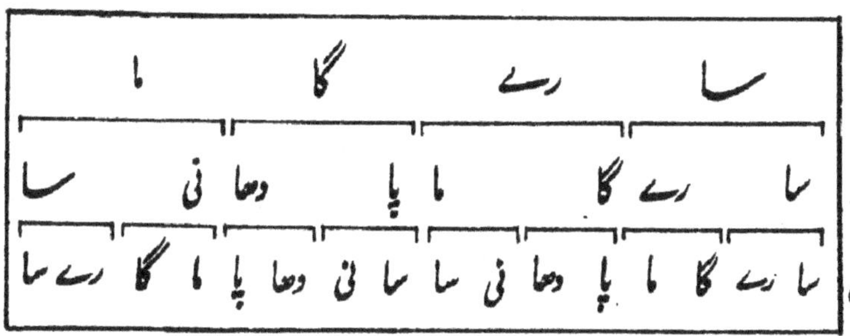

Sā, Re, Gā, Mā in single, double, and quadruple tempos (*vīlamb, made, drut*)

For the amount of time that four notes require in *vīlamb kāl* there will be eight notes in *made kāl* and sixteen in *drut kāl.* If one extemporizes in the intervals between counts while singing or playing and does not proceed according to the regular spaces but moves in an irregular manner, this is called *āṛ kī lay.* And if one moves in an irregular manner from one cycle to the next extending over both clapped divisions (*tāl*) and *sam*, this is called *kuāṛ kī lay.* This is the equivalent of playfulness (*bānkpan*) in music.

Grah

Grah is a Hindi word for place. In music, *grah* is of four types. The first is *sam grah.* This is the name for a situation where one begins and ends an extemporization (*ūpaj*) on *sam.* The second is *visham grah*, which is when one begins an extemporization before *sam* or before a clapped measure (*tāl*) and ends on *sam.* The third is *atīt grah*, when one begins an extemporization after the *sam* or *tāl.* The fourth is *anāghāt grah* in which the place one begins has no relation to the time or *tāl.* The singer or player begins where he wants and ends on *sam.* This happens when the singer or instrumentalist is so engaged in his work that he loses his attentiveness and the extemporization begins spontaneously at any time.

Yatī

Ways of using words (*bol*) along with melody (*sur*) is called *yatī*. There are five types of *yatī*, which are all manifest through tempo (*lay*). The first is *sam yatī*. In this *yatī* a syllable begins at *sam* and ends after moving over two notes. The notation is . In singing *Sā Re* in this notation

the mark for *sam* appears below *Sā*, so that is where the *yatī* begins. One sings the syllable *lā* and slides over the notes *Sā* and *Re*. In other words, the voice is extended over two notes. The second is *vīsham yatī*, in which the words begin before *sam* and end on *sam*.

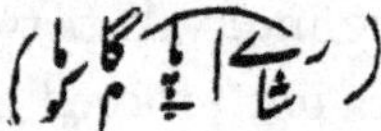

In this example the syllable *shā* begins on *Re* before *sam* and ends on *Pā* on *sam*. This is *visham yatī*. The third is *mridang yatī* and its symbol is . The notes that have this sign should be sung louder and softer as the shape of the notation indicates.

In this example the *mridang yatī* is written over eight notes: , The syllable *ā* written below the first note should be stretched over all the notes. The *Sā* at the beginning should be sung softly; the voice should be a bit stronger when it reaches *Gā*, and by *Mā* the voice should be fully open. After the *Pā*, which should be more open, the second *Mā* should be a bit softer; then the volume should be gradually decreased until *Re* has the same softness as at the beginning. Sometimes a half-*mridang yatī* is written. When it appears like this, one should sing according to the shape of the *yatī*. Sing the syllable *nū* which is written below the *Sā*, and stretch it over the three notes. Since the mouth of the notation is wider near the *Sā*, the voice should be fully open at the *Sā*, less so at the *Re,* and soft at the *Gā*. If the notation is written over just one note, it should be sung according to the shape of the notation.

If it appears like this, one should begin the syllable *ḍā* softly, then increase the volume. If it is written like this

one should begin the syllable *ṛā* which is written below the *Mā* by singing loudly and then becoming softer. The fourth type is the *gopūcca yatī*, in which several syllables are sung to one note. In the example below

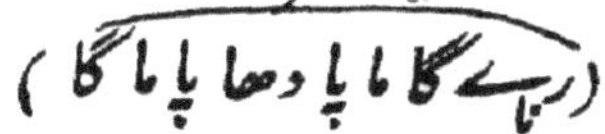

the syllable *nā* is stretched across all the notes *Re Gā Mā Pā Mā Gā*. In this type of *yatī* there are no restrictions as to variety or length. Often, extemporizations (*tān*s and *palṭa*s) are written with this *yatī*. Aside from the four types of *yatī*s, a *yatī* can be used to join notes. In the example there is a *yatī* over two *Sā*'s so they should be sung as one, but the *Sā* should have the beauty of two. The fifth is the *plut yatī*: . The notes that have this *yatī* indicated should be sung with a *khaṭkā* ornament on them. In the example

the syllable *yā* is begun on *Gā* then continued on the other notes *Re Mā Gā*, but each of these notes should be sung with a *khaṭkā* ornament. This *yatī* can be used in the low and middle *saptak*s.

Chapter Seven
The Notation of Music

In India music training is based on singing or listening, but a thing can't be properly impressed on the mind just by hearing it. Such things as *sur* and *lay* are very difficult to hear and thoroughly understand until they are put into writing. Often people do not give it time and patience and choose to avoid it, which is why so few students of this art are produced. Compositions of the old masters are in current practice today, but they differ with each person's performance. If ten singers were to sing an old composition, each one's song would be different. Because everyone cannot remember a single version correctly, each one who plays or sings a composition adds something of one's own to it, so the real forms of the old compositions are not to be found. Likewise, if an artist should wish to preserve vocal compositions or *gats*, *parans*, *toṛās*, or *ṭhekas* of his own making, he is forced to bring a student to an understanding of his version with a great deal of labor and long training. If he can, fine, otherwise it is a lost cause. Because of this, many people will have nothing to do with this art. The practitioners of the art cannot propagate their compositions in writing because there is no system for it. Some time ago my maternal grandfather, the late Professor Maula Bakhsh, instituted in the (Baroda) College a system of notation for the musical art. He also published books in the notation, which is a blessing for our era. The name of this is *tahrīr-i mūsīqī*, or "Notation." Its real virtue is that, just as by learning the alphabet the reader of a letter comes to know the well-being of the writer, or the reader of a book reads it and can understand the message of the author, similarly through musical notation someone can write a letter to another about his way of thinking and make it known. A person who knows the system can sing or play whatever is written, and can write for himself any style to which he has taken a liking. It is like a photo of music. For the educated person this system makes the art of music not difficult and obscure but very easy to learn. When a person becomes thoroughly practiced in it, *rāg* and *tāl* certainly become his loyal followers. The compositions for vocal and instrumental music that appear in Part Two of this book are written in this system.

The Current Method of Musical Notation

مولا This symbol occurs at the beginning of each sequence. It is the identifying signature of this musical notation, and it is a sign to begin the composition in the middle register (*mada saptak*).

واو If this sign occurs at the beginning of the segment, one should begin the composition in the low register (*mandra saptak*).

واو If a segment begins with this sign, the composition should begin in the high register (*tār saptak*).

V. This is the sign for a flat note (*komal sur*).

V گا The sign is written on a note like this. If, as in this example, it occurs with *Gā*, the *Gā* is *komal*.

\ This is the sign of a sharp note (*tīvra sur*).

When the mark occurs with a note like this, for example *Madham*, the *Mā* is *tīvra*.

This is a sign of a natural note (*shuddh sur*). It is used in rare cases.

Otherwise, *shuddh surs* are written without any notation. Here since there is no sign for *komal* or *tīvra* with *Pā*, one should understand it to be *shuddh*.

This sign is placed below a note of the low octave (*mandra saptak*) and above a note of the high octave (*tār saptak*).

For example, since it is below the *Dhā*, one knows that the *Dhā* is in the *mandra saptak*.

Here the sign is above the *Re* so one should know that the *Re* is in the *tār saptak*.

Here the *Nī* has the sign for the *mandra saptak* and also a dot. This designates the extra-low register (*mandratar saptak*).

The dot which appears above the *Gā* along with the sign for the *tār saptak* indicates the extra-high register (*tārtar saptak*).

سا If the *kāgpad* sign is given with the *Sā*, it indicates that the *Sā* should be held steadily for eight *mātrās*.

رے If the *devguru* sign appears with the *Re*, it should be held for four *mātrās*.

گا If the *guru* sign appears with the *Gā*, it should be held for two *mātrās*.

ما If there are none of the above-mentioned signs, such as here given with *Mā*, it is one *laghu* in length and will be held for one *mātrā*.

پا If there is a *drut* sign with *Pā*, it should be held for a half *mātrā*.

دھا If *Dhā* has a sign for *anādrut* with it, it should be held for one quarter of a *mātrā*.

نی This *Nī* has one-and-a-half *devgurus* with it. Therefore it should have four *mātrās* for the *devguru* and two for the dot. Altogether a hold of six *mātrās* is indicated.

The *guru* sign on *Sā* indicates two *mātrās*; the first dot indicates one *mātrā* and the second dot indicates a half *mātrā*, altogether making three-and-a-half. So it will be held for three-and-a-half *mātrās*.

Notations for rest (*bisrām)* occur where the sections of the *tāl* are empty. In other words, one should understand it to be a rest when marks appear as shown below without a *sur.*

This sign is called *kāgpad*. It has eight *mātrās*. One should rest on it for a count of eight.

This is a *devguru*. It has four *mātrās*.

This is a *guru*. It has two *mātrās*.

This is a *laghu bisrām*. It has one *mātrā*.

This is a *drut*. It has a half *mātrā*.

This is *anādrut*. It has one quarter of a *mātrā*.

Where the *bisrām* signs are written, one should count as many *mātrās* as are indicated and stop for that amount of time before beginning to sing or play again.

This mark of an arc is called *yatī*. The syllable *bā* which is written at the bottom should be stretched over all the four notes.

This is a sign of a *yatī* on two *Pā*'s. If any note is written twice together with a *yatī* on it like this, the notes should not be sung two times. Both *Pā*'s are *laghu,* and two *laghus* together equal a *guru*, therefore one must hold *Pā* for that much time, in other words for two *mātrās*. This is also called the *bīsham yatī*.

These signs refer to the *mridang yatī*. The notes written below it should be sung and played loudly or softly, according to its shape.

The notation for the structure (*surūp*) of a *tāl* is given at the beginning of each composition.

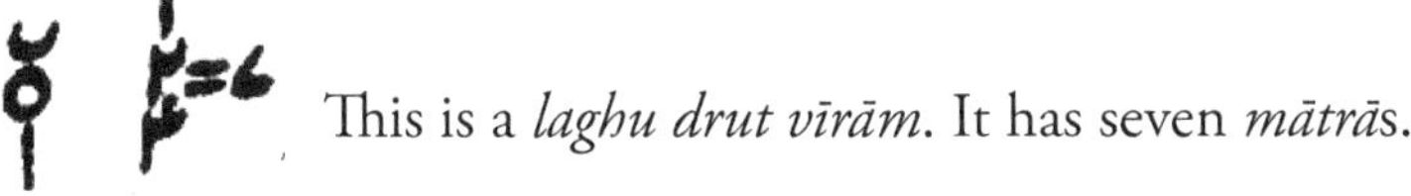

This is a *laghu drut vīrām*. It has seven *mātrās*.

This is a *laghu vīrām*. It has five *mātrās*.

This is a *drut vīrām*. It has three *mātrās*.

This is a *guru*. It has eight *mātrās*.

This is a *laghu*. It has four *mātrās*.

This is a *drut*. It has two *mātrās*.

This is a *vīrām*. It has one *mātrā*.

This is the sign for the *sam* of the *tāl*. A forceful clap is given here.

This is a sign for the *tāl*. A clap should be given.

This is the sign for *khālī*. This juncture is shown by a lowering of the hand.

This straight line indicates the divisions of the *tāl*. It is called a "bar.

Tetāla, for example, has sixteen *mātrās*. It is divided into four sections made up of three claps (*tāl*) and one *khālī*. Sixteen *mātrās* are completed by writing four *mātrās* in each section so each section is written with a bar as follows:

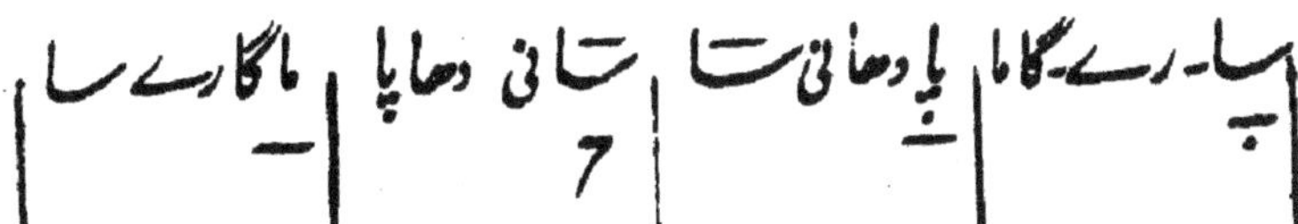

If this sign is written on the right side of the bar, the piece of music written on the right should be repeated.

| سارے گاما | پادھا پاما | گاما پاما | گارے سا ||

If notated as above, one should sing *S R G M P D P M* two times, then sing *G M P M G R S* -- one time.

If this sign is to the left of the bar, one should sing the music written to the left two times.

| سانی دھاپا | ماگارے گا | ماپا ماپا | دھاپا |

If written as above, one should sing *Ṡ N D P M G R G* and then sing *M P M P D - P* -- two times.

If this sign is attached to both sides of the bar, one should repeat the music that is written both to the right and the left of the bar.

It is called a double bar. It indicates a section of a song. If notated as above, one should sing *S R M P P G M P* twice, then sing *N D M P M G R S -* twice.

┌۱┐ ┌۲┐ These signs are often found together with or near the repeat signs. When any music is repeated, the first time through one should omit the notes written below the ┌۲┐ sign. When it is repeated, one should omit the notes written below the ┌۱┐ sign. For example:

Here, one should sing *G R G M P M G M P D P M P D Ṡ -* the first time. When repeating, sing *G R G M P M G M P D P M*, then omit ┌۱┐ and sing *N D P M*.

This mark written on each side of a portion of a song indicates that that portion should be sung twice.

سارے گارے | پا ما گا رے | دھا پا نی دھا | رے نی سا ||

If written as above, sing *S R G R P M G R D P N D*, then again sing the section *P M G R D P N D*, and finally sing *Ṙ N Ṡ* - .

This sign indicates the end of a piece.

This sign often is written near the end sign. When it appears, one should begin the song from here,

and end the song at this sign.

A note that has this sign receives a rest for as long as one wishes.

A set of *surs* (*sargam)* that has this sign above it should be sung in accordance with the *sargam* but using the words of the verses indicated by the same sign.

Praise to God!

End of Part One

The Late Professor Maula Bakhsh Sahab

Verse in Praise of Maula Baksh Sahab

A gift (*bakhsh*) of God was this fine man,
  my maternal grandfather, the great Maula Bakhsh.
In the art of song, unequalled during his time;
  in instrumental music, extraordinary in his composing
  (*gatkārī*).
Dancers were awed by his energy.
  the banner of his stature was the lofty firmament.
His melodies contained the power of his soul,
  alluring among mankind, with beautiful speech
A record of his deeds is yet to be done;
  he must be strolling in the garden of paradise.
His grace is my support;
  from him alone is my great good fortune.
It is gift (*'ināyat*) enough, this longing
  for the blessings of my Sheikh.

Part One

The Practice of Music

(*Sangīt kalā*)

Maharaj Sir Kishen Pershad Bahadur
Prime Minister of Hyderabad

Verse in Praise of Sir Kishen Pershad

The Exalted One of the proud court, the Power of Command, the Great One of the Deccan province, His Excellence, "Happy One" (*shād*), Prince among princes, Ruler among rulers, Sir Kishen Pershad Bahadur, Prime Minister, Commander-in-Chief, may his shadow endure.

How great is this worldly lord's countenance!
  His face turns the affairs of the world toward order.
The tongue of the unseen says of him, "O Lord,
  may Kishen Pershad hold sway throughout the era."
By his policy, the ornamentation of the state gains luster.
  By his authority, the Deccan has become the envy of
  the rose garden.
O God, may the domain of Asif be happy (*shād*),
  full of the fortunate, for ages to come.
Inayat, sovereignty is the door to your desire.
  Under the faithful rule of Shad, may you smile
  in happiness.

In the Name of the Merciful, the Compassionate

In the name of the One who taught the soul music,
and with the clamor of the soul's music set the world ablaze.
How can language describe Ahmad, when God Himself
found it necessary to pronounce "*Ya sīn*?"
"Inayat, introduce the second part:
you are the revealer of the secret of song"
O God, I am inexpert in secrets and their telling,
and in my failure am in need of your perfection.

Among Muslims music has always been considered a genteel art. It is regrettable that during the time of the Muslim decline, music was made into a sport or game, and its position was let fall to such a degree that the dignity of musicians was reduced to the designation "masters of pleasure" (*arbāb-i nishāṭ*).[1] Muslims have closely studied the arts of the entire world and have shown their own great achievements in music as well. For as long as there was discussion among Muslims, a great many books and useful explanations were done by them and became known to the world. You gentlemen will have seen in the pages of history the extent to which the Muslims took an interest in music. This is clearly illustrated by the example that when a certain musician heard about the renown of the Khalifa Abd al-Rahman and came to meet him, the Khalifa personally came out of his palace to welcome him. In Qurtuba (Cordoba), a music college functioned under royal patronage, which produced unparalleled teachers. Music was practiced during the time of the Abbasid rule as well, and there were many improvements made to musical instruments. The country of the Arabs is ancient in its self-determinacy. Among the people there, the desert wanderers and devotees have cultivated music

1 Both Maula Bakhsh and Inayat Khan's disapproval of the use of this term by royal patrons are noted in *Biography*, 26, 62.

since ancient times. It was very much practiced and still is. The truth is that every country's tastes have developed in various ways. History tells us that among the Arabs composers of musical verse were the very first kind of artists. Arabs have always been well-spoken and eloquent, and their connection with sweet modulation is clear. Quranic reading was established on this basis, and its pronunciations have *sur* and *tāl* as well. Every European traveler who has heard the call of our marvelous muezzin can understand the close connection between the rules of music and recitation.

Music was a highly approved science and one considered near to God, since God gave the gift of his voice to Da'ud by way of a miracle. In the following era music became a part of the equipment of battle, as it is today indeed, an important and necessary part. And it was a proud part of the accouterments of the Muslim emperors. To the extent that a simple Muslim like myself can understand the holy Qur'an, though I am not qualified for formal exegesis, I have found nothing against music there. The Muslims were not unmindful of the effect that music has on the mind and heart. But it is regrettable that the art was made into such a contemptible object that no respectable person would give it attention. If one looks closely, music is in the chanting of elegies and burial services, but this has not been taken into account. Imam Muhammad Ghazali—God's mercy be upon him—in his book *Kīmiyā-i Sa'ādat* presents a discussion about listening to music (*sama'*), saying that it is worthy of respect in every way, and because of this the dignity of music is approved in the Muslim view. Among the noble Sufis to this day *sama'* is called "the nourishment for the soul." In fact, its vestiges are preserved especially among their orders. It is true that sometimes ill-intentioned people imitate them, but the worth of jewels is not diminished by superficial impurities. Our future intellectual and artistic progress is entirely dependent on our young students. If a little effort and attention were to be paid, the ugly stain that despicable and ill-mannered people have given to music would quickly be erased. Change to one's attractions and influences comes about through music. When music seems to be merely stimulation, one should remember that good qualities and education depend on training. People who are well-educated and courteous will be engaged in the genteel arts to a higher degree, and such fundamental aims are not misguided.

Music was practiced during the period of Muslim rule in Hindustan, but it is regrettable that no record of it has been preserved. Anyone who has an interest in the history of the Eastern rulers can easily ascertain that the harem women of the Muslim emperors were all acquainted with music. The wealthy Muslims of Hindustan were often proficient in this science. In the subsequent era, a philosopher was not fully accomplished without the knowledge of music. Likewise, up until the last century knowledge of it was a necessity. Hakim Abu Ali Sina was a great master of music, so it is said that the *sīnā'ī*, or *surnā'ī*, or *shahnā'ī*, was his invention.

Aurangzeb has often been given a bad name for the strictness of his religious ordinances. In his era, however, many Muslims were highly accomplished in music. Mir Abd al-Jalil was without equal in music. Mir Abd al-Jalil's sister's son, Sayyid Ghulam Nabi, was also without equal in music. *Nakh Sikh* and *Rasprabodh* are among his writings. Mir Nizam al-din was another scholar of music during the reign of Aurangzeb. Among his books on music, *Nādcandrīkā* and *Madhnāyaksingār* are noteworthy. Music is practiced even now in Islamic countries. In Egypt, for example, the honorable men and women there are engaged in music, and it has had no harmful effects on their culture.

Chapter One
Vocal Music (*gāyan*)

Sangīt has three fundamentals: vocal music, instrumental music, and dance (*gāyan, vādan, nart*), but vocal music is primary because it is a God-given gift. No instrument can accomplish it perfectly, and if it does it is an imitation of the real thing. Vocal music is of two types: professional and amateur (*ustādī* and *a'ṭāī*). In *ustādī* vocal music there are higher and lower levels. *Dhrupad* singing, for example, is very difficult and is considered the highest level. *Kh̲ayāl*, also called *āstāī*, singing is considered to be below that, and *ṭhumrī* and *gh̲azal* are below that. Masters of earlier times sang *chand, praband, gīt*, and *kīvat*, but now that practice has ended. *Ustād*s made use of the four composition types: *dhamār, dhrupad, dhuvā*, and *māṭhā*. Later, that is in the present era, they began to sing *dhrupad, kh̲ayāl, ṭappa, ṭhumrī, gh̲azal, tarāna, horī* and the like, which are still current.

During the era of the acknowledged masters, styles of singing were distinct from each other, for which the technical term is *bānī*. There are four types. The first is *Kandahārī*, in which the *dhrupad* style is sung, often in *mārg rāg*s. These are the *rāg*s that are sung and played alike in every region. This can be called "Universal Mode." The late Mir Nasir Ahmad of Delhi brought this *bānī* into practice. The second is *Goharmārī*. This *bānī* is the name for the style of Tansen, who brought it into practice. The third is called *Ḍāgar*. This is sung with a great many notes wound together in *ākār*. Shahab Khan of Delhi brought this into practice. The fourth is *Nauhār*. It is the singing style of the late Madar Khan, and he is the main creator of this style. Aide from these, there are two more *bānī*s, which are called *mīrāṣ̲* and *dhaḍ*. These *bānī*s are not current today, and there does not seem to be any great necessity for them.

There are four ancient categories of musician. The first is *gāyak*, the second *gunī*, the third *gandharv*, the fourth *nāyak*. A *gāyak* is one who can sing a composition learned from a master in correct *tāl* and *sur*. A *gunī* is one who understands correctly what he is singing and sings in tune and in rhythm. A *gandharv* is one who can understand both his own and another's singing, who can train another, and who has the competence to make compositions. A *nāyak* is one who has not only completely mastered the essence of *rāg* and *tāl* but who can invent *rāg*s and *tāl*s himself. He is so perfectly attuned to *sur* that he can instantly realize the *sargam* of any sound that falls on his ears, and he can make vocal compositions. He is perfectly competent in the science of the musical art, unequalled in both speaking and writing about music, and good in training and teaching. The *nāyak* category in all these matters is the highest.

In India a break occurred in the ranking of these categories when disagreements about the art arose. This happened when the methods used in each household (*ghar*) became different and each household had a different *ustād*. Who would pay attention to categories when people objected to each other's achievements? So the categories began to disappear and everything was lumped together. Not only did the sense of excellence and accomplishment disappear, but whosoever managed to produce high and low notes began to consider themselves *ustād*s.

These days, improvements in music have been going on in Europe, and universities and degrees have been set up there in which there are these four highest levels: "Associate of Music," "Licentiate of Music," "Bachelor of Music," and the highest category, "Doctor of Music."

In general the levels of a singer are said to be three: best (*uttam*), middle (*madham*), and low (*adham*). *Uttam* is one who has no need for any instrument while singing. *Madham* is one who needs an instrument. *Adham* is one who sings poorly even with an instrument.

Defects of a Vocalist

To gnash the teeth while singing; to have a meager voice; to sing with restlessness; to open the mouth more than necessary; to sing with fear; to have a trembling, shrill, or harsh voice; to lift the head while singing; to have a ponderous voice; to shake the head while singing; to allow the voice to break; to sing with the head bowed; to wave the hands more than necessary while singing; to sing with the eyes closed; to sing unpleasantly; to make faces while singing; to sing with a thin voice; to become separated from *tāl* or *sur*; to sing contrary to the rules; to sing with a nasal voice; to change the natural fashion of the voice; to repeatedly take breaths while singing.

It is imperative to keep the above-mentioned faults in mind while singing because the effort of performance makes the limbs such as the hands, neck and head move involuntarily, and this affects the face as well. The same thing affects listeners, that is, their hands, head and neck tend to shake, so why should it not happen to the singer? Even in conversation the hands, head, neck and face display sense and motion, but such movements are acceptable only to a certain degree.

Virtues of a Vocalist

The singing should have impact; the singer should have received training from a competent master and have aptitude in learning; the singer should be obedient to the master and make students obedient to him; his skill should be such as to please himself and others; he should have good fortune and be of pleasing manner; he should have a clear voice that is pleasing to those familiar with the art and to others; there should be sweetness in his singing; his voice should be neither too loud or too soft and in good tune; his voice should produce three octaves clearly; his singing should produce a feeling of calm; there should be feeling (*dard*) in his singing; his singing should be delicate; his voice should carry long distances; his lung capacity (*dam*) should be strong; his voice should not become hoarse from singing just a little; the voice should be expansive; the breath should not break while singing nor should the rhythm be interrupted; the voice should be like a cuckoo—this is a quality of the voice box; the singing should be commensurate with the song and be in accord with the rules.

The above-mentioned virtues should always be kept in mind by one who pursues the art. Nowadays often a thin sort of male voice is cultivated, and people enjoy the display (*takal-lufi*). Likewise, some women make their voices deep and sing *tān*s like a man, and they consider that good. But when one really thinks of it, this is a big mistake. When God gives one the strength, stature and form of a man it is only proper that his singing or other work be of the same sort; he should not produce a feminine voice and make feminine movements. If his singing and motions are suited to his form and face, they look better, otherwise it is silliness, and these things are rejected in the circles of the art experts. The Europeans call this type of voice "unnatural," that is, contrary to innate disposition, and it is a serious fault.

The Sixteen Adornments (*singār*) of the Vocalist

To pronounce the words correctly; to demonstrate *sam* in the song; to sing with authority; to sing without fear; to sing in a masterly way; to have a good memory; to sing at appropriate times; to have some familiarity with poetry as well; to sing a *rāg* correctly and to know its notes; to use the *grah*s such as *sam, visham* and *atīt* and have a good rhythmic sense; to be able to bring out the form of the *rāg* clearly and show it through *ālāp*; to be good-hearted; to be well-practiced; to be well versed in writing and speaking about singing; to have good fortune and be personable; to be free of addiction to any intoxicant. If one should ask which of all these things is the highest, however, it is the presence of the grace of God. One's style should be such as to be acceptable at a shrine dedicated to love of the Divine. And through this work alone one should reach one's desired goal.

Training in singing is often given with the accompaniment of a *tānpūra*. There is no more noble accompaniment instrument for singing, because no instrument but the *tānpūra* can truly accompany a song. The reason I say this is that when one sings with an instrument, the singing is necessarily constrained because of it. Since only the *sur* rings out from the *tānpūra*, one can sing freely. The *tānpūra* often gives problems both to the student in learning and to the teacher in teaching; but after a long while the voice performs the *sur* correctly and real proficiency in *sur* develops. *Sur* is quickly learned with the harmonium and the *sitār*, and this method is easier than the *tānpūra*. The *tānpūra, sārangī*, harmonium, fiddle, and the like are often used in vocal music, and the *tabla* or *pakhāvaj* is often used to help keep the *tāl*. *Tabla* is suitable for *khayāl* and *pakhāvaj* for *dhrupad*. Ordinary (*ma'muli*) songs are also accompanied by such instruments as *sitār, ektārā, ḍhol,* and *daf*.

Types of Current Vocal Compositions

Dhrupad—This is an old type of song composition. It is difficult to sing, and those who sing it are held in esteem. *Dhrupads* are composed in difficult *rāgs* and *tāls*. They are often sung in *tāls* such as *Cautālā, Āṛā Cautālā, Dhīmā* (slow) *Tetālā, Tevrā, Rudhar,* and *Lachmī*. The *pakhāvaj*, that is the *mridang*, is often played with it. *Dhrupad* has four sections of which the first is called the *dhrupad āstāī*. The beginning of the *rāg* is articulated in this section. The second part is the *antarā*, in which all the rest of the notes of the *rāg* are shown. The third part is the *bhog* in which the notes of the upper register are explored. The fourth section is the *sancārī* in which the composition joins back with the *āstāī*. All four parts of the *dhrupad* should be of similar weight, and extemporization is done exclusively in rhythms of double and triple time, and showing *sam* and *visham*. It is not the practice to sing fast runs (*tān*). *Dhrupad* is a serious song style, so when performing it one should be attentive that no light techniques (*halkī tarkīb*) be allowed to come from the throat. In the old courts, to sing anything more ordinary than *dhrupad* was considered a breach of court etiquette.

Khayāl—This is also called *āstāī*. Its practice spread later than that of *dhrupad*, but *ustāds* have sung it so excellently that now it is more prevalent. *Khayāl* has two sections. The beginning section is *āstāī* and the final section is the *antarā*. *Khayāl* is usually sung in *tāls* such as *Tetālā, Jhūmrā* and *Āṛā Cautālā*. Its performance is somewhat similar to *dhrupad*, but runs, note clusters, and words (*tān, palṭā, bol*) are used for extemporization.

Ṭappā—Miyan Shori brought *ṭappā* into practice. *Ṭappās* are often sung in the Panjab region and often composed in the Panjabi language. *Ṭappā* is a style sung with *tāns* and *palṭās*. Its singing method is completely distinct from *dhrupad* and *khayāl* and its drum accompaniment (*ṭhekā*) is also different. To sing *ṭappā* one must have a practiced voice.

Ṭhumrī—Among the song types this one is enjoyed by the common people. It is practiced a lot in the east, but there is no region in India where *ṭhumrī* is not sung. *Ṭhumrī* is usually composed in poetic Hindi (*bhāshā*), its subject is often the love of Kanaiya and the *gopīs*, and it is set to common *rāgs* and *tāls*. They sing *ṭhumrī* during dance performances.

Kaharva—This is a type of *ṭhumrī* sung in *Kaharva tāl*. The dance of the peacock is done to this type of song.

Dādrā—This is another type of *ṭhumrī* sung in *Dādrā tāl*. It is often used in dance.

Horī—This is a song type whose subject is the month of *phāgun* (February-March). There are two types of *horī*. One is *horī dhamār*, which is in the style of *dhrupad* and is sung only by *ustāds*. The second is *cāncar kī horī*, which is commonly practiced in the east; in fact every Easterner knows *horī*. It is in the style of *ṭhumrī*, its *tāl* is often *Dīpcandī*, and it is also used in dance.

Ghazal—*Ghazal*s are in Persian and Urdu and are sung in many styles. Their *tāls* and rhythmic styles are also of several sorts.

Alāp—Singing a composition or doing extemporization is not sufficient to fully open up and show the character of a *rāg*. *Ustād*s therefore often do *ālāp* before singing a *dhrupad* or *khayāl* to make its complete picture clear. This is a wonderful achievement (*kamāl*). Syllables such as *ay, ne, te, rī, rā, nā, tā, nom, tom*, are sung. The restriction of *tāl* does not hold here.

Tarāna—This is of the same style as *ṭhumrī* but it uses syllables such as a*u, re, tā, nā, tan, dīm, dere, nādere, tādere, dānī, tanadir, nā.* The syllables of the *tarāna* are formed in such a way that it can reach speeds difficult for any other song. Often extemporizations are done using the syllables of *tāl* and *sargam.* Another sort of *tarāna* is a composition called *tillānā* in which in addition to the syllables of *tarāna*, ones like *yal, lūm, yalalī yalā, lā,* and *lāle* are used.

Tirvaṭ—When *tabla* syllables such as *dhirakiṭa, tirakiṭa, dharadhinnā* are set to notes and sung as a song it is called *tirvaṭ.*

Caturang—This means "four colors." In this type of song some words have meanings, some are from *tarāna*, some are from *tirvaṭ,* and some are *sargams*.

Sargam—*Ustāds* in India have used the syllables *Sā Re Gā Mā Pā Dhā and Nī* in a song style and called it *sargam.*

Garbā—In the region of Gujarat during the festival of *naurāt*, Hindu women form a circle and sing *garbā* while moving in a circle. The *ḍhol* or sometimes the *naqāra* is played, and often a shared miraculous state is created. In Kathiavar they also sing a song similar to *garbā* —*rāsṛā*—which also has a powerful effect.

Women sing a song similar to *garbā* called *hinc* while they rock their babies. *Hinc* is called *lorī* in northern India.

Bhajan—Jogis sing songs of their own making with the *ektārā* and these are called *bhajans*. They often sing them in temples. In English this is called "hymn." Another song of a similar sort is called *ārtī*. Hindus sing this while moving the flame before the divine image.

Lāvanī—This is mostly practiced among the Marāṭhi people and is sung to some extent in the east as well. They make a rhymed verse and expand on it with different melodies from beginning to end. There are two types of *lāvanī*: *tambura kī lāvanī*, and *ḍholkī kī lāvanī*. Marāṭha mimics often sing them in their street fairs (*tamāshā*). *Cakaṛ* is another style of *lāvanī* in which often the content is indecent language (*gālī*). In the east, *lāvanī* singers sing questions and answers back and forth, of which there are two methods, *kalghī*, and *ṭura*.

Kāfi—It is sung in Sindh. Its form is something like *bhajan*.

Pad—These are composed in Sanskrit, Prakrit, Marāṭhi or Gujarati. When a song is made to be sung in the meter of a verse it is called *pad*. Nowadays songs for Marāṭhi plays are also called *pad*.

Ashṭapadī—This is also a type of *pad*. It is considered sacred by the Hindus and they sing it with great ardor. The poet Jaidev Kavi is famous for composing *ashṭapadīs*. Singing this is common practice in southern India.

Kirtan—This is also called *kritī*. For the people of the Karnatak region this is like *dhrupad*, and really this song type is very nice. Tyagaraj and Dikshit are the inventors of *kirtan*.

Varnam—There are two types: *tāl varnam* and *cok varnam*, also called *pad varnam*. When *tāl varnam* is sung or played, one uses fast techniques of the voice or hands. *Cok varnam* is sung in a dance performance.

Pallavī—This type of song is sung by Karnatak *ustāds*. They extemporize with *sargam*, and to sing it is considered a wonderful skill. Its method is somewhat like *ṭappa*.

Jāvalī—This is also sung in the Karnatak region. It is used with dance. Its style is something like *ṭhumrī*.

Chapter Two
Systematic Notations of Vocal Compositions

In the notations below the words of the songs are given in syllables which have been separated to correspond with the musical tones (*sargam*). The words are given without the *sargam* as well at the beginning of each notation so that readers can easily read the song.

Dhrupad
Rāg Khammāc[1]

لاگ رہی توسے لگن - لاگو رہت ہے سمرن - عاصیون کی آس پورن - تو ہی کرن ہار وہے
بنا ساتھیون کے ساتھ - ڈوبت کو دیوے ہاتھ - بے وارث کو تو ناتھ - تیر و ہی سہار وہے
ٹوٹت ہمت بندھاوے - دُکھ مین تو ہی کام آوے - روت کو تو ہنساوے - تیر و ہی آدھار وہے
عالم تیرو محتاج - راجن پہ تیرو راج - تو ہی رکھے تو رہے لاج - عنایت دار وہے

I am stricken with love for You. Thoughts of You are constantly with me.
You are the fulfiller of hopes and the defeater of sorrow.
You give companionship to the companionless, a hand to those who are drowning.
You are savior to the helpless; You alone are their support.
You give strength to those whose courage has failed;
in their sorrow You alone can help.
Those who weep, You make them smile;
they depend on You alone.
The world is Your crown jewel.
Your dominion is above that of the kings.
When You cause it, joy is sustained. Inayat is Your servant.

---

1 A recording of this song is to be found in *Inayat Khan: the Complete Recordings of 1909,* CD 2, track 8.

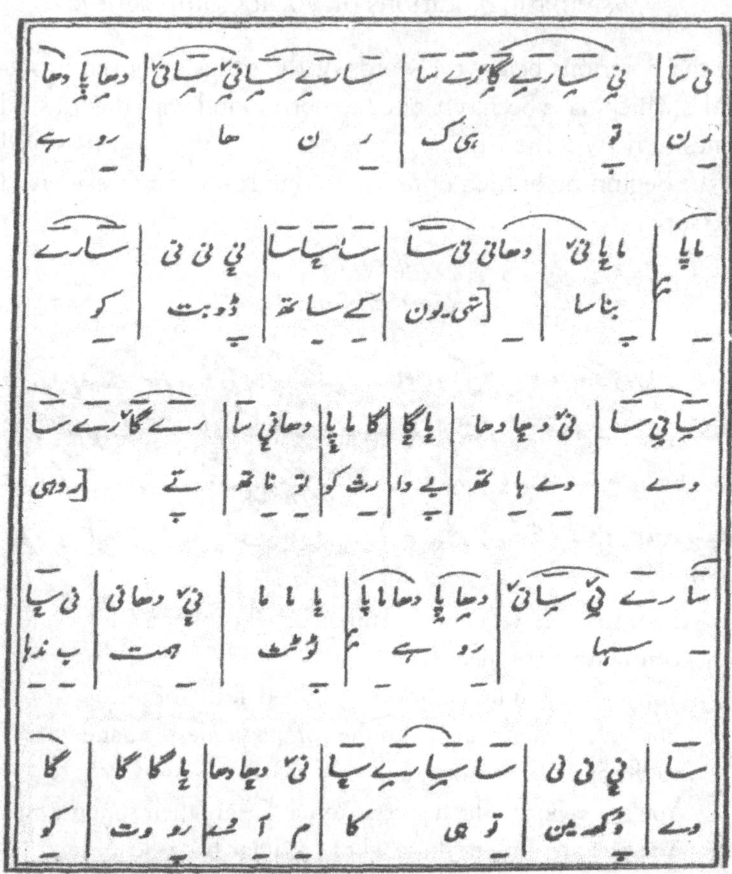

Dhrupad, Rāg Khammāc
(Inayat R., 102)

1. Dhrupad, Rāg Khammāc, Tāl Catūsra Jātī Cautālā, middle speed, twelve *mātrās*

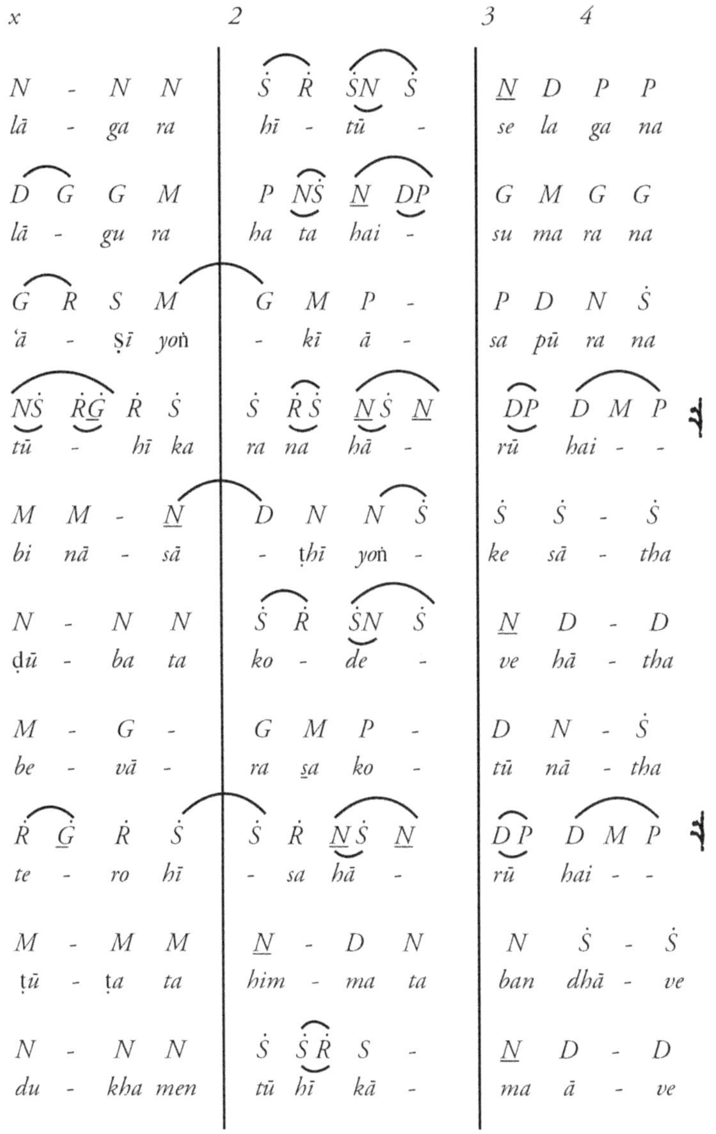

x				2				3		4	
N	-	N	N	Ṡ	Ṙ	ṠN	Ṡ	N̲	D	P	P
lā	-	*ga*	*ra*	*hī*	-	*tū*	-	*se*	*la*	*ga*	*na*
D	G	G	M	P	NṠ	N̲	DP	G	M	G	G
lā	-	*gu*	*ra*	*ha*	*ta*	*hai*	-	*su*	*ma*	*ra*	*na*
G	R	S	M	G	M	P	-	P	D	N	Ṡ
'ā	-	*ṣī*	*yoṅ*	-	*kī*	*ā*	-	*sa*	*pū*	*ra*	*na*
NṠ	ṘĠ̲	Ṙ	Ṡ	Ṡ	ṘṠ	N̲Ṡ	N̲	DP	D	M	P
tū	-	*hī*	*ka*	*ra*	*na*	*hā*	-	*rū*	*hai*	-	-
M	M	-	N̲	D	N	N	Ṡ	Ṡ	Ṡ	-	Ṡ
bi	*nā*	-	*sā*	-	*ṭhī*	*yoṅ*	-	*ke*	*sā*	-	*tha*
N	-	N	N	Ṡ	Ṙ	ṠN	Ṡ	N̲	D	-	D
ḍū	-	*ba*	*ta*	*ko*	-	*de*	-	*ve*	*hā*	-	*tha*
M	-	G	-	G	M	P	-	D	N	-	Ṡ
be	-	*vā*	-	*ra*	*ṣa*	*ko*	-	*tū*	*nā*	-	*tha*
Ṙ	Ġ̲	Ṙ	Ṡ	Ṡ	Ṙ	N̲Ṡ	N̲	DP	D	M	P
te	-	*ro*	*hī*	-	*sa*	*hā*	-	*rū*	*hai*	-	-
M	-	M	M	N̲	-	D	N	N	Ṡ	-	Ṡ
ṭū	-	*ṭa*	*ta*	*him*	-	*ma*	*ta*	*ban*	*dhā*	-	*ve*
N	-	N	N	Ṡ	ṠṘ	S	-	N̲	D	-	D
du	-	*kha*	*men*	*tū*	*hī*	*kā*	-	*ma*	*ā*	-	*ve*

Dhrupad, Rāg Khammāc

x				2				3		4	
M	-	G	G	G	M	P	-	D	N	ṠN̲	Ṡ
ro	-	*va*	*ta*	*ko*	-	*tū*	-	*han*	*sā*	-	*ve*
Ṙ	Ġ̲	Ṙ	Ṡ	Ṡ	Ṙ	N̲Ṡ	N̲	DP	D	M	P
te	-	*ro*	*hī*	-	*ā*	*dhā*	-	*rū*	*hai*	-	-
Ṙ	Ġ̲	Ṙ	Ṡ	Ṡ	-	Ṡ	D	N̲	D	-	D
‘ā	-	*lam*	-	*te*	-	*ro*	*muḥ*	-	*tā*	-	*ja*
M	-	P	P	N	Ṡ	N̲	D	P	M	G	G
rā	-	*ja*	*na*	*pe*	-	*te*	-	*ro*	*rā*	-	*ja*
G	S	S	M	G	M	P	P	D	N	Ṡ	Ṡ
tū	*hī*	*ra*	*khe*	-	*to*	*ra*	*hī*	-	*lā*	-	*ja*
Ṙ	Ṙ	Ġ̲	Ṙ	Ṡ	Ṙ	N̲Ṡ	N̲	DP	D	M	P
I	*nā*	-	*ya*	-	*ta*	*vā*	-	*rū*	*hai*	-	-

Dhrupad
Rāg Sārang

میری ری انکھیان میری میری آنن میرو آت اب میری ناہین جب دیکھی تب نرکھی پیا
تن در کی انکھیان میری ری انکھیان۔
جیو جیو من مین بیاپت تیو تیو جنائے بیٹھی آگما بیروکہی جات گو پر گھر کی اکھیان
میری ری انکھیان۔
انجن کاری کرت ہرت پیا پران اندر بھان چھب چُرائے جوبن جنائے بیٹھی
پان کھات پیاری لگت۔
پیا سکھ جیا گن گنگ جٹ سدھنگ مانو تال سُر راگ نایک مدن پیا پیارے گمن کین
لے درپن دیکھن لاگی اپنی چھب دیکھ دیکھ ری جل بھرتی انکھیان میری ری انکھیان۔

Oh my eyes, my face, my very self, are no longer my own. Wherever I look, the beloved is right there. Oh, my eyes, my eyes.

As soon as the turmoil stirs my heart everyone comes to know. My family honor, oh, my eyes, my eyes.

I've tried ointment, but the light of the dazzling beloved defeats me. Turning away her face, showing her youth, she sits there eating *pān* and looks adorable.

Pleasing to the beloved, hair tied up like Shiva's, beautiful, like *tāl, sur* and *rāg,* Nayak Madan Piya approaches the beloved. She begins to look in the mirror and seeing her own face her eyes fill with tears. Oh my eyes, my eyes.

2. *Dhrupad, Rāg Sārang, Tāl Catūsra Jātī Cautālā*
middle speed, twelve *mātrās*

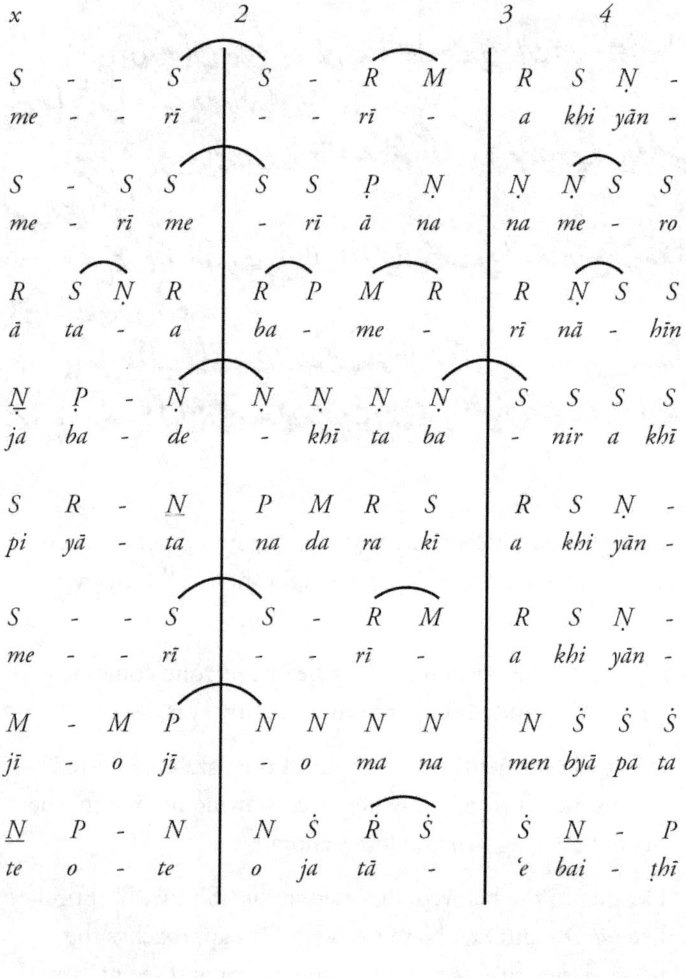

x				2				3		4	
S	-	-	S	S	-	R	M	R	S	Ṇ	-
me	-	-	*rī*	-	-	*rī*	-	*a*	*khi*	*yān*	-
S	-	S	S	S	S	P̣	Ṇ	Ṇ	Ṇ	S	S
me	-	*rī*	*me*	-	*rī*	*ā*	*na*	*na*	*me*	-	*ro*
R	S	Ṇ	R	R	P	M	R	R	Ṇ	S	S
ā	*ta*	-	*a*	*ba*	-	*me*	-	*rī*	*nā*	-	*hīn*
Ṇ̲	P̣	-	Ṇ	Ṇ	Ṇ	Ṇ	Ṇ	S	S	S	S
ja	*ba*	-	*de*	-	*khī*	*ta*	*ba*	-	*nir*	*a*	*khī*
S	R	-	N̲	P	M	R	S	R	S	Ṇ	-
pi	*yā*	-	*ta*	*na*	*da*	*ra*	*kī*	*a*	*khi*	*yān*	-
S	-	-	S	S	-	R	M	R	S	Ṇ	-
me	-	-	*rī*	-	-	*rī*	-	*a*	*khi*	*yān*	-
M	-	M	P	N	N	N	N	N	Ṡ	Ṡ	Ṡ
jī	-	*o*	*jī*	-	*o*	*ma*	*na*	*men*	*byā*	*pa*	*ta*
N̲	P	-	N	N	Ṡ	Ṙ	Ṡ	Ṡ	N̲	-	P
te	*o*	-	*te*	*o*	*ja*	*tā*	-	*'e*	*bai*	-	*ṭhī*

Dhrupad, Rāg Sārang

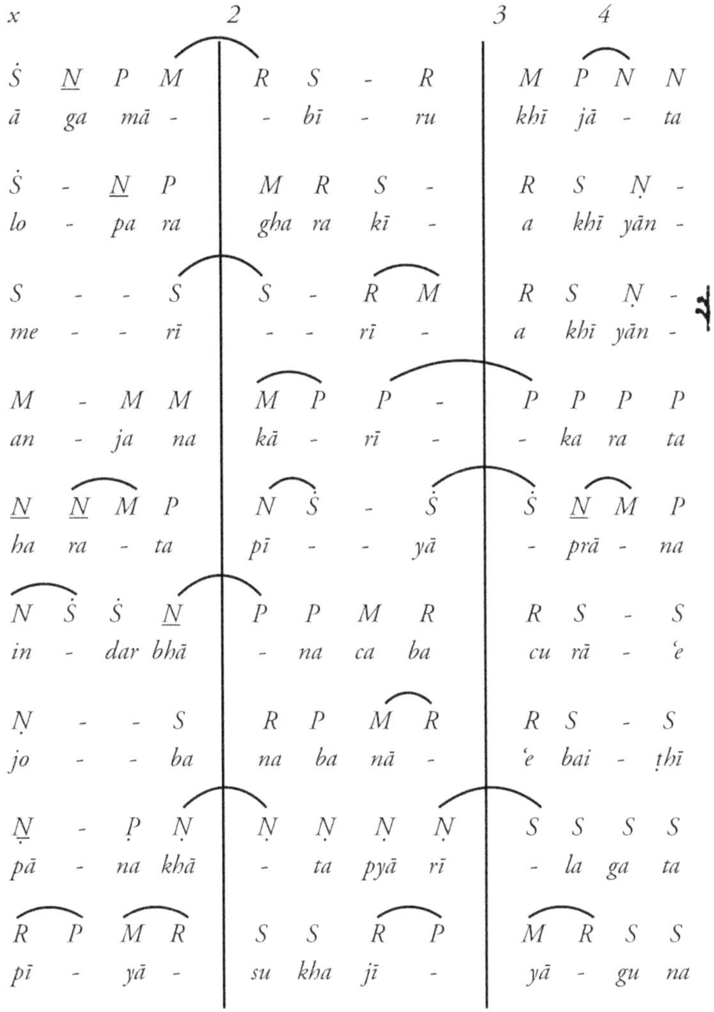

x				2				3		4	
Ṡ	N̲	P	M	R	S	-	R	M	P	N	N
ā	*ga*	*mā*	-	-	*bī*	-	*ru*	*khī*	*jā*	-	*ta*
Ṡ	-	N̲	P	M	R	S	-	R	S	Ṇ	-
lo	-	*pa*	*ra*	*gha*	*ra*	*kī*	-	*a*	*khī*	*yān*	-
S	-	-	S	S	-	R	M	R	S	Ṇ	-
me	-	-	*rī*	-	-	*rī*	-	*a*	*khī*	*yān*	-
M	-	M	M	M	P	P	-	P	P	P	P
an	-	*ja*	*na*	*kā*	-	*rī*	-	-	*ka*	*ra*	*ta*
N̲	N̲	M	P	N	Ṡ	-	Ṡ	Ṡ	N̲	M	P
ha	*ra*	-	*ta*	*pī*	-	-	*yā*	-	*prā*	-	*na*
N	Ṡ	Ṡ	N̲	P	P	M	R	R	S	-	S
in	-	*dar*	*bhā*	-	*na*	*ca*	*ba*	*cu*	*rā*	-	*ʿe*
Ṇ	-	-	S	R	P	M	R	R	S	-	S
jo	-	-	*ba*	*na*	*ba*	*nā*	-	*ʿe*	*bai*	-	*ṭhī*
Ṇ̲	-	P̣	Ṇ	Ṇ	Ṇ	Ṇ	Ṇ	S	S	S	S
pā	-	*na*	*khā*	-	*ta*	*pyā*	*rī*	-	*la*	*ga*	*ta*
R	P	M	R	S	S	R	P	M	R	S	S
pī	-	*yā*	-	*su*	*kha*	*jī*	-	*yā*	-	*gu*	*na*

Dhrupad, Rāg Sārang

x				2				3		4	
Ṇ̲	-	Ṇ̲	Ṇ̲	Ṇ̲	Ṇ̲	Ṇ̲	S	S	Ṇ̲	-	P̣
gan	-	*ga*	*ja*	*ṭa*	*su*	*dha*	-	*-nga*	*mā*	-	*no*
Ṇ	-	-	Ṇ	Ṇ	Ṇ	Ṇ	S	S	S	-	-
tā	-	-	*la*	*su*	*ra*	*rā*	-	-	*ga*	-	-
-	M	-	R	R	S	-	S	S	R	Ṇ	S
-	*Nā*	-	*ya*	-	*ka*	-	*Ma*	-	*da*	-	*na*
-	R	R	M	P	P	P	N	N	N	Ṡ	Ṡ
-	*Pi*	*yā*	*pi*	*yā*	*re*	*ga*	*ma*	*na*	*kī*	-	*īn*
N̲	M	P	N	N	Ṡ	Ṙ	Ṙ	Ṡ	N̲	-	P
le	-	*da*	*ra*	*pa*	*na*	*de*	*kha*	*na*	*lā*	-	*gī*
P	Ṙ	Ṙ	-	N	Ṡ	N̲	M	M	P	N	N
a	*pa*	*nī*	-	*cha*	*ba*	*de*	-	*kha*	*de*	-	*kha*
Ṡ	-	N̲	P	M	R	S	-	R	S	Ṇ	-
rī	-	*ja*	*la*	*bha*	*ra*	*tī*	-	*a*	*khī*	*yān*	-
S	-	-	S	S	-	R	M	R	S	Ṇ	-
me	-	-	*rī*	-	-	*rī*	-	*a*	*khī*	*yān*	-

Dhrupad
Rāg Bhīmpalās

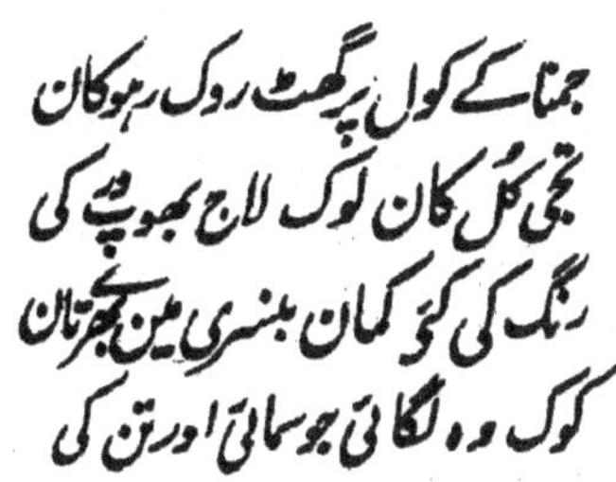

Kanha stopped me on the way to the bank of the Jamuna.
Have you no shame for the sake of lineage, family, or king?
He fills his flute with melodies and flings arrows of love.
He gives a shrill cry, and it pains all the more.

3. Dhrupad, Rāg Bhīmpalās, Tāl Catūsra Jātī Cautālā
middle speed, twelve *mātrās*

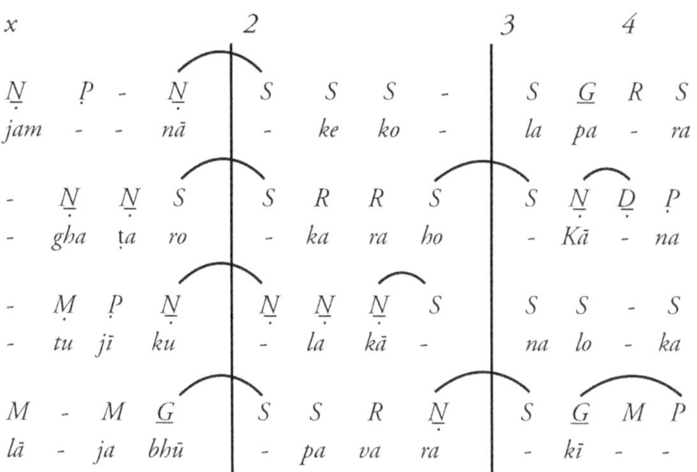

Dhrupad, Rāg Bhīmpalās

x				2				3		4	
M	G̲	R	S	S	S	Ṇ	S	M	G̲	R	S
jam	-	-	*nā*	-	*ke*	*ko*	-	*la*	*pa*	-	*ra*
-	P	P	G̲	M	P	N̲	-	N̲	N̲	Ṡ	Ṡ
-	*ra*	*-nga*	*kī*	-	*ka*	*‘ī*	-	*ka*	*mā*	-	*na*
N̲	-	N̲	Ṡ	Ṡ	Ṙ	Ṙ	Ṡ	Ṡ	N̲	D̲	P
ban	-	*su*	*rī*	-	*men*	*bha*	*re*	-	*tā*	-	*na*
-	P	Ṙ	Ṙ	Ṙ	N̲	Ṡ	-	Ṡ	N̲	D̲	P
-	*kū*	*ka*	*voh*	-	*la*	*gā*	-	*‘ī*	*jo*	-	*sa*
P	N̲	D̲	P	D̲	P	P	M	G̲	M	G̲	P
mā	-	*‘ī*	*au*	-	*ra*	*ta*	*na*	-	*kī*	-	-
M	G̲	R	S	S	S	Ṇ	S	M	G̲	R	S
jam	-	-	*nā*	-	*ke*	*ko*	-	*la*	*pa*	-	*ra*

Dhrupad
Rāg Sindhūrā

پچ برد کو بچار نام کی لاج بھیک کی ٹیک سرن کی پچ برد کو بچار
اترن کو تارن بے گن کو گن دین موڑھ کو گیان نردھن کے قتار
روگ کو اَوُکھت چنتا کے ہارن ہار تی مان سو مان دین کی رچھ
الیاس کاج سدھار لے سو کون ہے شکر شا جا کے چرن میں بہت نسدن

Consider the five honors, of name, pride, possessions,
support, protection.
To lift the fallen, give goodness to those without,
knowledge to the ignorant, wealth to the poor.
To give comfort to the sick, relief to the troubled, honor to
the honorable, to be the protector of the faith.
If your work is successful, Ilyas, who is the one to thank?
In whose protection do you live night and day?

4. Dhrupad, Rāg Sindhūrā, Tāl Tīsra Jātī Tevrā
middle speed, seven *mātrās*[1]

x			*2*		*3*		*x*			*2*		*3*	
												P	*P*
												pa	*ca*
+										ن			
D	*M*	*P*	*N*	-	*N*	-	*Ṡ*	-	-	*Ṡ*	-	*P*	*P*
bi	*ra*	*da*	*ko*	-	*bi*	-	*cā*	-	-	*ra*	-	*pa*	*ca*

1 I have reproduced flats and naturals as they appear in the *Minqār* except for clearly typographical errors, such as where *shuddh Ni* occurs between two *komal Ni's*.

Dhrupad, Rāg Sindhūrā

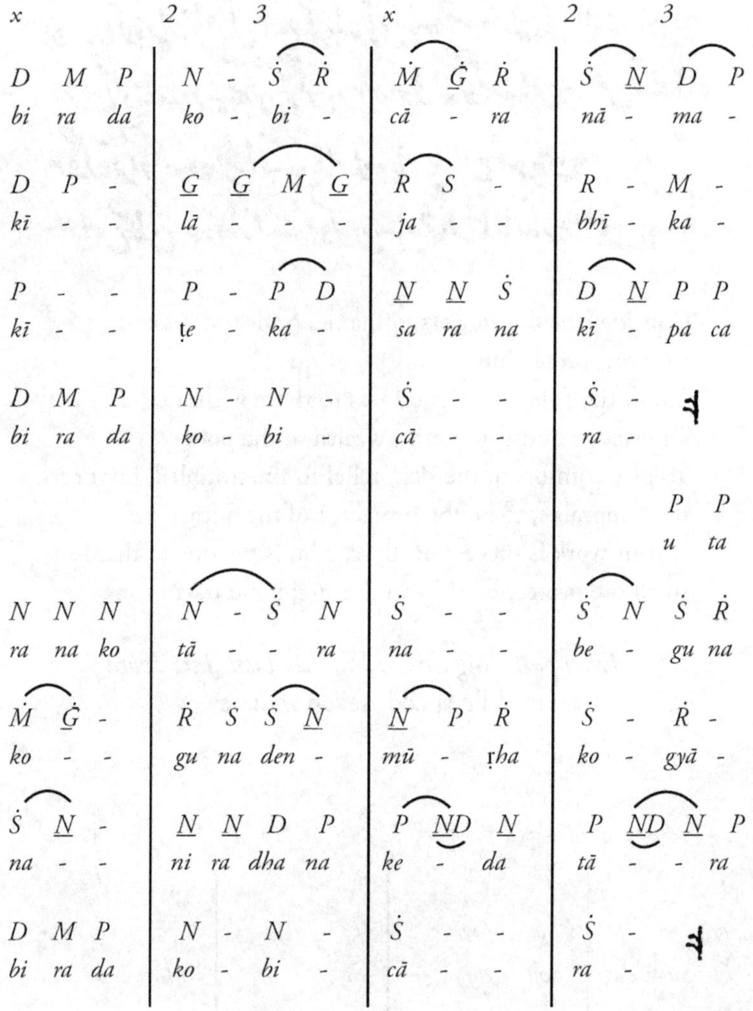

x	*2 3*	*x*	*2 3*
D M P	*N - Ṡ Ṙ*	*Ṁ Ġ̲ Ṙ*	*Ṡ N̲ D P*
bi ra da	*ko - bi -*	*cā - ra*	*nā - ma -*
D P -	*G̲ G̲ M G̲*	*R S -*	*R - M -*
kī - -	*lā - - -*	*ja - -*	*bhī - ka -*
P - -	*P - P D*	*N̲ N̲ Ṡ*	*D N̲ P P*
kī - -	*ṭe - ka -*	*sa ra na*	*kī - pa ca*
D M P	*N - N -*	*Ṡ - -*	*Ṡ -*
bi ra da	*ko - bi -*	*cā - -*	*ra -*
			P P
			u ta
N N N	*N - Ṡ N*	*Ṡ - -*	*Ṡ N Ṡ Ṙ*
ra na ko	*tā - - ra*	*na - -*	*be - gu na*
Ṁ Ġ̲ -	*Ṙ Ṡ Ṡ N̲*	*N̲ P Ṙ*	*Ṡ - Ṙ -*
ko - -	*gu na den -*	*mū - ṛha*	*ko - gyā -*
Ṡ N̲ -	*N̲ N̲ D P*	*P N̲D N̲*	*P N̲D N̲ P*
na - -	*ni ra dha na*	*ke - da*	*tā - - ra*
D M P	*N - N -*	*Ṡ - -*	*Ṡ -*
bi ra da	*ko - bi -*	*cā - -*	*ra -*

Dhrupad, Rāg Sindhūrā

x	2 3	x	2 3
M - M	M - M -	P P -	P P D -
ro - ga	*ko - au -*	*kha ta -*	*cin tā - -*
N̲ - Ṡ	D N̲ P P	Ṡ - Ṡ	Ṡ N̲ D P
ke - bi	*ḍā - ra na*	*hā - ra*	*nī - mā -*
M G̲ -	G̲ - M G̲	R - S	R - M M
na - -	*so - - -*	*mā - na*	*dī - na kī*
P - -	P - M M	M - P	N - N N
ra - -	*ccha - Il i*	*yā - sa*	*kā - ja su*
Ṡ - Ṡ	Ṡ N Ṡ Ṙ	Ṁ Ġ̲ Ṙ	Ṡ - Ṡ -
dhā - ra	*ai - so -*	*kau - na*	*hai - shā -*
Ṙ N̲ -	D - P -	P - N̲	N̲ D N̲ -
kar - -	*shā - jā -* +	*ke - ca*	*ra na men -*
P D N̲	D P P P		
ra ha ta	*ni sa di na*		

Dhrupad
Rāg Bahār

گرو بن گیان سکھانیے سمرن چیلا بن کئے مادہ کہین نر بن سہائے —
بہلائے کہین یار کہین عیار بن کہین عمر بھر دکھ مین رہے سگر کہین سکھ پائے
بن شاہ حکم عدل کئے خادم کہین کہلائے مان باپ بن پرو بجے کہین پوت بن جائے
محتاج کہین سرتاج کہین کیا کھیل کھیل دکھائے کہین راگ سن رامنی بجے کہین گیت عنایت گا

Becoming a *guru* he teaches knowledge;
  becoming a disciple, he learns.
Here he becomes a woman, and there
  a man to be her companion.
Sometimes he is a tempter, sometimes a friend,
  and sometimes he is mischievous.
He may live in sadness for a lifetime,
  or he may attain pleasure.
He becomes an emperor and rules,
  or he may be known as a servant.
Here, as mother and father he is the protector,
  and there he chooses to become the son.
Sometimes he is a beggar and sometimes a lord.
Sometimes he displays all kinds of playfulness.
  Sometimes he listens to a *rāg* and is pleased.
Sometimes Inayat sings a song.

5. Dhrupad, Rāg Bahār, Tāl Tīsra Jātī Tevrā
middle speed, seven *mātrās*[1]

1 I have reproduced the flats and sharps here are as they appear in the *Minqār*.

Dhrupad, Rāg Bahār

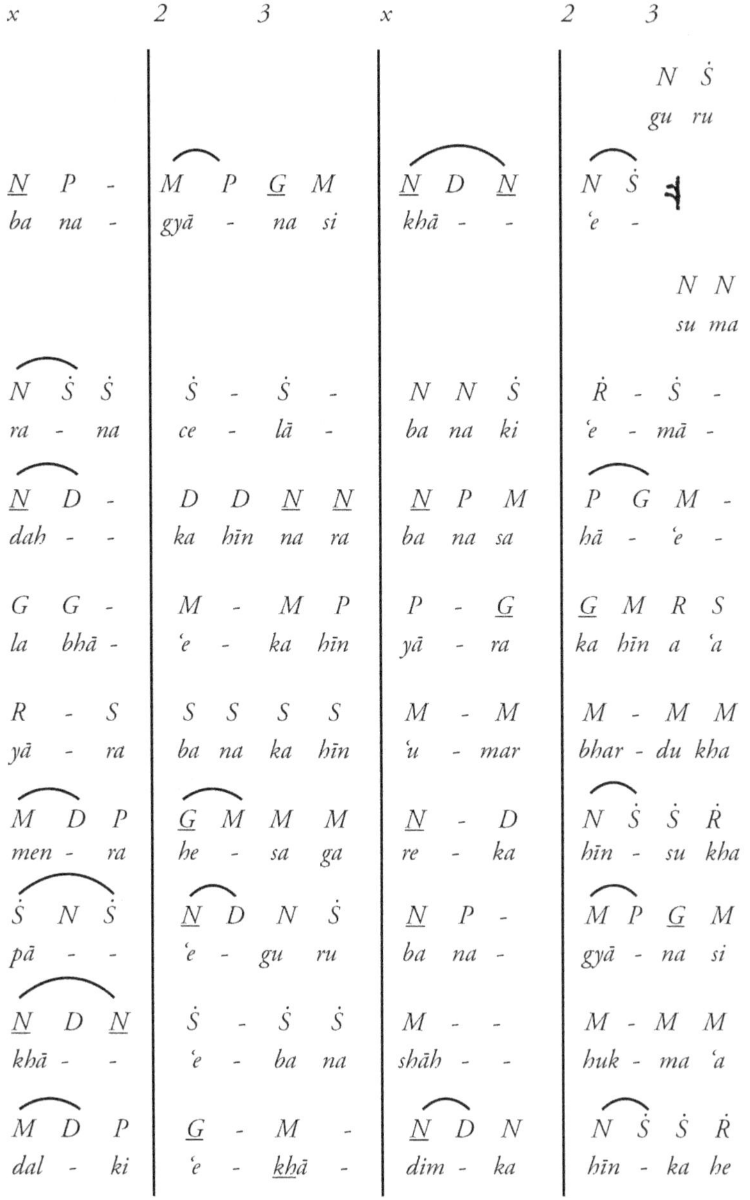

x	2 3	x	2 3
			N Ṡ
			gu ru
N P -	M P G M	N D N	N Ṡ
ba na -	*gyā - na si*	*khā - -*	*‘e -*
			N N
			su ma
N Ṡ Ṡ	Ṡ - Ṡ -	N N Ṡ	Ṙ - Ṡ -
ra - na	*ce - lā -*	*ba na ki*	*‘e - mā -*
N D -	D D N N	N P M	P G M -
dah - -	*ka hīn na ra*	*ba na sa*	*hā - ‘e -*
G G -	M - M P	P - G	G M R S
la bhā -	*‘e - ka hīn*	*yā - ra*	*ka hīn a ‘a*
R - S	S S S S	M - M	M - M M
yā - ra	*ba na ka hīn*	*‘u - mar*	*bhar - du kha*
M D P	G M M M	N - D	N Ṡ Ṡ Ṙ
men - ra	*he - sa ga*	*re - ka*	*hīn - su kha*
Ṡ N Ṡ	N D N Ṡ	N P -	M P G M
pā - -	*‘e - gu ru*	*ba na -*	*gyā - na si*
N D N	Ṡ - Ṡ Ṡ	M - -	M - M M
khā - -	*‘e - ba na*	*shāh - -*	*huk - ma ‘a*
M D P	G - M -	N D N	N Ṡ Ṡ Ṙ
dal - ki	*‘e - khā -*	*dim - ka*	*hīn - ka he*

Dhrupad, Rāg Bahār

x	*2 3*	*x*	*2 3*
Ṡ N Ṡ	*N̲ D N Ṡ*	*Ġ̲ - Ṁ*	*Ṙ Ṙ Ṡ -*
lā - -	*ʿe - mān -*	*bā - pa*	*ba na pa ri*
Ṙ Ġ̲ Ṙ	*Ṡ - N Ṡ*	*Ṙ Ġ̲ Ṙ*	*Ṡ N Ṡ Ṙ*
va ra bha	*ʿe - ka hīn*	*pū - ta*	*ba na ma na*
Ṡ N Ṡ	*N̲ D N Ṡ*	*N̲ P -*	*M P G̲ M*
bhā - -	*ʿe - gu ru*	*ba na -*	*gyā - na si*
N̲ D N̲	*N Ṡ Ṡ -*	*M - M*	*M M M -*
khā - -	*ʿe - muḥ -*	*tā - ja*	*ka hīn sar -*
M D P	*G̲ G̲ M M*	*N̲ - D*	*N - Ṡ Ṙ*
tā - ja	*ba na ka hīn*	*khe - la*	*khe - la di*
Ṡ N Ṡ	*N̲ D N Ṡ*	*Ṁ Ġ̲ Ṁ*	*Ṙ Ṙ Ṡ -*
khā - -	*ʿe - ka hīn*	*rā - ga*	*su na rā -*
Ṙ Ġ̲ Ṙ	*Ṡ - N Ṡ*	*Ṙ Ġ̲ Ṙ*	*Ṡ N Ṡ Ṙ*
z̤ī - bha	*ʿe - ka hīn*	*gī ta ʿI*	*nā - ya ta*
Ṡ N Ṡ	*N̲ D N Ṡ*	*N̲*[1] *P -*	*M P G̲ M*
gā - -	*ʿe - gu ru*	*ba na -*	*gyā - na si*
N̲ D N̲	*N Ṡ*		
khā - -	*ʿe -*		

1 *Shuddh Ni* in the text.

Āstāī
Rāg Darbārī Kānaṛā

کہاں تاب درس کی آنکھین کو — جو نہار سکین من موہن کو
نہین ہاتھ پاؤن واکو گہ سکین — من بدھی چت آہنکار تھکین
نہین ٹھور ٹھاون جہان خاص بسے — رنگ روپ بنا وہ کہان کو دسے
جن باتھ مین دوؤ جہان گہو — سج رج مین وہی سمائے رہو
جون دیپ پرکاس نے دکھلائیو — تیون ہی عنایت کے من بھائیو

Where can my eyes find a glimpse of the radiance?
Where might I behold my heart's desire?
Hands and feet can't reach him.
Spirit, intellect, consciousness, and ego are exhausted.
There's no fixed place where he particularly resides.
Without color or form, indeed how could he show?
In whose arms both worlds are hidden in every particle of dust, stay patient there.
Whatever light and the flame might show,
with that let Inayat's heart be satisfied.

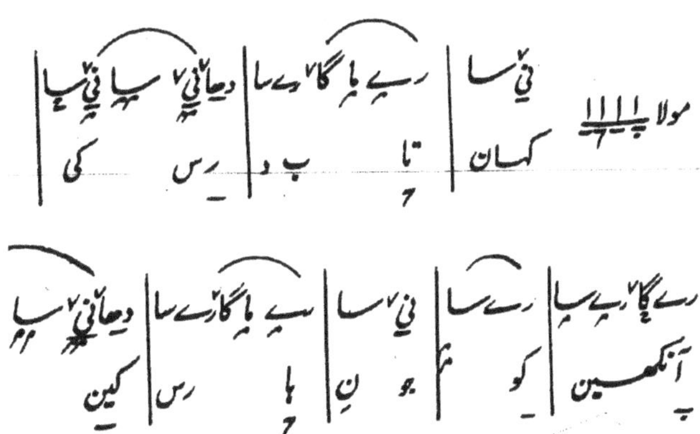

Āstāī, Rāg Darbārī Kānaṛā, (Khan, Inayat R., 117)

6. Āstāī, Rāg Darbārī Kānaṛā, *Tāl Tetāla,* middle speed, *sixteen mātrās*

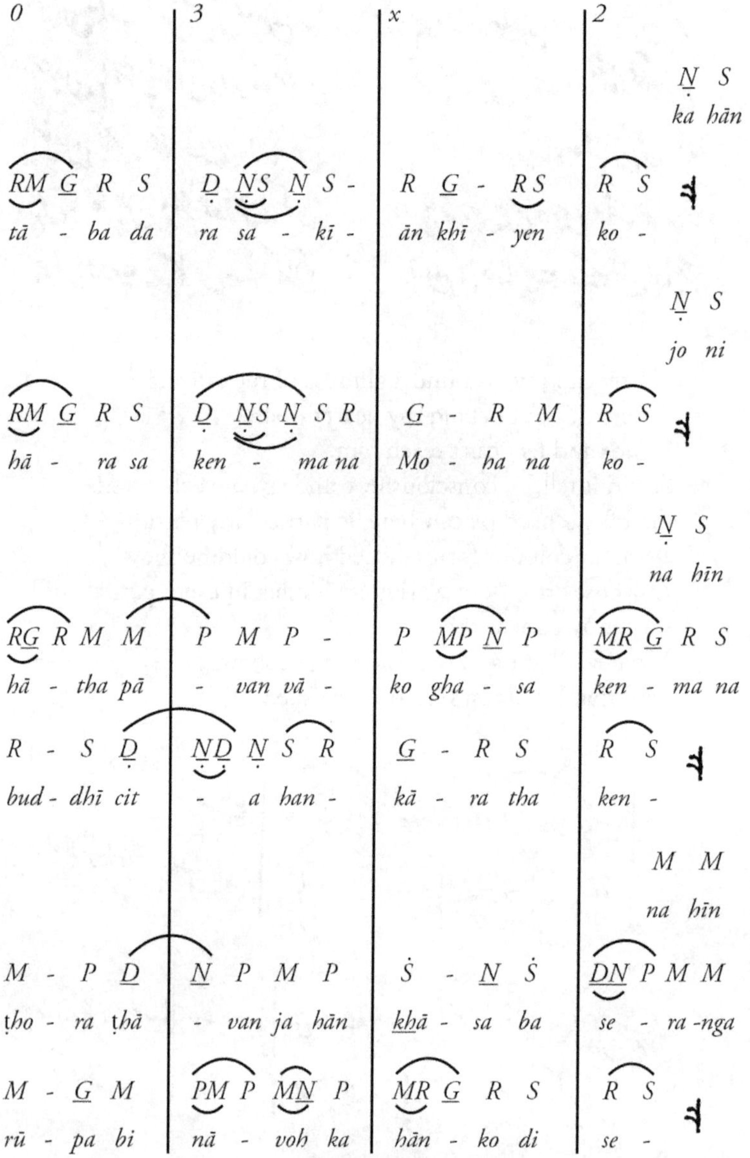

0	3	x	2	
				Ṇ S
				ka hān
RM G R S	Ḍ ṆS Ṇ S -	R G - RS	R S	ł
tā - ba da	*ra sa - kī -*	*ān khī - yen*	*ko -*	
				Ṇ S
				jo ni
RM G R S	Ḍ ṆS Ṇ S R	G - R M	R S	ł
hā - ra sa	*ken - ma na*	*Mo - ha na*	*ko -*	
				Ṇ S
				na hīn
RG R M M	P M P -	P MP N P	MR G R S	
hā - tha pā	*- van vā -*	*ko gha - sa*	*ken - ma na*	
R - S Ḍ	ṆḌ Ṇ S R	G - R S	R S	ł
bud - dhī cit	*- a han -*	*kā - ra tha*	*ken -*	
				M M
				na hīn
M - P D	N P M P	Ṡ - N Ṡ	DN P M M	
ṭho - ra ṭhā	*- van ja hān*	*khā - sa ba*	*se - ra -nga*	
M - G M	PM P MN P	MR G R S	R S	ł
rū - pa bi	*nā - voh ka*	*hān - ko di*	*se -*	

Āstāī, Rāg Darbārī Kānaṛā

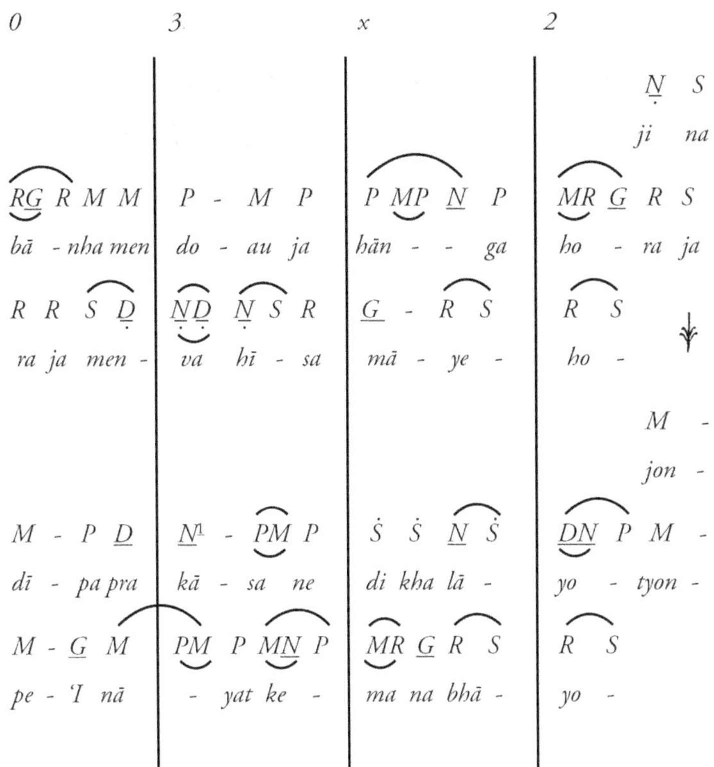

1. *Shuddh Ni* in the text.

Āstāī
Rāg Basant

ات چھب دیکھت پت چھانڈے مائی　　مہاراج بسنت کری بے
محلان کوٹ رُت مائی　　رانی داسی سہون چیڑی سون

King Basant, seeing the beauty of the full moon,
celebrates the season surrounded by women,
inadvertently taunting the queens and ladies of the court.

7. *Āstāī, Rāg Basant, Tāl Chatūsra Jātī Tetālā*
middle speed, sixteen *mātrās*

0	*3*	*x*	*2*
M̍ D̲ Ṡ N	*M̍ G M G*	*M̍ D̲ D̲ ND̲*	*ṠṘ̲ NṠ ND̲ P*
a ta ca ba	*de - kha ta*	*pa ta chān -*	*ḍe - mā ī*
N Ṙ̲ - Ṙ̲	*Ṙ̲ Ṡ Ṡ -*	*- N N D̲*	*ṠṠ ND̲N- M̍ G*
ma hā - rā	*- ja ba -*	*- san ta ka*	*rī - je -*
Ṙ̲ - N -	*D̲ - M̍ -*	*G R̲ R̲ -*	*S - SN̲ S*
maḥ- lā na	*ko - ṭa -*	*ru ta mā -*	*nī - rā -*
S - - N	*N M̍ - D̲*	*Ṡ - ṠR̲ NṠ*	*N D̲ PM̍ P*
nī - - dā	*- sī - sa*	*hūn - ce -*	*rī - son -*

Āstāī
Rāg Kaunsī Kānaṛā

سر مور کے پنکھ دھرے چراوت گیان بن مین - گوپال کے سر مور کے پنکھ دھرے
کانن کنڈل مکٹ براجے - ہاتھ لئے مرلی بن مین

Sporting a peacock feather on his head, he steals away one's wits in the forest. Gopal, with a peacock feather, rings in his ears, a crown on his head, is splendid. He holds a flute in his hands in the forest.

8. *Āstāī, Rāg Kaunsī Kānaṛā, Tāl Catūsra Jātī Tetālā*
middle speed sixteen *mātrās*

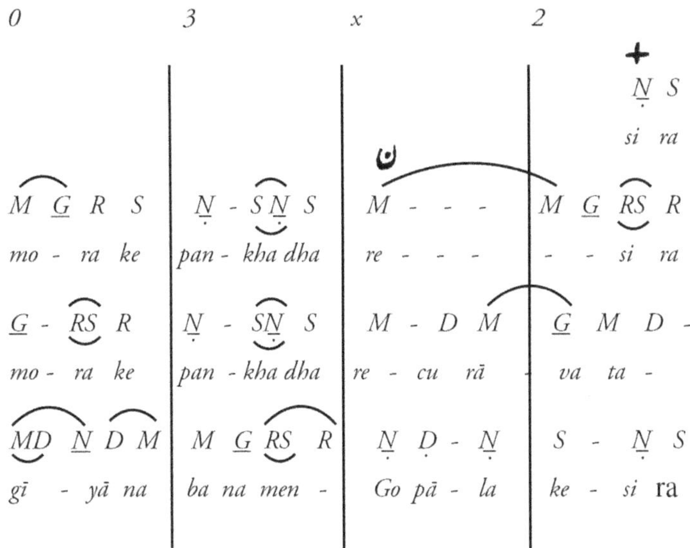

Āstāī, Rāg Kaunsī Kānaṛā

0	3	x	2
M G R S	*Ṇ - SṆ S*	*M - - -*	*M G - -*
mo - ra ke	*pan - kha dha*	*re - - -*	*- - - -*
G M D N	*Ṡ - N Ṡ*	*Ṙ Ṡ N*[1] *D*	*MD N D M*
kā - na na	*kun - da la*	*mu ku a bi*	*rā - je -*
M G R S	*R Ṇ SṆ S*	*M G GM G*	*R S* +
hā - tha lī	*ye - mu ra*	*lī - ba na*	*men -*

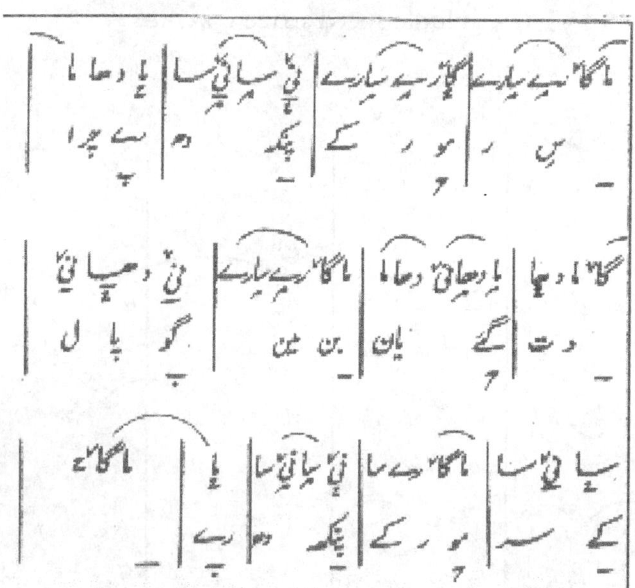

Āstāī, Rāg Kaunsī Kānaṛā, (Khan, Inayat R., 120)

1 This and the following *Ni* are notated as *shuddh* in the text.

Āstāī
Rāg Devgandhār

رب میرا وہی سکل جگت کو پیدا　　کرن ہارا وہی ہے رب میرا وہی
نہ کوئی مات نہ تات بھرات　　پوتی نہین کوئی سُت سب وہی ہے

My Lord is the one who created the entire universe;
He alone is the maker, my very Lord.
There's no mother, father or brother,
nor any daughter or son. He is everything.

9. *Āstāī, Rāg Devgandhār, Tāl Catūsra Jātī Tetālā*
middle speed, sixteen *mātrā*s

3 +	x	2	0
R M P Ṡ	N D P -	P - - -	M P D M
ra ba me rā	*vo - hī -*	*- - - -*	*sa ka la ja*
P G R S	R S - S	R M PN DP	M G R S
ga ta ko pai	*dā - - ka*	*ra na hā rā*	*vo - hī hai*
R M P Ṡ	N D P -	P - - -	M P P D
ra ba me rā	*vo - hī -*	*- - - -*	*ko 'ī - mā*
D D Ṡ -	ṠṘ Ġ Ṙ Ṡ	Ṙ S D D	Ṡ - N Ṡ
- ta na -	*tā - ta bhrā*	*- ta ja va*	*tī - na hīn*
N D P -	M P D P	M G R S	S - - - +
ko - 'ī -	*su ta sa ba*	*vo - hī hai*	*- - - -*

Āstāī
Rāg Bihāg

بلہار جاؤن مین آلِ نبی اولادِ علی پر بار بار — اُمت کے بخشاون ہارے
فاطمہؓ کے دلِ جان دُلارے — حسنؑ حسینؑ اللہ کے پیارے کیجئے عنایت سردار

I humble myself to the dynasty of the Prophet,
offspring of Ali, again and again.

Of the race of forgivers, dear to the heart of Fatima,
Hasan Husain, beloved of Allah,
make Inayat his chief server.

10. *Āstāī, Rāg Bihāg, Tāl Catūsra Jātī Tetālā*
middle speed, sixteen *mātrā*s

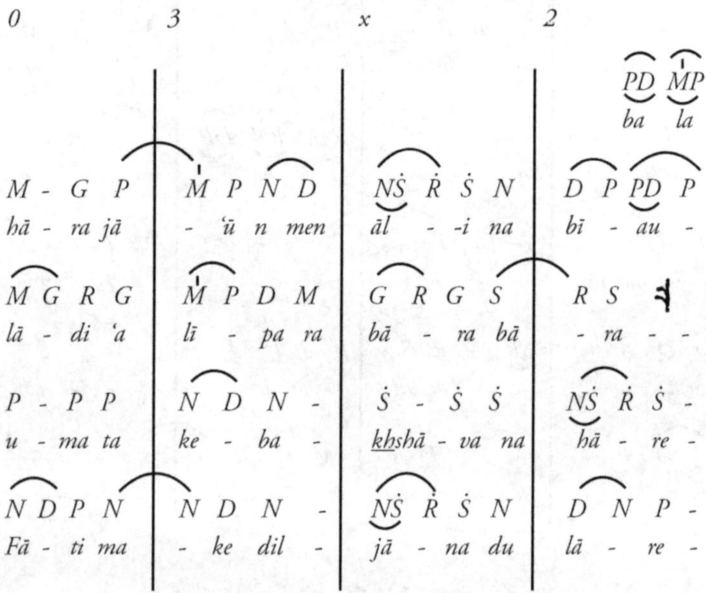

Āstāī, Rāg Bihāg

0	3	x	2
D Ṡ D P	M - M G	R M - M	P - P -
Ha sa na Hu	sai - na ‘A	- lla - ke	pyā - re -
P - N N	N - Ṡ -	Ṙ Ṡ - N	D P
kī - je ‘I	nā - yat -	sa ra - dā	- ra

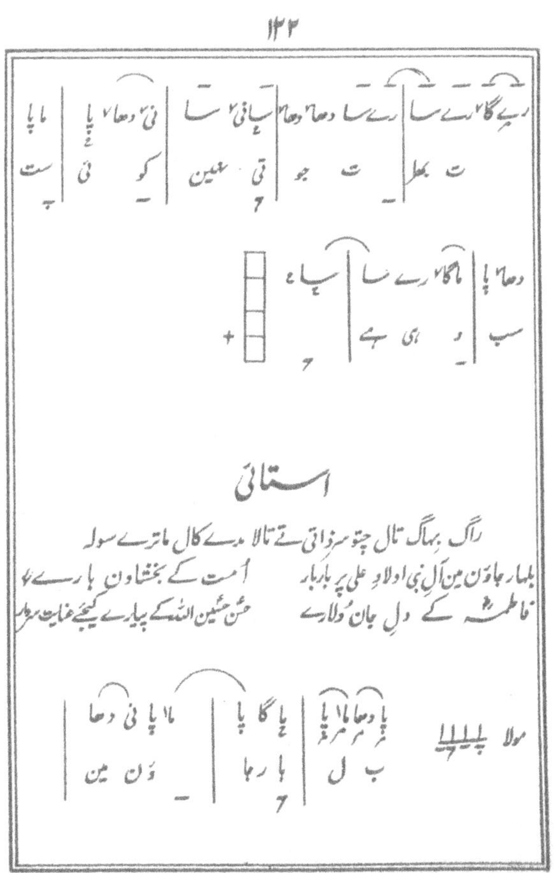
۱۲۲

استائی

راگ بہاگ تال چتو سرزاتی تے تالا مدے کال ماترے سولہ

بلہار جاؤن مین آلِ نبی اولادِ علی پر بار بار اُمت کے بخشاون ہارے
فاطمہؓ کے دل جان دُلارے حسن حسین اللہ کے پیارے کیجے عنایت سردار

Āstāī, Rāg Bihāg, (Khan, Inayat R., 122)

Ṭhumrī
Rāg Ẕila'

موری نازنی کلائی مرکائی مس کائی
بانہہ پکر کی نی رنگ بھینی اور چریاں مُرکائیں مرجھائیں مسکائیں

He grabs my delicate wrists and smiles.
Holding my arms he drenches me with color and twists,
breaking my bangles, laughing.

11. *Ṭhumrī, Rāg Ẕila', Tāl Catūsra Jātī Tetālā*
middle speed, sixteen *mātrās*

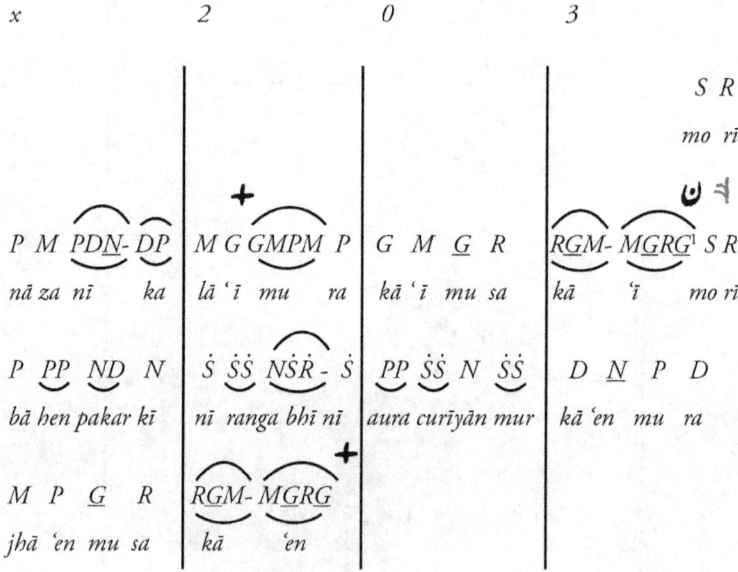

1 *Shuddh Ga* in the text.

Ṭhumrī
Rāg Khamāj[10][1]

وہ تو مدھوا پئے مست وارو دئیلی　　چلو چلو ری سکھی وا کے منہ نا لگو
مدھوا پیکے دھوم مچاوے　　گاؤن ہنست ہے سارو دئیاری

He's drunk some wine and is in quite a state.
Hurry, let's go, girlfriend, don't catch his glance.
When he drinks wine he makes a commotion.
The whole village is laughing.

12. *Ṭhumrī, Rāg Khamāj, Tāl Dīpcandī*
middle speed, fourteen *mātrās*[2]

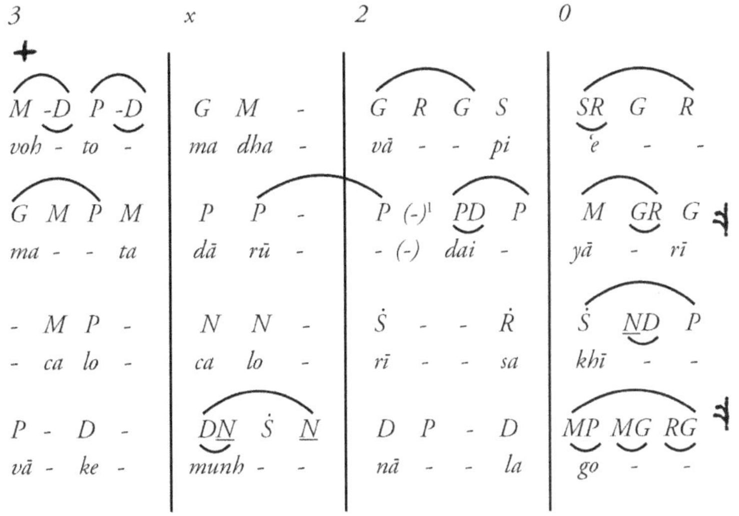

3 +	x	2	0
M -D P -D	G M -	G R G S	SR G R
voh - to -	*ma dha -*	*vā - - pi*	*‘e - -*
G M P M	P P -	P (-)[1] PD P	M GR G
ma - - ta	*dā rū -*	*- (-) dai -*	*yā - rī*
- M P -	N N -	Ṡ - - Ṙ	Ṡ N̲D P
- ca lo -	*ca lo -*	*rī - - sa*	*khī - -*
P - D -	DN̲ Ṡ N̲	D P - D	MP MG RG
vā - ke -	*munh - -*	*nā - - la*	*go - -*

1 This *rāg* name appears in two forms in the *Minqār*. It is *Khammāc* in *dhrupad* song. In the *rāgā* list it is *Khamāj*.
2 (-) are rests added.

Ṭhumrī, Rāg Khamāj

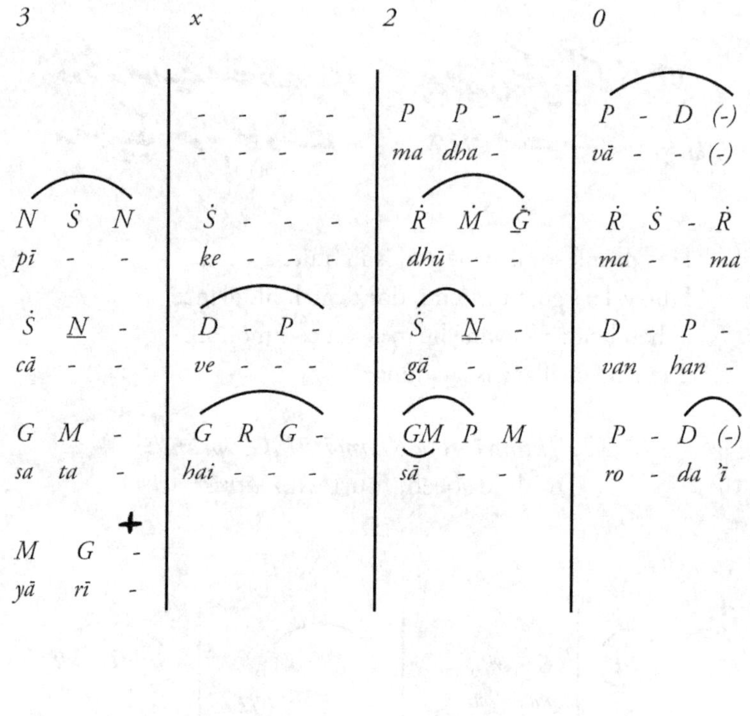

Ṭhumrī
Rāg Bihārī

بنگ ری موری مروڑی رے کانہا　　چڑیاں موری پھوری رے کانہا
لپٹ جھپٹ موسوں کرت ہے نٹ ور　　چاند لاکھوں برسوں جیے کانہا

Oh, Kanha has grabbed my arm
Oh, my bracelets, he's broken them, Kanha has
He pounces and embraces me, that trickster.
May he live a hundred thousand years, Kanha!

13. *Ṭhumrī, Rāg Bihārī, Tāl Dādrā*
middle speed, six *mātrā*s

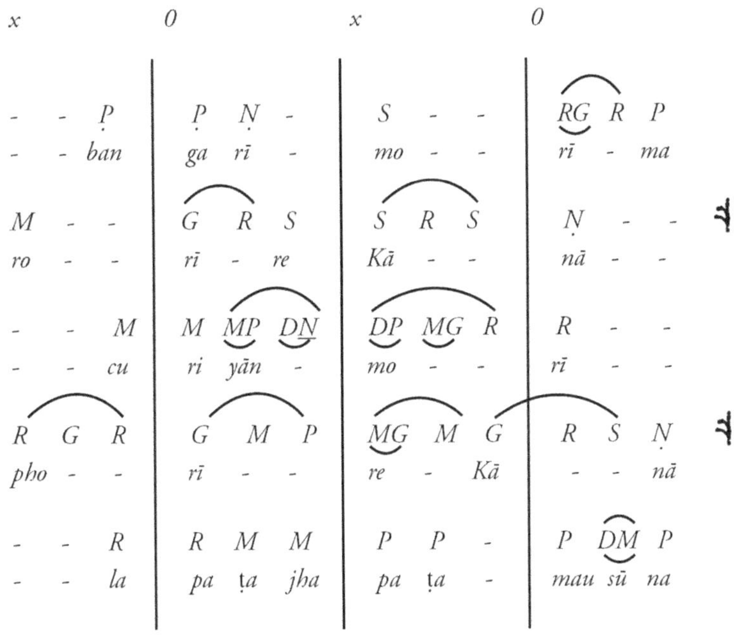

x	*0*	*x*	*0*
- - P̣	P̣ Ṇ -	S - -	RG R P
- - *ban*	*ga rī* -	*mo* - -	*rī* - *ma*
M - -	G R S	S R S	Ṇ - -
ro - -	*rī* - *re*	*Kā* - -	*nā* - -
- - M	M MP DṆ	DP MG R	R - -
- - *cu*	*ri yān* -	*mo* - -	*rī* - -
R G R	G M P	MG M G	R S Ṇ
pho - -	*rī* - -	*re* - *Kā*	- - *nā*
- - R	R M M	P P -	P DM P
- - *la*	*pa ṭa jha*	*pa ṭa* -	*mau sū na*

Ṭhumrī, Rāg Bihārī

x			0			x			0		
-	-	*R*	*R*	*M*	*P*	*P*	*MP*	*D$\underline{N}$*	*DP*	*MG*	*R*
-	-	*ka*	*ra*	*ṭa*	*hai*	*na*	*ṭa*	-	*va*	*ra*	-
-	-	*P̣*	*Ṇ*	-	*Ṇ*	*S*	-	-	*R*	*P*	-
-	-	*cān*	*da*	-	*lā*	*khon*	-	-	*ba*	*ra*	-
M	-	-	*G*	*R*	*S*	*S*	*R*	*S*	*Ṇ*	-	-
son	-	-	*de*	-	-	*Kā*	-	-	*nā*		

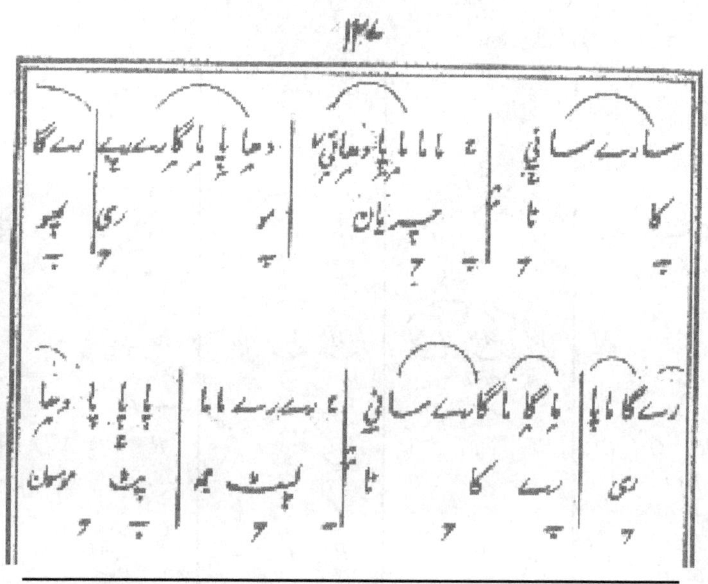

Ṭhumrī, Rāg Bihārī, (Khan, Inayat R., 127)

Ṭhumrī
Rāg Kāfī[1]

کچھ عجب کھیل ہینگے اس پاک پروردگار کے
کوئی کو راج تاج ہے پہنایا کوئی عاجز فقیر بنایا کوئی شان کو جان نہ پایا
نکٹ بھید ستار کے ۔ کچھ نہ بنے خود آپ سدھارے روہی ہووے جو مالک دھارے
کیوں غم کرے عنایت گارے بلہار لو نہار کے۔

Some marvelous game it is, that of this perfect God.
One he clothes as king or emperor, another he makes a lowly *faqīr*. Another attains no life of distinction.
It's a great, concealed mystery. If you don't become something, you might improve yourself, but only what the master gives you will be. Why grieve, Inayat? Sing, won't you, as an offering to the new day.

14. *Ṭhumrī, Rāg Kāfī, Tāl Tetālā*
middle speed, sixteen *mātrā*s

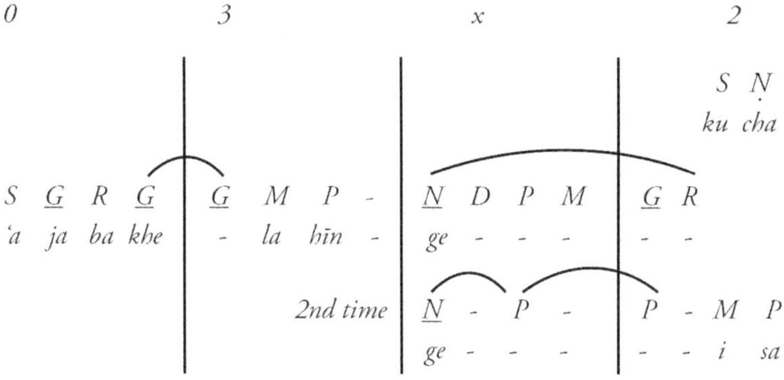

1 A recording of this song is to be found in *Inayat Khan: the Complete Recordings of 1909*, CD 1, track 6. In the recording the refrain is *kuch ajab khel suhāge*.

Ṭhumrī, Rāg Kāfī

0	3	x	2
N Ṡ - Ṡ	*N̲ P M P*	*G̲ G̲ M G̲*	*R S S Ṇ*
pā - - ka	*pa ra va ra*	*di gā - ra*	*ke - ku ch*
S G̲ R G̲	*G̲ M P -*	*N̲ - P -*	*P - - -*
‘a ja ba khe	*- la hīn -*	*ge - - -*	*- - - -*
M M - M	*P N̲ P N*	*N N Ṡ N*	*Ṡ N Ṡ -*
ko ‘ī - ko	*rā - ja tā*	*- ja hī pah*	*nā - yā -*
N̲ - P N	*N Ṡ N Ṡ*	*Ṙ - N Ṡ*	*N̲ - P -*
ko ‘ī - ‘ā	*- ja za fa*	*qī - ra ba*	*nā - yā -*
P Ṙ - Ṙ	*Ṙ Ṙ Ṡ -*	*N - Ṡ Ṡ*	*N̲ - P -*
ko ‘ī - shā	*- na ko -*	*jā - na na*	*pā - yā -*
P N Ṡ N̲	*N̲ P M P*	*G̲ - M G̲*	*R S S Ṇ*
bi ka ṭa bhe	*- da sa -*	*ttā - - ra*	*ke - ku cha*
S G̲ R G̲	*G̲ M P -*	*N̲ - P -*	*P - - -*
‘a ja ba khe	*- la hīn -*	*ge - - -*	*- - - -*
M M M M	*P (-) P N*	*N (-) Ṡ N*	*Ṡ N Ṡ -*
ku cha na ba	*ne - k̲h̲u da*	*ā - pa su*	*dhā - re -*
N̲ - P N	*N Ṡ N Ṡ*	*Ṙ - N Ṡ*	*N̲ - P -*
vo - hī ho	*- ve jo -*	*mā - li ka*	*dhā - re -*
P Ṙ Ṙ -	*Ṙ Ṡ - Ṙ*	*N - Ṡ Ṡ*	*N̲ - P -*
kyon - gha ma	*ka re - ‘I*	*nā - ya ta*	*gā - re -*
P N Ṡ -	*N̲ P M P*	*G̲ - M G̲*	*R S*
ba la hā -	*ra nau - na*	*hā - - ra*	*ke -*

Ṭhumrī
Rāg Gauṛ Malhār

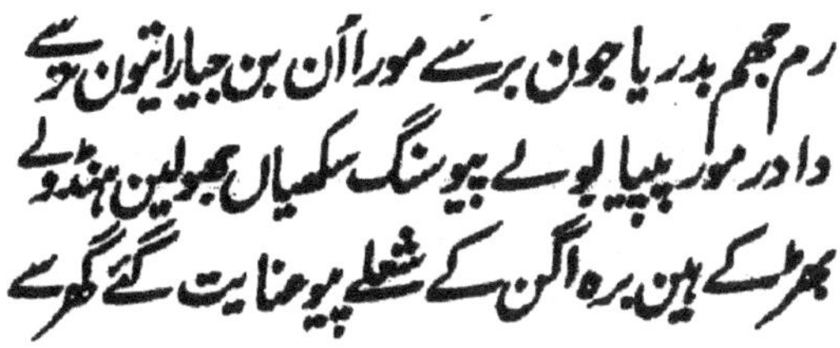

When the clouds clamor and pour rain
I suffer at night without him.
Frogs, peacocks, cuckoos call, and my friends
are all enjoying swings with their beloveds.
The flames of separation flash.
Inayat's Beloved has left the house.

15. *Ṭhumrī, Rāg Gauṛ Malhār, Tāl Catūsra Jātī Tetālā*
middle speed, sixteen *mātrās*

0				3				x				2			
														P	-
														ram	-
M	G	R	G	M	P	MG	M	G	R	S	Ṇ	S	-	[illegible]	
jham		-	ba	da	ri	yā	-	jon	-	ba	ra	se	-		
														Ṇ	S
														mo	ra
R	R	M	M	P	P	N	-	NṠ	Ṙ	Ṡ	Ṡ	ND	P	-	-
u	na	bi	na	ji	'e	rā	-	tyon	-	ta	ra	se	-		
P	-	P	P	D	ND	N	N	Ṡ	-	Ṡ	-	NṠ	Ṙ	Ṡ	-
dā	-	da	ra	mo	-	ra	pa	pī	-	hā	-	bo	-	le	-

Ṭhumrī, Rāg Gauṛ Malhār

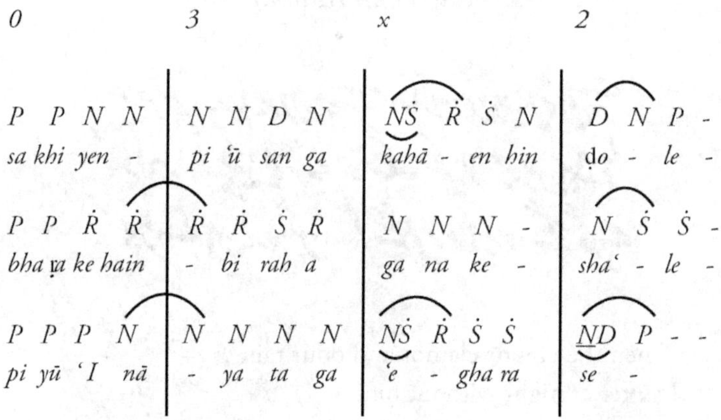

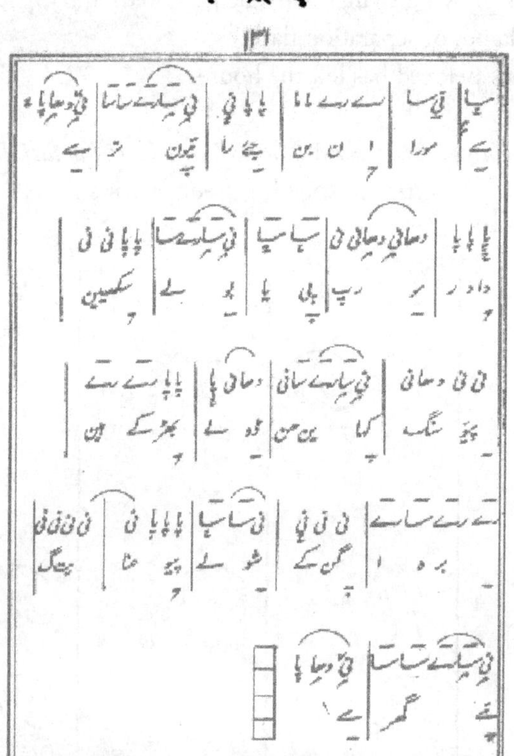

Ṭhumrī, Rāg Gauṛ Malhār 9 (Khan, Inayat R., 131)

Horī-Dhamār
Rāg Darbārī Kānaṛā

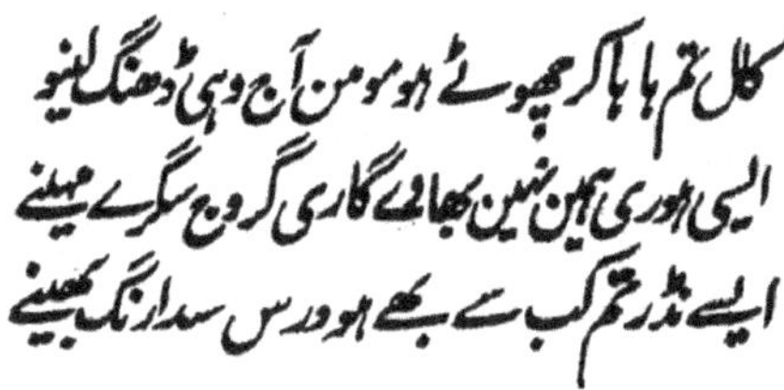
کل تم ہا ہا کر چھوٹے ہو موہن آج وہی ڈھنگ لینو
ایسی ہوری ہمیں نہیں بھاوے گاری گروج سگرے مہینے
ایسے نڈر تم کب سے بھئے ہو ورس سدا رنگ بھینے

Once you were an imploring child, Mohan. Now you've taken to your other ways. I don't like that kind of Holi, being taunted all month long. Since when have you become so fearless? Sadarang ("the ever colorful") is drenched from your sprinkling.

16. *Horī-Dhamār, Rāg Darbārī Kānaṛā, Tāl Dhamār*
middle speed, fourteen *mātrā*s

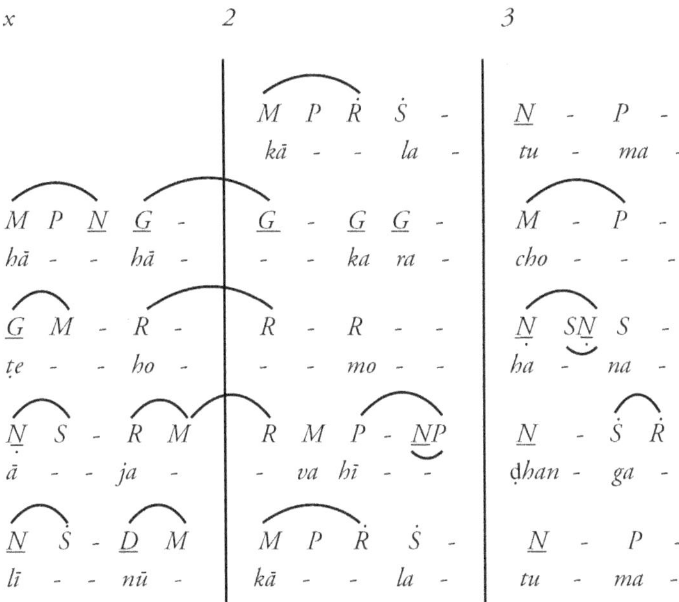

Horī-Dhamār, Rāg Darbārī Kānaṛā

x	2	3
M - - M -	M - M P -	P - P -
ai - - sī -	- - ho - -	rī - ha -
N̲ D̲ (-) D̲ N̲	P - M P -	G̲ - - -
men - (-) na -	hīn - bhā - -	ve - - -
G̲ M - R -	R - S R -	Ṇ̲ - S -
gā - - rī -	- - ga ro -	- - ja -
R M - M -	M - M P -	G̲ - M -
sa ga - re -	- - ma hī -	ne - - -
M - - P -	N̲ - P N̲ N̲	Ṡ - Ṡ -
ai - - se -	- - na ḍa ra	tu - ma -
N̲ Ṙ - Ṡ -	Ṡ Ṙ N̲ Ṡ -	N̲ D̲[1] P -
ka ba - se -	- bha ʻe - -	ho - - -
M M - M -	M - P N̲ P	N̲ - Ṡ Ṙ
va ra - sa -	Sa - dā - -	ran - ga -
N̲ Ṡ - N̲ M		
bhī - - ne -		

1 *Shuddh* in the text.

Horī, Cāncar kī
Rāg Sindhūrā[1]

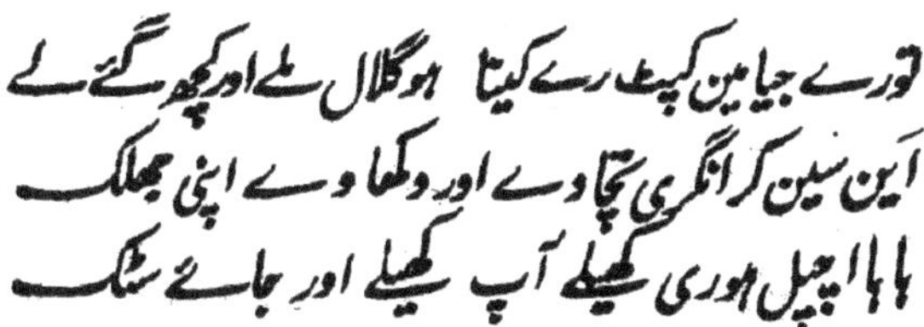
تورے جیا مین کپٹ رے کینا ہو گلال لے اور کچھ گئے لے
اَین سین کر انگری تچاوے اور دکھاوے اپنی جھلک
ہا ہا اچپل ہوری کھیلے آپ کھیلے اور جائے سٹک

There's guile in your heart, Kanaiya. You've found red powder and you're up to something. With winks of your eyes you're sending scorching sparks and showing your radiance. Ha Ha, Achpal is playing Holi. You play and run away.

17. *Horī, Cāncar kī, Rāg Sindhūrā, Tāl Dīpcandī*
middle speed, fourteen *mātrās*

3	*x*	*2*	*0*
G̲ - M -	P - P	+ P - P -	N̲ D̲ -
to - re -	*jī - yā*	*men - ka -*	*pa ṭa -*
P D̲ - M	P - -	N̲ - - -	D̲N̲ Ṡ -
re - - ka	*na'i - -*	*yā - - -*	‿ - -
N̲ Ṙ Ṡ -	N̲ D̲ -	P - N̲ -	D P -
to - re -	*jī yā -*	*men - ka -*	*pa ṭa -*
G̲M G̲M P M	P - -	N̲ - - -	D̲ N̲ Ṡ -
re - - ka	*na'i - -*	*yā - - -*	- - - -
P - N̲ -	N̲ Ṡ -	Ṡ - - Ṙ	Ṡ N̲ -
ho - gu -	*lā - -*	*la - - mi*	*le - -*

1 A recording of this song is to be heard on *Inayat Khan: The Complete Recordings of 1909*, CD 2 track 7.

Horī, Cāncar kī, Rāg Sindhūrā

3	x	2	0
D̲ - P -	G̲ M -	G̲M P G̲ -	R S -
au - ra -	*ku cha -*	*ga ‘e - - -*	*le - -*
- - - -	- - -	N̲ - N̲ N̲	Ṡ Ṡ -
		ā - īn se	*- na -*
Ṡ - Ṡ -	- - -	N̲ N̲ N̲ Ṡ	ṘṘ ṠN Ṡ
ka - ra -		*an ga rī na*	*cā - -*
D̲ - P -	- - -	N̲ - Ṡ -	D̲ - -
ve - - -		*aur - di -*	*khā - -*
P D̲ M -	P N̲ -	N̲ - N̲ -	Ṡ Ṡ -
ve - - -	*a pa -*	*nī - jha -*	*la ka -*
N̲ - Ṡ -	- - -	N̲ N̲ N̲ -	- - -
hā - hā -	- - -	*a ca pal -*	- - -
N̲ - Ṡ -	ṘṘ ṠN̲ Ṡ	D̲ - P -	P - -
ho - rī -	*khe - -*	*le - - -*	- - -
- - - -	P Ġ̲ -	Ṙ Ṡ Ṙ -	Ṡ N̲ -
- - - -	*ā - -*	*pa - khe -*	*le - -*
N̲ - Ṡ -	P N̲ -	Ṡ - ṠṘ G̲	Ṙ Ṡ -
aur - - -	*jā - -*	*‘e - sa -*	*ṭa ka -*
N̲ - Ṡ -	N̲ D̲ -		
to - re -	*ji yā -*		

Ṭappa
Rāg Bhairavīn

وے تو ساڈے نال گلاں کر کے چلا میاں رانجا تینڈا ہو بھلا
جے مین جاندی جانے نہ دیندی اب کی کروں تواڈا گلہ

Come and talk to us before you go
Miyan Ranja, may you be well.
If I had known, I would not have let you go
But now, how can I complain to you?

18. *Ṭappa, Rāg Bhairavīn, Tāl Panjābī*
middle speed, sixteen *mātrās*

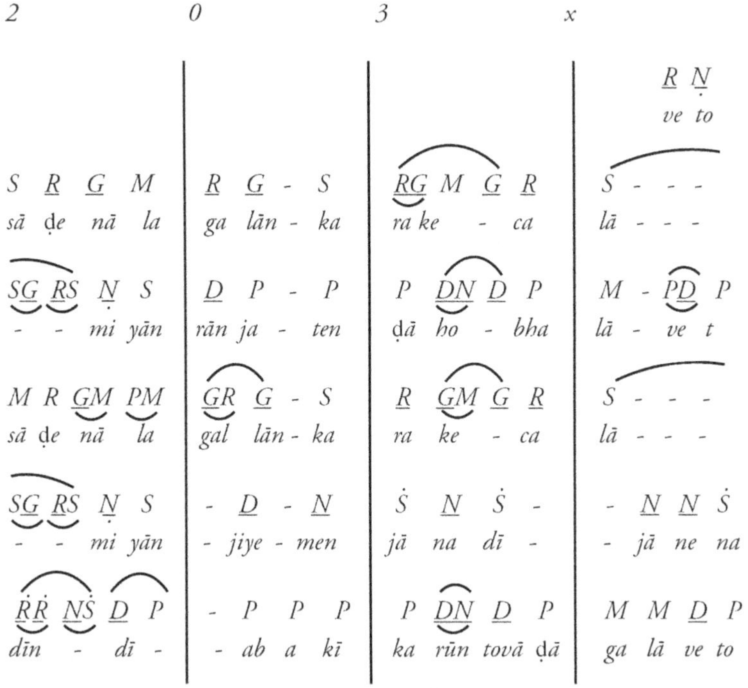

2	0	3	x
			R Ṇ
			ve to
S R G M	R G - S	RG M G R	S - - -
sā ḍe nā la	*ga lān - ka*	*ra ke - ca*	*lā - - -*
SG RS Ṇ S	D P - P	P DN D P	M - PD P
- - mi yān	*rān ja - ten*	*ḍā ho - bha*	*lā - ve t*
M R GM PM	GR G - S	R GM G R	S - - -
sā ḍe nā la	*gal lān - ka*	*ra ke - ca*	*lā - - -*
SG RS Ṇ S	- D - N	Ṡ N Ṡ -	- N N Ṡ
- - mi yān	*- jiye - men*	*jā na dī -*	*- jā ne na*
ṘṘ NṠ D P	- P P P	P DN D P	M M D P
dīn - dī -	*- ab a kī*	*ka rūn tovā ḍā*	*ga lā ve to*

Ṭappa, Rāg Bhairavīn

2				0				3				x	
M	*R*	*G*	*M*	*R*	*G*	-	*S*	*R*	*GM*	*G*	*R*	*S*	-
sā	*ḍe*	*nā*	*la*	*ga*	*lān*	-	*ka*	*ra*	*ke*	-	*ca*	*lā*	-

Tarānā
Rāg Bihāg[1]

دانی نا دِر دِر دیم تن تنا تن دِر نا ت دارے دانی یا لا لوم یا لا لوم یا لا لوم لا لا لے
تک دیم تَ تَ نَ نَ نَ دِر نا ت دار دانی تا رِت دارے دانی -
شنو شنو کہ ترا رسم دلربائی نیست   بیا بیا کہ مرا طاقتِ جدائی نیست

dā nī nā di ra di ra dīm ta na ta nā ta na di ri nā ta dā re dā nī yā lā lūm yā lā lūm yā lā lūm lā lā le tak dīm ta ta na na na di ri nā ta dā ri dā nī tā ri ta dā re dā nī -

shanau shanau ki turāra sim dil rubā'ī nīst
biyā biyā kih marā ṭāqat-i judā'ī nīst

Hear me, hear me! This coquetry is not your way.
Come to me, come to me! I cannot bear your being away.

1 A recording of this song is to be heard on *Inayat Khan: The Complete Recordings of 1909*, CD 1 track 13. Songs 19 and 20 are examples of *tarānā* and *tirvat*, genres that use non-meaningful syllables as lyrics. *Tarānā* syllables are specific to the genre. This one includes a Persian couplet. *Tirvat* lyrics consist of drum syllables.

19. Tarānā, Rāg Bihāg, Tāl Catūsra Jātī Tetālā
fast speed, sixteen *mātrās*

2	*0*	*3*	*x*
			M̍ P
			dā nī
G M G P	*P N D Ṡ*	*N - - D*	*P - M G*
nā dira dira dīm	*- ta na ta*	*nā - - -*	*- - ta na*
M P D M	*G R Ṇ S*	*S Ṇ S S*	*G R M G*
di ri nā ta	*dā ri dā nī*	*yā lā lū ma*	*yā lā lū ma*
P M̍ P D	*M - G R*	*S N - N*	*Ṡ Ṙ Ṡ N*
yā lā lū ma	*lā - lā le*	*tak dīm - ta*	*ta na na na*
D P M̍ P	*G M GR G*	*GM PD P M*	*G R Ṇ S*
di ri nā ta	*dā ri dā nī*	*tā - re ta*	*dā re dā nī*
P P - P	*N D N N*	*Ṡ - Ṡ -*	*Ṡ Ṡ - Ṡ*
sha nau - sha	*nau - ki tu*	*rā - ra -*	*sim dil - ru*
N D N Ṡ	*N D M̍ P*	*M G R G*	*GM P M G*
bā - ʿī -	*nīst - - -*	*bi yā - bi*	*yā - kih ma*
S - G -	*M P - P*	*N D N Ṙ*	*ṠṘ ṠN DP M̍P*
rā - ṭā -	*qat -i - ju*	*dā - ʿī -*	*nīst*

Tirvaṭ, Rāg Kedārā

دھا گینا دھا دھا دھا توتا نا   دھا گینا دھا دھا دھا تونا
دھا گینا دھا دھا دھا تونا   ترکٹ تک دھے دّھے نا
دھا کِٹ تک دُھم کٹ تک   دِھت تّا دھا سکھ رنگ
کڑان کڑان دھا دھا دھا   کڑان کڑان دھا دھا دھا
کڑان کڑان دھا دھا دھا   ترکٹ تک دِھے دّھے نا

dhā gī nā dhā dhā dhā tū nā dhā gī nā dhā dhā dhā tū nā
dhā gī nā dhā dhā dhā tū nā tira kiṭa taka dhe dhe nā
dhā kiṭatakadhuma kiṭataka dhit tā dhā sa kha ran ga
kṛān kṛān dhā dhā dhā kṛān kṛān dhā dhā dhā
kṛān kṛān dhā dhā dhā tira kiṭa taka dhe ddhe nā

20. Tirvaṭ, Rāg Kedārā, Tāl Catūsra Jāti Tetālā

fast speed, sixteen *mātrā*s

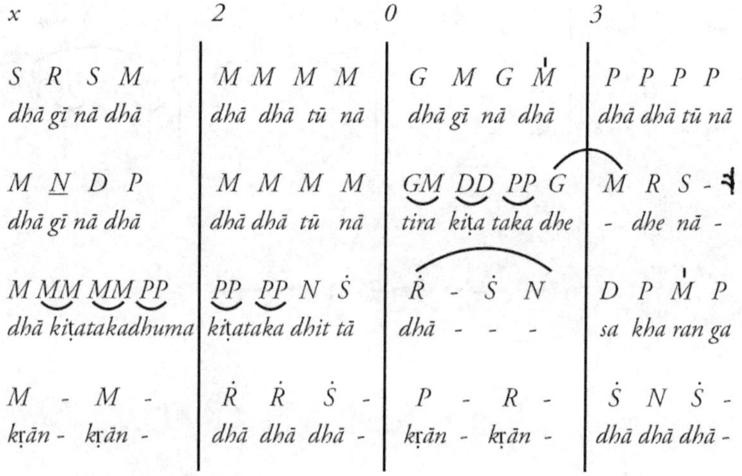

x	*2*	*0*	*3*
S R S M	*M M M M*	*G M G M̍*	*P P P P*
dhā gī nā dhā	*dhā dhā tū nā*	*dhā gī nā dhā*	*dhā dhā tū nā*
M N̲ D P	*M M M M*	*GM DD PP G*	*M R S -*
dhā gī nā dhā	*dhā dhā tū nā*	*tira kiṭa taka dhe*	*- dhe nā -*
M MM MM PP	*PP PP N Ṡ*	*Ṙ - Ṡ N*	*D P M̍ P*
dhā kiṭatakadhuma	*kiṭataka dhit tā*	*dhā - - -*	*sa kha ran ga*
M - M -	*Ṙ Ṙ Ṡ -*	*P - R -*	*Ṡ N Ṡ -*
kṛān - kṛān -	*dhā dhā dhā -*	*kṛān - kṛān -*	*dhā dhā dhā -*

Tirvaṭ, Rāg Kedārā

x	2	0	3
P M Ṡ N	*D P M -*	*GM DD PP G*	*M R S -*
kṛān - kṛān -	*dhā dhā dhā -*	*tirakiṭa takadhe*	*- ddhe nā -*

Chok Varnam, Rāg Kharaharapriyā

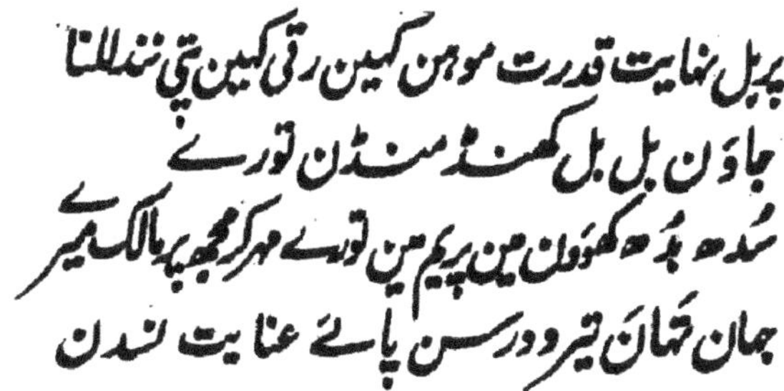
پربل نہایت قدرت موہن کہین رتی کہین پتی نندللا
جاؤن بل بل گہنڈ منڈن تورے
سُدھ بُدھ کھووں مین پریم مین تورے مہر کر مجھ پر مالک میر
جہاں تہاں تیرو درسن پاۓ عنایت نسدن

Utmost in strength and power, Mohan, sometimes a lover sometimes a lord, beloved son of Nanda.

Let me become a nightingale among your adornments. I say clearly and knowingly—in your love have favor on me, my Lord.

Wherever I might catch a glimpse of you, there Inayat will be, day and night.

21. Chok Varnam, Rāg Kharaharapriyā, Tāl Chatūsra Jātī Ektālā middle speed, four *mātrās*

x	x	x	x
N D N Ṡ	Ṡ - Ṡ Ṡ	G[1] Ṙ Ṡ N	N D P M
pra ba la ni	*hā - ya ta*	*qu da ra ta*	*mo - ha na*
+ P P P D	N D P M	M P M P	G R S -
ka hīn ra tī	*ka hīn pa tī*	*nan - - da*	*la la nā -*
S - Ṇ -	S G G M	G M P M	P G R S
jā - 'ūn -	*bu la bu la*	*khan - - ḍa*	*man - ḍa na*
S - S -	P - M G	M G (-) R	G - R S
to - re -	*sudh - bu dha*	*kah 'ūn (-) men*	*pre - ma men*
S - S -	P P M G	P M G R	G - R S
to - re -	*mi har ka ra*	*mu jh pa ra*	*mā - li ka*
S - S -	S G R G	M G M -	M N D N
me - re -	*ja hān ta hān*	*te - ro -*	*da ra sa na*
P D N Ṡ	N Ṙ Ṡ N	N D P M +	
pā - 'e 'I	*nā - ya ta*	*ni sa di na*	

1 Likely should be high octave.

Ghazals in Various Styles

This section contains various types of *ghazals* both old and contemporary. Two couplets of each are shown in the notation but one should sing the entire *ghazal* with the melody. One Urdu and one Persian *ghazal* is given for each selection. In consideration of the general opinion that the *ghazal* is of popular interest, various *ghazals* are included in this book.

Ghazals of Amir and Hafiz

Amir[1]

خودی سے بیخودی مین آ جو شوقِ حق پرستی ہے
جسے تو نیستی سمجھا ہے اے غافل وہ ہستی ہے

خبردار اے مسافر خوف کی جا راہِ ہستی ہے
ٹھگون کا بیٹھکا ہے جا بجا چورونکی بستی ہے

خمارِ نشۂ مے سے نگاہین انکی کہتی ہین
یہان کیا کام تیرا یہ تو متوالون کی بستی ہے

جوانی داغ دیجائیگی ناز اس پر نہ کر غافل
برنگِ مستی طاؤس کوئی دم کی مستی ہے

امیر اس راستے سے جو گزرتے ہین وہ لٹتے ہین
محلہ ہے حسینون کا یہ قزاقون کی بستی ہے

Come from self-regard to selflessness, which is the ardor of worship. That which you take for nothingness,
O heedless one, is the real being.

Traveler beware, the road of being is a fearsome stretch.
Here are the camps of cutthroats, there are the hideouts
of thieves.

Languid with wine, her eyes say "What business have you here? This is the district of drunks."

---

1 A translation of this *ghazal* is to be found in Khan and Westbrook, 1996, 12.

Youth will leave a scar; do not glorify it heedlessly. Is the proud strut of the peacock any sort of ecstasy?

Amir, all those who travel this road are plundered. It is the neighborhood of beauties, and the quarter of thieves.

Hafiz

الا یا ایها الساقی ادر کأسا و ناولها — که عشق آسان نمود اول ولی افتاد مشکل‌ها
بوی نافه‌ای کاخر صبا زان طره بگشاید — ز تاب جعد مشکینش چه خون افتاد در دل‌ها
به می سجاده رنگین کن گرت پیر مغان گوید — که سالک بی‌خبر نبود ز راه و رسم منزل‌ها
مرا در منزل جانان چه امن عیش چون هر دم — جرس فریاد می‌دارد که بربندید محمل‌ها
حضوری گر همی خواهی از او غایب مشو حافظ — متی ما تلق من تهوی دع الدنیا و اهملها

O Saqi, pass around the cup of wine, and offer it,
for love at first seemed easy, but then came the difficulties.

Awaiting the perfume the morning breeze may, at last, loosen from her hair. Hearts are drenched in blood by the twisting of her musky black curls.

Stain your prayer carpet with wine if the Magian elder bids you, for the wayfarer is not unfamiliar with the road and the customs of its stations.

How could I enjoy tranquility in this caravanserai, when the bells are always crying, "Pack up your loads!"

Hafiz, if you desire her presence, do not yourself be absent: when you meet the one you love, abandon the world and let it go.

22. *Rāg Husainī Kānaṛā, Tāl Qavālī*
middle speed eight *mātrās*

x	x	x	x
			M
			khu
R - S -	S R - R	R - RS R	G - - M
dī - se -	*- be - khu*	*dī - men -*	*ā - - jo*
R - S -	- M - M	M P P M	G - - M
shau - q-i -	*- haq - pa*	*ras - tī -*	*hai - - ji*
R - S -	S R - -	R - RS R	G - - M
se - tū -	*- nīs - -*	*tī - sam -*	*jhā - - hai*
R - S -	- M - M	M P P M	G - - R
aye - ghā -	*- fil - vo*	*has - tī -*	*hai - - kha*
M - M -	M P - N	N - Ṡ -	Ṡ Ṡ N D
bar - dār -	*- aye - mu*	*sā - fir -*	*- khauf - -*
P D P -	- M - M	M P P M	G - - M
kī - jā -	*- rāh - i*	*has - tī -*	*hai - - ṭha*
R - S -	S R - R	R - RS R	G - - M
gon - kā -	*- bai - ṭha*	*kā - hai -*	*jā - - ba*
R - S -	- M - M	M P P -	G - -
jā - co -	*- ron - kī*	*bas - tī -*	*hai - -*

*Ghazal*s of Sauda and Muhi

Sauda[1]

کیون نہ تسکین دل اے یار کرون یا نہ کرون
نالہ جا کر پسِ دیوار کرون یا نہ کرون

سن لے ایک بات مری تو کہ رمق باقی ہے
پھر سخن تجھ سے ستمگار کرون یا نہ کرون

سخت مشکل ہے مین صیاد سے جا کر یارو
ذکر مرغان گرفتار کرون یا نہ کرون

حال باطن کا نمایان ہے مرے ظاہر سے
مین زبان اپنے سے اظہار کرون یا نہ کرون

کوچۂ یار کو مین رشک چمن اے سودا
جا کے با دیدۂ خونبار کرون یا نہ کرون

Why not ease my heart, O beloved, should I or not?
Should I go at last and wail by the wall or not?

Hear me out this once, for I have only this last breath.
After this, my tormentor, will I talk with you or not?

It is a real dilemma. Should I go to the hunter, friends,
and speak to him of the birds trapped in his net, or not?

My inner state is obvious from my appearance.
Should I express it with my tongue or not?

O Sauda, shall I go and make my beloved's lane the envy of
the flower bed with my blood-weeping eyes, or not?

1 A translation of this *ghazal* is to be found in Khan and Westbrook, 1996, 43.

Muhi

بے حجابانہ درآ از درِ کاشانۂ ما   کہ کسے نیست بجز دردِ تو در خانۂ ما

گر بیائی بسرِ تربتِ ویرانۂ ما   بینی از خونِ جگر آب زدہ خانۂ ما

فتنہ انگیز مشو کاکلِ مشکین مکشا   تاب زنجیر ندارد دلِ دیوانۂ ما

شکر اللہ نمردیم و رسیدیم بدوست   آفرین باد برین ہمتِ مردانۂ ما

محی بر شمع تجلی جمالش میسوخت   دوست میگفت زہے ہمتِ پروانۂ ما

Into my abode, come without a veil
for no one is home but the sorrow of your absence.

Visiting my lonely graveside, you would see
my life-blood sprinkling the house in your honor.

Don't raise a riot—don't unbraid your musky black hair!
My maddened heart cannot bear the chains.

Allah be thanked, I reached the friend without dying.
Such manly determination—well done!

As the candle of her beauty's luster burned up Muhi,
the friend said, "Bravo for my moth's determination!"

23. *Rāg Jhinjhoṭī, Tāl Qavālī*
middle speed, eight *mātrās*

x	x	x	x
G G G M	*P - D P*	*M M M G*	*R G R -*
kyon- na tas	*kī - - -*	*ni dil aye -*	*- - yā -*
R R RS R	*G - - M*	*G R G R*	*SN S - -*
ra ka rūn -	*yā - - -*	*na ka rūn -*	*- - - -*
G G G M	*P - D P*	*M M M G*	*R G R -*
nā lah jā -	*kar - - -*	*pas -i dī -*	*- - vā -*
R R RS R	*G - - M*	*G R G R*	*SN S - -*
ra ka rūn -	*yā - - -*	*na ka rūn -*	*- - - -*
G G G M	*P - - -*	*M D P -*	*P - - -*
su na le ek	*bā - - -*	*ta me rī -*	*- - - -*
G G M P	*D - - -*	*D Ṡ N D*	*P - - -*
to kih ra maq	*bā - - -*	*- - qī -*	*hai - - -*
G G G M	*P - D P*	*M M M G*	*R G R -*
phir su khun -	*tujh - - -*	*se si tam -*	*- - gā -*
R R RS R	*G - - M*	*G R G R*	*SN S - -*
ra ka rūn -	*yā - - -*	*na ka rūn -*	*- - - -*

Ghazals of Zamin and Tarki

Zamin[1]

رخ روشن کو ہم اسکے تجلی خدا سمجھے تھا / بجا سمجھے حقیقت میں جو راز انبیا سمجھے
سمجھکر بوجھکر اے دل ہوئے غافل وہ کیا سمجھے / جو تھا مخفی اُسے ظاہر جو ظاہر تھا چھپا سمجھے
سمجھ ہے اپنی اپنی اور عقیدہ اپنا اپنا ہے / کوئی اس بت کو کچھ سمجھے ہم اس بت کو خدا سمجھے
اصول معرفت ذات خدا اے عاشقو یہ ہے / فنا کو جو بقا سمجھے بقا کو جو فنا سمجھے تھا
رضا مندی سے جان دینا نہ کچھ خواہش مری جانی / شہادت کا مزا ضامن شہید کربلا سمجھے

I understood her bright countenance to be a manifestation of God. They understood rightly, in truth, who understood the prophetic mystery.

O my heart, aware as she was, though heedless, what did she understand? What was concealed was clear to her, and what was plain she thought was hidden.

Everyone's understanding is one's own; everyone has one's own belief. Some saw this image as a mere thing; I saw this idol as God.

The foundation of the knowledge of the divine essence is this, O lovers: to see subsistence in annihilation and annihilation in subsistence.

Give up your life willingly, asking nothing, my dear. Learn the pleasure of sacrifice, Zamin, from the martyr of Karbala.

---

1 A translation of this *ghazal* is to be found in Khan and Westbrook, 1915, 14.

Turki

ے داغ جگر سوزان وگرنه زخم جگر بینیم — بهار تازه هر دم در غمت ای سیمبر بینیم
امشب این قدر از فراقش درد جگر باشد — مدار امید ای همدم که من روی سحر بینیم
دارم سر فتراک لیکن این قدر خواهم — که در پای تو از شمشیر چوگان گوی سر بینیم
ب مه هم کنار من چو آن رشک قمر باشد — مبادا چشم من روشن اگر سوی سحر بینیم
ذاهم بادهٔ وصلش مگر میخواهم ای ترکی — که امشب بی حجاب آن چشم میگون یک نظر بینیم

When my heart is not burning in pain, I see it slashed,
but always in my grief over you, silver-bosomed one,
I see lush spring.

If without you tonight I must face this much heartache,
O you most near to my life, abandon the hope that
I will live to see dawn.

My head is nothing special, but I ask this much
that severed at your foot, I see it as a polo ball.

When on a moonlit night, she whom the moon envies is
beside me, let the light fade from my eyes if I look
toward the dawn.

I do not ask for the wine of her embrace, but Turki,
I do ask that tonight I see a glimpse of her
wine-dark eyes unveiled.

24. *Rāg Shāhāna, Tāl Qavālī*
middle speed, eight *mātrās*

x	x	x	x
			S *ru*
S - S - *kh̲-i - ro -*	R - - M *shan - - ko*	P - D Ṙ *ham - us -*	Ṡ N̲D N̲ D *ke - - ta*
P - M P *jal - lī -*	G̲R G̲ - R *-e - - kh̲u*	Ṇ S RM RG̲ *dā - sam -*	R - - S *jhe - - ba*
S - S - *jā - sam -*	R - - M *jhe - - ḥa*	P - D Ṙ *qī - qat -*	Ṡ N̲D N̲ D *men - - jo*
P M P - *rā - z-i -*	G̲R G̲ - R *an - - bi*	Ṇ S RM RG *yā - sam -*	R - - M *jhe - - sa*
M - P - *majh - kar -*	N - - N *bū - - jh*	N - N - *kar - aye -*	Ṡ - - N̲ *dil - - hu*
N̲ - DP D *'e - gh̲ā -*	N̲ - - Ṙ *fil - - voh*	ṠN Ṡ N̲ D *kyā - sam -*	P - - S *jhe - - jo*
S - S - *thā - makh̲ -*	R - - M *fī - - u*	P - D Ṙ *se - ẓā -*	Ṡ N̲ DN̲ D *hir - - jo*
P - M P *ẓā - hir -*	G̲R G̲ - R *thā - - chu*	Ṇ S RM RG *pā - sam -*	R - - *jhe - -*

Ghazals of Amir and Shad

Amir[1]

یہ تو مین کیونکر کہون تیرے خریدارون مین ہون
تو سراپا ناز ہے مین ناز بردارون مین ہون

وہ کرشمے شانِ رحمت نے دکھائے روزِ حشر
چیخ اٹھا ہر بے گنہ مین بھی گنہگارون مین ہون

اونچے اونچے مجرمون کی ہوگی پرسش حشر مین
کون پوچھیگا مجھے مین کن گنہگارون مین ہون

بے گناہون مین چلا زاہد جو اسکو ڈھونڈھنے
مغفرت بولی ادھر آ مین گنہگارون مین ہون

پھول مین پھولون مین ہون کانٹو نمین کانٹا ہون امیر
یار مین یارون مین ہون عیار عیارون مین ہون

How could I say that I am among your customers?
You are coquetry from head to foot; I am one of your
whim bearers.

That amorous glance with the radiance of mercy evoked
the Day of Resurrection. All the sinless ones cried out "I
am among the sinners!"

The great transgressors will be interrogated in the resurrection. Who will ask after me? I am merely among the
minor sinners.

Among the sinless ones the ascetic went in search of Him.
Forgiveness called, "Come here, I am among the sinners."

Among flowers I am a flower, Amir, among thorns a thorn;
among friends I am a friend, among scoundrels a
scoundrel.

1 A translation of this *ghazal* is to be found in Khan and Westbrook, 1996, 15.

Shad

شوقِ خودآرائیِ خود را تماشا دیده ایم
در وجودِ خویشتن رنگِ تمنا دیده ایم

وحشیِ رم آرزو را حلقهٔ اش دامے گشت
پا بزنجیرِ جنونِ زلفِ چلیپا دیده ایم

جذوه در وادیِ ایمن که موسیٰ دیده بود
لمعهٔ آتش فروزش در کلیسا دیده ایم

عشوه اش بسمل نمود و خنده اش جانم فزود
در ادائے یار اعجازِ مسیحا دیده ایم

از غبارِ غیر روے آئینه صاف است شاد
دیدهٔ حیرت گشودیم و سراپا دیده ایم

I have seen the spectacle of my vanity's ardor;
in my own essence, I have seen the color of desire.

The wild beast of the herd? Desire made his stomping
ground a net. I have seen her ringlets binding his hooves
with the chains worn by the mad.

The kindling which Moses had seen in the wadi of Aiman,
in the church, I have seen the glow of its fire.

Her blandishments—night—brought death, and her smile
—dawn—renewed my life: in the coquetry of the friend,
I have seen the miracles of the Messiah.

Shad, the mirror is untainted by the mist of another's face:
I have opened the eyes of rapture, and seen from
head to toe.

25. *Rāg Eman, Tāl Qavālī*
middle speed, eight *mātrās*

x	*x*	*x*	*x*
- P - G	*G R G M̍*	*PD M̍P - R*	*G R SR ṆS*
- yeh - to	*men - kyon -*	*kar - - ka*	*hūn - te -*
- Ṇ - R	*R - RS R*	*G - - M*	*G R SṆ S*
- re - k̲h̲a	*rī - dā -*	*ron - - men*	*hūn - - -*
- P - G	*G R G M̍*	*PD M̍P - R*	*G R SR ṆS*
- tū - sa	*rā - pā -*	*nā - - z*	*hai - men -*
- Ṇ - R	*R - RS R*	*G - - M*	*G R SṆ S*
- nā - z	*bar - dā -*	*ron - - men*	*hūn - - -*
- P - G	*P - D -*	*- Ṡ - Ṡ*	*Ṡ Ṙ Ṡ -*
- voh - ki	*rish - me -*	*- shā - ni*	*raḥ - mat -*
- N - N	*D - DP D*	*N - - Ṡ*	*N D PM̍ P*
- ne - di	*khā - 'e -*	*rū - - zi*	*ḥa shr - -*
- P - G	*G R G M̍*	*PD M̍P - R*	*G R SR ṆS*
- cīk̲h̲ - u	*ṭhā - har -*	*be - - gu*	*na - men -*
- Ṇ - R	*R - RS R*	*G - - M*	*G R SṆ S*
- bhī - gu	*na - gā -*	*ron - - men*	*hūn - - -*

Ghazals of Asif and Maghribi

Asif[1]

تہمت تمہارے عشق کی ہم پر لگی ہوئی — یارب بجھیگی آگ یہ کیونکر لگی ہوئی
لاؤ تو قتل نامہ مرا مین بھی دیکھ لون — کس کس کی مہر ہے سرِ محضر لگی ہوئی
جائینگے کس اُمید پہ ہم اسکے کوچہ مین — کافی ہے ہمکو پہلی ہی ٹھوکر لگی ہوئی
الفت کا جب مزا ہو کہ دونوں ہوں بیقرار — دونو طرف ہو آگ برابر لگی ہوئی
آصف ذرا سمجھ کے یہاں کیجئے مقام — منزل ہے اور دوسری سر پر لگی ہوئی

The accusation of loving you has been leveled against me.
Oh God, this fire, how will it be quenched, which has
started in me?

Bring me my death decree, would you? Let me, too,
see which heads of assembly are they whose seals
are stamped there.

With what hope will I go to her lane? It is enough for me
to have stumbled against it already at the outset.

When the pleasure of intimacy is such that both are ill at
ease, let the fire burn on both sides equally.

Asif, think a bit before settling here.
You have a home; a second is a heavy burden.

1 A translation of this *ghazal* is to be found in Khan and Westbrook, 1996, 19.

Maghribi

ہر سو کہ دویدیم ہمہ سوئے تو دیدیم
ہر جا کہ رسیدیم ہمہ کوئے تو دیدیم

از باد صبا بوئے تو دوش شنیدیم
با بادِ صبا قافلۂ بوئے تو دیدیم

روئے ہمہ خوبانِ جہان را بتماشا
دیدیم و لے آئینۂ روئے تو دیدیم

وز ظاہر و باطن بہ مجاز و بہ حقیقت
خلق دو جہان را ہمہ رو سوئے تو دیدیم

اے مغربی احوال مپرسید کہ او را
سودا زدہ ترکی و ہندو تو دیدیم

Wherever I ran, I always looked to you.
Wherever I found myself, I always looked to your lane.

In the breeze last night I breathed your sweet fragrance.
In the city of the breeze I saw the caravan of your fragrance.

I gazed admiringly on the faces of all the world's beauties,
but it was all a mirror of your face that I saw.

Without and within, metaphorically and in fact
I saw the creatures of both worlds all turned toward you.

Do not ask Maghribi how he is doing.
I saw his mood darkened like a Turk or Hindu over you.

26. *Rāg Jaijaivantī, Tāl Dādrā*
middle speed, six *mātrās*

x 0	x 0	x 0	x 0	
				D N
				to ha
S - R G - M	*RG M G R R G*	*SR G R S ND N*	*S - - -*	
mat-tumhā - re	*'ish - q kī ham -*	*par - la gī - hu*	*'ī - - -*	
				D N
				yā -
S - R G - M	*RG M G R R G*	*SR G R S ND N*	*S - - -*	
rab- bu jhe - gī	*ā - ga yeh kyon-*	*kar - la gī - hu*	*'ī - - -*	
				G -
				lā -
MG RS S S - R	*M - M M M -*	*G - G R - R*	*SR G MG RS*	
'o - to qa- tal	*nā - meh me rā -*	*men - bhī de - kh*	*lūn - - -*	
				D N
				kis -
S - R G - M	*RG M G R R G*	*SR G R S ND N*	*S - - -*	
kis - kī mu - har	*hai - sar i mah -*	*zar - la gī - hu*	*'ī - - -*	

Ghazals of Shad and Shams

Shad

یہ سب دیر و حرم کے لوگ اپنے دیکھے بھالے ہیں
عدم آباد یک بستی ہے وہاں کے رہنے والے ہیں

بگڑنا اور منہ بنانا ذرا سی بات پر اس کا
یہ سارے ڈھنگ اس بت کے خدائی سے نرالے ہیں

بتائیں کیا تمہیں ہم کون ہیں اتنا سمجھ جاؤ
تمہیں پر جان دیتے ہیں تمہیں پر مرنے والے ہیں

امیدوں کا کسی کے اے فلک کیوں خون کرتا ہے
مٹاتا ہے ہمیں کیوں تو کہ آخر مٹنے والے ہیں

تصدق جائیے اے شادؔ اس صانع کی صنعت کے
حسینانِ جہاں جتنے ہیں اک سانچے میں ڈھالے ہیں

I have seen all these temple-goers and hajj-pilgrims before.
"Lost-ville" is a town, and they are its people.

The anger and tantrums of hers at the slightest thing,
all these sorts of behaviors are separate from that idol's divinity.

What can I tell you about who I am? Just understand this much: I give my life for you; I am the one who is dying for you.

O Fate, why do you murder someone's hopes?
Why do you efface me now, who will anyway be effaced in the end?

O Shad, devote yourself to the art of the Artist.
As many beauties as there are in the world, all are cast from a single mold.

Shams[1]

ـا از اغیار خالی کن چو عـــزم کوے ما داری — میفگن نظر بر غیرے چو قصد روے ما داری
ـوق از لا به الا رو که تا لالاے ما گردی — صدف کن گوهر خودرا اگر لولوے ما داری
ـن آن شمع ام که در مجلس مرا پروانه بسیار اند — بسوزان خویش را تو چون اگر خود بوے ما داری
ـدن باطن خودرا به نور ما منور کن — اگر چه ظاهر خودرا بجست و جوے ما داری
تیر غمزه ات مستم که از جانم گذر کرده — کمال شمس دین بینی چو تو بازوے ما داری

Rid the road of strangers if you would approach my lane.
Do not look at another if you long for my face.

By tasting, go from "no god..." (*lā*) to "...but God" (*illā*),
til you return to my splendor (*lālā'ī*). Remove the shell of
your essence if you would have my pearl.

I am the candle in a soiree teeming with moths.
Burn that self, if you would have my own fragrance.

Illuminate your inner being with my light
if on the outside you cherish and seek me.

I am intoxicated by the arrow of your wink, which has
healed my soul. Behold the perfection of Shams ud-din,
when you have my strength.

---

1 Jalal ad-Din Rumi often used the pen name "Shams" in tribute to his spiritual mentor, Shams-i-Tabrizi.

27. *Rāg Pahāṛī, Tāl Qavālī*
middle speed, eight *mātrās*

x	*x*	*x*	*x*
			N
			yah
N - N -	*- Ṡ - Ṡ*	*NṠ Ṙ Ṡ N*	*D - - P*
sab - dai -	*- ro - ḥa*	*ram - ke -*	*lo - - g*
D - P -	*MG RS R R*	*G M GR GR*	*SṆ S - N*
ap - ne -	*de - - khe*	*bhā - le -*	*hain - - ʿa*
N - N -	*- Ṡ - Ṡ*	*NṠ Ṙ Ṡ N*	*D - - P*
dam - ā -	*- bā - d*	*ek - bas -*	*tī - - hai*
D - P -	*MG RS R R*	*G M GR GR*	*SṆ S - G*
vahān - ke -	*rah - - ne*	*vā - le -*	*hain - - bi*
G - G -	*- P - P*	*P - D -*	*Ṡ - - P*
gaṛ - nā -	*- au - r*	*mun - jā -*	*nā - - ẓa*
P - D -	*Ṡ Ṙ - Ṙ*	*ṠṘ G Ṙ Ṡ*	*N D - N*
rā - sī -	*bā - - t*	*par - us -*	*kā - - yeh*
N - N -	*- Ṡ - Ṡ*	*NṠ Ṙ Ṡ N*	*D - - P*
sā - re -	*- ḍha - ng*	*us - bu t*	*ke - - khu*
D - P -	*MG RS R R*	*G M GR GR*	*SṆ S -*
dā - ʿī -	*se - - ni*	*rā - le -*	*hain - -*

Ghazals of Amir and Iraqi

Amir[1]

آنکھون مین نور تیرا دل مین سرور تیرا
دروازے سے ہے گھر تک سارا ظہور تیرا

اے چشم شوق وہ تو ہر رنگ مین ہے نمایاں
اب بھی جو تو نہ دیکھے تو ہے قصور تیرا

مین آئینہ ہون تیرا تو آئینہ ہے میرا
تجھ مین ظہور میرا مجھ مین ظہور تیرا

یہ بیخودی ہے جس سے ہوتا ہے قرب حاصل
غائب جو آپ سے ہو پائے حضور تیرا

نادان امیر ناحق امیدوار ہے تو
دل لیکے پھیر دے گا وہ اب ضرور تیرا

Your light is in my eyes; your joy is in my heart.
From the gate to the inner chambers, all is a manifestation of you.

O eye of desire, he is manifest in every hue.
If you still have not seen him the fault is yours.

I am your mirror, and you are mine.
My manifestation is in you, and yours is in me.

This is rapture, which results in your nearness.
The one who is absent to himself attains your presence.

Foolish Amir, you hold out hope in vain
Having taken your heart, now he will surely return it.

1 A translation of this *ghazal* is to be found in Khan and Westbrook, 1996, 14.

Iraqi

صنما رهِ قلندر سزد ار بمن نمائی — که دراز و دور دیدم ره و رسم پارسائی
بطواف کعبه رفتم بحرم رهم نه دادند — که برون در چه کردی که درون خانه آئی
بزمین چو سجده کردم ز زمین ندا برآمد — که مرا خراب کردی تو بسجدهٔ ریائی
به خمارخانه رفتم همه پاکباز دیدم — چو بصومعه رسیدم همه یافتم دغائی
درِ دیر چون زدم من ز درون ندا برآمد — که بیا بیا عراقی تو ز خاصگان مائی

O idol, show me the rapid road of the Qalandar
for I have seen that the road of piety is interminable.

I went to circle the Ka'ba, but they barred me from the precincts saying, "With a ring in there, you expect to come in here?"

When I prostrated myself on the ground, the ground cried out: "You have ruined me with your sanctimonious prostration!"

I went to the tavern and saw people reveling innocently.
When I went to the monastery I found only pretense.

When I knocked on the door of the idol-temple, a call came from within: "Come, come, Iraqi! You are one of our chosen."

28. *Rāg Jhinjhoṭī, Tāl Qavālī*
middle speed, eight *mātrās*

x	x	x	x	
				P̣ Ḍ
				ān -
S - - -	*Ḍ S - R*	*SR GM G -*	*SG MR G -*	
khon - - -	*men nū - r*	*te - rā -*	*- - dil -*	
S - - -	*R SR G R*	*S Ṇ Ḍ -*	*ṆḌ Ṇ*	*P̣ Ḍ*
men - - -	*su rū - r*	*te - rā -*	*- -*	*dar -*
S - - -	*Ḍ S - R*	*SR GM G -*	*SG MR G -*	
vā - - -	*ze se - hai*	*ghar - tak -*	*- - sā -*	
S - - -	*R SR G R*	*S Ṇ Ḍ -*	*ṆḌ Ṇ*	*G -*
rā - - -	*ẕu hū - r*	*te - rā -*	*- -*	*aye*
M - - -	*M GM PD P*	*M - G -*	*MG M R G*	
cash - - -	*mi shau - q*	*voh - to -*	*- - har -*	
S - - -	*R SR G R*	*S Ṇ Ḍ -*	*ṆḌ Ṇ*	*P̣ Ḍ*
rang - - -	*- men - hai*	*ẓā - hir -*	*- -*	*ab -*
S - - -	*Ḍ S - R*	*SR GM G -*	*SG MR G -*	
bhī - - -	*jo tū - na*	*de - khe -*	*- - to -*	
S - - -	*R SR G R*	*S Ṇ Ḍ -*	*ṆḌ Ṇ*	
hai - - -	*qu ṣū - r*	*te - rā -*	*- -*	

Ghazals of Nasim and Bedil

Nasim[1]

تیری ذات پاک ہے اے خدا تری شان جل جلالہٗ
ترا نام مالک و کبریا تری شان جل جلالہٗ

ہے چمن میں تو ہی تو رنگ و بو ہے زبان پہ طوطی کے تو ہی تو
پڑھے کیوں نہ بلبل خوشنوا تری شان جل جلالہٗ

جسے چاہے مردہ بناوے تو جسے چاہے زندہ اٹھا تو
ترے ہاتھ میں ہے فنا بقا تری شان جل جلالہٗ

کوئی شاہ کوئی امیر ہے کوئی بینوا و فقیر ہے
جسے چاہا جیسا بنا دیا تری شان جل جلالہٗ

یہ گناہ گار نسیم ہے تو کریم ہے تو رحیم ہے
اسے بخش صدقہ رسول کا تری شان جل جلالہٗ

Your essence is pure, O God—may Your splendor be glorified! Your name is the Master and the Mighty One—may Your splendor be glorified!

You are the color and the fragrance of the flower bed, You are on the parrot's tongue. Why should the sweet-voiced nightingale not utter "may Your splendor be glorified!"?

Destroy as You will and raise up as You will. Annihilation and subsistence are in Your hands—may Your splendor be glorified!

One is a king, one an *amīr*, another is an outcast or a *faqīr*. You made us as You willed—may Your splendor be glorified!

This sinner is Nasim. You are Karim (the Kind) and Rahim (the Merciful). Your generous gift to me is the Prophet—may Your splendor be glorified!

1 A translation of this *ghazal* is to be found in Khan and Westbrook, 1915, 16–17.

Bedil

ستم است اگر هوست کشد که بسیر سرو سمن درآ ‌ ‌ ‌ تو ز غنچه کم ندمیدهٔ در دل کشا بچمن درآ

پی نافه‌های رمیده بو مپسند زحمت جستجو ‌ ‌ ‌ بخیال حلقهٔ زلف او گره خور و بختن درآ

نفست اگر بفسون دمد بتعلقه هوس جسد ‌ ‌ ‌ ده دامن تو که میکشد که درین لباس کهن درآ

غم انتظار تو برده‌ام بره خیال تو مرده‌ام ‌ ‌ ‌ قدمی به پرسش من کشا نفسی تو جان ببدن درآ

بدرآی بیدل ازین قفس اگر آن طرف کشدت هوس ‌ ‌ ‌ تو بغربت آن همه خوش نیی که نگویمت بوطن درآ

If desire calls you to wander among the cypress and jasmine, it is purposeful: come. You've not bloomed less than the rosebud; in your heart's expansion come into the garden.

Don't set your sights on malodorous musk-pods. Dreaming of her perfumed and knotted curls, come out to musk-rich Khotan.

Your ego may be weaving its sensuous spell, but who is pulling the hem of your robe, saying "Come in these old clothes?"

I have borne the pain of waiting for you; I have died in the path of dreaming of you. Take one step toward me, one breath; like soul to body, come.

If desire pulls you out of this cage, O Bedil, your removal will not be a happy one until I say "Come home."

29. *Rāg Soraṭ, Tāl Tīsra Jātī Tīvrā*
middle speed, seven *mātrās*

x	0 0	x	0 0
			S S
			te rī
G - G	G - G G	G̲M̲ P M	M̲G̲ R R R
zā - t	pā - k hai	aye - k̲h̲u	dā - te rī
G - P	D - Ṡ Ṡ	N̲ D P	M G ↲ S S
shā - n	jal - la ja	lā - lu	hu - te rā
G - G	G - G G	G̲M̲ P M	M̲G̲ R R R
nā - m	mā - li k	kib - ri	yā - te rī
G - P	D - Ṡ Ṡ	N̲ D P	M G ↲ M M
shā - n	jal - la ja	lā - lu	hu - hai ca
M - P	N - N N	Ṡ - Ṡ	N̲Ṡ Ṙ N̲ N̲
man - men	tū - hī tū	rang - va	bū - hai za
N̲ D P	G P N Ṡ	N̲ D P	M G ↲ S S
bān - pe	ṭū - ṭī ke	tū - hī	tū - paṛ he
G - G	G - G G	G̲M̲ P M	M̲G̲ R R R
kyon - na	bul - bul i	k̲h̲ush - na	vā - te rī
G - P	D - Ṡ Ṡ	N̲D P M	G -
shā - n	jal - la ja	lā - lu	hu -

Ghazals of Asif and Hafiz

Asif

تم مرے حال پریشاں کو نہیں جانتے کیا
اثر گردش دوران کو نہیں جانتے کیا

ایسے بھولے ہو کہ باتیں نہیں آتیں تمکو
عہد کو قول کو پیمان کو نہیں جانتے کیا

گو وہ کم سن ہیں مگر اتنے بھی نادان نہیں
مری حسرت مرے ارمان کو نہیں جانتے کیا

ہاں کے معنی تو نہیں رکھے ہیں تونے ظالم
ہم ترے روز کے ہاں ہاں کو نہیں جانتے کیا

عاشقِ زار تمہارا تو وہی آصف ہے
میر محبوب علی خان کو نہیں جانتے کیا

Don't you know of my anxious state?
Don't you know the effect of fortune's reversal?

Are you so innocent that you don't comprehend?
How can you not know of your oath, your word, your promise?

She may be of tender years, but she is not *that* naive.
How can she not know of my longing, my yearning?

You haven't observed the sense of "yes," my oppressor.
Don't I know about your everyday "yes, yes?"

Your groaning lover is none other than Asif.
Don't you know Mir Mahbub Ali Khan?

Hafiz

دوش در حلقهٔ ما قصهٔ گیسوی تو بود تا دلِ شب سخن از سلسلهٔ موی تو بود
دل که از ناوکِ مژگانِ تو در خون می‌گشت باز مشتاق کمان خانهٔ ابروی تو بود
عالم از شور و شرِ عشق خبر هیچ نداشت فتنه انگیز جهان غمزهٔ جادوی تو بود
بگشا بند قبا تا بگشاید دلِ من که گشادی که مرا بود ز پهلوی تو بود
به وفای تو که بر تربت حافظ بگذر کز جهان میشد و در آرزوی روی تو بود

Last night in our circle the story was of your hair.
Into the heart of the night went words of the chains
of your tresses.

The heart, that was made to bleed by the darts of your eyelashes, was again seized with desire for the bow-house
of your eyebrow.

Of the hue and cry of love, the world was unaware.
But then your bewitching wink raised its sedition.

Open the fastening of your gown, that my heart may open
in joy, for joy was always mine at your side.

In your faithfulness, pass by the tomb of Hafiz,
who left the world and who longed to see your face.

30. *Rāg Kāfī, Tāl Qavālī*
middle speed, eight *mātrās*

x	x	x	x
G R SN S	R - - -	R G M P	G R S R
tum me re -	*ḥā - - -*	*l pa re -*	*shān - - -*
M M M PM	P - - -	P M PD P	M G M -
ko na hīn -	*jān - - -*	*- - te -*	*kyā - - -*
G R SN S	R - - -	R G M P	G R S R
a ṣar -i -	*gar - - -*	*dish -i dau -*	*rān - - -*
M M M PM	P - - -	P M PD P	M G M -
ko na hīn -	*jān - - -*	*- - te -*	*kyā - - -*
M N D -	D - - -	D N Ṡ -	NṠ ND P -
ai se bhū -	*le - - -*	*ho kih bā -*	*ten - - -*
R M M -	P - - -	D P M -	M G M -
na hīn ā -	*ten - - -*	*tum - ko -*	*- - - -*
G R SN S	R - - -	R G M P	G R S R
ʿa had ko -	*qau - - -*	*l ko pai -*	*mān - - -*
M M M PM	P - - -	P M PD P	M G M -
ko na hīn -	*jān - - -*	*- - te -*	*kyā - -*

Ghazals of Navab and Saib

Navab

جھومتا ناز سے جس دم وہ پریزاد آیا   کیسی حالت ہوئی میری کہ خدا یاد آیا

حسن شیرین نے کسے ناز و ادا سے مارا   پھٹتا قبر سے جس کے لئے فرہاد آیا

شاد تھا وصل مین کیسا دل غمگین میرا   کیون غمِ ہجر ترا ہائے مجھے یاد آیا

ابھی دعوی بہت انصاف کا ہے داور حشر   سیر ہو جائے گی گر وہ ستم ایجاد آیا

غش مین کیا لیٹے ہو نواب ذرا کھولو آنکھ   دیکھو تو بہرِ عیادت وہ پریزاد آیا

The moment that fairy-born beauty sauntered in, so sure of himself, such a state came over me that God came to mind!

The beauty of Shirin struck with such coquetry and blandishments that, his tomb shattered, Farhad came out of his grave.

How could my mournful heart be happy in the attainment of your intimacy? For even then, alas, I remembered the sorrow of being far from you.

Lord of the Apocalypse, for now your claim is very appropriate. The oppressed will be contented once Creation comes.

Enough of this swooning, Navab, open your eyes a bit. Look! Inquiring after your health, that fairy-born beauty has come.

Saib

هردم آزردگی غیر سبب را چه علاج
ما گذشتیم ز لطف تو غضب را چه علاج

میتوان داشت نهان عشق ز مردم لیکن
زردهٔ رنگ و رخ و خشکی لب را چه علاج

فرض کردم که بیاد تو دلم خورسند است
لیکن این دیدهٔ دیدار طلب را چه علاج

کہا عنایت سو کہوں کہتے آوے لاج
پگ روکوں تب من پھرے یاکو کہا علاج

گیرم از هر دو جهان چشم بپوشم صائب
دل دیوانهٔ معشوق طلب را چه علاج

What cure is there for incessant, unjustified vexation?
It's your courtesy that allows us to pass; what cure is there for your wrath?

Love can be hidden from a man, but then what cure is there for the pallor of cheeks and the dryness of lips?

I have insisted that my heart be content with your memory, but what cure is there for these eyes, always seeking a glimpse of you?

[Urdu interpolation]
Inayat said, I will tell you, though I am ashamed to say, though I halt my feet, my heart wanders on—what cure is there?

Saib, I seized from both worlds eyes to wear.
What cure is there for a mad heart, always seeking the Beloved?

31. *Rāg Bhairavī, Tāl Pashto*[1]
middle speed, fourteen *mātrās*

x							0						
-	-	-	G	R	G	-	GG	RR	SṆ	S	-	-	M
-	-	-	*jhū*	*m*	*tā*	-	*nāz*	-	-	*se*	-	-	*jis*
GR	G	R	S	S	R	Ṇ	S	-	R	M	-	-	-
dam	-	-	*voh*	*pa*	*rī*	-	*zād*	-	*ā*	*yā*	-	-	-
S	-	-	D	P	-	-	NN	DD	P	M	-	-	M
kai	-	-	*sī*	*ḥā*	-	-	*lat*	-	*hu*	*'ī*	-	-	*me*
GM	PD	P	M	G	MP	M	G	-	M	G	R	S	-
rī	-		*kih*	*khu*	*dā*	-	*yād*	-	-	-	-	-	-
S	-	R	M	-	-	-	-	-	-	P	D	N	-
-	-	*ā*	*yā*	-	-	-	-	-	-	*ḥu*	*sn*	*shī*	-
Ṡ	-	Ṡ	Ṙ	Ṙ	Ṡ	-	N	-	-	N	N	Ṡ	-
rīn	-	*ne*	-	*ki*	*se*	-	*nā*	-	-	*z-o*	*a*	*dā*	-
Ġ	Ġ	-	Ṙ	Ṙ	Ṡ	N	N	Ṡ	D	-	P	-	-
se	-	-	-	-	-	-	-	*mā*	*rā*	-	-	-	-
S	D	P	-	S	D	P	N	N	D	D	P	M	M
pīṭ	*a*	*tā*	-	*pīṭ*	*a*	*tā*	*qabr*	-	-	*se*	-	*ji*	*s*
GM	P	D	PM	GM	P	M	G	-	M	G	R	S	-
ke	-	-	-	*li'e*	*Far*	-	*hād*	-	-	-	-	-	-
S	-	R	M	-	-	-	-	-	-	-	-	-	-
-	-	*ā*	*yā*	-	-	-	-	-	-	-	-	-	-

1 *Shuddh* and *komal* notes are reproduced as they appear in the text. The rhythmic setting of the lyrics is somewhat ambiguous.

Gh̲azals of Momin and Sharaf

Momin[1]

ناوک انداز جدھر دیدۂ جانان ہونگے — نیم بسمل کئی ہونگے کئی بیجان ہونگے

تو کہان جائیگی کچھ اپنا ٹھکانا کر لے — ہم تو کل خواب عدم مین شبِ ہجران ہونگے

ہم نکالینگے سن اے بادِ صبا بل تیرا — اُسکی زلفون کے اگر بال پریشان ہونگے

تاب نظارہ نہین آئینہ کیا دیکھنے دون — اور بنجائینگے تصویر جو حیران ہونگے

عمر ساری تو کٹی عشق بتان مین مومن — آخری وقت مین کیا خاک مسلمان ہونگے

Wherever the glance of the Beloved casts its arrows,
some will be half slain; others will lose their lives.

Where will you go? Make some arrangement for yourself.
As for me, tomorrow during the night of separation I'll be
in the dream of nonbeing.

Listen wind, I will straighten you out if the curls of her
tresses are disarrayed.

The sight of her is too much to bear: should I let her look
in the mirror? In her bedazzlement she will become still
more of a picture.

You have spent your whole life in the love of idols, Momin.
At the end am I then to become the dust of a Muslim?

1 A recording of this song is to be found in *Inayat Khan: the Complete Recordings of 1909*, CD 2 track 4.

Sharaf

غیرت از چشم برم روئے تو دیدن ندهم
گوش را نیز حدیثِ تو شنیدن ندهم

گر شبِ دست دهد وصل تو از غایت شوق
تا قیامت نه شود صبح دمیدن ندهم

دبۂ زلف تو گر ملک دو عالم بدهند
یعلم الله که سرِ موئے تو دیدن نه دهم

گر بیاید ملک الموت که جانم ببرد
تا نه بینم رخِ تو روح رمیدن نه دهم

شرف ار باد وزد مایۂ زلفش ببرد
باد را نیز ز کوئے تو وزیدن ندهم

Jealous of my own eye, I do not let it see your face, nor do I allow my ear to hear any news of you.

If some night I attain your intimacy, in the profusion of my passion, until the Day of Resurrection I will not allow dawn to break.

Should the Lord of both worlds give me the gift of your curls, Allah knows, I will not allow even a single tip to be seen.

If the Angel of Death comes to wrap up my life, as long as your face remains in my sight I will not allow my soul to be alarmed.

Sharaf moved her wealth of curls from the thrashing wind: I do not even allow the wind to blow in her lane.

32. *Rāg Pīlū, Tāl Dādrā*
middle speed, six *mātrās*

x			*0*			*x*			*0*		
-	-	*M*	*N̲*	*DP*	*D*	*DṠ*	*N̲*	*D*	*P*	*M*	*MP*
-	-	*nā*	*vak*	*an*	-	*dāz*	-	-	-	*ji*	*dhar*
G̲M	*G̲*	*R*	*S*	*SR*	*G̲R*	*S*	*Ṇ*	*S*	*RG̲*	*R*	-
dī	*dah*	*e*	-	*jā*	-	*nān*	-	-	*hon*	*ge*	-
-	-	*M*	*N̲*	*DP*	*D*	*DṠ*	*N̲*	*DP*	*M*	*M*	*P*
-	-	*nī*	*ma*	*bis*	-	*mil*	-	*ka ‘e*	-	*hon*	-
G̲M	*G̲*	*R*	*S*	*SR*	*G̲R*	*S*	*Ṇ*	*S*	*RG̲*	*R*	-
ge	*ka*	*‘e*	-	*be*	-	*jān*	-	-	*hon*	*ge*	-
-	-	*M*	*M*	*P*	*D*	*N*	*Ṡ*	*N*	*Ṡ*	*Ṡ*	-
-	-	*tū*	*ka*	*hān*	-	-	*jā*	*‘e*	*gī*	*kuch*	-
N̲	-	*D*	*D*	*D*	-	*DN̲*	*Ṡ*	*N̲*	*D*	*P*	-
ap	-	*nā*	*ṭhi*	*kā*	-	*nā*	-	-	*kar*	*le*	-
-	-	*M*	*N̲*	*DP*	*D*	*DṠ*	*N̲*	*DP*	*M*	*M*	*P*
-	-	*ham*	*to*	*kal*	-	*k̲h̲vāb*	-	*-i*	*‘a*	*dam*	-
G̲M	*G̲*	*R*	*S*	*SR*	*G̲R*	*S*	*Ṇ*	*S*	*RG̲*	*R*	-
men	-	*shab-i*	*hij*	-		*rān*	-	-	*hon*	*ge*	-

Ghazals of Dagh and Hashimi

Dagh

اے فلک چاہیے جی بھر کے نظارا ہم کو
جا کے آنا نہین دنیا مین دو بارا ہم کو

جوش کے اُن سے ہوئے اور زیادہ مضطر
مَرَضِ عشق کے پرہیز نے مارا ہم کو

شکر صد شکر کہ اب قبر مین ہم آ پہونچے
توسنِ عمر نے منزل پہ اوتارا ہم کو

بد سلوکی مین مزا کیا ہے مزا ہے اس مین
کہ ہمارا ہو تمھین پاس تمھارا ہم کو

بحر ہستی مین ہوئے کشتیِ طوفانی ہم
نہین ملتا ہے کہین داغ کنارا ہم کو

O fate, we ought to take in the view to our heart's content, for once we leave this world there will be no coming back.

Compared to the grumblings of anger from her, even more distressful was the disease of abstention from love's malady that felled me.

Thanks one hundred-fold that at last I've arrived at the grave. The high-blooded steed of age has set me down me at the goal.

What pleasure is there in bad behavior? Pleasure is in this: for you, all that's mine, and for me, nearness to you.

In the ocean of existence, I am a storm-struck boat.
Dagh, nowhere is to be found a stretch of shore.

Hashimi

شرر شعلهٔ عشقش سر جانم باقیست　　نه برون ماند بجائی نه نهانم باقیست
بسرودند چون وی زمزمهٔ عشق هنوز　　لذت نغمه بسر گوش روانم باقیست
بسر وصل کسی سر بسر خاک شدم　　بدل خاک مگر حسرت آنم باقیست
همه تن جان بشدم از اثر جام صفاش　　تا ابد منت آن پیر مغانم باقیست
هاشمی سوخت مرا آنچه که بود از من و تو　　شکر ایزد که مگر عشق بتانم باقیست

A spark of the flame of my love for Him, my innermost spirit endures. It does not linger outside; in a place unhidden to me it endures.

Whenever they intone the murmered chant of love,
in the ear of my spirit, the joy of melody endures.

At the height of union, I was reduced to dust,
and yet with this heart of dust, my longing for being endures.

Tasting the cup of His purity, my whole body became spirit. For all eternity, my gratitude to that Magian elder endures.

Hashimi, all there was of "you" and "I" has been burned from me. God be thanked if by some chance my love of idols endures.

33. *Rāg Tilak Kāmod, Tāl Pashto*
middle speed, fourteen *mātrās*

x	x
	S Ṇ S -
	a ʿe falk -
GM P M P P - -	GP DṠ ND P G M -
cā - hi ʿe jī - -	*bhar - - ke na ẓā -*
GR G - GM P G M	GR G - D N̲ D -
rā - - ham - - -	*ko - - jā ke ā -*
DN̲ ṠṠ N̲D N̲ - D P	GP DṠ N̲D P G M -
nā - na hīn - dun -	*yā - - men dū bā -*
GR G - GM P G M	GR G - G M P -
rā - - ham - - -	*ko - - jo ru ke -*
P - N N Ṡ - -	N - - - N N -
un - se ho ʿe - -	*aur - - - za yā -*
ṘṘ ṠN Ṡ N D P -	MP MG RG N N Ṡ -
dah - - mu z̤ ṭar -	*- - - ma ra z̤ -*
DṠ N̲ D P P - (-)	GP DṠ N̲D P G M -
ʿishq - - ke par - (-)	*hez - - ne mā - -*
GR G - GM P G M	GR G -
rā - - ham - - -	*ko - -*

Ghazals of Rasikh and Iraqi

Rasikh

یہان تک روئی ہے حسرت ہماری — کہ ہے موتی محل تربت ہماری

ترے جوڑے کی لینی ہین بلائین — اکٹھی آئی ہے شامت ہماری

گرینگے سر کے بل اس سنگ در پر — کھولیگی پھوٹ کر قسمت ہماری

ہمین ہم ہین جو سیدھا ہو مقدر — تمھین تم ہو جو پلٹے مت ہماری

ہزارون انگلیان اُٹھتی ہین راسخ — بہت بدنام ہے شہرت ہماری

My longing has produced such tears
that I have a shrine of pearls for a tomb.

I will have to give your groom my blessings.
My bad luck has sprung up again.

I will fall headlong on that stone threshold.
Then will my destiny burst open.

It had to be I who was destined to be straight
and you alone who would turn my disposition.

Thousands of fingers are raised, Rasikh;
your reputation is quite notorious.

Iraqi

نخستین باده کندر جام کردند — ز چشم مست ساقی وام کردند
چو گوی حسن در میدان نهادند — بیک چوگان دو عالم رام کردند
بعالم هر کجا درد و بلا بود — بهم کردند و عشقش نام کردند
ندیمان را مگر هشیار دیدند — شراب بیخودی در جام کردند
ز خود کردند سر خویشتن فاش — عراقی را عبث بدنام کردند

First they filled the cup with wine
borrowed from the *sāqī*'s drunken gaze.

They tossed the ball of beauty onto the field
and with one crack of the stick tamed heaven and earth.

Pain and affliction were everywhere in the world.
They put them together and called it "love."

Whenever they found revelers still sober
they filled their cup with the wine of ecstasy.

They themselves divulged their own secret.
In vain they give Iraqi a bad name.

34. *Rāg Tilang, Tāl Qavālī*
middle speed, eight *mātrās*

x	0	x	0
- - - S	G - MD P	M - - R	G R SṆ S
- - - ya	*hān - tak -*	*ro - - 'ī*	*hai - ḥas -*
SR G - R	GM PD P -	- - - P	N - Ṡ -
rat - - ha	*mā - rī -*	*- - - kih*	*hai - mo -*
Ṡ DṠ N̲ D	P - P D	MP MG R G	GM PD P -
- tī - ma	*ḥal - tur -*	*bat - - ha*	*mā - rī -*
- - - M	G - M -	M P - P	N - N -
- - - te	*re - jo -*	*ṛe - - kī*	*le - nī -*
ṘṘ ṠN Ṡ D	N - P -	- - - P	N - Ṡ -
hain - - ba	*lā - 'en -*	*- - - i*	*kaṭ - ṭhī -*
Ṡ DṠ N̲ D	P - P D	MP MG R G	GM PD P -
- ā - 'ī	*hai - shā -*	*mit - - ha*	*mā - rī -*

<u>Gh</u>azals of Akhtar and Maghribi

Akhtar

دل بچے کیونکر نگاہِ ناز سے
الاماں اس تیر بے آواز سے

خفتہ بختون کی بھی سُن لینا ذرا
تم کو فرصت ہو جو خوابِ ناز سے

اُس نے دنیا بھر کو اپنا کر لیا
شوخیون سے ناز سے انداز سے

اُسکے مُنہ مین پھر زبان گویا نہ تھی
جو ہوا واقف تمہارے راز سے

شکر ہے آختر کہ اِس حالت مین بھی
لوگ لیتے ہین تمھین اعجاز سے

How did my heart survive her amorous glance?
God save us from that silent arrow!

Listen a little also to those whose luck is sleeping,
when you have a moment from your dreams of coquetry.

She made the whole world her own, with her
blandishments, with her coquetry, with her posturing.

It was as though he lost his tongue,
whoever became privy to your secret.

Gratitude is due, Akhtar, that even in this state
people hold you in wonderment.

Maghribi

اے تو مخفی در ظہورِ خویشتن   اے رُخت پنہان بنورِ خویشتن
بعض چندے در تماشاگاہِ ناز   جنتِ خود بود حورِ خویشتن
تا کند بر خود تجلّا ہم ز خود   موسیِٔ خود بود طورِ خویشتن
جملہ کارستان خود در خود بدید   در عجب ماند از امورِ خویشتن
بر سرِ راہ بے خبر اُفتادہ دید   مغربی را در عبورِ خویشتن

O You who are concealed in Your own manifestation!
O You whose face is hidden in Your own brilliance!

Amid the spectacle of coquetry, only a few
are their own paradise, themselves their own nymph.

Until one reveals Us from himself to himself,
he remains his own Moses, himself his own Mt. Sinai.

Seeing the whole factory of self in himself,
he was astonished by his own productions.

Lying senseless at the head of the road,
he saw Maghribi, crossing over himself.

35. *Rāg Kāfi, Tāl Qavālī*
middle speed, eight *mātrās*

x	0	x	0
- M - G	M G M P	M - - G	R S R -
- *dil* - *ba*	*ce* - *kyon* -	*kar* - - *ni*	*gāh* - -*i* -
G MP DN D	P - - -		
- *nāz* - - -	*se* - - -		
- M - G	M G M P	M - - G	R S R -
- *al* - *ā*	*mān* - - *is*	*tīr* - - -	*be* - *ā* -
G MP DN D	P - - -		
- *vāz* - - -	*se* - - -		
- M - N	D - D -	PD N - D	P - M -
- *khuf* - *teh*	*bakh* - *ton* -	*kī* - - *bhī*	*sun* - *le* -
G[1] MP DN D	P - - -		
- *nā* - - *za*	*rā* - - -		
- M - G	M G M P	- M - G	R S R -
- *tum* - *ko*	*fur* - *ṣat* -	- *ho* - *jo*	*khvāb* - *i* -
G MP DN D	P - - -		
- *nāz* - -	*se* - - -		

1 *Shuddh* in text.

Ghazals of Nasikh and Shad

Nasikh

دل مین پوشیدہ تپِ عشقِ بتان رکھتے ہین
آگ ہم سنگ کے مانند نہان رکھتے ہین

ایک مدت سے تمنا ہے قدم بوسی کی
سر ٹپکتا ہون صنم پاؤن جہان رکھتے ہین

مثلِ پروانہ نہین کچھ زر و مال اپنے پاس
ہم فقط تجھ پہ فدا کرنے کو جان رکھتے ہین

طائرِ روح کو کر دیتے ہین کیونکر بسمل
تیر رکھتے ہین پری رو نہ کمان رکھتے ہین

عوضِ ملکِ جہان ملکِ سخن ہے ناسخ
ہاتھ مین نقدِ سخن طبعِ روان رکھتے ہین

I keep the heat of my love for idols hidden in my heart.
I keep fire concealed in the like of rock.

For long I have yearned to kiss her feet.
Instead I dash my head wherever my idol steps.

Like a moth, I have no money or possessions.
I keep only my life to sacrifice for you.

How does she slaughter the bird of my soul?
The fairy-faced one has arrows and doesn't need a bow.

Instead of world dominion, Nasikh, you have dominion of the word. You have on hand the cash of a flowing stream of speech.

Shad

لله الحمد که از عشق صنم دل شادم — صوفی المشربم از دیر و حرم آزادم

گرد آراستگی کوچهٔ ذوقم در هجر — نقش خاکِ کفِ جانانا شده افتادم

طایر گلشنِ توحید بعلمش بودم — نالهٔ درد شده در دلِ خود آبادم

پرتوِ مهرِ تجلیِ الستم ز ازل — سوزشِ داغ محبت نرود از یادم

وا شد از فضل خدا عقدهٔ مالاینحل — شاد از غیب رسیده است مبارکبادم

Allah be praised, my heart delights in the love of an idol. A Sufi by creed, I have no need of temple or Ka'ba.

In my exile I've become an ornament in the lane of pleasure. I have fallen into the footprint of the Beloved.

Knowing Him, I am a bird in the garden of the divine Unity. A squall of pain has sounded in my indwelling heart.

I am a ray from the Sun of the epiphany of "Am I not,"[1] since pre-eternity. The burning of love's wound does not leave my mind.

By God's grace the inexplicable knot has been opened: Shad has arrived from the Unseen—I am blessed.

1 "Am I not Your Lord?" Qur'an 7:172.

36. *Rāg Bihārī, Tāl Dādrā*
middle speed, six *mātrās*

x	0	x	0	x	0
- - R	P M GR	R G GR	S S R	Ṇ - Ṇ	S R -
- - *dil*	*men po* -	*shī* - *dah*	*tap* -*i* -	*ʿish* - *q-i*	*bu tān* -
SR G MG	RS R S	♩			
rakh - -	- *te hain*				
- - R	P M GR	R G GR	S S R	Ṇ - Ṇ	S R -
- - *āg*	- *ham* -	*san* - *ga-*	*ke mā* -	*nan* - *ni*	*hā n* -
SR G MG	RS R S	♩			
rakh - -	- *te hain*				
- - S	S S -	RG R M	M P -	R - R	M P -
- - *ek*	- *mu* -	*dat* - *se*	*ta man* -	*nā* - *hai*	*qa dam* -
MP DN DP	MG R -	♩			
bo - -	*sī kī* -				
- - R	P M GR	R G GR	S S R	Ṇ - Ṇ	S R -
- - *sir*	*pa ṭak* -	*tā* - *hūn*	- *ṣanam*	*pā* - *ʿun*	*ja hān* -
SR G MG	RS R S				
rakh - -	- *te hain*				

G̲hazals of Zahir and Hafiz

Zahir

پاتے نہین ہین تجھکو چاتر گیان والے
عاجز ہین عقل والے گم ہین گمان والے

تجھکو ہے کبریائی تیری ہے سب خدائی
سب تجھکو مانتے ہین جتنے ہین مان والے

ہر جا پہ تو مکین ہے شہ رگ سے تو قرین ہے
اور پھر کہین نہین ہے اے آسمان والے

کوئی نہین رہیگا تو ہی مکین رہے گا
ہین نیست ہونے والے جتنے ہین جان والے

سب خاک ہی مین ملتے دیکھے ظہیر ہم نے
حورون کی شکل والے پریون کی شان والے

Wise sages do not attain You.
Men of reason are helpless and speculators are lost.

You have magnificence; all divinity is Yours.
Everyone believes in You, as many as have belief.

You inhabit every place; You dwell within the heart's vein,
and yet You are nowhere, O Heavenly One.

When no one remains, still You will abide,
all are to become non-existent, as many as have lives.

We have seen all things turn to dust, Zahir,
those with the figures of nymphs and those with the beauty of fairies.

Hafiz

دل میرود ز دستم صاحبدلان خدارا   دردا که راز پنهان خواهد شد آشکارا
ده روز مهر گردون افسانه است افسون   نیکی بجاے یاران فرصت شمار یارا
آسایش دو گیتی تفسیر این دو حرف است   با دوستان تلطف با دشمنان مدارا
گر مطرب حریفان این پارسی بخواند   در رقص حالت آرد پیرانِ پارسارا
حافظ بخود نپوشد این خرقۂ مے آلود   اے شیخ پاکدامن معذور دار مارا

O love's faithful, by God, my heart is getting out of control. Alas that my hidden secret should be revealed!

The kindness of fortune is a magical romance for all of ten days. My friend, count the goodness of friends as a consolation.

Ease in this world and the next is the explanation of these two words: with friends *kindness*; with enemies, *courtesy.*

Should the singer of an assembly recite this Persian, all the pious old men would come out dancing.

Hafiz did not dress himself in this wine-stained robe. O unsullied Shaikh, consider us excused.

37. *Rāg Devgirī Bilāwal, Tāl Qavāli*
middle speed, eight *mātrās*

x	0	x	0
- - M -	M - - -	M M - M	GM PD D -
- - pā -	*te - - -*	*na hīn - hain*	*tujh - ko -*
D - P M	M G R -	R SR G R	GM GR S -
- - - cā	*tur - - -*	*gyā - - n*	*vā - le -*
- - M -	M - - -	M M - M	GM PD D -
- - ‘ā -	*jaz - - -*	*hain ‘a - ql*	*vā - le -*
D - P M	M G R -	R SR G R	GM GR S -
- - gum -	*hain - - -*	*gū mā - n*	*vā - le -*
- - N -	Ṡ - - -	Ṡ Ṡ - Ṙ	ṠṘ ĠṘ Ṡ -
- - tujh -	*ko - - -*	*hai ki - bri*	*yā - ‘ī -*
Ṡ - ṠṘ ṠN	D - - -	D PD N D	NṠ ND P -
- - te -	*rī - - -*	*hai sab - <u>kh</u>u*	*dā - ‘ī -*
- - M -	M - - -	M M - M	GM PD D -
- - sab -	*tujh - - -*	*ko mā - n*	*te - hain -*
D - P M	M G R -	R SR G R	GM GR S -
- - ji ta	*ne - - -*	*hain mā - n*	*vā - le -*

Ghazals of Amir and Khusrau

Amir

مرے بس مین یا تو یارب وہ ستم شعار ہوتا
یہ نہ تھا تو کاش دل پر مجھے اختیار ہوتا

وہ مزا دیا تڑپ نے کہ یہ آرزو تھی یارب
میرے دونو پہلوؤں مین دل بیقرار ہوتا

مرے دل کو یون مٹایا کہ نشان تک نہ رکھا
مین لپیٹ کے رو تو لیتا جو کہین مزار ہوتا

جو نگاہ کی تھی ظالم تو پھر آنکھ کیون چرائی
وہی تیر کیون نہ مارا جو جگر کے پار ہوتا

مری خاک بھی لحد مین نہ رہی امیر باقی
انھین مرنے ہی کا اب تک نہین اعتبار ہوتا

O Lord, would that my oppressor were under my control,
or failing that, that I might have control of my heart.

She bestowed on me such pleasurable agony, O Lord, that I desired restless hearts on both sides of my chest.

She so completely obliterated my heart that not even a mark remains. That I might at least weep and embrace the grave wherever it might be.

The one who glanced at me, the cruel one, why did she then look away? Why did she not shoot that arrow which would have pierced my heart?

Not even dust remains of me in my grave,
while she has not yet given credit even to my dying.

Khusrau

خبرم رسید امشب کہ مزار خواہی آمد   سر من فدای راہی کہ سوار خواہی آمد
ہمہ آہوانِ صحرا سر خود نہادہ بر کف   بامید آنکہ روزی بشکار خواہی آمد
بلبم رسید جانم تو بیا کہ زندہ مانم   پس از آنکہ من نمانم بچہ کار خواہی آمد
کششی کہ عشق دارد نگذاردت بدین سان   بجنازہ گر نیائی بمزار خواہی آمد
بیک آمدن ربودی دل و دین و صبر خسرو   چہ شود اگر بدانسان دو سہ بار خواہی آمد

The news reached us today: you will come to my grave.
I am the sacrifice of the road by which, on horseback,
you will come.

The gazelles of the desert carry their heads in their palms
in the hope that one day on a hunt you will come.

My soul teeters on the brink of my lips—while I still live,
come! After I am no more, to what purpose will you come?

Love's allure did not pass you up. On this account
if you will not come for my funeral, perhaps to my grave
you will come.

Coming once, you plundered Khusrau's heart, faith, and
forbearance. How will it be if two or three times like this
you come?

38. *Rāg Bihāg Kalyān, Tāl Qavālī*

middle speed, eight *mātrās*

x	*0*	*x*	*0*
			MD PD
			me re
MP GM M -	*GR GR S R*	*GM PD MP MG*	*RG R G M*
bas - - -	*men yā - to*	*yā - rab -*	*- - voh si*
P - - -	*P GP DN D*	*P DP MP MG*	*RG - ‖ MD PD*
tam - - -	*she ʿār - -*	*ho - tā -*	*- - yeh na*
MP GM M -	*GR G RS R*	*GM PD MP MG*	*RG R G M*
thā - - -	*to kā - sh*	*dil - par -*	*- - mu jhe*
P - - -	*P GP DN D*	*P DP MP MG*	*RG - ‖ DP D*
ikh - - -	*ti yār - -*	*ho - tā -*	*- - voh ma*
Ṡ - - -	*Ṡ Ṡ - Ṡ*	*NṠ Ṙ Ṡ -*	*ND PD -*
zā - - -	*di yā - ta*	*ṛap - ne -*	*- kih yeh -*
Ṡ - Ṙ Ṡ	*N D - N*	*D PD MP GM*	*GR G ‖ MD PD*
ā - - -	*r zū - thī*	*yā - rab -*	*- - me re*
MP GM M -	*GR GR S R*	*GM PD MP MG*	*RG R G M*
do - - -	*no pah - lū*	*on - men -*	*- - dil -i*
P - - -	*P GP DN D*	*P DP MP MG*	*RG -*
be - - -	*qa rār - -*	*ho - tā -*	*- -*

Ghazals of Rasikh and Khusrau

Rasikh

نگراں کبھو نہ یہ جانب رخ دل فریب پری ہی
مری چشم مندتے مندتے تک تری محو جلوہ گری رہی

نہیں ہوش والونپہ کچھ حسد مجھے رشک ہے تو انہیں پہ ہے
جنھیں تیرے جلوے کے سامنے مری طرح بے خبری رہی

یہ جواب ہے آخر عاشقی کبھی ہوش ہو کبھی رفتگی
نہ وہ گریۂ دل شب رہا نہ وہ زاری سحری رہی

مجھے سونپ کر غم ہجر دے ہوئے یوں جدا کہ نہ پھر ملے
مرے دل میں تا دم واپسیں وہ امانت انکی دھری رہی

نہ کبھی چشم راسخ خستہ دل کبھی خالی اشک سے دوستاں
شب و روز جام پُرآب کی روش آنسوؤں سے بھری رہی

I never cast my glance toward that fairy's alluring face.
The power of your splendor went only as far as my well-covered eyes.

I do not at all envy the ones whose senses are intact.
If I am jealous, it is of those who, like me, fell senseless at the sight of your splendor.

In the end, this is the lover's reward, whether he is mindful or faraway: no longer is there weeping in the heart of the night and wailing at dawn.

She entrusted me with the pain of separation, saying we will never meet again. Until my last breath, that charge of hers remained held in my heart.

Friends, the eyes of brokenhearted Rasikh were never dry of teardrops. Night and day, like cups brimming with water, they were always full of tears.

Khusrau

اے چہرۂ زیبائے تو رشکِ بتانِ آذری   ہر چند وصفت میکنم لیکن ازان بالاتری

آفاقہا گردیدہ ام مہرِ بتان ورزیدہ ام   بسیار خوبان دیدہ ام لیکن تو چیزے دیگری

من تو شدم تو من شدی من تن شدم تو جاں شدی   تاکس نگوید بعد ازین من دیگرم تو دیگری

صورت گرِ زیبائے چین رو صورتِ یارم ببین   یا صورتِ کش این چنین یا ترک کن صورت گری

خسرو غریب است و گدا افتادہ در شہرِ شمار   باشد کہ از بہرِ خدا سوئے غریبان بنگری

O you whose lovely face is the envy of Azar's idols,[1]
however much I praise you, you are far above it.

I have roved the horizons and become acquainted with the moon among idols; I have seen many beauties, but you are something else.

I became you and you became me; I became your body and you my soul, so neither of us anymore says "you and I are different."

Painter of Chinese beauties, go, behold my friend;
render one like this or abandon your craft!

Khusrau is one of the poor, fallen a beggar in love's quarter.
Is it possible, for the sake of God, you might spare a glance on the poor?

1 Azar, father of Abraham, was a maker of idols.

39. *Rāg Bihārī, Tāl Pashto*
middle speed, fourteen *mātrā*s

x	*x*
	S S
	ni ga
R - S Ṇ - P̣ Ḍ	*S - S R - P M*
rān - ka bhū - na yeh	*jā - nab -i - ra kh-i*
G - G S - S R	*SR G R S - Ṇ S*
dil - fa rī - b pa	*rī - ra hī - me rī*
G - G G - G G	*GM G R S - P M*
ca - shma mun - da te	*mun da te tak - te rī*
G - R GR S R G	*RM G R S - Ṇ S*
ma - ḥa vi jal vah ga	*rī - ra hī - na hīn*
R G R M - M M	*PD N D P - P P*
ho - sh vā - lon pe	*kuch - ḥa sad - mu jhe*
D - Ṡ Ṡ N D -	*DṠ N D P - P D*
ra - shk gar hai to -	*in - pe hai - jin hen*
N - N D - P D	*PM G R S - S S*
te - re jal - vah ke	*sām - ne - - me rī*
RG M M GR S S R	*SR G R S -*
ṭar - aḥ be - kha ba	*rī - ra hī -*

Ghazals of Shamshad and Ishrati

Shamshad

سرمست ترنم ہون نہ سرگرم فغان ہون — مین بلبلِ شوریدۂ گم کردہ زبان ہون
قطرہ تو سمندر مین ہے مین کس مین نہان ہون — کھلتا نہین یہ بھید کہ مین کیا ہون کہان ہون
کیون صرفۂ ارباب نظر ہے مری مٹی — ہان کشتۂ تیغ نگہِ ناز بتان ہون
سمجھا ہون اقامت جسے وہ عین سفر ہے — ظاہر مین تو بیٹھا ہون حقیقت مین روان ہون
ظاہر ہے مری شورش مستانہ روی سے — شمشاد گلستانِ تمنائے جوان ہون

Neither am I a drunken song nor a passionate groan.
I am a melancholy nightingale who has lost his tongue.

A drop is in the ocean, but where am I concealed?
It does not reveal itself, this mystery of what and where I am.

Why is the clay of my grave of interest to spectators?
Oh yes, I am a victim of the sword of idols' alluring glances.

I have mistaken for rest that which is the very essence of travel: it appears that I am sitting, but in reality I am moving.

My inner turmoil is obvious from my drunken expression.
Shamshad, I am a garden of youthful desire.

Ishrati

از پنجهٔ من چاک گریبان گله دارد　　وز گریهٔ من گوشهٔ دامان گله دارد
گه بت شکنم گاه به مسجد زنم آتش　　از مذهب من گبر و مسلمان گله دارد
دامانِ نگه تنگ گل حسن تو بسیار　　گل چین بهارِ تو ز دامان گله دارد
در بزمِ وصال تو به هنگام تماشا　　نظاره ز جنبیدنِ مژگان گله دارد
گه گریه و گه خنده و گه آه جگرسوز　　ای عشرتی از وضع تو جانان گله دارد

Against my hand, my torn collar has a grievance.
Against my weeping, the soaked hem of my robe has
a grievance.

Sometimes I break idols. Other times I set fire to mosques.
Against my creed, both Zoroastrians and Muslims have
a grievance.

The skirt of a look is narrow, and the roses of beauty
profuse; against this skirt, the gathering of your springtime
flowers has a grievance.

In the feast of union with you, there is much to see right
away. Against the eyelashes' chewing, inspection has
a grievance.

Now weeping, now laughing, now sighing with a burning
heart, O Ishrati, against your lifestyle the sweetheart has
a grievance.

40. *Rāg Ẕila^c, Tāl Dādrā*

middle speed, six *mātrās*

x 0	x 0	x 0	x 0	
				Ḍ Ṉ̣
				sar -
S - R G M -	G - R R G̱ -	R - S Ṉ̣ Ḍ Ṉ̣	S - - -	
mast- ta ra n -	*num - hūn na sar -*	*gar - m fi ghān -*	*hūn - - -*	
				Ḍ Ṉ̣
				men -
S - R G M -	G - R R G̱ -	R - S Ṉ̣ Ḍ Ṉ̣	S - - -	
bul - bul -i sho -	*rī - da h-i gam -*	*kar - voh za bān -*	*hūn - - -*	
				P -
				qaṭa
P - M M M -	M - G G G -	G - R R R -	SR GM GR S	
rah - to sam un -	*dar- men hai men-*	*kis - men ni hān -*	*hūn - - -*	
				Ḍ Ṉ̣
				khul
S - R G M -	G - R R G -	R - S Ṉ̣ Ḍ Ṉ̣	S - - -	
tā - na hīn ye -	*bhe - d kih men -*	*kyā- hūn ka hān -*	*hūn - - -*	

1 *Shuddh* in the text.

Ghazal of Zafar

نہین عشق مین اسکا تو رنج ہمین کہ قرار و شکیب ذرا نہ رہا
غمِ عشق تو اپنا رفیق رہا کوئی اور بلا سے رہا نہ رہا
مین نے چاہا تھا اُسکو مین روک رکھون مری جان بھی جائے تو جانے دون
کئے لاکھون فریب ہزارون فسون نہ رہا نہ رہا نہ رہا نہ رہا
دیا اپنی خودی کو جو ہم نے مٹا وہ جو پردہ کے بیچ مین تھا نہ اُٹھا
رہا پردے مین اپنے وہ پردہ نشین کوئی دوسرا اُسکے سوا نہ رہا
نہ تھی حال کی جب ہمین اپنی خبر رہے دیکھتے اورون کے عیب و ہنر
پڑی اپنی بُرائیون پہ جبکہ نظر تو نگاہ مین کوئی بُرا نہ رہا
ظفر اُسکو نہ آدمی جانیگا وہ جو ہووے نہ صاحبِ فہم و ذکا
جسے عیش مین یادِ خدا نہ رہی جسے طیش مین خوفِ خدا نہ رہا

I was not so aggrieved in my love for her that no trace of patience or resolve remained. The pain of love remained my companion, whether or not anyone else remained.

I had wanted to stop him in his tracks, and even should my spirit leave me, not let him go. How many millions of enchantments, how many thousands of deceptions! He did not stay, he did not stay.

The one to whom I gave my self expired. He who was within the veil did not rise. He remained behind the veil, withdrawn. Except for him no one else remained.

When I have no clue of my own state, I observe the flaws and merits of others. But when my glance falls on my vices, no one else in view seems bad.

Zafar, he will not be seen as a man who lacks wisdom and insight, who does not retain in gratification the thought of God, and in anger the fear of God.

41. *Rāg Kāfī Ẕilaʿ, Tāl Qavālī*
middle speed, eight *mātrās*

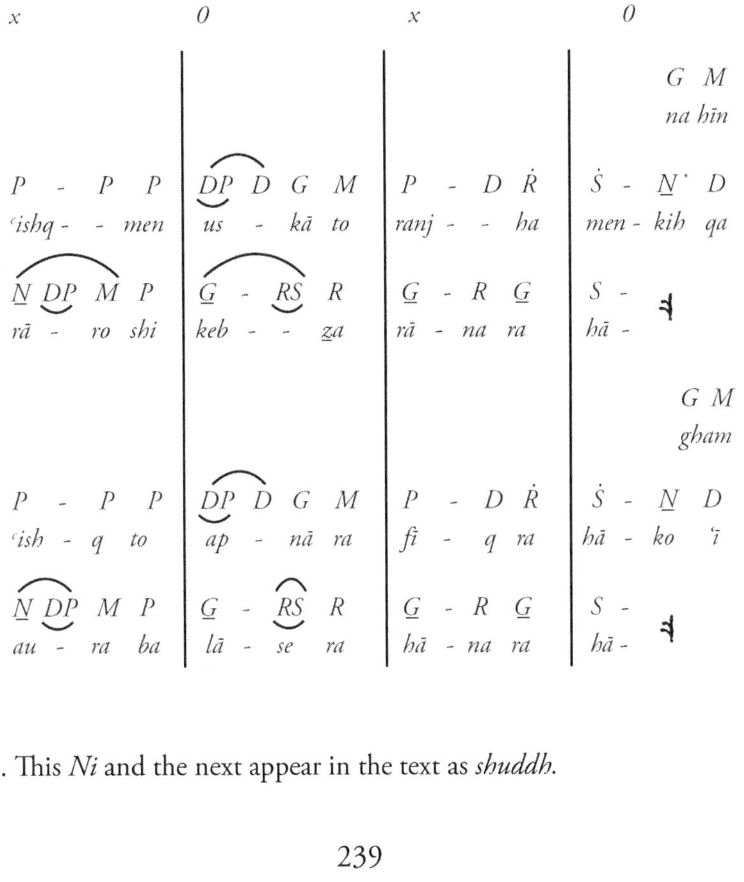

x	0	x	0
			G M
			na hīn
P - P P	DP D G M	P - D Ṙ	Ṡ - N[1] D
ʿishq - - men	*us - kā to*	*ranj - - ha*	*men - kih qa*
N DP M P	G - RS R	G - R G	S -
rā - ro shi	*keb - - za*	*rā - na ra*	*hā -*
			G M
			gham
P - P P	DP D G M	P - D Ṙ	Ṡ - N D
ʿish - q to	*ap - nā ra*	*fi - q ra*	*hā - ko ʾī*
N DP M P	G - RS R	G - R G	S -
au - ra ba	*lā - se ra*	*hā - na ra*	*hā -*

1. This *Ni* and the next appear in the text as *shuddh.*

Rāg Kāfī Ẓila[c]

x	0	x	0
			G M
			men ne
P - N N	*Ṡ - N Ṡ*	*Ṁ Ġ Ṙ Ġ*	*Ṡ - P D*
cā - hā thā	*us - ko men*	*ro - k ra*	*khūn - me rī*
N̲ - DP D	*N̲ - Ṡ Ṙ*	*ṠN Ṡ N̲ D*	*P -* ने
jān - - bhī	*jā - ʿe to*	*jā - ne na*	*dūn -*
			G M
			ka ʿe
P - P P	*DP D G M*	*P - D Ṙ*	*Ṡ - N̲ D*
lā - khon fi	*re - b ha*	*zā - ron fa*	*sūn - na ra*
N̲ DP M P	*G̲*[1] *- RS R*	*G̲ - R G̲*	*S -*
hā - na ra	*hā - na ra*	*hā - na ra*	*hā -*

1 This *Ga* appears in the text as *shuddh*.

Ghazals of Asif and Hazin

Asif

نرگس کو چشم مست سے مستانہ کر دیا
عارض پہ تو نے شمع کو پروانہ کر دیا

آئینہ خانہ کو جو پری خانہ کر دیا
جلوے نے تیرے کس کو نہ دیوانہ کر دیا

رکھا نہ ایک حال پہ عاشق کا اس نے دل
کعبہ بنا دیا کبھی بت خانہ کر دیا

وہ سختیاں اٹھائیں محبت کی راہ میں
نام اپنا تو نے ہمت مردانہ کر دیا

بیٹھے بٹھائے آج یہ کیا دل میں آ گئی
آصف نے ترک مشرب رندانہ کر دیا

With your drunken eyes, you intoxicated the narcissus.
With your appearance, you made the candle into a moth.

You, who made the house of mirrors into a fairy-house,
who has not been driven mad with your splendor?

He did not keep his lover's heart in a single state:
Now he built the Ka'ba, now he made it an idol-house.

I have suffered such hardships on the road of love.
You've made my name stand for manly courage.

What is this that unexpectedly came over me today?
Asif has renounced his creed of roguery.

Hazin

هجران رسیده کی برد از روزگار فیض　　شاخ بریده را نبود از بهار فیض

مستان اگر برند ز ابر بهار فیض　　ما می بریم از مژهٔ اشکبار فیض

بی زخم ناوکی چه کشی صید عشق را　　دل می برد ز غمزهٔ عاشق شکار فیض

اقلیم بیخودی همه فصل است خوش هوا　　دیوانه می برد ز خزان و بهار فیض

نبود حزین بروز نه ز صبح چشم ما　　ایجاد می کند دل شب زنده دار فیض

Separation has reached the point where it takes the grace out of fortune. For the broken branch, there is no springtime of grace.

If inebriates find grace in the clouds of spring,
I find it in lashes laden with tears.

Without inflicting an arrow wound how will you kill love's prey? The heart finds grace in the wink of the lover's hunter.

The climate of ecstasy is all temperate bounty:
the madman finds grace in autumn and spring.

Let my eyes not be sad (*hazīn*) in the morning or in the day: the heart of night elates one who is alive in grace.

42. *Rāg Ẕilaᶜ, Tāl Dādrā*
middle speed, six *mātrās*

x 0	x 0	x 0	x 0
			Ḍ N̲̣
			nar -
R - R R - G̲	MR G̲ R S Ṡ R	M - PM PN̲ - P[1]	MR G̲ R -
gis - ko ca - shm	*mast - - se ma -*	*stā - na kar - di*	*yā - - -*
			Ḍ N̲̣
			'ā -
R - R R - G̲	MR G̲ R S Ṡ R	M P M P N̲ P	MR G̲ R -
riz - pe tū - ne	*sham - 'a ko par -*	*vā - nah kar - di*	*yā - - -*
			N̲ -
			ā -
D - D D - D	ṠD N̲ D P P D	M - P MP N̲ P	MR G̲ R -
'e - na khā - nah	*ko - jo pa rī -*	*k̲h̲ā - nah kar - di*	*yā - - -*
			Ḍ N̲̣
			jal -
R - R R - G̲	MR G̲ R S Ṡ R	M - P MP N̲ P	MR G̲ R -
vah - ne te - re	*kis - ko na dī -*	*vā - nah kar - di*	*yā - - -*

1 The rhythm of this phrase differs in its reoccurances, likely representing various options.

Ghazals of Kaifi and Qudsi

Kaifi

گنجایش کلام کہان خیر و شر مین ہے
جب تو بشر مین ہے تو سبھی کچھ بشر مین ہے

بندہ بشر ہے عفو خطا کا امیدوار
بے بس معاملات قضا و قدر مین ہے

مین جانتا ہون اب وہ مری عزت آبرو
میری نظر مین ہے نہ تمہاری نظر مین ہے

دیوانہ پن مرا ترے جلوہ سے کم نہین
یہ بھی تو ایک بھیڑ ترے رہ گذر مین ہے

کیفی ہے سو برون کا برا پھر بھی سچ کہو
ایسا بھی کوئی شخص تمہاری نظر مین ہے

What room for disputation is there in good and evil (*shar*)?
Since you are in man (*bashar*), everything is in man.

This creature is a man hopeful of forgiveness for his faults.
He is helpless in matters of destiny and fate.

I know now that my honor
does not rest in my opinion or yours.

My madness is no less than your splendor.
This too is cause for a crowd in your street.

So Kaifi is the worst of the worst, but still, tell the truth:
in your view is there really anyone like him?

Qudsi

من لذتِ دردِ تو بدرمان نفروشم
کفرِ سرِ زلفِ تو بایمان نه فروشم

در دل ز خیالِ گلِ روئے تو خلیده
خارے که بصد گلشنِ رضوان نه فروشم

صد جان نستانم که دهم دامنت از دست
دشوار بدست آمد و آسان نفروشم

کام دو جهان در عوضِ غم نستانم
این جنس گرامی بکس ارزان نه فروشم

قدسی من و تر دامنیِ عشق چو زاهد
هرگز بکسے پاکیِ دامان نه فروشم

In exchange for the cure, I will not sell the pleasure of my sorrow over you. For faith, I will not sell the infidelity of your wink.

Visualizing the rose of your face, my heart is pierced. For a hundred gardens of paradise, I will not sell that thorn.

Not for life a hundredfold would I unhand the train of your robe. It came with great difficulty, and I will not sell it easily.

For the desire of both worlds, I would not exchange my grief. This precious commodity I will not sell to anyone cheaply.

It's just me and the guilt of love, Qudsi.
But like the renunciate, my innocence I will not sell ever to anyone.

43. *Rāg Ẕila[c], Tāl Dādrā*

middle speed, six *mātrās*

x 0	x 0	x 0	x 0	
				Ḍ Ṉ̣
				gun
S - S S - R	SR G̲ R SṈ̲ Ḍ Ṉ̣	R - S RG M R	G̲ - RS R	꠲
jā - - īsh - ka	*lā - m ka hān -*	*k͟hair- o shar - men*	*hai - - -*	
				Ḍ Ṉ̣
				jab
S - S S - R	SR G̲ R SṈ̲ Ḍ Ṉ̣	R - S RG M R	G̲ - RS R	꠲
tū - ba shar - men	*hai - to sa bhī -*	*kuch- ba shar - men*	*hai - - -*	
				S -
				ban
R G̲ R M - M	PD N̲ D P P -	M - P MP N̲ P	G̲ - RS R	
dah - ba shar - hai	*ʿaf - ū k͟haṯa -*	*kā - u mī - d*	*vār - - -*	
				Ḍ Ṉ̣
				be -
S - S S - R	SR G̲ R SṈ̲ Ḍ Ṉ̣	R - S RG M R	G̲ - RS R	
bas - mu ʿā - ma	*lā - t qa ẕā -*	*va - qa dar men -*	*hai - - -*	

Ghazals of Niyaz and Qutb

Niyaz

عشق میں تیرے کوہ غم سر پہ لیا جو ہو سو ہو
عیش و نشاط زندگی چھوڑ دیا جو ہو سو ہو

عقل کے مدرسے سے ہو عشق کے میکدہ میں آ
جام فنا و بے خودی اب تو پیا جو ہو سو ہو

لاگ کی آگ لگ چکی پنبہ طرح سا جل گیا
خطِ وجود جان و تن کچھ نہ بچا جو ہو سو ہو

ہجر کی سب مصیبتیں عرض کیں اس کے روبرو
ناز و ادا سے مسکرا کہنے لگا جو ہو سو ہو

دنیا کے نیک و بد سے کام ہم کو نیاز کچھ نہیں
آپ سے جو گذر گیا پھر اسے کیا جو ہو سو ہو

Loving you, I took a mountain of woe on my head, come what may. I gave up the comforts and pleasures of life, come what may.

You may be from the seminary of reason, but come into the tavern of love. I've now drunk from the cup of annihilation and ecstasy, come what may.

Touched by the fire of love, I burned like cotton. Nothing was spared, not body, soul, nor any mark of life, come what may.

Face to face with him, I detailed all the hardships of separation. Smiling coyly, he said, "Come what may."

Niyaz, I have no use for the good or bad of the world. After what has passed with you, how could that affect me, come what may?

Qutb

شاہ یکے سپاہ یکے یار یکے سخن یکے — مہر یکے ماہ یکے یار یکے سخن یکے

دلبر جاویدان یکے جلوہ گر بتان یکے — پوشیدہ و عیان یکے یار یکے سخن یکے

صنم و بینوا یکے پادشاہ و گدا یکے — بیدل و دلبر یکے یار یکے سخن یکے

ملت و مذہبم یکے باہمہ مشربم یکے — نالہ و زار یکے یار یکے سخن یکے

صدر شریعتم یکے قطب طریقتم یکے — سر حقیقتم یکے یار یکے سخن یکے

King and army are one, the Beloved and poetry, one;
sun and moon are one, the Beloved and poetry, one.

The eternal sweetheart and most lustrous of beauties are one; the concealed and revealed are one, the Beloved and poetry, one.

The idol and the indigent are one, the king and the beggar, one; love's victim and the sweetheart are one, the Beloved and poetry, one.

Sect and creed are one, I am one with every way;
sigh and groan are one, the Beloved and poetry, one.

I am one with the heart of the Law, one with the pole (*qutb*) of the Way; I am one with the secret of the Truth, the Beloved and poetry, one.

44. *Rāg Bhairavī, Tāl Dādrā*
middle speed, six *mātrās*

x *0*	*x* *0*	*x* *0*	*x* *0*
M D̲ D̲ P - D̲	*M - P G̲ - -*	*S S R̲ G̲ - M*	*R̲ - G̲ S - -*
'ishq - men te - re	*koh - i gham - -*	*sar par li yā - jo*	*ho - so ho - -*
M D̲ D̲ P - D̲	*M - P G̲ - -*	*S S R̲ G̲ - M*	*R̲ - G̲ S - -*
'aish-o ni shā - ṭ	*zin - da gī - -*	*choṛ - di yā - jo*	*ho - so ho - - -*
M D̲ D̲ D̲ - N̲	*Ṡ - Ṙ̲[1] Ṡ - -*	*N̲ N̲ N̲ Ṡ - Ṡ*	*Ṙ̲ Ṡ - D̲ P -*
'a ql ke mad - ra	*se - se ho - -*	*'ishq - ke mī - k*	*dah men- ā - -*
* *M D̲ D̲ P - D̲*	*M - P G̲ - -* *	*S S R̲ G̲ - M*	*R̲ - G̲ S - -*
jā m fa nā - va	*be - khū dī - -*	*ab to pi yā - jo*	*ho - so ho - -*

1 This *Re* reads *shuddh* in the text.
* begin and end here.

Ghazals of Jura't and Hafiz

Jur'at

پھرتا ہون تجھ بغیر مین ہو کے دیوانہ ہو بہ ہو — شہر بہ شہر دہ بدہ خانہ بخانہ کو بہ کو

چھوٹے وہ کس طرح سے دل آہ ہوا ہو جو اسیر — زلف بہ زلف خم بہ خم پیچ بہ پیچ مو بہ مو

روئے ہین ہم جو نوحہ گر پہنچے ہین تا اشک چشم تک — بحر بہ بحر یم بہ یم دجلہ بہ دجلہ جو بہ جو

واہ نصیب ایک شب اُس سے ہوئے تاکہ ہم — دست بدست لب بہ لب سینہ بہ سینہ رو بہ رو

دیکھا چمن مین جرأت اب جلوہ عیان ہے یار کا — شاخ بہ شاخ گل بہ گل غنچہ بہ غنچہ بو بہ بو

I wander without you, lost to reason, come what may,
city to city, town to town, house to house, lane to lane.

How can that heart gain freedom which, alas, has been
taken captive, curl by curl, lock by lock, plait by plait,
hair by hair?

I have wept with such lamentation that my tears have
surged up to my eyes, ocean by ocean, sea by sea,
lake by lake, stream by stream.

Ah fate, spare me one night relieved of sighs on her
account, hand to hand, lip to lip, breast to breast,
face to face.

Jur'at saw now in the flowerbed that there is a
manifestation of the friend, branch to branch, rose to rose,
bud to bud, scent to scent.

Hafiz

مطرب خوش نوا بگو تازه بتازه نو بنو ۔ باده دل کشا بجو تازه بتازه نو بنو

با صنمی چون لعبتی خوش بنشین بخلوتی بوسه ستان و کام از و تازه بتازه نو بنو

بر ز حیات کی خوری گر نه مدام میخوری باده بخور بیاد او تازه بتازه نو بنو

شاهد دلربای من میکند از برای من نقش و نگار و رنگ و بو تازه بتازه نو بنو

باد صبا چون بگذری بر سر کوی آن پری قصهٔ حافظش بگو تازه بتازه نو بنو

Sweet singer, intone a song—afresh, anew;
seek out heart-expanding wine—afresh, anew.

Sit in privacy with an idol like a dressed-up doll,
stealing kisses and your desire—afresh, anew.

How do you enjoy the fruit of life if you do not drink
wine? To her memory, drink wine—afresh, anew.

My heart-ravishing beloved displays for me: ornament,
embellishment, color, and fragrance—afresh, anew.

Morning breeze, when you pass over that fairy's lane,
tell her the tale of Hafiz—afresh, anew.

45. *Rāg Shankarābharan, Tāl Dādrā*

middle speed, six *mātrās*

x *0*	*x* *0*	*x* *0*	*x* *0*
Ḍ Ḍ Ḍ S - R	G - D P - -	G G R S - R	SR G R S - -
phirtā hūn tujh- ba	*ghai - r men - -*	*ho ke dī vā - nah*	*hū - ba hū - -*
P D N Ṡ - G	M - D P - -	G G R S - R	G - R S - -
sha hr ba sha hr	*dih - ba dih - -*	*khānah ba khā-nah*	*kū - ba kū - -*
Ḍ S S S - R	G - D P - -	D D D D - P	N - D P - -
chū ṭe voh kis - ṭa	*raḥ- se dil - -*	*ā h hū ā - ho*	*jo - u ser - -*
P D N Ṡ - G	M - D P - -	G G R G - S	R - Ṇ S - -
zulf- ba zul - f	*kham- ba kham - -*	*pe c ba pe - c*	*mū - ba mū - -*

Ghazals of Siraj and Sharif

Siraj

خبر تحیر عشق سن نہ جنون رہا نہ پری رہی
نہ تو تو رہا نہ تو میں رہا جو رہی سو بیخبری رہی

شہ بیخودی نے عطا کیا مجھے اب لباس برہنگی
نہ خرد کی بخیہ گری رہی نہ جنون کی پردہ دری رہی

وہ عجب گھڑی تھی کہ میں جس گھڑی لیا درس نسخۂ عشق کا
کہ کتاب عقل کی طاق میں جوں دھری تھی تیوں ہی دھری رہی

ترے جوش حیرت حسن کا اثر اس قدر سے یہاں ہوا
نہ تو آئینہ میں جلا رہی نہ پری میں جلوہ گری رہی

لیا خاک آتش عشق نے دل بینوائے سراج کو
نہ خطر رہا نہ حذر رہا جو رہی سو بے خبری رہی

Listen to the news of love's wonderment: neither madness remained nor the fairy remained. Neither was there you nor I. All that was left was oblivion.

The Shah of ecstasy has lately conferred on me the robe of nakedness. Neither the stitching of wisdom remained nor the rending of madness.

It was an hour of such amazement when I studied the manuscript of love, that the book of intellect sitting on the shelf stayed there for good.

The wonder of your beauty had such an effect here, that no sheen remained to the mirror, no splendor to the fairy.

Love's fire made ashes of the poor heart of Siraj. Neither attention nor presence remained. All that was left was oblivion.

Sharif

نه رسید طرز گشاده گل بلطافت دل تنگ ما | که بهار طرز چمن دهد ز ره تحیر رنگ ما
نگه عتاب بهم شود همه برق خرمن مهر و ماه | چه قیامت است اگر جهد شرری ز آتش سنگ ما
چو به جنگ نفس نظر کنم بتأمل شده رو نما | همه صلح سازش نفس دون به کمین نهفته ست جنگ ما
بنوازش کرم ازل شده وقف سامع تا ابد | دو جهان ست جلوهٔ شعبهٔ ز صدای نغمهٔ چنگ ما
نظر شریف یگانه بین نه فتاده است به روی کس | به تجلی دل صاف ما شده عکس غیر تو زنگ ما

The rose could not bloom on account of my enfeebled heart, for spring's path through the garden is directed by its amazement with my color.

Eyes met in reproach: lightning met the haystack, the sun met the moon. What chance is there of resurrection if a spark of fire flies up from my flint?

When I incline toward war against my ego, my intention in plain sight, my ego is all diplomacy, while behind it lies in ambush.

The hearer is rapt in the music of eternal grace until the end of time. Both worlds are emanations of the sound of my harp's melody.

Observe Sharif's singular glance; it does not alight on just anyone's face. In the mirror of my pure heart the reflection of anything but you is rust.

46. *Rāg Des, Tāl Pashto*
middle speed, fourteen *mātrās*

x	*0*	*x*	*0*

	S S
	kha b
NS RG R M - P P	*N Ṡ N Ṡ Ṙ N D*
ri - ta ḥai - yur -	*'ish q sun - - nah ju*
P - R R GR G M	*PṠ ND PM GR G M*
nūn - ra hā - na pa	*rī - ra hī - -*
	S S
	na to
NS RG R M - P P	*N Ṡ N Ṡ Ṙ N D*
tū - ra hā - na to	*men - ra hā - jo ra*
P - R R GR G M	*PṠ ND PM GR G*
hī - so be - kha ba	*rī - ra hī -*
	M M
	sha 'eh
P - P N - N N	*N Ṡ N Ṡ - D D*
be - khū dī - ne 'a	*ṭā - ki yā - mu jhe*
ṠN D P D N Ṡ Ṡ	*NṠ N D P -*
ab - li bā - s be	*rah na - ngī -*
	S S
	na khi
NS RG R M - P P	*N Ṡ N Ṡ Ṙ N D*
rū - kī bakh yah ga	*rī - ra hī - na ju*
P - R R GR G M	*PṠ ND PM GR G*
nū - n kī par dah da	*rī - ra hī -*

<u>Gh</u>azals of Amir and Ali

Amir

موقوف جرم ہی پہ کرم کا ظہور تھا
بندے اگر قصور نہ کرتے قصور تھا

میرے عمل تو قابلِ دوزخ ہی تھے مگر
کرتا جو وہ نہ رحم تو رحمت سے دور تھا

اے برقِ حسنِ یار یہ اچھا ظہور تھا
دیدار کو کلیم تھے جلنے کو طور تھا

آجائے بس میں وہ تو کہوں شبِ وصال میں
وہ شوخیاں کہاں گئیں جن پر غرور تھا

اک نیم جان کا کام نہ پورا ہوا امیر
قاتل کو تیغ ناز پہ ناحق غرور تھا

The manifestation of mercy depended on the sin:
if this slave had not fallen short, it would have been
a shortcoming.

The deeds I have committed qualify me for hell, but
he who does not act with mercy is distant from
God's mercy.

O lightning-bolt of the friend's beauty, this was a good
manifestation! It was like Moses to seeing, and like
Mount Sinai to burning.

If ever I have her in my grasp, on the night of union I will
say, "Where have those blandishments gone, of which
you were so proud?"

The work of one half dead is not yet complete, Amir.
The executioner was unduly proud of the sword of her
coquetry.

Ali

آن بیوفا که آمد و یکدم نشست و رفت
پرسید دل کجاست بگفتم شکست و رفت

تا چشم او فتاد بمن کرد رو بغیر
گویا غزال بود که فی الحال جست و رفت

خونش حلال شد عوض بادهٔ حرام
یعنی که محتسب خُم مے را شکست و رفت

شوخی چنانکه یاد توام در دلم نماند
از خاطرم خیال تو چون برق جست و رفت

دل بستگی ست حلقهٔ زنجیر زندگی
عالی خوش آنکسے که ازین قید جست و رفت

That faithless one—who came and having sat for a moment,
left—asked "How is your heart?" I said, "Broken." And she
left.

When her eye fell on me, she turned away.
You might say a gazelle sprang up at once,
and left.

His blood became lawful, as redress for unlawful wine.
In other words, the officious meddler broke the wine jar,
and left.

The provocative allure once yours lingers no longer in my
heart. Like lightning your image struck my mind,
and left.

The ring of life's chain is the confinement of the heart.
Ali, he is happy who escaped this bondage,
and left.

47. *Rāg Pīlū, Tāl Dādrā*
middle speed, six *mātrās*

x 0	x 0	x 0	x 0	
				S
				mau
G - R G R -	G R M G R G	S - R GM P M	GR G - MG RS	
qū - f jur m -	*hī - peh ka ram -*	*kā - ẓu hū - r*	*thā - - - -*	
				S
				ban
G - R G - R	G R M G R G	S - R GM P M	GR G - MG RS	
de - a gar - qa	*sū - r na kar -*	*te - qa sūr - -*	*thā - - - -*	
				S
				me
R G R M - M	PD N D P P -	M - P MP D P	M - GR G -	
re - 'a mal - to	*qā - bil do - -*	*zakh - hī the - ma*	*gar - - - -*	
				S
				kar
G - R G - R	G R M G R G	S - R GM P M	GR G - MG RS	
tā - jo voh - nah	*raḥ - m to - raḥ*	*mat - se dū - r*	*thā - - - -*	

Ghazals of Shadan and Jami

Shadan

سنین تمہاری جو ایسی باتین کہان ہے ایسا دماغ ہمکو   صنم کی باتون مین پھنس رہے ہین نہین ہے اتنو فراغ ہمکو
چمکتے ہین ستارے شب کو عجب طرح کی بہار دیکھی   پیا لایا ہے گھر ہمارے تو بھر دے ساقی ایاغ ہمکو
اگر وہ گوہر سا سامنے تھا مگر وہ ہمکو نظر نہ آیا   اندھیری راتون مین بھولتے تھے بتا دیا ہے چراغ ہمکو
تمہاری خاطر ہمارے پیارے ذرا تو دیکھو کیا ہے کیا کچھ   بھٹکتے پھرتے تھے رات اور دن ملا ہے اب تو سراغ ہمکو
اُسکی دولت سے عیش گھر گھر کہان ہے ایسا بتا دے شادان   شہ سکندر سوار ہووے تو کیون نہ جنگل ہو باغ ہمکو

How could a mind such as mine take in such words as yours? I am caught in the idol's speech, and don't have the chance.

At night, the stars twinkling, I beheld a wondrous sight: the beloved has come home—Saqi, fill our cup.

Though that jewel-like beauty was before me, I could not see him. In the dark nights I forgot, until the lamp reminded me.

My love, consider a little your affection for me. What is it all about? Having wandered after you day and night now I find only your footprint.

Tell me Shadan, why, despite his fortune, isn't there pleasure in every household? If we were Shah Alexander on horseback, wouldn't the jungle be a garden for us?

Jami

صبا ز کوی مدینه آمد نماند هوش و حواس برجا — به بوی آن زلف عنبرافشان دماغ جان گشت پر سودا

اهن نه شوقاً الی دیارٍ لقیت فیها جمال سلمی — که میرساند از آن نواحی نوید وصلت بجانب ما

بوادی غم منم فتاده زمام فکرت ز دست داده — نه بخت یاور نه عقل رهبر نه تن توانا نه دل شکیبا

حریم کوی تو کعبهٔ دل جمال روی تو قبلهٔ جان — فان سجدنا الیک نسجد وان سعینا الیک نسعی

بر آستانت کمینه جامی مجال بودن ندید از آن رو — بکنج فرقت نشست محزون بکوی محنت گرفت ماوی

A zephyr came from the lanes of Medina; all awareness was transported. By the fragrance of that ambergris-wafting hair, mind and spirit went black.

I long for the place where I met the beauty of the south wind, for from those environs I was sent the promise of union.

I am fallen in the riverbed of sorrow, the reins of your memory released from my hand. Without the friendship of fortune, the guidance of intelligence, strength of body or forbearance of heart.

The sanctuary is your lane, the Ka'ba of the heart. Beauty is your face, the prayer-niche of the soul.
Truly we have bowed down to you, truly we have aspired to you.

Servile at your threshold, Jami did not behold the breadth of Being, for he sat in the corner of your separation and took refuge in the lane of your affliction.

48. *Rāg Jogī Āsāvarī, Tāl Qavālī*
middle speed, eight *mātrās*

x	*0*	*x*	*0*
R M - M	M PM P -	M P D M	P D Ṡ -
su nen - tum	*hā - rī -*	*jo ai - sī*	*bā - ten -*
PD Ṡ - N	D - P D	M MP D P	MP GM G -
ka hān - hai	*ai - sā -*	*di mā - gh*	*ham - ko -*
R M - M	M PM P -	M P D M	P D Ṡ -
ṣa nam - kī	*bā - ton -*	*men phans - ra*	*he - hain -*
PD Ṡ - N	D - P D	M MP D P	MP GM G -
na - hīn - hai	*ab - to -*	*fa rā - gh*	*ham - ko -*
M P - D	N ṠN Ṡ -	Ṙ Ṡ - Ṙ	N - ṠṘ NṠ
ca mak - ra	*he - hain -*	*si tā - re*	*shab ko -*
D NṘ Ṡ N	D - P D	M PN D P	M G M G
'a jab - ṭa	*rah - kī -*	*ba hā - r*	*de - khī -*
R M - M	M PM P -	P P D M	P D Ṡ -
pi yā - rā	*ā - yā -*	*hai ghar - ha*	*mā - re -*
P D Ṡ N	D - P D	M MP D P	MP GM G -
to bhar - de	*sā - qī -*	*a yā - gh*	*ham - ko -*

Ghazals of Iqbal and Jami

Iqbal

سختیان کرتا ہون دل پر غیر سے غافل ہون مین
ہائے کیا اچھی کہی ظالم ہون مین جاہل ہون مین

مین جب ہی تک تھا کہ تیری جلوہ پیرائی نہ تھی
جو نمود حق سے مٹ جاتا ہے وہ باطل ہون مین

ذات ہی میری ہے کچھ میری شرافت کی دلیل
جسکی غفلت کو ملک روتے ہین وہ غافل ہون مین

جانتا ہون جلوۂ بے پردہ ہے کاشانہ سوز
سادگی دیکھو تو پھر دیدار کا سائل ہون مین

ڈھونڈتا پھرتا ہون اے اقبال اپنے آپکو
آپ ہی گویا مسافر آپ ہی منزل ہون مین

I treat my heart with harshness, oblivious to all else.
Alas, how well you said it: I am a tyrant, I am a fool.

I existed only until you arrayed your splendor. That which is erased by the appearance of truth, I am that void.

The only proof of my nobility is my inner self: I am that heedless one for whose heedlessness the angels weep.

I know that your splendor unveiled would burn down the house. But look at my simplicity: I am begging for the sight.

I wander about in search of myself, O Iqbal,
as though I am myself the traveler, I myself the destination.

Jami

کی بود یارب که رو در یثرب و بطحا کنم   گه بمکه منزل و گه در مدینه جا کنم
یا رسول الله بسوی خود مرا راه نما   تا ز فرق سر قدم سازم ز دیده پا کنم
آرزوی جنت الماوی برون کردم ز دل   جنتم این بس که در خاک درت ماوی کنم
خام از سودای پابوست نیم سر دو جهان   یا به پایت سر نهم یا سر درین سودا کنم
هر دم از شوق تو معذورم اگر هر لحظه‌ای   جامی آسا نامهٔ شوق دگر انشا کنم

O Lord, when shall I set eyes on Yathrib and Batiha,
dwell for a time in Mecca, and then in Medina?

O Messenger of Allah, show me the road in your direction,
that I may set out from separation and step beyond what I have seen.

All desire for the refuge of paradise I put out of my heart.
For me, taking refuge in the dust of your doorway is paradise enough.

O zenith of both worlds, I'm not uncooked when it comes to to the blackness (*sauda'i*) of kissing your feet. Either I place my head on your feet or I succumb to madness (*sauda*).

In my desire for you, I am always full of vain hopes.
Like Jami, every moment I draft another love letter.

49. *Rāg Sohinī, Tāl Pashto*
middle speed, fourteen *mātrās*

x			0				x			0			
G	-	*G*	*M*	*PM*	*P*	-	*D*	-	*P*	*M*	-	*P*	-
sakh	-	*ti*	*yān*	-	*kar*	-	*tā*	-	*hūn*	*dil*	-	*par*	-
M	-	*G*	*M*	-	*P*	-	*M*	-	*G*	*G*	*RN*	*S*	-
ghai	-	*r*	*se*	-	*ghā*	-	*fil*	-	*hūn*	*men*	-	-	-
G	-	*G*	*M*	*PM*	*P*	-	*D*	-	*P*	*M*	-	*P*	-
hā	-	*'e*	*kyā*	-	*a*	-	*chī*	-	*ka*	*hī*	-	*ẓā*	-
M	-	*G*	*M*	-	*P*	-	*M*	-	*G*	*G*	-	*RN*	*S*
lim	-	*hūn*	*men*	-	*jā*	-	*hil*	-	*hūn*	*men*	-	-	-
D	-	*N*	*N*	-	*Ṡ*	-	*N*	-	*D*	*P*	*M*	*P*	-
men	-	*jab*	*hi*	-	*tak*	-	*thā*	-	*kih*	*te*	-	*rī*	-
M	-	*G*	*M*	-	*P*	-	*M*	-	*G*	*G*	-	*RN*	*S*
jal	-	*vah*	*pai*	-	*rā*	-	*'ī*	-	*na*	*thī*	-	-	-
G	-	*G*	*M*	*PM*	*P*	-	*D*	-	*P*	*M*	-	*P*	-
jo	-	*na*	*mū*	-	*di*	-	*ḥaq*	-	*se*	*miṭ*	-	*jā*	-
M	-	*G*	*M*	-	*P*	-	*M*	-	*G*	*G*	-	*RN*	*S*
tā	-	*hai*	*voh*	-	*bā*	-	*ṭil*	-	*hūn*	*men*	-	-	-

Ghazal of Zafar

Zafar

ترے جو پازیب سر کا جھومر زمین پہ گوہر فلک پہ اختر
ہوئے ہین جلوہ نما چمک کر زمین پہ گوہر فلک پہ اختر
وفور اشکون کا ہے ہمارے نکلتے بالون مین ہین شرارے
نہ کیونکہ ہون عرش پہ نچھاور زمین پہ گوہر فلک پہ اختر
ذرا جبین عرق فشان پر تو اپنی افشان دکھا دے چن کر
کہان نظر آوین ماہ پیکر زمین پہ گوہر فلک پہ اختر
نہ سیر دہ گل نہ جوش شبنم نہ چمکے جگنون ہوا پہ ہر دم
نہ شب کو آتے تھے مجھکو یکسر زمین پہ گوہر فلک پہ اختر
زمین نہایت ہی تھی وہ مشکل ظفر ہے استاد پر وہ کامل
غرض دکھا دے وہی بنا کر زمین پہ گوہر فلک پہ اختر

Your anklet, your tiara, which are a gem in the earth, a star
in the sky, shining have become a resplendent sight,
a gem in the earth, a star in the sky.

In my copious tears, and falling hair are sparks of fire,
not because I am coins scattered at the throne.
a gem in the earth, a star in the sky.

As sweat streams from my forehead, show me a little of
your own diffusion, having gathered it so that it reflects
your moon-like face:
a gem in the earth, a star in the sky.

The rose does not bloom, nor does the dew surge, nor the
firefly glitter in the breeze all the time. At night they did
not used to come to me all in one place:
a gem in the earth, a star in the sky.

The earth was the very boundary; it is a difficult victory
(*ẓafar*), accomplished through the skill of the teacher.
Reveal your aim, having made it that:
a gem in the earth, a star in the sky.

50. *Rāg Jaunpūrī, Tāl Qavālī*
middle speed, eight *mātrās*

x	*0*	*x*	*0*
R M - M	M PM P -	P D - M	P DṘ ṠN̲ DP
te rī - jo	*pā - ze -*	*b sar - kā*	*jhū - mar -*
P N̲ - P	MP M G̲R G̲	R M PN̲ P	G̲ R S -
za mīn - peh	*gau - har -*	*fa lak - peh*	*ak̲h̲ - tar -*
R M - M	M PM P -	P D - M	P DṘ ṠN̲ DP
hū 'e - hain	*jal - vah -*	*nu mā - ca*	*mak - kar -*
P N̲ - P	MP M G̲R G̲	R M PN̲ P	G̲ R S -
za mīn - peh	*gau - har -*	*fa lak - peh*	*ak̲h̲ - tar -*
M M - M	P - N -	N Ṡ - Ṡ	ṀG̲ ṘṠ Ṡ -
va fū - r	*ash - kon -*	*kā hai - ha*	*mā - re -*
N D - D	N - Ṡ -	Ṙ Ṡ - Ṙ	ṠN̲ DP P -
ni kal - te	*bā - lon -*	*men hain - sha*	*rā - re -*
R M - M	M PM P -	P D - M	P DṘ ṠN̲ DP
na kyon - kih	*hūn - 'ar -*	*sh se - ni*	*chā - var -*
P N̲ - P	MP M G̲R G̲	R M PN̲ P	G̲ R S -
za mīn - peh	*gau - har -*	*fa lak - peh*	*ak̲h̲ - tar -*

Ghazals of Faiz and Nizami

Faiz

کرین ہم کسکی پوجا اور چڑھائین کسکو چندن ہم ۔ صنم ہم دیر ہم بتخانہ ہم بت ہم برہمن ہم
در و دیوار ہے نظرون مین اپنے آئینہ خانہ ۔ کیا کرتے ہین گھر بیٹھے ہی اپنا آپ درشن ہم
ہدایت ہم سے ہے پیدا ضلالت ہم سے ہے شیدا ۔ کبھی ہین رہنما اپنے کبھی ہین اپنے رہزن ہم
رہا کرتے ہین پہرون محوِ نظارہ میں ہم اپنے ۔ سراپا ہو رہے ہین اب تو اپنے آپ درپن ہم
ہوا اے فیض معلوم ایک مدت سے ہمین تھے وہ ۔ جپا کرتے تھے جسکے نام کی دنرات سمرن ہم

Whose *pūjā* shall I perform and to whom should I offer sandalwood? I am the statuary, the temple, the altar, the idol, and myself the Brahman.

In my eyes, home is my own palace of mirrors. What do I do sitting right at home? I am my own royal audience.

I inspire guidance and I provoke error. Sometimes I am my own pathfinder, other times my own highway robber.

I remain for hours dazzled by my own sight.
From head to toe, I am now becoming my own mirror.

You there, Faiz, for long I have understood: I chanted night and day the name of the one whose remembrance I am.

Nizami

شدم بر صورتِ عاشق که بر مه میکند غوغا — چه صورت صورتِ دلبر چه دلبر دلبرِ زیبا

اگر رویش نمی بینم دو چشمم چشمه گردد — چه چشمه چشمهٔ لولو چه لولو لولوئے لاله

خیالے را که می دارم غمم را همدمے باشد — چه همدم همدمِ محرم چه محرم محرمِ دلها

نگاهِ من بصد خوبی دو زلفش نگهتے دارد — چه نگهت نگهتِ عنبر چه عنبر عنبرِ سارا

مرا از بهرِ جانانہ نظامی شربتے باید — چه شربت شربتِ قابل چه قابل قابلِ جانا

The face made me a lover who howls at the moon.
What face? The face of the beloved. What beloved?
The beautiful beloved.

When I do not see her my eyes become a fountain
What sort of fountain? A fountain of pearls.
What sort of pearls? Pearls like tulips.

My thoughts seem to be the intimate friend of my grief.
What sort of intimate friend? An intimate friend who is a
confidant. What sort of confidant? A confident of hearts.

My eyes caught a glimpse of the hundredfold beauty of her
two braids. What glimpse? A glimpse of ambergris.
What ambergris? The ambergris of Sara.

On account of the beloved, Nizami, I am in need of a
draught of medicine. What medicine? A suitable medicine.
Suitable for what? Suitable for the soul.

51. *Rāg Bihāg, Tāl Qavālī*
middle speed, eight *mātrās*

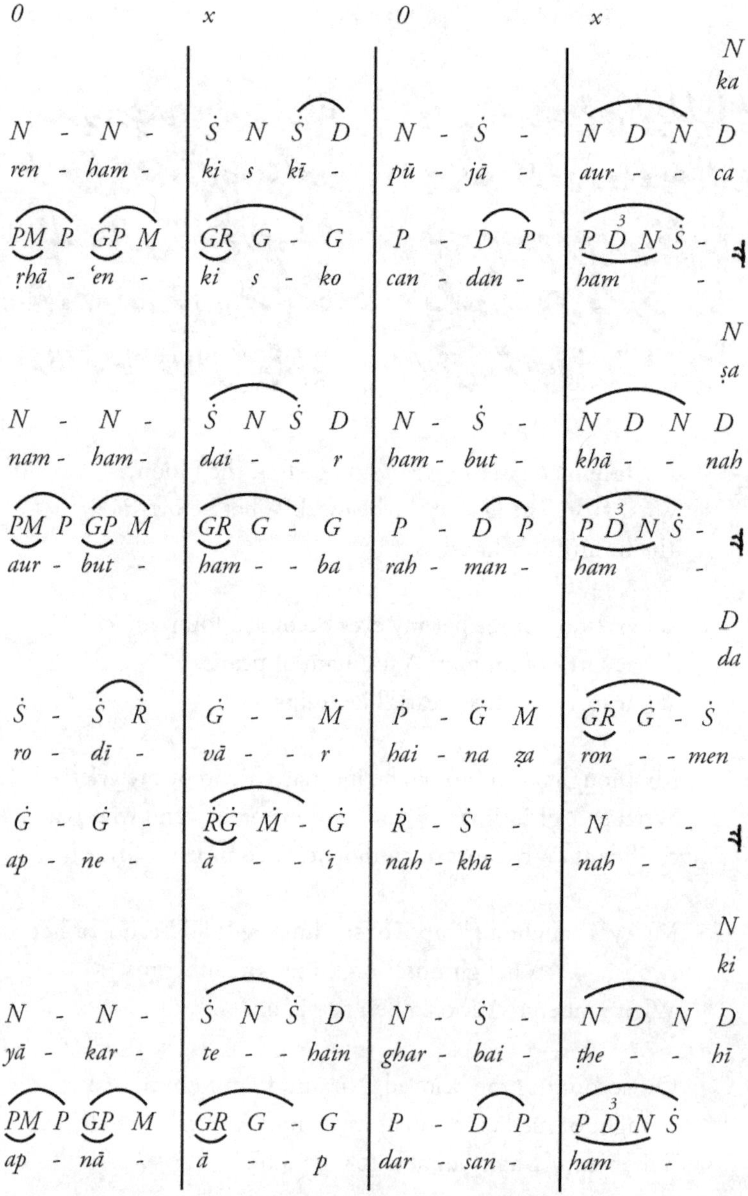

0	x	0	x	
				N
				ka
N - N -	Ṡ N Ṡ D	N - Ṡ -	N D N D	
ren - ham -	*ki s kī -*	*pū - jā -*	*aur - - ca*	
PM P GP M	GR G - G	P - D P	P D N Ṡ -	
ṛhā - 'en -	*ki s - ko*	*can - dan -*	*ham -*	
				N
				ṣa
N - N -	Ṡ N Ṡ D	N - Ṡ -	N D N D	
nam - ham -	*dai - - r*	*ham - but -*	*khā - - nah*	
PM P GP M	GR G - G	P - D P	P D N Ṡ -	
aur - but -	*ham - - ba*	*rah - man -*	*ham -*	
				D
				da
Ṡ - Ṡ Ṙ	Ġ - - Ṁ	Ṗ - Ġ Ṁ	ĠṘ Ġ - Ṡ	
ro - dī -	*vā - - r*	*hai - na ẓa*	*ron - - men*	
Ġ - Ġ -	ṘĠ Ṁ - Ġ	Ṙ - Ṡ -	N - -	
ap - ne -	*ā - - 'ī*	*nah - khā -*	*nah - -*	
				N
				ki
N - N -	Ṡ N Ṡ D	N - Ṡ -	N D N D	
yā - kar -	*te - - hain*	*ghar - bai -*	*ṭhe - - hī*	
PM P GP M	GR G - G	P - D P	P D N Ṡ	
ap - nā -	*ā - - p*	*dar - san -*	*ham -*	

Ghazals of Asif and Hasan

Asif[1]

جب اسکے کام کا نہ مرے کام کا ہے دل — پھر کس مرض کی بار خدایا دوا ہے دل

اس سنگدل کے جور و جفا پر فدا ہے دل — کمبخت میرے جان کے پیچھے پڑا ہے دل

اکسیر کے تلاش مین کیون خاک چھانئے — کشتہ کرے جو نفس کو پھر کیمیا ہے دل

کچھ وسعتِ زمین و فلک کی نہین بساط — گر حوصلہ ہو دل مین تو سب سے بڑا ہے دل

آصف کا امتحان تو کیا منصفی بھی کر — یہ ہر کسی کا حوصلہ ہر ایک کا ہے دل

When the heart is of no use either to her or to me,
then, O God, for what sickness is the heart the remedy?

My heart is the sacrifice to that stone-hearted one's anger
and violence. The miserable thing has come after my life,
that heart.

In the quest for elixir, why sift through dust?
Eliminate the ego, and the heart is the potion.

The sprawl of earth and heaven has no expanse.
When it holds aspiration, the heart is vaster than all.

Though it be Asif on trial, so what, you must still exercise
justice. My aspiration is like everyone's; everyone has
a heart.

---

1 This poem sung in a different *rāg* and *tāl* is to be heard on *Inayat Khan: The Complete Recordings of 1909*, CD 1, track 10.

Hasan

ے طالب فردوس برو سوئے محمد — چون خلد برین آمده در کوئے محمد
ے کعبہ طلب چند کنی قطع بیابان — چون کعبۂ عشاق بود روئے محمد
الشمس چہ باشد صفت وجہ شریفش — ولیل چہ باشد صفت موئے محمد
ے کعبۂ عشاق خداوند تعالے — میباش بہر حال ثنا گوئے محمد
ند حسن اینست اگر گوش بداری — اے طالب فردوس برو سوئے محمد

O seeker of paradise, go toward Muhammad,
for heaven reaches its utmost in the lane of Muhammad.

O seeker of the Ka'ba, how long will you traverse the desert? For the Ka'ba of lovers is the face of Muhammad.

How can the sun compare with his noble countenance?
How can the night compare with the hair of Muhammad?

O Ka'ba of lovers, God Most High, may one always remain a praiser of Muhammad.

Hasan's advice is this, if you have ears to hear: O seeker of paradise, go toward Muhammad.

52. *Rāg Janglā, Tāl Dādrā*

middle speed, six *mātrās*

x 0	x 0	x 0	x 0
			- S R
			- *ja b*
P - G M - P	G̲ - R S N̲̣Ḍ Ṇ̲	S - R RM G̲ R	S - - -
is - ke kā - m	*kā - na me re -*	*kā - m kā - hai*	*dil - - -*
			- S R
			- *phi r*
P - G M - P	G̲ - R S N̲̣Ḍ Ṇ̲	S - R RM G̲ R	S - - -
kis - ma raẓ - kī	*bā - r k͟hu dā -*	*yā - da vā - hai*	*dil - - -*
			- Ḍ Ṇ̲
			- *u s*
S - S G - G	RG MP M G M -	R - R G̲ - P	MM G̲R S R
san - g dil - ke	*jo - rū ja fā -*	*par - fi dā - hai*	*dil - - -*
			- S R
			- *ka m*
P - G M - P	G̲ - R S N̲̣Ḍ Ṇ̲	S - R RM G̲ R	S - - -
bak͟h- t me - rī	*jā - n ke pī -*	*che - pa ṛā - hai*	*dil - - -*

Ghazals of Zafar and Khusrau

Zafar

جلایا آپ ہم نے ضبط کر کر آہ سوزان کو — جگر کو سینہ کو پہلو کو دل کو جسم کو جان کو
جگہ کن کن کو دون دل مین ترے ہاتھون سے اے قاتل — کٹاری کو چھری کو بانک کو خنجر کو پیکان کو
ترے دندان و لب نے کر دیا بیقدر عالم مین — گہر کو لعل کو یاقوت کو ہیرے کو مرجان کو
نہ ہو جب تو ہی اے ساقی بھلا پھر کیا کرے کوئی — ہوا کو ابر کو گل کو چمن کو صحن بستان کو
بنایا اے ظفر خالق نے کب انسان سے بہتر — ملک کو دیو کو جن کو پری کو حور و غلمان کو

I burned myself up holding back my ardent sighs—
my heart, my breast, my body, and my soul.

Who-all should I give a place to in my heart, O murderer,
through your hands: the dagger, the knife, the scimitar,
the spear-tip?

Your lips and teeth have caused to be devalued in the world
the pearl, the ruby, the garnet, the diamond, and coral.

When even you are not in good spirits, O Saqi, what is
anyone to do with the breeze, the clouds, the rose,
the flowerbed, and the garden lawn?

O Zafar, when did the Creator ever make better than man
an angel, a demon, a jinn, a fairy, or a nymph?

Khusrau

تو ئی در ملک جان خسرو چه خسرو خسرو خوبان   بود نخل قدت فتنه چه فتنه فتنهٔ دوران
جمالت مجمع باشد چه مجمع مجمع خوبان   چه خوبی خوبی یوسف چه یوسف یوسف کنعان
دهانت غنچه باشد چه غنچه غنچهٔ دلکش   چه دلکش دلکش خرم چه خرم خرم خندان
بسر زلفت یکی هندو چه هندو هندوی کافر   چه کافر کافر رهزن چه رهزن رهزن ایمان
چو خسرو بندهٔ باشد چه بنده بندهٔ عاشق   چه عاشق عاشق بیدل چه بیدل بیدل هجران

In the realm of spirit, you are a king. What king?
The king of beauties. Your palmlike figure is an upheaval.
What upheaval? The upheaval of fate.

Your loveliness is a throng. What throng?
The throng of beauties. What beauty?
The beauty of Yusuf. What Yusuf? Yūsuf of Canaan.

Your mouth is a grape. What sort of grape?
A delicious grape. How delicious? Delicious as blooming.
What blooming? The blooming of laughter.

With your provocative glance, you are a Hindu. What sort
of Hindu? An infidel Hindu.
What manner of infidel? An infidel highwayman.
What kind of highwayman? A highwayman of faith.

Be, like Khusrau, a slave. What sort of slave?
A slave that is a lover. What kind of lover?
A heartsick lover. Heartsick how?
Heartsick of separation.

53. *Rāg Ẕilaᶜ, Tāl Pashto*
middle speed, fourteen *mātrās*[1]

x	0	x	0	
				PMGM-
				ja lā - yā -
P - P P - D -	*ṠṠ N̲D N̲D P MG M*	*D - P D N̲ Ṡ Ṙ*	*N̲Ṡ N̲D*	
ā - p ham - ne -	*ẓa - but kar - kar -*	*āh - so - zān - -*	*ko -*	
				PMGM-
				ji gar - ko -
P - P P - D -	*ṠṠ N̲D N̲D P MG M*	*D - P D N̲ Ṡ Ṙ*	*N̲Ṡ N̲D*	
sī - na ko - pah -	*lū - ko dil - ko -*	*jis - m ko - jān -*	*ko -*	
				N N - N -
				ja gah - kin -
N - N N - D N	*NṠ Ṙ N Ṡ - Ṡ -*	*N D P D N̲ S Ṙ*	*N̲Ṡ N̲D*	
kin - ko dūn - dil -	*men - te re - hā -*	*thon - se aye - qā -*	*til -*	
				P M G M -
				ka ṭā - rī -
P - P P - D -	*ṠṠ N̲D N̲D P MG M*	*D - P D N̲ Ṡ R*	*N̲Ṡ N̲D*	
ko - churī - ko -	*bān - k ko - k̲h̲an -*	*jar - ko pai - kā n*	*ko -*	

1 The melody is nearly identical to song no. 60.

Ghazals of Amir and Shams

Amir

کریگا یاد اے غم ہمکو بعدِ مرگ تو برسون
کھلایا ہے جگر برسون پلایا ہے لہو برسون

تڑپ کر دل نے میرے مدتون رسوا کیا مجھکو
بہا کر اشک آنکھون نے ڈوبائی آبرو برسون

نہ کر اے یاس یون برباد میرے خانۂ دلکو
اسی گھر مین جلایا ہے چراغِ آرزو برسون

فنا کے بعد ایسے بیکسون کو کون پوچھے گا
مگر اے بیکسی رویا کرے گی مجھکو تو برسون

امیر اک مصرعۂ تر تب کہین صورت دکھاتا ہے
بدن مین خشک جب ہوتا ہے شاعر کا لہو برسون

Sorrow, you will remember me after my passing, year after year. I've been fed my heart and given my blood to drink, year after year.

Fluttering, my heart tainted my reputation again and again. The flood of my tears drowned my honor, year after year.

Despair, do not thoughtlessly ransack the abode of my heart. In this house has been kindled the lamp of hope, year after year.

After we are gone, who will ask about such lonely souls? But you, O loneliness, will weep for me, year after year.

Amir, a solid verse only then sometimes shows its face when the blood in the poet's body has run dry, for years.

Shams[1]

چه تدبیرے مسلمانان که من خود را نمی دانم
نه ترسا و یهودیم نه گبرم نه مسلمانم

نه شرقیم نه غربیم نه بحریم نه بریم
نه از ملکِ عراقیم نه از خاکِ خراسانم

نه از خاکم نه از آبم نه از بادم نه از آتش
نه از آدم نه از حوا نه از فردوس رضوانم

مکانم لامکان باشد نشانم بے نشان باشد
نه تن باشد نه جان باشد نه باشد عشق جانانم

الا یا شمس تبریزی چرا مستی درین عالم
بجز مستی و مدهوشی نباشد هیچ سامانم

What can be done, O Muslims? For I do not know
myself; I am neither Christian, nor Jew, nor Zoroastrian,
nor Muslim.

I am not of the East nor of the West, neither of land
nor of sea; I am not of the kingdom of Iraq
nor of the land of Khorasan.

I am not of earth, nor of water, nor of air, nor of fire;
I am not of Adam nor of Eve, nor of Paradise.

My place is the placeless, my trace is the traceless;
I have no body, no soul, not even love for the Beloved.

O Shams Tabrizi, why in the world this drunkenness?
Drunkenness and bewilderment aside, I have no possessions.

1 See footnote on 197.

54. *Rāg Shāhānā, Tāl Qavālī*
middle speed, eight *mātrās*

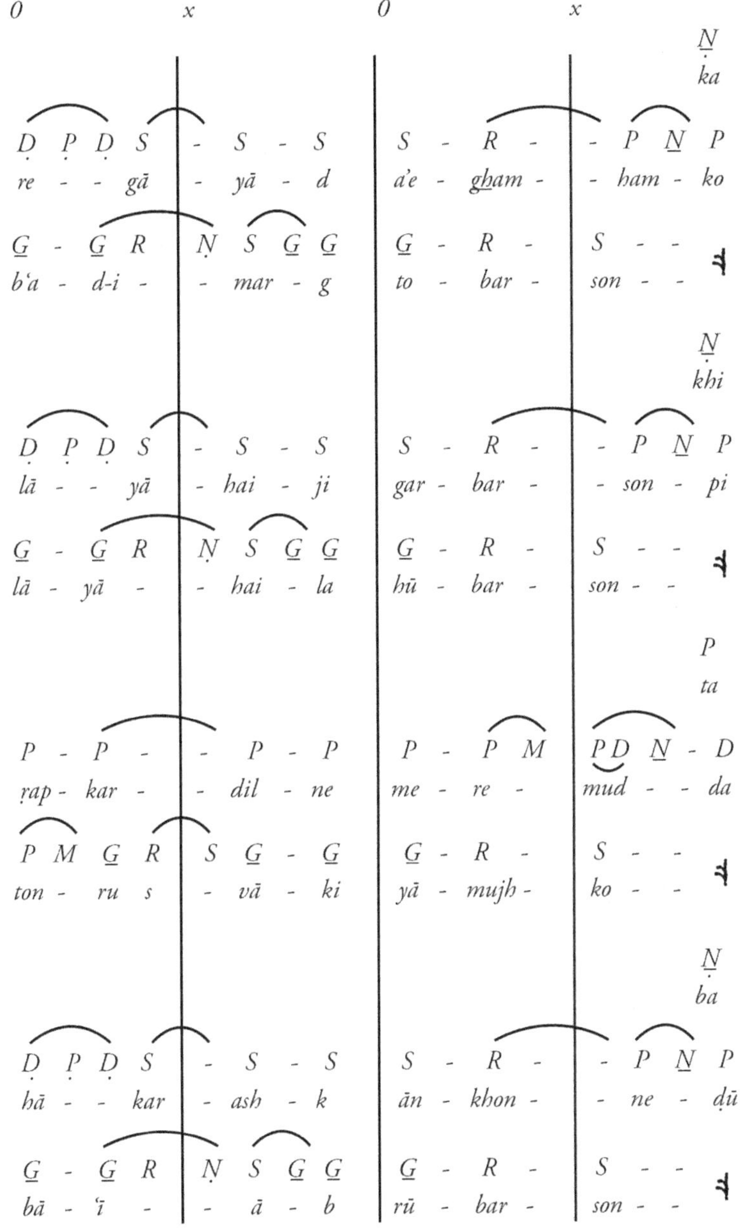

Ghazals of Asif and Saʹdi

Asif

لیتے ہیں ہنس ہنس کے میرا نام اُٹھتے بیٹھتے
پیار سے دیتے ہیں وہ دشنام اُٹھتے بیٹھتے

غیر کی تعریف میرا شکوہ اپنی خوبیاں
وہ بیان کرتے ہیں صبح و شام اُٹھتے بیٹھتے

میرے کہنے پر عمل کرتے تھے وہ دن اور تھے
اب تو ہیں ہر بات پر الزام اُٹھتے بیٹھتے

نعت میں کن مشکلوں سے طے ہوئی راہِ شوق
پہونچے ہیں منزل پہ ہر ہر گام اُٹھتے بیٹھتے

دل ہی جب بےچین ہو آصف تو کوئی کیا کرے
چلتے پھرتے ہی نہ ہے آرام اُٹھتے بیٹھتے

She takes my name laughing heartily, all the time.
She ridicules me fondly, all the time.

Another's praise, my shortcomings, her own merits:
these she discusses morning and evening, all the time.

Those days are past when my instructions were followed.
Now my word is scorned, all the time.

What problems befall one taking shelter on the road of
passion! They arrive at the lodging in each and every town,
all the time.

When the heart itself is restless, Asif, what can anyone do?
Going about one's business there's no relief, at any time.

Sa'di

ایکه می گوئی بخوبان آشنائی مشکل است   آشنائی میتوان کردن جدائی مشکل است
پیش بی دردان گریبان پاره کردن مشکل است   دل که شد بیچاره اورا چاره کردن مشکل است
زندگانی در جهان بی یار کردن مشکل است   راز دل با هر کسی اظهار کردن مشکل است
دل که رنجید از کسی خورسند کردن مشکل است   شیشه بشکسته را پیوند کردن مشکل است
سعدیا سهل است با هر کس گرفتن دوستی   لیک چون پیوند کردی باز گشتن مشکل است

O you who complain that intimacy with beauties is difficult;
intimacy is manageable—separation is difficult.

In the face of unfeeling ones, tearing your collar is difficult;
helping a heart made helpless is difficult.

To live in this world without a friend is difficult;
revealing secrets of the heart to all and everyone is difficult.

For the heart brooding over someone, cheer is difficult.
To restore a broken glass is difficult.

Sa'di, it is easy to make friends, but once joined,
to leave them again is difficult.

55. *Rāg Bhairavī, Tāl Pashto,* middle speed, fourteen *mātrās*

0	x	0	x
R̲ - S Ḏ̣ - - Ṉ̣		G̲ - R G̲ R G̲ -	
le - te hain - - hans		*hans - ke me - rā -*	
R̲G̲ R̲S Ṉ̣ S R̲ G̲ M		G̲R G̲ R̲ S Ṉ̣ S -	
nā - m u ṭh te -		*bai - ṭh te - - -*	
S - Ḏ P - Ḏ -		PM Ḏ P G̲ R G̲ -	
pyā - r se - de -		*te - hain voh - dish -*	
R̲ - Ṉ̣ S R̲ G̲ M		G̲R G̲ R̲ S Ṉ̣ S -	
nā - m u ṭh te -		*bai - ṭh te - - -*	
Ḏ - P Ḏ - Ṉ -		Ṡ Ġ̲ Ṙ̲ Ṡ Ṉ Ṉ Ṡ	
ghai - r kī - t'a -		*rīf - - me - rā -*	
Ṉ - Ṉ Ṉ - Ṡ -		Ġ̲Ġ̲ Ṙ̲Ṡ Ṉ̲Ṡ Ḏ - P -	
shak - vah ap - nī -		*k̲h̲ū - bī yān - - -*	
S - Ḏ P - Ḏ -		PM Ḏ P G̲ R G̲ -	
voh - ba yān - kar -		*te - hain ṣu ba ḥ-o -*	
R̲ - Ṉ̣ S R G̲ M		G̲R G̲ R̲ S Ṉ̣ S -	
shā - m u ṭh te -		*bai - ṭh te - - -*	

Ghazals of Hashimi and Qudsi

Hashimi

میرے مکی مدنی پیارے رسول عربی
رخ انور پہ تصدق ترے اُمّی و ابی

انس و جن پر ہی نہیں تیری نبوت کا ثبات
وحش بھی دیکھ کے کہتے ہیں تجھے انت نبی

نفسی نفسی میں ہیں جبکہ پیمبر سارے
سب پہ کھل جائیگی اس دن تری عالی نسبی

تری سرکار ہے سرکار الہی بخدا
سبھی بندے ہیں ترے کیا عجمی کیا عربی

تیرے ہی وصف میں اے شاہ مرا بھلا ہو
یہ ترا ہاشمیِ نالہ کشِ نیم شبی

My Meccan, Medinan, beloved Arabian Messenger,
I would offer up my mother and father to your luminous face.

Your prophetic mission is not confined to man and jinn alone. Beasts too, seeing you, declare "You are the Prophet."

When all the message-bearers are crying "my soul, my soul!" on that day your high descent will be made obvious to all.

Your master is the divine Master, by God!
All are your slaves, whether Arab or Aryan.

O my king, my success comes from praising you.
It is I, your midnight-groaning Hashimi.

Qudsi

مرحبا سید مکی مدنی العربی — دل و جان باد فدایت که عجب خوش لقبی
من بیدل بجمال تو عجب حیرانم — الله الله چه جمال است بدین بوالعجبی
نسبتی نیست بذات تو بنی آدم را — بهتر از عالم و آدم تو چه عالی نسبی
نسبت خود بسگت کردم بس منفعلم — زانکه نسبت بسگ کوی تو شد بی ادبی
سیدی انت حبیبی و طبیبی قلبی — آمده سوی تو قدسی پی درمان طلبی

Hail to you, Meccan Medinan Arabian lord! May my heart and soul be your sacrifice, for awe is an agreeable remainder.

Lovesick, by your beauty I am awestruck. Allah, Allah! What beauty there is in this "Father of Awe!"

Your essence is not of the pedigree of Adam: in your high descent, you surpass the world and humanity.

I traced my lineage to your dog—bashfully, for fear that a link to the dog of your lane might seem impertinent.

My lord, you are my beloved, and the physician of my heart. Qudsi has approached you in need of a cure.

56. *Rāg Kāfī Ẕila*[c], *Tāl Dādrā*

middle speed, six *mātrās*

x 0	x 0	x 0	x 0
			S R M -
			me re ma -
GM P M P P -	*D - M P P D*	*Ṡ N̲ D P MR G̲*	*R -*
kkī - - mad nī -	*pyā - re ra sū -*	*l-i - ʿa r bī -*	*- -*
			M G M -
			ru kh̲-i an -
GM PD M G̲ R -	*RM G̲ R S N̲D N̲̣*	*S - R P M G̲*	*R -*
var - peh ta ṣa -	*dduq te re u - -*	*mī - va a bī -*	*- -*
			R M M -
			ins va jin -
GM P M P P -	*D - M P P D*	*Ṡ N̲ D P MG̲ RG̲*	*R -*
par - hī na hīn -	*te - rī na bū -*	*vat - s̲ā - but -*	*- -*
			M G M -
			vaḥsh bhī -
GM PD M G̲ R -	*RM G̲ R S N̲D N̲̣*	*S - R P M G̲*	*R -*
de - kh ke kah -	*te - hain tū an -*	*ta - - na bī -*	*- -*

Ghazals of Shamshad and Mahmud

Shamshad

جب سادگی مین حُسن ہو زیور سے کیا غرض　　تیغ نظر کو زینتِ جوہر سے کیا غرض
آنکھون مین دل مین اسکی تجلی کہان نہین　　خلوت مین ہمکو شمع منور سے کیا غرض
جب دل مین تو نہو تو ہمین دل سے کام کیا　　سودا ترا جو سر مین نہین سر سے کیا غرض
مشتاق روے یار کو جنت سے کام کیا　　دیدار مست کو مئے کوثر سے کیا غرض
شمشاد ہمکو سنبلِ ریحان سے واسطہ　　مشتاق زلف یار کو عنبر سے کیا غرض

When there is beauty in simplicity, what point is there in jewelry? What point is there in ornamenting with art the sword of a glance?

In the eyes, in the heart, where isn't his splendor? In my hermit's cell, what point is there in a lighted lamp?

When you are not in my heart, then what good is the heart? What point is there in a mind that is not deranged by you?

What use has the desirer of the friend's face for paradise? For drunken eyes, what point is there in the wine of paradise's fountain?

Shamshad, in the name of sweet-smelling hyacinth, tell me: for the desirer of the friend's tresses, what point is there in ambergris?

Mahmud

امروز دیگرم بفراق تو شام شد   در آرزوے وصل تو عمرم تمام شد
آمد نماز شام و نیامد نگار من   اے دیدہ پاس دار کہ خفتن حرام شد
بستم بسے خیال کہ بینم جمال دوست   آن ہم نشد میسر و سودائے خام شد
خال تو دانہ دانہ و زلف تو دام دام   مرغیکہ دانہ دید گرفتار دام شد
محمود غزنوی کہ ہزاران غلام داشت   عشقش چنان گرفت غلام غلام شد

On another day without you evening has fallen.
Amid the hope of attaining you, my life has ended.

The evening prayer-time came, but not my idol.
Eyes of mine, keep alert, for sleep is forbidden.

I fantasized again and again of looking on the beauty of the
friend, but even thus she could not be had,
and the business was bungled.

Your beauty mark is a seed, your tresses a net.
The bird which spies the seed is for the net's taking.

Mahmud Ghaznavi, with his thousands of slaves,
in the grips of love became the slave of a slave.

57. *Rāg Jhinjhoṭī Ẕilaᶜ, Tāl Dādrā*

middle speed, six *mātrās*[1]

x 0	x 0	x 0	x 0
			Ṇ -
			jab -
S - R SN S Ṉ	D - P MP MG M	P D P PD NS N	S - - -
sā - da gī - men	*ḥu - san ho - ze*	*var - se kyā - gha*	*raẓ - - -*
			Ṇ -
			te -
S - R SN S Ṉ	D - P MP MG M	P D P PD NS N	S - - -
gh-i na ẕar - ko	*zī - - nat - jau*	*har - se kyā - gha*	*raẓ - - -*
			ṆS
			ān -
R - R R - R	SR GM G RG S R	G - M GR G R	S - - -
khon-men dil-men	*is - kī - ta jal*	*lī - ka hān - na*	*hīn - - -*
			Ṇ -
			khal -
S - R SN S Ṉ	D - P MP MG M	P D P PD NS N	S - - -
vat- men ham - ko	*sham-ʿa mu - na*	*var - se kyā - gha*	*raẓ - - -*

1 A number of rhythmic marks are missing in this notation, making interpretations necessary.

Ghazals of Amir and Hafiz

Amir

دو عالم کے سرتاج اللہ والے — مجھے اب تو قدمون مین اپنے بلالے
جفاکار دنیا جفا جو زمانہ — پڑا ہون مین دو بیوفاؤن کے پالے
کہین مجھکو ٹھنڈا نہ کردین جلا کر — مری سرد آہین مرے گرم نالے
کرے کون فریاد کس سے تمھین ہو — معیبت زدون پر ترس کھانیوالے
جدائی کے صدمے ضعیفی کا عالم — کہان تک امیر اپنے دل کو سنبھالے

Holy crown-wearer of both worlds,
Call me now to your feet.

The world is an oppressor, and the age is oppressive.
I have fallen into the clutches of two betrayers.

May they not freeze me after burning me—
my cold sighs, my hot groans.

To whom but you can anyone call out?
You, who take pity on the afflicted.

The shell of isolation, the globe of frailty:
Amir, just how long can you protect your heart?

Hafiz

دلم پے جمالت صفائی نہ دارد — چو بیگانہ کاشنائے نہ دارد
متاعِ دل پاک عشاق مسکین — بہ بازار حُسنش بہائے نہ دارد
دلا جام ساقی کل رخ طلب کن — کہ چون کل زمانہ بقائے نہ دارد
اگر چہ دلم رفت لیکن غمش نیست — بجز آن سر زلف جائے نہ دارد
چون ماہ است روشن کہ بیمہر رویت — دل و جان حافظ صفائے نہ دارد

On account of your beauty, my heart has no contentment,
just like a stranger, who has no friend.

The wares of the pure hearts of rueful lovers,
in the bazaar of her loveliness have no value.

O my heart, seek the saqi's cup from every (*kul*) face,
for like a balding head (*kal*), the world has no endurance.

Though my heart left me, she is not bothered.
Nothing more than a wink came to pass.

Like a moon, without your face's sun to light it,
the heart and soul of Hafiz have no contentment.

58. *Rāg Harī Kāmodī, Tāl Jhaptālā*
middle speed, ten *mātrās*

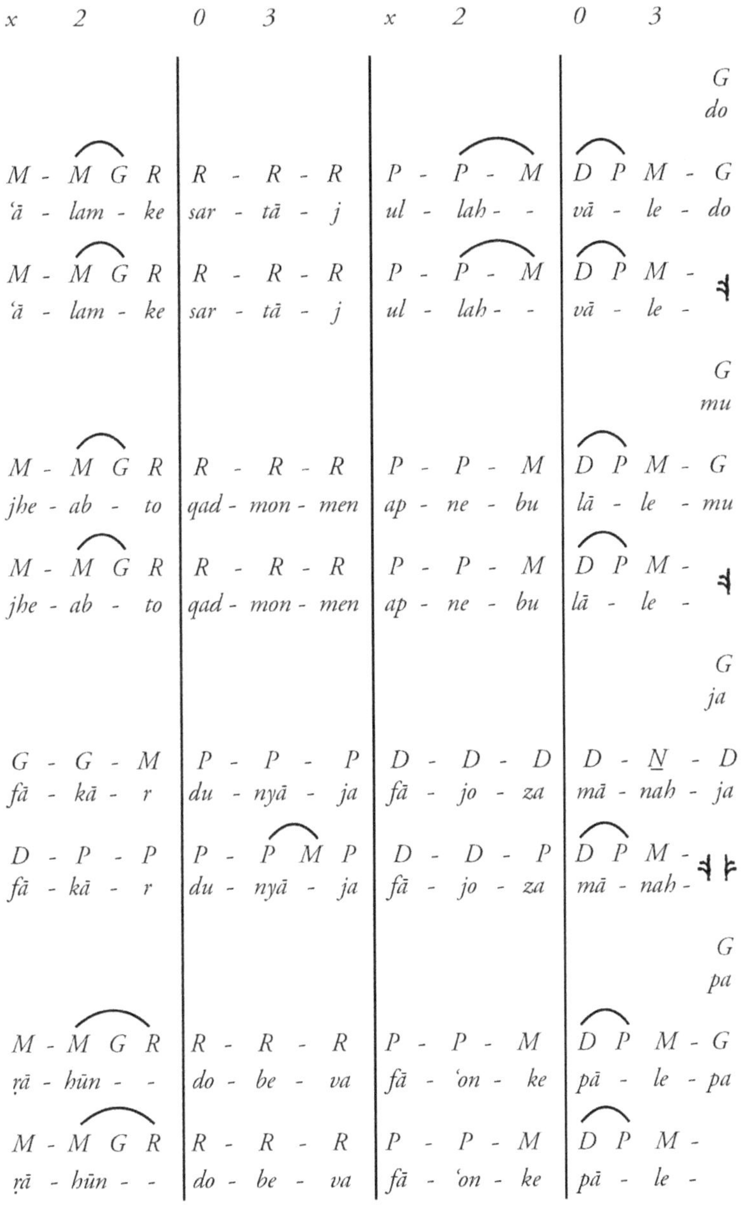

x 2	0 3	x 2	0 3	
				G
				do
M - M G R	R - R - R	P - P - M	D P M - G	
'ā - lam - ke	*sar - tā - j*	*ul - lah - -*	*vā - le - do*	
M - M G R	R - R - R	P - P - M	D P M -	
'ā - lam - ke	*sar - tā - j*	*ul - lah - -*	*vā - le -*	
				G
				mu
M - M G R	R - R - R	P - P - M	D P M - G	
jhe - ab - to	*qad - mon - men*	*ap - ne - bu*	*lā - le - mu*	
M - M G R	R - R - R	P - P - M	D P M -	
jhe - ab - to	*qad - mon - men*	*ap - ne - bu*	*lā - le -*	
				G
				ja
G - G - M	P - P - P	D - D - D	D - N̲ - D	
fā - kā - r	*du - nyā - ja*	*fā - jo - za*	*mā - nah - ja*	
D - P - P	P - P M P	D - D - P	D P M -	
fā - kā - r	*du - nyā - ja*	*fā - jo - za*	*mā - nah -*	
				G
				pa
M - M G R	R - R - R	P - P - M	D P M - G	
ṛā - hūn - -	*do - be - va*	*fā - 'on - ke*	*pā - le - pa*	
M - M G R	R - R - R	P - P - M	D P M -	
ṛā - hūn - -	*do - be - va*	*fā - 'on - ke*	*pā - le -*	

Ghazals of Ashna and Hafiz

Ashna

یہ مانا ہم نے بیارِ محبت کی دوا تم ہو
نہ آئے کام جب اپنے تو دردِ لادوا تم ہو

وفا کی ہم نے پوری بانتے جور و جفا تم ہو
نبھیگی کس طرح ہم باوفا ہین بیوفا تم ہو

ہمین یہ رشک بھی منظور ہے تم غیر کو چاہو
بھلا ہو درد الفت مین تو لذت آشنا تم ہو

خدا کو بھی پسند آتا نہین ناز و غرور اتنا
نہ بولو گے کسی سے تم تو کیا کوئی خدا تم ہو

بھروسہ غیر کو ہو گا تمہارے آشنائی کا
جو ہم سے بیوفائی ہے تو کسکے آشنا تم ہو

I supposed you were the remedy for the malady of love.
It did not work, for my pain without remedy is you.

I had complete faith in your oppression and cruelty.
How can this go on: I with faith and you, faithless.

I am also allowed to be jealous, if you love others.
If there is good in the pain of intimacy, then you are
the lover's delight.

Even God is not pleased with this much vainglory.
You won't speak to anyone—so you are some sort of god?

Will others rest assured in your friendship?
You who have betrayed me, whose friend (*āshnā*) are you?

Hafiz

اگر آن ترک شیرازی بدست آرد دل ما را بخال هندوش بخشم سمرقند و بخارا را
بده ساقی مے باقی که در جنت نخواهی یافت کنار آب رکنا باد گل گشت مصلّے را
ز عشق ناتمام ما جمال یار مستغنی است باب و رنگ و خال و خط چه حاجت روی زیبا را
حدیث از مطرب و می گو و راز دهر کمتر جو که کس نگشود و نگشاید بحکمت این معما را
غزل گفتی و در سفتی بیا و خوش بخوان حافظ که بر نظم تو افشاند فلک عقد ثریا را

If that Turk of Shiraz would lay hold of my heart, I would give Samarqand and Bukhara for her dark mole.

Saqi, pour what remains of the wine, for in heaven is not to be found the banks of the river Ruknabad, nor the rose of the garden Muṣall^{c}a.

The beauty of the friend can do without our imperfect love: what need has a beautiful face of luster and color, mole and line?

Tell the tale of singer and wine; worry less about the secret of fate, for wisdom never helped anyone solve this puzzle, and never will.

You spoke a *ghazal*, you threaded pearls; Hafiz, come, sing sweetly that the heavens may scatter over your verse the stringed Pleiades.

59. *Rāg Bhairavī, Tāl Qavālī*
middle speed, eight *mātrās*

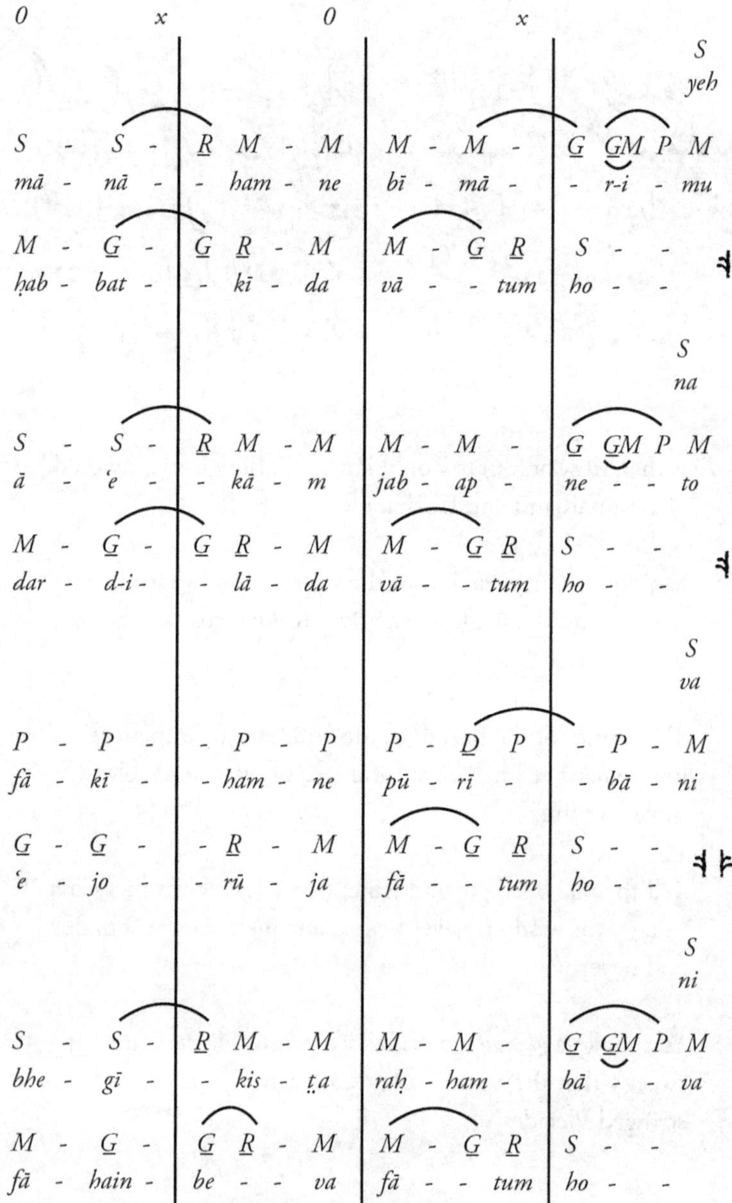

Ghazals of Mir Iqbal and Qudsi

Mir Iqbal

مجھے دنیا مٹانے کے لئے کیا کیا ترستی ہے
کہ گویا صورتِ نقشِ کفِ پا میری ہستی ہے

ہزاروں حسرتیں رونق فزائے خانۂ دل ہیں
مرے اجڑے ہوئے گھر میں بڑی مخلوق بستی ہے

نہیں کھلتا کہ میں کس واسطے ہوں کون ہوں کیا ہوں
عجب سرِ نہاں دنیا میں یا رب میری ہستی ہے

تری نظروں پہ چڑھ جانا تری نظروں سے گر جانا
سرِ راہِ محبت یہ بلندی ہے وہ پستی ہے

نہ پوچھ اے زاہدِ نافہم تو اقبال کا مذہب
کہ کعبہ کی طرح اس میں بھی جائز بت پرستی ہے

How I wish the world might be swept away
for being seems to be the form of my footprint.

The heart houses thousands of festive desires.
In my ruined home, the host lies listless.

It is not clear who I am, what I am, and what I am for.
O Lord, what a wonderful secret in the world is
my existence!

Being lifted by your glances and falling at your glances,
on the road of love, this is the exaltation and that is
the humility.

Witless moralist, do not ask about Iqbal's creed
that like to the Ka'ba, it also allows obeisance to the idol.

Qudsi

برائے سوختن یک شعله کافی نیست داغم را   صد آتش خانه باید تا کند روشن چراغم را
یکے سرگشتۂ شوق چراغِ آرزوے گل   چرا از بلبل و پروانه می جوئی سراغم را
زچشم چند جو شد خون دل چون بادهٔ ساقی   برغم دیدهٔ پُر خون بیا پُر کن ایاغم را
پریشان شد دماغم اے نسیم صبحدم برخیز   ز بوے سنبلِ زلفش معطر کن دماغم را
دلم را طاقتِ محرومیِ غم کے بود قدسی   فراقِ صحبتِ پروانه می سوزد چراغم را

A single candle is not enough to scorch my wound: to light my lamp, no less than a hundred fire-temples will do.

I am a passionate wanderer, a lamp of desire for the rose. Why do you seek signs of me among the moths and nightingales?

From my eyes how much of my heart's blood poured forth, like the saqi's wine. In spite of my blood-filled eyes, come and fill my cup.

My mind has become disturbed, O early morning breeze, arise. Perfume my mind with the hyacinth fragrance of her hair.

How does my heart have the strength to bear the frustration of its grief, Qudsi? Separation from the company of the moth is what burns my lamp.

60. *Rāg Kāfī, Tāl Pashto*
middle speed, fourteen *mātrās*[1]

0 x	*0 x*	*0 x*	*x*
			M M - G M
			mujhe - duni
P - P P - D -	*ṠṠ N̲D N̲D P M̲G M*	*D - D P D NṠ Ṙ*	*N̲D P̲D*
yā - mi ṭā - ne -	*ke - li ʿe - kyā -*	*kyā- ta ras - tī -*	*hai -*
			M M - G M
			kih go - yā -
P - P P - D -	*ṠṠ N̲D N̲D P M̲G M*	*D - D P D NṠ Ṙ*	*N̲D P̲D*
ṣū - ra ta - naq -	*sh-i - kaf-i - pā -*	*me - rī has - tī -*	*hai -*
			N N - N -
			ha zā - ron -
N - N N - D N	*NṠ Ṙ N Ṡ - Ṡ -*	*N̲ D P D N Ṡ Ṙ*	*N̲D P̲D*
ḥus-ra ten - rau -	*nak - fa zā - ʿe -*	*khā - na-e - dil -*	*men -*
			M M - G M
			me re - u ja
P - P P - D -	*ṠṠ N̲D N̲D P M̲G M*	*D - D P D NṠ Ṙ*	*N̲D P̲D*
ṛe - hu ʿe - ghar -	*men - ba ṛī - makh -*	*lū - q bas - tī -*	*hai -*

1 The melody is nearly identical to that of no.53.

Ghazals of Inayat and Munir

Inayat

دیوانہ ازل سے ہوں میں مکّی مدنی کا
مقصد ہے انھیں سے مرا ربِ ارنی کا

دکھلائے جو محبوب کو یا رب تو نہ چاہوں
جلوہ میں سرِ طور وہ ربِ ارنی کا

دوزخ کا ہے ڈر مجھکو نہ جنت کی ہے پروا
پروانہ ہوں کشتہ ہوں چراغِ یمنی کا

گم نام مرا نام ہے اور عشق مرا کام
عاشق ہوں ابو ہاشم سید مدنی کا

ہے جان محمدؐ کی مرے تن میں عنایت
مشرب ہے مرا طرز اویسِ قرنی کا

I am eternally mad with love for the one from Mecca and Medina. He is the answer to my cry, "Lord, reveal Thyself to me!"[1]

Grant me a glimpse of that Beloved, Lord, and I will not desire the epiphany you revealed to Moses on Mount Sinai. I neither fear hellfire nor hope for paradise.

I am a moth, consumed by the lamp of the one from Yemen. My name is no-name, my profession is love.

I am the lover of Abu Hashim Sayyid Madani.
The soul of Muhammad is the grace (*'ināyat*) in my body.
My way is the wellspring of 'Uwais al-Qaranī.'

1 Qur'an 7:143.

Munir

بینست چه رخ خوبی گل پیرهنی را — هرگز نکند دعوی نازک بدنی را
شوق سفر سیر گلستان مدینه — کردست فراموش خیال وطنی را
ای شمع رس روشنی خانهٔ کعبه — فخر عجمی و عربی و یمنی را
این خاک شود خاک زهی عرش بطحی — روی شب معراج رسول مدنی را
بر حال منیر جگر افگار کرم کن — از واسطهٔ روی حسن و حسینی را

It is clear which face, in its rose-adorned beauty,
never has a need to vaunt its delicacy.

The desire for an excursion to the rose garden of Medina
has left all thoughts of homeland forgotten.

O candle that brings forth the Ka'ba's light,
Pride of the 'Ajami, and of the 'Arab and Yamani.

Just imagine! My dust mingling with the dust of Batiha
in the path of the night ascent of the Medinan Messenger.

Have mercy on the condition of the broken-hearted Munir
in the name of the faces of Hasan and Husain.

61. *Rāg Bhairavī, Tāl Dādrā*
middle speed, six *mātrās*

x 0 | x 0 | x 0

S R
dī -

Ṇ - S G M - | P D P P P - | P M P DN D P
vā - nah a zal - | se - hūn men ma - | kī - ma da nī -

M - M PD P M | G - G MP M G | R - R GM GR SN | S - - -
kā - ma da nī - | kā - ma da nī - | kā - ma da nī - | kā - - -

S R
maq -

Ṇ - S G M - | P D P P P - | P M P DN D P
ṣad - hai un hīn - | se - me rā ra - | b-i - a ra nī -

M - M PD P M | G - G MP M G | R - R GM GR SN | S - - -
kī - a ra nī - | kā - a ra nī - | kā - a ra nī - | kā - - -

P -
dikh -

D - P D D N | Ṡ - R Ṡ Ṡ - | N - N ṠR Ṡ N | D - P -
lā - i jo maḥ - | bū - ba ko yā - | rabb - to na cā - | hūn - - -

P D
jal -

P - P P P - | P D P M - M | P M P DN D P
vah - men - sir - | ṭor - - voh - rab | b-i - a ra nī -

M - M PD P M | G - G MP M G | R - R GM GR SN | S - - -
kā - a ra nī - | kā - a ra nī - | kā - a ra nī - | kā - - -

Chapter Three
Instrumental Music

The term for instrumental playing is *vādan* and it ranks next after vocal music. The beauty of music not complete without instruments, because instruments satisfy the need for sounds stronger or fuller than those produced by the human voice. The sounds of brass instruments such as the *qurnā* and *tūtārī*, for instance, are several times greater than that of the human voice and reach long distances. Likewise, the sounds of the *sitār* and the *sārangī* are more full than the human voice. Instruments are of four types.

The first, *tat*, consists of those that use strings made of steel, iron, brass, gut, or silk such as the *bīn, sitār,* and *sārangī*. The second type, *vitat*, consists of instruments with a skin covering. The *daf, ḍhol, ṭabla* and *mridang* are of the *vitat* type. The third is *sūshir*, which consists of instruments played by blowing, such as the *shahnā'ī, pungī, bānsurī,* and *bherī*. The fourth type is *ghan*, and all the remaining instruments such as the *jhānjh, kaṛtāl, jaltarang* and *ghaṛā* are in this category.

Instruments have been used for several thousand years in India since the time of Mahadev and the other Hindu gods. Since the period of Muslim rule in this country instruments from such foreign countries as Egypt, Arabia, Persia, and Afghanistan as well have come into use here, and those ancient instruments have been in use ever since. There have been neither improvements nor new inventions made. This is so, firstly, because musicians have paid little attention to improvements, and secondly because of a lack of awareness and lassitude on the part of our instrument makers. Europeans have made great improvements to their instruments. In my opinion no country can rival Europe in this regard. Their military band instruments have been constructed so systematically and with such excellence that nations all over the world have appreciated and taken to playing them. Likewise, how beautifully the violin, viola, mandolin and the like are constructed, and with such good sound! And improvements are topics of discussion all the time. These days lakhs or even crores of rupees of trade in instruments is going on, and shops have been set up specifically for making instruments, in which thousands of men work.

Detailed List of Contemporary Instruments

Rudra bīn or *bīn*

This is an ancient instrument which Shivji put into circulation. This instrument has two gourds and a fingerboard *(ḍanḍī)*. It is mostly used in north India where it is called *bīn*. Its sound is soulful and pleasant. Playing it requires practice and discipline. The playing of *ālāp, dhrupad* style, and the techniques of pulling and sliding *(mīnṛ-sūnt)* are extensively done on this instrument.

Sarasvatī bīn or *vīnā*

This instrument is almost like the *bīn*. It is the Hindu goddess Sarasvati's instrument. Its lower part is like a *ṭambūrā* and the upper part has a gourd attached to the neck. This instrument is mostly found in south India, where the people revere it as holy.

Nārad bīn, ṭanbūrā, or *ṭanbūrī*

This instrument has a large gourd at its lower end, and it is a close brother to singing because its sound is customarily heard-with vocal music. It is an invention of the sage Narada. It is called *ṭanbūrā*, and a smaller instrument of the same type is called *ṭanbūrī*.

Tumburu bīn

This instrument is of the same shape as the *ṭanbūrā*. It is played with a slide *(baṭṭā)*. It is not very common. It is said to have been invented by the sage Tumburu.

Surbīn or *kamānca*
This instrument is very rarely seen.

Kachap bīn, sarod, rabāb, or *cikārā*
This instrument is shaped somewhat like a tortoise *(kachuā)*. It has gut strings and a skin-covered belly *(ṭablī)*. It is used not only in India but in Persia and Afghanistan as well. It is played with a plectrum *(javā)*. It is also called *sarod* or *rabāb*. A small instrument of this type is called *cikārā*.

Brahm bīn, surmanḍal or *qānūn*
This instrument has a four-cornered shape. One side is raised and a great many strings and sympathetic strings *(tarab)* are attached. It is played with a slide, or with two thin pieces of wood, or with a *mizṛāb* on the finger. *Brahm bīn* is an ancient name, but in contemporary times it is called *surmanḍal* or *qānūn*.

Kinnar bīn or kinarī
This instrument has three gourds attached to a single neck *(ḍānḍ)*. It is used in south India by village people and often by *jogīs*. This instrument is said to be holy.

Sharab bīn or *sharbat*
This is an instrument like the *vīnā*. Its belly *(ṭablī)* is skin-covered. It is used in south India.

Sehtār, sitār, sitārī or *sundarī*
This instrument is very widespread in the country. It is easy and enjoyable to play. *Joṛ* is played on it and *gats* are played on it too. It was invented by Janab Amir Khusrau. In common language it is called *sitār*, and a small version is called *sitārī* or *sundarī*.

Ṭāūs
The lower portion of this instrument has the shape of a peacock, and the upper portion is shaped like a *sitār*. Its belly is skin-covered and it is played with a bow.

Dilrubā

This differs from the *ṭāūs* only in shape and there is no difference in its playing technique. This instrument does not have the peacock's head.

Isrār

This is prevalent in Bengal. It is a type of *dilrubā* but its lower portion is round like a *sitār*.

Sārangī

This instrument is very common. Its usage is widespread in India. Its lower portion is skin-covered. It has gut strings and is played with a bow. It has sympathetic strings. The sound of the *sārangi* is especially well suited to female singers because of its delicacy and sweetness.

Sārinda

This instrument is constructed in the shape of a mango. It also has gut strings and is played with a bow.

Sursanghār

The lower portion of this instrument is shaped like a large *ṭanpūrā*, and the neck is very broad. Its sound is resonant. Because it does not have frets it requires practice to play. The technique *ṣūt* (slide) can sound good on this instrument and the *rabāb* style (*bāj*) can also be played. It is played with a *javā* plectrum.

Sursoṭā

This is current in the southern region. It is used in place of the *ṭanpūrā*. There is no gourd attached to it. It is shaped like a club.

Ektārā

It comes in two kinds. One is the southern *(dakhini) ektārā* in which the lower portion is like a round box, the bottom of which is covered with skin. The second type is made from a gourd. People of Marvar, Gujarat and Kathiavar sing devotional *bhajans* with it and strum its string in time with the *tāl*.

Tabla or *tabla-bāyān*
This is a set consisting of two pieces and it is very widely used. The beauty of singing and instrumental music is not fully achieved without it. The real job of the *tabla* is to provide the *tāl*, but it also provides support for the tone *(sur)*. Vocal and instrumental music without it is like soup *(dāl)* without salt.

Mridang or *pakhāvaj*
This instrument requires practice. It is like a *tabla-bāyān* set joined to each other. It is often played in accompaniment to *horī* and *dhrupad*. Its style is somewhat different from that of the *tabla*. In south India it is used not only with vocal music but with dance as well.

Naqāra, naghāra, naubat, ḍanka, daf, or *dundubhī*
This is a very ancient skin-covered instrument. In India it is played in the temples, but in former times it was played on the field of battle. In fact, messages were sent to the emperors through the *naqāra*. A small instrument of this type called *naubat* is played at the entranceway to a nobleman's home. The same type of instrument, carried with the emperor's entourage and placed on each side of the elephant or horse, is called *ḍanka*. *Daf* is a small instrument of the same sort. It was introduced here by the Arabs. Sanskrit poets call it the *dundubhī*.

Ḍhol, ḍholak, ḍholkī or *ḍhak*
The *ḍhol* is bound with leather straps and has skin covering on both ends. It is played along with the *shahnā'ī* at weddings. The *ḍholak* is a smaller instrument. It is often played at weddings by women as they sing. A small *ḍholak* is called *ḍholkī* or *ḍhak*.

Khanjarī or *ḍhapṛā*
This has skin mounted on a wide frame. It has small cymbals attached which add a *chan chan* to the sound of the skin when the drum is played. It is used in accompaniment to dance. Watchmen also play this. The *ḍhapṛā* is a large instrument of the same sort. Marvaris play it during the *holī* festival, and it

is also played to accompany *lāvanī* folk songs. It does not have cymbals on it.

Tāsha

This is a clay vessel covered with skin and played with two thin wooden sticks. It is played at weddings. The experts play it very well.

Ḍugḍugī, ḍamaru, ḍorū, budhbudī or *kā'īṛkā*

This instrument is very old. It is small and skin-covered on both sides. It is held in the middle with the hand and played by shaking it back and forth. It is said to have been invented by Hanuman. Jugglers play it during their shows. In Hindi it is called *budhbudī*, *ḍamaru*, or *ḍorū*. In the region of Malabar, several instruments of this type are played in ensemble in the temples. I saw a large instrument of the same type in Telangana which the priests and devotees of the Mother Goddess were playing with wooden sticks and which produced a terrific resonating sound. The people of that sect go into an ecstatic trance from that sound.

Sharnā'ī, shahnā'ī, mukhbīn, nāgsur, sur, na'e, or *alg̱hoza*

The *sharnā'ī* is used in every part of India. It is also played in ensembles along with the *naubat*. It is like a wooden *na'e* but its lower portion is wide. It is called *sunā'ī* in Marathi. In the language of Telangana it is called *nāgsur*. A small *sharnā'ī* is called *mukhvīnā*. There is a large instrument of this type used for keeping the drone, which is called *sur*.

Bānsurī, bansī, pāvā, murlī, na'e, or *alg̱hoza*

This is hollow and has holes. Its sound is intoxicating and alluring. One feels a sort of rapture upon hearing it. Krishna was its inventor. In Prakrit it is called *bansī*, in Marathi *pāvā*, in Sanskrit *murlī*, in Urdu *na'e*, and in Pashto *alg̱hoza*. The *murlī* or *bansī* is played held crossways to the lips. The *alg̱hoza* is held straight from the lips. There is also a practice of playing two *alg̱hozas* together.

Tūtārī, tura'ī, nafīrī, sīng, karnāh or *qurnā*
The *tūtārī* is a thin curved instrument with a wide mouth. It is also called *tura'ī*. Another instrument, the *nafīrī*, is tapered and its mouth is wide and open. Another, the *sīng*, is the same sort of instrument but is curved like a horn and is tapered. It is hung around the neck with a string. The fourth, *karnāh*, is of the same sort and is shaped something like a pestle. These four instruments are played in temples, in royal processions, and in the entourages of Rajput ladies. They are also ancient military instruments. Only two or three notes and a few improvised syllables can be played, and their sound is harsh.

Pungī
The *pungī* is made of two small pipes attached to a small gourd. Snake charmers often have one, and they use it to catch snakes. Its sound is remarkably appealing.

Mashk or surtī apang
This is an instrument made of a skin resembling a bellows. Two pipes are attached below the skin and have holes in them. The *mashk* is played by filling it with air. It is especially used in south India. This instrument is also used for giving the drone in dance. Another name for it is *surtī apang*.

Sankh
Its sound reaches very far. One feels the enjoyment of the beginningless divine in the sound of this instrument.

> What can Inayat say—Allah, Allah
> Hari is in every chant (*har*) and Allah in Allah.
>
> If there is any truth in what the eye sees,
> when destruction is destroyed, immortality remains.
>
> Every little thing of this place is protected by God;
> Truly, reality is His and every tone is Allah.

The *sankh* is often found in the entourages of *jogīs* and it is played in their establishments and temples. It produces only one note. There are some that when placed in a windy spot will produce a sound of their own accord.

Karṭāl or *caṭka*
This is made of two small flat pieces of wood. It is played by holding the pieces in one hand, or it can be played with two hands. It keeps the rhythm steady. It is also used with *bhajans*. *Bhajan* singers attach small cymbals *(manjīrā)* to them.

Jhānjh
These are cymbals, made of metal. They are played along with *ḍhol* and *tāsha*. *Manjīras* are similar but very small. Another name for this instrument is *tāl*. It is used in dance.

Jaltarang
Jaltarang is a set of china dishes filled with water and played with two wooden sticks.

Nastarang
This instrument is made like two *sharnā'īs*. It is played by placing it next to the throat and singing with the mouth closed. The sound of the singing resonates through the two instruments.

Ghanṭa, ghanṭī, cang, ghunguru, jhānjar, jhunjhūnā
The bell, *ghanṭa*, is played in the temple. A small *ghanṭa* is a *ghanṭī*. A *cang* is the same shape as a *jhunjhunā*. A very small *cang* is called *ghunguru*, which is tied to the leg in dance. *Jhānjhar* is also tied to the leg, and *jhunjhunā* is of the same family.

List of English Musical Instruments.

Accordeon	Flageolet	Piano
Ariel	Flute	Piccolo
Bagpipe	Guitar	Seraphone
Banjo	Harmonium	Symphonion
Bugle	Mandoline	Tambourine
Castagnets	Melodeon	Viola
Clarionet	Metronome	Violin
Concertina	Oboe	Violoncello
Cornet	Ocarina	Zither
Double Basse		

Sitar

Chapter Four
Rules for Playing the *sitār*

In north India the *sitār* is very widely played and there is enthusiasm for it everywhere. This chapter covers the method for playing the *sitār* along with compositions and variations *(gat, toṛā)* given systematically and in notation.

Tuning the *sitār*

The first string is tuned to *Ma* in the lower octave *(mandra saptak)*. The second and third strings are tuned to the lower *Sā*. The fourth string is tuned to lower *Pa* and the fifth to low *Pa* an octave below the fourth string. The sixth string, called *cikārī*, is tuned to middle *(mad saptak) Pa*. The seventh, called *papīyā*, is tuned to high *(tār saptak) Sā*.

The notes produced on the fourth string are *P̤ D̤ N̤̲ N̤*
The notes on the second and third strings are *Ṣ Ṛ G̣̲ G̣*
The notes produced on the first string are
Ṃ Ṃ̍ P̣ Ḍ Ṇ̲ Ṇ S R G M M̍ P D N Ṡ Ṙ Ġ . See the drawing.

Positioning the Frets

There are two systems for positioning the frets on a *sitār:* the moveable *(cal) ṭhāṭ* and the immoveable *(acal) ṭhāṭ*. In the *acal ṭhāṭ* there is no need to move any frets from their original positions to play any *rāg* because the flat and sharp *(komal, tīvra)* frets are all in place. This system is not very common. With the *cal ṭhāṭ* there are fewer frets and the frets must be moved according to the *rāg*. If one wants to place a fret in the *komal* position in the *cal ṭhāṭ* one slides the fret from its original position halfway toward the preceding fret. In the *cal ṭhāṭ* there are two frets for the *Ma*. The first is *shudh Ma* and the second is *tīvra Ma* so one does not have to move the *Ma* fret. When playing the *sitār* a *miẓrāb* is worn on the right forefinger.

Kneeling is a good position for playing the *sitār*. Otherwise any position can be used. While playing, one must keep the gourd pressed with the right arm so the *sitār* doesn't fall.

Open the right hand and place the thumb on the neck. The first finger of the right hand plays the string. The other three fingers should be kept together to assist the first. The hand and the fingers should be kept relaxed, that is they should not be rigid. The first finger of the left hand is placed on the fret and the other fingers are kept open and together alongside it. The thumb is positioned behind the neck.

The strokes *(bol)* of *sitār* playing are *dā*, *ṛā*, and *diṛ*. In *dā*, the finger of the right hand strokes inward towards oneself. In *ṛā,* the finger strokes in the opposite direction. When one plays the two strokes quickly, the sound of both blends together to become *diṛ*.

Two styles of *sitār* playing, called *bāj*, are well known. One is the *Musīdkhvānī*, in which the (*dhrupad*-style) techniques *mīnḍ*, *masak*, and *gamak* are used. The second style is *Fīrozkhvānī* or Eastern *(pūrbī)* in which everything is played with speed and playfulness.

Compositions called *gats* are played on the *sitār* in all the various *rāgs*. Fixed variations are called *toṛā*, and the variations that are extemporized by the player are called *fiqrā*.

Sitting Position for a *sitār* Player
(The Author's Father, the Late Rahmat Khan Sahab)

Chart of the Twelve *ṭhāṭs*

Number	Name	Notes
1	*Kalingṛā*	*S R̲ G M P D̲ N*
2	*Bhairavīn*	*S R̲ G̲ M P D̲ N̲*
3	*Sind Bhairavīn*	*S R G̲ M P D̲ N̲*
4	*Devgirī Bilāval*	*S R G M P D N*
5	*Jhinjhoṭī*	*S R G M P D N̲*
6	*Kāfī*	*S R G̲ M P D N̲*
7	*Pīlū*	*S R G M P D̲ N*
8	*Ṭoṛī*	*S R̲ G̲ M̍ P D N*
9	*Rāt kī Pūriyā*	*S R̲ G M̍ P D N*
10	*Din kī Pūriyā*	*S R̲ G M̍ P D̲ N*
11	*Kalyān*	*S R G M̍ P D N*
12	*Rāmkalī*	*S R̲ G M P D N*

Ten types of *gamak*

Gamak is a type of beautifying ornament (*singār*) in singing and instrumental music and there are ten varieties. Detailed explanations are given in the chart below.

Number	*Name*	*Notation*	*Method*
1	*tān (āroh)*	*SRGMPDNS* سارے گاما پا دھانی سا	The notes move upward.
2	*palṭā (avaroh)*	*SNDPMGRS* سانی دھا پا ما گا رے سا	The notes move downward.
3	*sūnth (ḍālū)*	*SG SM SP*	The finger is kept pressed down while moving from one note to another. This is called *sūntnā*, "to slide." One should not lift the finger while sliding.
4	*zamzama (sphurat)*	*RS GR MG*	The first note is sounded with the right hand and the second note is played with the left hand alone.
	murkī (sphurat)	*GRS- MGR-PMG-*	The first note is sounded with a right hand stroke, and the second and third notes are played with the left hand alone.
5	*giṭkiṛī (sphurat)*	*SNSR- RSRG- GRGM-*	The first note is sounded with the right hand, and the other three notes are played with the left hand alone.
6	*larzā (kampat)*	*S-SSSSS*	With the finger pressed down on one fret one should shake the string.
7	*gamak (āhat)*	*SRRGMGGR*	The first note is stroked with the right hand and all the other notes are produced with the left hand

Number	Name	Notation	Method
8	*ghasīṭ (pratyāhat)*	SGR-- سا گا رے	After playing the first note, play the highest note by pulling on the next fret, then return to lower note on that fret.
9	*masak (tripunca)*	SGR-- سا گا رے	All three notes are produced on one fret.
10	*mīnḍ (āndolan)*	SRG RGM GMP سا رے گا رے گا ما گا ما پا	All the notes up to the fourth are played by pulling from the fret of the first note.

Gats to Play on the *sitār*

62. *Gat*

Rāg Kāliṅgṛā, Tāl Catūsra Jātī Tetālā,
middle speed, sixteen *mātrās*

	3	x	2	0
R̲R̲	*Ṇ SS R̲ G*	*R̲ G G MM*	*G R̲R̲ S R̲*	*Ṇ S S*
diṛ	*dā diṛ dā ṛā*	*dā dā ṛā diṛ*	*dā diṛ dā dā*[1]	*dā dā ṛā*
GG	*M D̲D̲ P M*	*G G G MM*	*G R̲R̲ S R̲*	*Ṇ S S*
diṛ	*dā diṛ dā ṛā*	*dā dā dā diṛ*	*dā diṛ dā ṛā*	*dā dā ṛā*
ṠṠ	*N D̲D̲ P M*	*G G G MM*	*G R̲R̲ S R̲*	*Ṇ S S*
diṛ	*dā diṛ dā ṛā*	*dā dā ṛā diṛ*	*dā diṛ dā ṛā*	*dā dā ṛā*

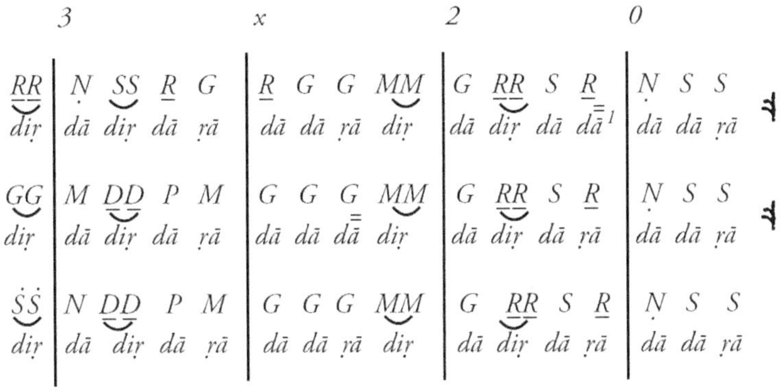

63. *Gat*

Rāg Gauṛ Mallār, Tāl Catūsra Jātī Tetālā,
middle speed, sixteen *mātrās*

x	2	0	3
M MM M G	*M PP M P*	*M G R MM*	*G RG Ṇ S*
dā diṛ dā ṛā	*dā diṛ dā ṛā*	*dā dā ṛā diṛ*	*dā diṛ dā ṛā*
R MM P D	*ṠN DP M P*	*M G R MM*	*G RR Ṇ S*
dā diṛ dā ṛā	*diṛ diṛ dā ṛā*	*dā dā ṛā diṛ*	*dā diṛ dā ṛā*

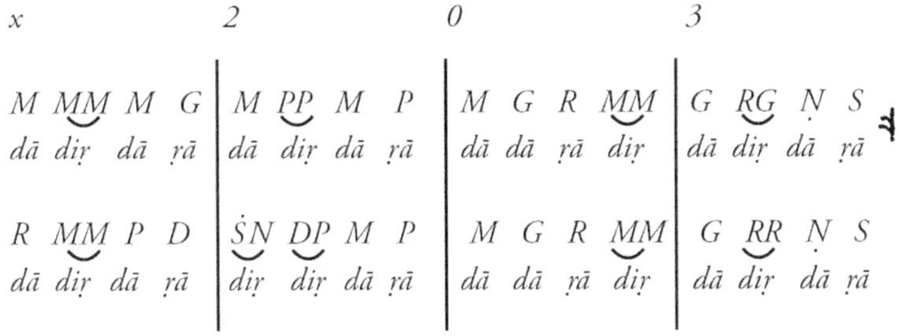

1 This notational mark is unexplained.

64. *Gat*

Rāg Sārang, Tāl Catūsra Jātī Tetālā

middle speed, sixteen *mātrās*

	3	x	2	0
N̲N̲	Ṃ P̣P̣ N̲ S	R R R PM	R SS N̲ S	R R S
diṛ	*dā diṛ dā ṛā*	*dā dā ṛā diṛ*	*dā diṛ dā ṛā*	*dā dā ṛā*
RR	M PP N̲ P	Ṡ N̲ P N̲N̲	M PM R P	M R S
diṛ	*dā diṛ dā ṛā*	*dā dā ṛā diṛ*	*dā diṛ dā ṛā*	*dā dā ṛā*

65. *Gat*

Rāg Miyān kī Malhār, Tāl Catūsra Jātī Tetālā

middle speed, sixteen *mātrās*

x	2	0	3
Ṇ ḌḌ Ṇ S	R RR R P	G̲M G̲M R SS	NS RS DN P̣
dā diṛ dā ṛā	*dā diṛ dā ṛā*	*diṛ diṛ dā diṛ*	*dā diṛ diṛ dā*
M PP D Ṡ	DN P MP DP	G̲M G̲M R S	NS RS DN P̣
dā diṛ dā ṛā	*diṛ dā diṛ diṛ*	*diṛ diṛ dā ṛā*	*diṛ diṛ diṛ dā*

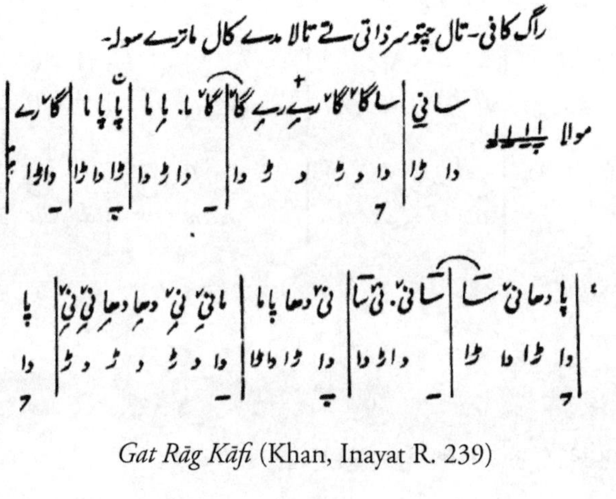

راگ کافی۔ تال چتوسر ذاتی تے تالا مدھے کال ماترے سولہ۔

Gat Rāg Kāfi (Khan, Inayat R. 239)

66. *Gat*

Rāg Jaijaivantī, Tāl Catūsra Jātī Tetālā
middle speed, sixteen *mātrās*

	3	x	2	0	
P	*R R R RR*	*R GG M P*	*M G G MM*	*G RR G S*	
ṛā	*dā dā ṛā diṛ*	*dā diṛ dā ṛā*	*dā dā ṛā diṛ*	*dā diṛ dā ṛā*	
	Ṇ SS R G	*R SS Ṇ Ḍ*	*Ṇ S S RR*	*S ṆṆ D*	
	dā diṛ dā ṛā	*dā diṛ dā ṛā*	*dā dā ṛā diṛ*	*dā diṛ dā*	
P	*S SS Ṡ Ṡ*	*N DD N Ṡ*	*ND PM GR RG*	*R SN Ḍ*	
ṛā	*dā diṛ dā ṛā*	*dā diṛ dā ṛā*	*diṛ diṛ diṛ diṛ*	*dā diṛ dā*	

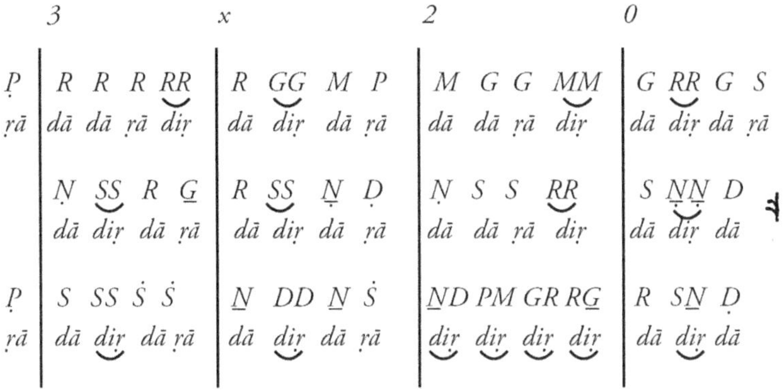

67. *Gat*

Rāg Kāfī, Tāl Catūsra Jātī Tetālā[1]
middle speed, sixteen *mātrās*

	0 ✚	3	x ٮ	2
S Ṇ	*S GG RR G*	*- M -M M*	*P - P M*	*G R*
dā ṛā	*dā diṛ diṛ dā*	*- dā -ṛ dā*	*ṛā - dā ṛā*	*dā ṛā*
- -	*P D N Ṡ*	*- N -N Ṡ*	*N D P M*	*M NN DD NN*
- -	*dā ṛā dā ṛā*	*- dā -ṛ dā*	*dā ṛā dā ṛā*	*dā diṛ diṛ diṛ*
	P D M P	*- M -M P*	*M - S Ṇ*	*S GG RR MM*
	dā ṛā dā ṛā	*- dā -ṛ dā*	*ṛā - dā ṛā*	*dā diṛ diṛ diṛ*
	✚ *G R*			
	dā ṛā			

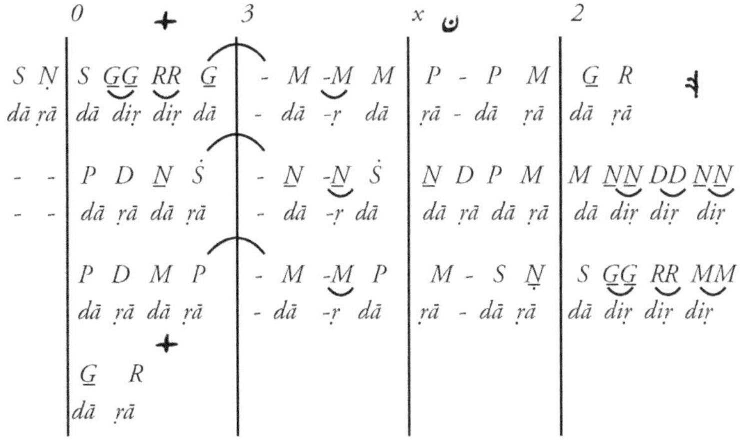

1 *Gats* 67 through 73 have stroke patterns and the fast tempo characteristic of the *purbī* style. Versions of *Gat* 67 in *rāg Kāfī* are found in virtually every oral and written collection. ✚ indicates a return to the first line at the corresponding point. ٮ indicates the end.

68. *Gat*
Rāg Ālaiyā Bilāval, Tāl Catūsra Jātī Tetālā
fast speed, sixteen *mātrās*

	2	0	3	x
S Ṇ *dā ṛā*	S GG RR SS *dā diṛ diṛ diṛ*	Ṇ ṆṆ -Ṇ ṆṆ *dā ṛdā -ṛ diṛ*	Ṗ ṖṆ -Ḍ Ṇ *dā ṛdā -ṛ dā*	S - *dā -*
P P *dā ṛā*	P DD PP PP *dā diṛ diṛ diṛ*	M MG -R G *dā ṛdā -ṛ dā*	M DD PP MM *dā diṛ diṛ diṛ*	G GR -R S *dā ṛdā -ṛ dā*
	Ṇ SS SS SS *dā diṛ diṛ diṛ*	Ṇ ṆṆ -Ṇ Ḍ *dā ṛdā -ṛ diṛ*	Ṗ ṖṆ -Ḍ Ṇ *dā ṛdā -ṛ dā*	S - *dā -*

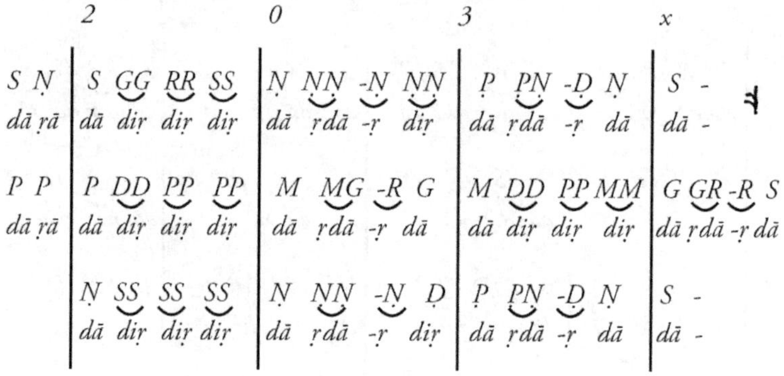

69. *Gat*
Rāg Gārā, Tāl Catūsra Jātī Tetālā
fast speed, sixteen *mātrās*

	2	0	3	x
Ṇ *dā*	Ṇ Ṇ Ṇ Ṇ *ṛā dā dā ṛā*	S GG RR SS *dā diṛ diṛ diṛ*	Ṇ ṆṖ -Ṗ Ḍ *dā ṛdā -ṛ dā*	S - - Ḍ[1] *dā - - ṛā*
	Ṗ Ḍ S R *ṛā dā dā ṛā*	G PP MM GG *dā diṛ diṛ diṛ*	R RS -S Ṇ *dā ṛdā -ṛ dā*	Ḍ RR SS R *dā diṛ diṛ dā*
	S R ṆṆ SS *ṛā dā diṛ diṛ*	Ṇ ṆḌ -Ḍ SS *dā ṛdā -ṛ diṛ*	Ṇ ṆḌ -Ṗ Ḍ *dā ṛdā -ṛ dā*	S - Ṇ Ṇ *dā - dā ṛā*
	Ḍ Ḍ Ṗ Ḍ *dā ṛā dā ṛā*	Ṗ G RR SS *dā dā diṛ diṛ*	Ṇ ṆṖ -Ṗ Ḍ *dā ṛdā -ṛ dā*	S - - *dā - -*

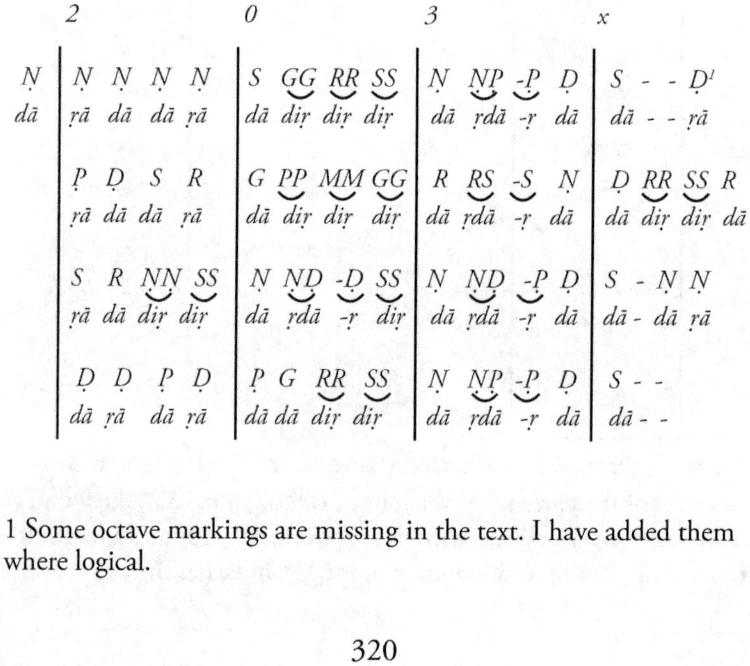

1 Some octave markings are missing in the text. I have added them where logical.

70. *Gat*
Rāg Tilak Kāmod, Tāl Catūsra Jāti Tetālā
fast speed, sixteen *mātrās*[1]

0	*3*	*x*	*2*
			- - SS ṆṆ *diṛ diṛ*
S G -G M *dā dā -ṛ dā*	*P Ṡ -Ṡ N* *dā dā -ṛ dā*	*P - G MM* *dā - dā diṛ*	*G R SS ṆṆ* *dā ṛā diṛ diṛ*
S G -G M *dā dā -ṛ dā*	*P Ṡ -Ṡ N* *dā dā -ṛ dā*	*P - [- -]* *dā - [- -]*	
			P M -R G *dā dā -ṛ dā*
M DD PP PP *dā diṛ diṛ diṛ*	*M MG -R G* *dā ṛdā -ṛ dā*	*Ṇ S R -* *dā ṛā dā -*	*G R G -* *dā ṛā dā -*
M G M - *dā ṛā dā -*	*G R G -* *dā ṛā dā -*	*P M P -* *dā ṛā dā -*	*P M P -* *dā ṛā dā -*
M G M - *dā ṛā dā -*	*G R G -* *dā ṛā dā -*	*P M P -* *dā ṛā dā -*	*P M P -* *dā ṛā dā -*
M G M - *dā ṛā dā -*	*G R G -* *dā ṛā dā -*	*G D -D N* *dā dā -ṛ dā*	*Ṡ ĠĠ ṘṘ ṠṠ* *dā diṛ diṛ diṛ*
N ND -D PP *dā ṛdā -ṛ diṛ*	*M MG -R G* *dā ṛdā -ṛ dā*	*M DD P M* *dā diṛ dā ṛā*	*G R* *dā ṛā*

1 This nice *gat* includes a repeating riff sometimes called *naghma*, traditionally played in lighter *rāgs* like *Tilak Kāmod*. The *tāl* markings are inconsistent in the book. I have added rests in brackets where they seem logical.

71. *Gat*

Rāg Sindhūṛā, Tāl Catūsra Jātī Tetālā

fast speed, sixteen *mātrās*

x	*2*	*0*	*3*
Ṡ N̲ Ṡ -	*Ṡ - P P*	*D ṘṘ ṠṠ N̲N̲*	*D DM̲ -M̲ P*
dā ṛā dā -	*dā - dā ṛā*	*dā diṛ diṛ diṛ*	*dā ṛdā -ṛ dā*
Ṡ - N̲ Ṡ	*- S P P*	*D ṘṘ ṠṠ N̲N̲*	*D DM̲ -M̲ P*
dā - ṛā dā	*- dā dā ṛā*	*dā diṛ diṛ diṛ*	*dā ṛdā -ṛ dā*
R - M -	*G̲ RR S S*	*S G̲G̲ RR MM̲*	*G̲ G̲R -R̲ S*
dā - dā -	*dā diṛ dā ṛā*	*dā diṛ diṛ diṛ*	*dā ṛdā -ṛ dā*
P - P M	*G̲ R Ṡ Ṡ*	*Ṡ ṠṠ N̲N̲ N̲N̲*	*D DM̲ -M̲ P*
dā - dā ṛā	*dā ṛā dā ṛā*	*dā diṛ diṛ diṛ*	*dā ṛdā -ṛ dā*

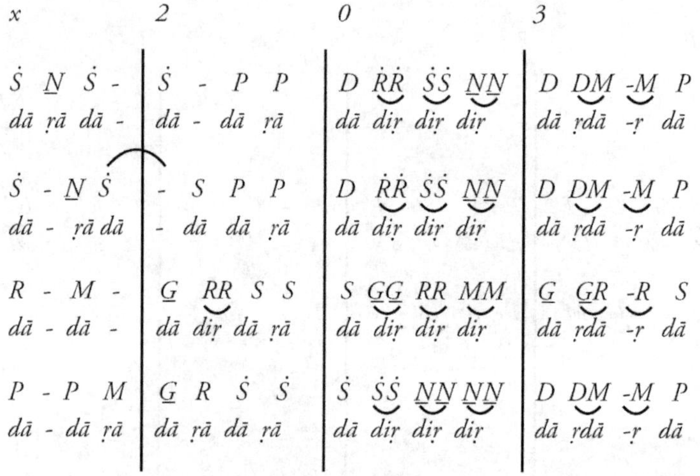

72. *Gat* and *Toṛā*

Rāg Pīlū Barvā[1], *Tāl Catūsra Jātī Tetālā*

fast speed, sixteen *mātrās*

0	*3*	*x*	*2*
Ṇ G̲G̲ R G̲	*- R̲ -S S*	*Ṇ ṆṆ SS R̲R̲*	*Ṇ ṆD̲ -D̲ P̣*
dā diṛ dā ṛā	*- dā -ṛ dā*	*dā diṛ diṛ diṛ*	*dā ṛdā -ṛ dā*
Ṃ P̣P̣ P̣P̣ Ṇ	*-Ṇ Ṇ SS SS*	*G̲ G̲R -R̲ S*	*R ṆṆ S S*
dā diṛ diṛ dā	*-ṛ dā diṛ diṛ*	*dā ṛdā -ṛ dā*	*dā diṛ dā ṛā*

Toṛā

Ṇ G̲G̲ R G̲	*- S -R R*	*G̲ MM PP MM*	*G̲ G̲R -R̲ S*
dā diṛ dā ṛā	*- dā -ṛ dā*	*dā diṛ diṛ diṛ*	*dā ṛdā -ṛ dā*

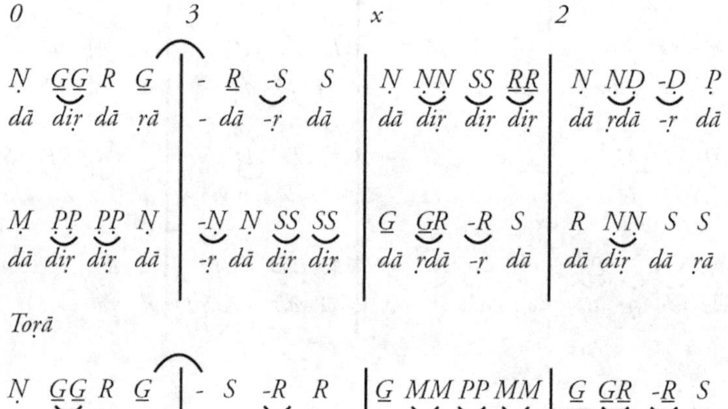

1 A vocal composition in this *rāg* can be heard on *Inayat Khan*, CD 2, track 11.

73. *Gat* and *Toṛā*
Rāg Bhairavīn, Tāl Catūsra Jātī Tetālā
fast speed, sixteen *mātrās*

3	x	2	0
N̲̣ SS G̲ M	P - P P	P PP D̲D̲ N̲N̲	D̲ D̲P -P D̲
dā diṛ dā ṛā	*dā - dā ṛā*	*dā diṛ diṛ diṛ*	*dā ṛdā -ṛ dā*
M PP G̲ M	G̲ N̲N̲ D̲D̲ PP	M MG̲ -G̲ MM	G̲ G̲R̲ -R̲ S
dā diṛ dā ṛā	*dā diṛ diṛ diṛ*	*dā ṛdā -ṛ diṛ*	*dā ṛdā -ṛ dā*

Toṛā

		D̲ D̲D̲ D̲D̲ N̲N̲	Ṡ ṠṠ -Ṡ Ṡ
		dā diṛ diṛ diṛ	*dā ṛdā -ṛ dā*
D̲ D̲D̲ D̲D̲ N̲N̲	Ṡ ṠṠ -Ṡ Ṡ	N̲ Ġ̲Ġ̲ Ṙ̲ Ġ̲	Ṡ Ṙ̲Ṙ̲ N Ṡ
dā diṛ diṛ diṛ	*dā ṛdā -ṛ dā*	*dā diṛ dā ṛā*	*dā diṛ dā ṛā*
D̲ N̲N̲ P D̲	M PP G̲ M	G̲ N̲N̲ D̲D̲ PP	G̲ G̲R̲ -R̲ S
dā diṛ dā ṛā	*dā diṛ dā ṛā*	*dā diṛ diṛ diṛ*	*dā ṛdā -ṛ dā*

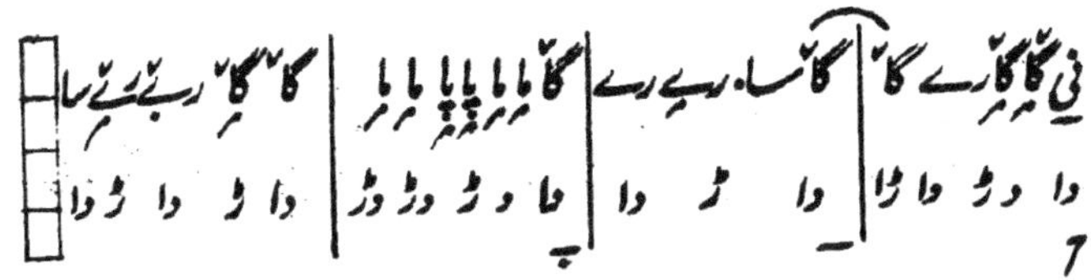

Toṛā, Rāg Pīlū Barvā
(Khan, Inayat R. 145)

74. *Gat* and *Toṛā*
Rāg Rāmkalī, Tāl Catūsra Jātī Tetālā,
middle speed, sixteen *mātrās*[1]

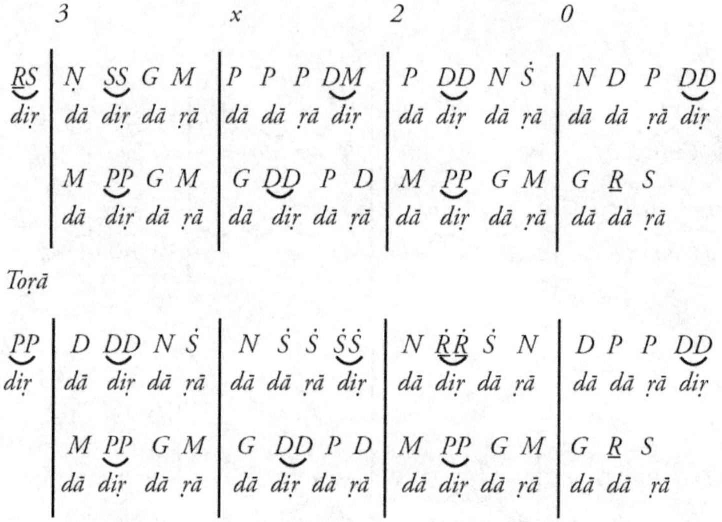

	3	x	2	0
R̲S *diṛ*	*Ṇ SS G M* *dā diṛ dā ṛā*	*P P P DM* *dā dā ṛā diṛ*	*P DD N Ṡ* *dā diṛ dā ṛā*	*N D P DD* *dā dā ṛā diṛ*
	M PP G M *dā diṛ dā ṛā*	*G DD P D* *dā diṛ dā ṛā*	*M PP G M* *dā diṛ dā ṛā*	*G R̲ S* *dā dā ṛā*

Toṛā

PP *diṛ*	*D DD N Ṡ* *dā diṛ dā ṛā*	*N Ṡ Ṡ ṠṠ* *dā dā ṛā diṛ*	*N Ṙ̲Ṙ̲ Ṡ N* *dā diṛ dā ṛā*	*D P P DD* *dā dā ṛā diṛ*
	M PP G M *dā diṛ dā ṛā*	*G DD P D* *dā diṛ dā ṛā*	*M PP G M* *dā diṛ dā ṛā*	*G R̲ S* *dā dā ṛā*

75. *Gat* and *Toṛā*
Rāg Jogiyā, Tāl Catūsra Jātī Tetālā
middle speed, sixteen *mātrās*

	3	x	2	0
SS *diṛ*	*R̲ MM P D̲* *dā diṛ dā ṛā*	*Ṡ Ṡ Ṡ ṠṠ* *dā dā ṛā diṛ*	*N Ṙ̲Ṙ̲ NN ṠṠ* *dā diṛ diṛ diṛ*	*N D̲ P ṠṠ* *dā dā ṛā diṛ*
	N D̲D̲ P P *dā diṛ dā ṛā*	*N D̲D̲ P M* *dā diṛ dā ṛā*	*D̲ PP M G* *dā diṛ dā ṛā*	*R̲ S S* *dā dā ṛā*

Toṛā

SS *diṛ*	*R̲ MM P D* *dā diṛ dā ṛā*	*ṠṠ NN ṠṠ NN* *diṛ diṛ diṛ diṛ*	*D̲D̲ PP MM GG* *diṛ diṛ diṛ diṛ*	*R̲ S S* *dā dā ṛā*

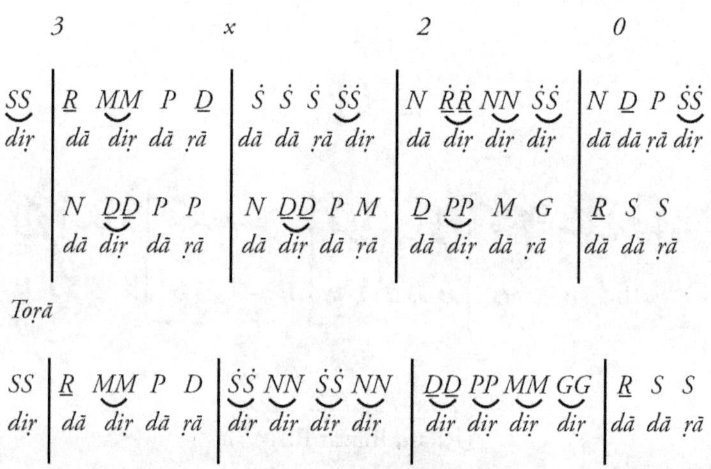

1 The stroke pattern identifies this and the next as a *Masītkhānī gat*

76. *Gat* and *Toṛā*
Rāg Pūrbī, Tāl Catūsra Jātī Tetālā
middle speed, sixteen *mātrās*

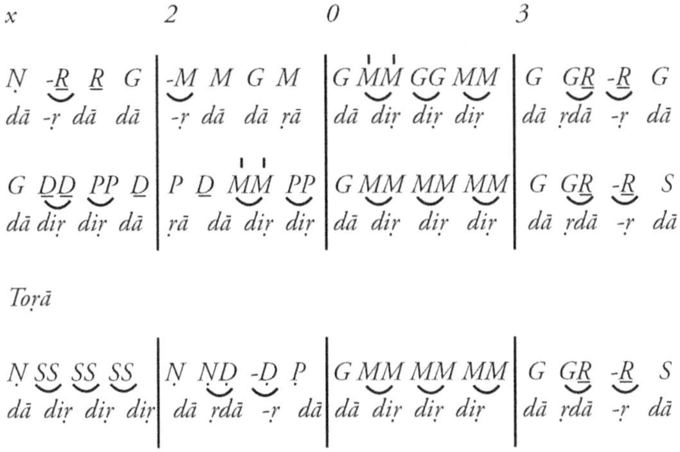

x	2	0	3
Ṇ -R R G	*-M M G M*	*G MM GG MM*	*G GR -R G*
dā -ṛ dā dā	*-ṛ dā dā ṛā*	*dā diṛ diṛ diṛ*	*dā ṛdā -ṛ dā*
G DD PP D	*P D MM PP*	*G MM MM MM*	*G GR -R S*
dā diṛ diṛ dā	*ṛā dā diṛ diṛ*	*dā diṛ diṛ diṛ*	*dā ṛdā -ṛ dā*

Toṛā

Ṇ SS SS SS	*Ṇ ṆḌ -Ḍ P̣*	*G MM MM MM*	*G GR -R S*
dā diṛ diṛ diṛ	*dā ṛdā -ṛ dā*	*dā diṛ diṛ diṛ*	*dā ṛdā -ṛ dā*

Chapter Five
Rules for Playing the Harmonium

Sitting Position for a Harmonium Player

The harmonium is played sitting in front of it just like at a table, as everyone knows.[1] Now, there are a few rules about how the hands and feet are moved when playing it. First, one should bring both hands to the keyboard, press the keys successively with the fingers and raise them immediately. Both hands should remain a little above the keyboard. The fingers should

1 The full-sized harmonium described here would soon be eclipsed in India by the "portable" harmonium pictured in the illustration. See Brockschmidt, Rahaim, Woodfield.

be kept somewhat relaxed and moved without using the entire hand. One should keep both feet on the pedals and move one foot after another, allowing the air to fill the intended parts. The feet should not be pressed too hard or too softly but at an ordinary weight. Pressing the pedals too hard results in a *phaṭ phaṭ* sound. The chart below shows the keys for each note.

Drawing of the Keyboard

Sargams to Play on the Harmonium[2]

77. Sargam
Rāg Shankarābharan, Tāl Tetālā

x				*2*				*0*				*3*			
S	-	*R*	-	*G*	-	*M*	-	*P*	-	*M*	-	*G*	-	*R*	-
S	-	*G*	-	*R*	-	*M*	-	*G*	-	*P*	-	*R*	-	*M*	-

2 These notations are found in the author's *Ināyat Hārmoniam Śikṣak*, written in Hindi (Khan, Inayatkhan, 1903b, 12–37)

78. *Sargam*
Rāg Shankarābharan, Tāl Tetālā

x	2	0	3
S - G -	R - S[1] -	R - M -	G - R -
G - P -	M - G -	R - M -	G - M -

79. *Sargam*
Rāg Shankarābharan, Tāl Tetālā

x	2	0	3
S - G -	R - S[1] -	R - M -	G - R -
G - P -	M - G -	R - M -	G - M -

80. *Sargam*
Rāg Shankarābharan, Tāl Tetālā

x	2	0	3
S - R[2] -	G - R -	G - M -	P - M -
P - M -	G - M -	G - R -	S - R -

81. *Sargam*
Rāg Shankarābharan, Tāl Tetālā

x	2	0	3
S R S R	G R G S	R G R G	M G M R
G M G M	P M P G	R G R G	M G M R

1 The *Minqār* reads *G*. A number of typographical errors appear in this chapter. The *Ināyat Hārmoniam Śikṣak* is the basis for most of the emendations I have made.
2. The *Minqār* reads *G*.

82. *Sargam*
Rāg Rāmkalī, Tāl Dādrā

x			0			x			0		
S	$\underline{R}$	G	M	G	$\underline{R}$	G	M	P	M	G	$\underline{R}$
S	G	S	$\underline{R}$	M	$\underline{R}$	G	P	G	$\underline{R}$	M	$\underline{R}$

83. *Sargam*
Rāg Kāfī, Tāl Dādrā

x			0			x			0		
S	R	S	R	$\underline{G}$	R	$\underline{G}$	M	P	M	P	M
$\underline{G}$	M	$\underline{G}$	R	$\underline{G}$	R	S	$\underline{G}$	R	S	M	$\underline{G}$
S	P	M	P	$\underline{G}$	M	P	R	$\underline{G}$	P	S	R

84. *Sargam*
Rāg Kalyān, Tāl Dādrā

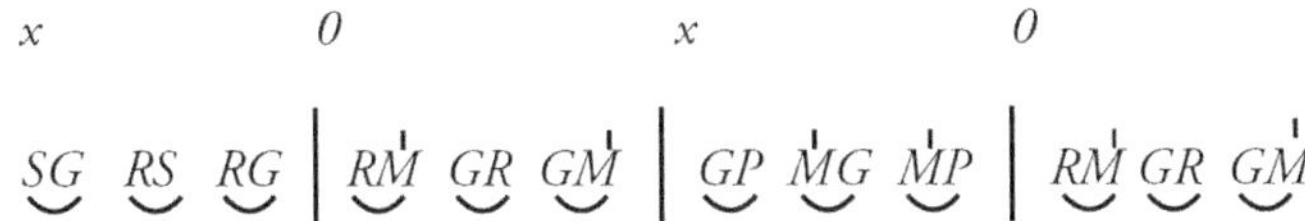

85. *Sargam*
Rāg Bhairavīn, Tāl Dādrā

x			0			x			0		
S$\underline{G}$	S$\underline{R}$	S$\underline{G}$	$\underline{R}$S	$\underline{G}$S	$\underline{R}$S	$\underline{R}$M	$\underline{R}\underline{G}$	$\underline{R}$M	$\underline{G}\underline{R}$	M$\underline{R}$	$\underline{G}\underline{R}$

86. *Sargam*
Rāg Toṛī, Tāl Dādrā

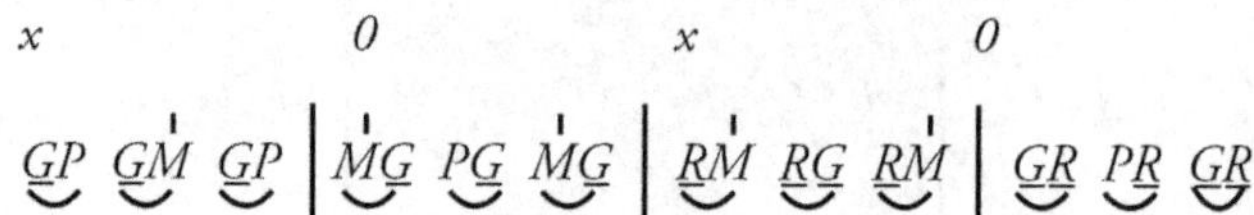

87. *Sargam*
Rāg Shankarābharan, Tāl Tetālā

x	2	0	3
S - - -	R - - -	G - - -	M - - -
P - - -	D - - -	N - - -	Ṡ - - -
Ṡ - - -	N - - -	D - - -	P - - -
M - - -	G - - -	R - - -	S - - -

88. *Sargam*
Rāg Shankarābharan, Tāl Tetālā

x	2	0	3
S - S -	R - R -	G - G -	M - M -
P - P -	D - D -	N - N -	Ṡ - Ṡ -
Ṡ - Ṡ -	N - N -	D - D -	P - P -
M - M -	G - G -	R - R -	S - S -

89. *Sargam*
Rāg Shankarābharan, Tāl Tisra Jātī Tetālā[1]

x	*2*	*0*	*3*
S S S	*R R R*	*G G G*	*M M M*
P P P	*D D D*	*N N N*	*Ṡ Ṡ Ṡ*
Ṡ Ṡ Ṡ	*N N N*	*D D D*	*P P P*
M M M	*G G G*	*R R R*	*S S S*

90. *Sargam*
Rāg Shankarābharan, Tāl Tetālā

x	*2*	*0*	*3*
S S S S	*R R R R*	*G G G G*	*M M M M*
P P P P	*D D D D*	*N N N N*	*Ṡ Ṡ Ṡ Ṡ*
Ṡ Ṡ Ṡ Ṡ	*N N N N*	*D D D D*	*P P P P*
M M M M	*G G G G*	*R R R R*	*S S S S*

1 Three notes are to be distributed over four beats.

91. *Sargam*
Rāg Shankarābharan, Tāl Rūpak[1]

x 2 0	*x 2 0*	*x 2 0*	*x 2 0*
S - R - G -	*R - G - M -*	*G - M - P -*	*M - P - D -*
P - D - N -	*D - N - Ṡ -*	*Ṡ - N - D -*	*N - D - P -*
D - P - M -	*P - M - G -*	*M - G - R -*	*G - R - S -*

92. *Sargam*
Rāg Shankarābharan, Tāl Ektālā[2]

x	*x*	*x*	*x*	*x*
S R G M	*R G M P*	*G M P D*	*M P D N*	*P D N Ṡ*
Ṡ N D P	*N D P M*	*D P M G*	*P M G R*	*M G R S*

93. *Sargam*
Rāg Shankarābharan, Tāl Misra Jātī Ektālā[3]

x	*x*	*x*
S R G S R G M	*R G M R G M P*	*G M P G M P D*
M P D M P D N	*P D N P D N Ṡ*	*Ṡ N D Ṡ N D P*
N D P N D P M	*D P M D P M G*	*P M G P M G R*
M G R M G R S		

1 This is six-beat *rūpaka tāl* of Karnatak music.
2 This is four-beat Karnatak *ekatāla.*
3 This is seven-beat Karnatak *ekatāla.*

94. *Sargam*
Rāg Shankarābharan, Tāl Tetālā

x	2	0	3
S - S S	R - R R	G - G G	M - M M
P - P P	D - D D	N - N N	Ṡ - Ṡ Ṡ
Ṡ - Ṡ Ṡ	N - N N	D - D D	P - P P
M - M M	G - G G	R - R R	S - S S

95. *Sargam*
Rāg Rāmkalī, Tāl Tetālā[1]

x	2	0	3
S S - S	R̲ R̲ - R̲	G G - G	M M - M
P P - P	D D - D	N N - N	Ṡ Ṡ - Ṡ
Ṡ Ṡ - Ṡ	N N - N	D D - D	P P - P
M M - M	G G - G	R̲ R̲ - R̲	S S - S

96. *Sargam*
Rāg Jhinjhoṭī, Tāl Tetālā

x	2	0	3
S S S -	R R R -	G G G -	M M M -
P P P -	D D D -	N̲ N̲ N̲ -	Ṡ Ṡ Ṡ -
Ṡ Ṡ Ṡ -	N̲ N̲ N̲ -	D D D -	P P P -
M M M -	G G G -	R R R -	S S S -

1 The text reads *ektālā*.

97. *Sargam*
Rāg Kālingṛā, Tāl Tetālā

x	2	0	3
SS S S S	*R̲R̲ R̲ R̲ R̲*	*GG G G G*	*MM M M M*
PP P P P	*D̲D̲ D̲ D̲ D̲*	*NN N N N*	*ṠṠ Ṡ Ṡ Ṡ*
ṠṠ Ṡ Ṡ Ṡ	*NN N N N*	*D̲D̲ D̲ D̲ D̲*	*PP P P P*
MM M M M	*GG G G G*	*R̲R̲ R̲ R̲ R̲*	*SS S S S*

98. *Sargam*
Rāg Kāfī, Tāl Tetālā

x	2	0	3
S SS S S	*R RR R R*	*G̲ G̲G̲ G̲ G̲*	*M MM M M*
P PP P P	*D DD D D*	*N̲ N̲N̲ N̲ N̲*	*Ṡ ṠṠ Ṡ Ṡ*
Ṡ ṠṠ Ṡ Ṡ	*N̲ N̲N̲ N̲ N̲*	*D DD D D*	*P PP P P*
M MM M M	*G̲ G̲G̲ G̲ G̲*	*R RR R R*	*S SS S S*

99. *Sargam*
Rāg Bhairavīn, Tāl Tetālā

x	2	0	3
S S SS S	*R̲ R̲ R̲R̲ R̲*	*G̲ G̲ G̲G̲ G̲*	*M M MM M*
P P PP P	*D̲ D̲ D̲D̲ D̲*	*N̲ N̲ N̲N̲ N̲*	*Ṡ Ṡ ṠṠ Ṡ*
Ṡ Ṡ ṠṠ Ṡ	*N̲ N̲ N̲N̲ N̲*	*D̲ D̲ D̲D̲ D̲*	*P P PP P*
M M MM M	*G̲ G̲ G̲G̲ G̲*	*R̲ R̲ R̲R̲ R̲*	*S S SS S*

100. *Sargam*
Rāg Kalyān, Tāl Ektālā[1]

x	2	0	3
S S S RG	*R R R GM̍*	*G G G M̍P*	*M̍ M̍ M̍ PD*
P P P DN	*D D D NṠ*	*Ṡ Ṡ Ṡ ND*	*N N N DP*
D D D PM̍	*P P P M̍G*	*M̍ M̍ M̍ GR*	*G G G RS*

101. *Sargam*
Rāg Toṛī, Tāl Tetālā

x	2	0	3
S S SR̲ G̲M̍	*R̲ R̲ R̲G̲ M̍P*	*G̲ G̲ G̲M̍ PD̲*	*M̍ M̍ M̍P D̲N*
P P PD̲ NṠ	*Ṡ Ṡ ṠN D̲P*	*N N ND̲ PM̍*	*D̲ D̲ D̲P M̍G̲*
P P PM̍ G̲R̲	*M̍ M̍ M̍G̲ R̲S*		

102. *Sargam*
Rāg Rāmkalī, Tāl Ektālā

x	x	x	x
D - - -	*P M G R̲*	*- S Ṇ S*	*R̲ M G P*
D N Ṡ N	*Ṙ̲ - Ṡ -*	*N DP MD PM*	*G R̲ S -*

1 The *tāl* divisions are for *tetālā*. The *Ināyat Hārmoniam Śikṣak* gives the *tāl* divisions of four-beat *ektālā* for this notation and the next.

103. *Sargam*
Rāg Jhinjhoṭī, Tāl Dādrā[1]

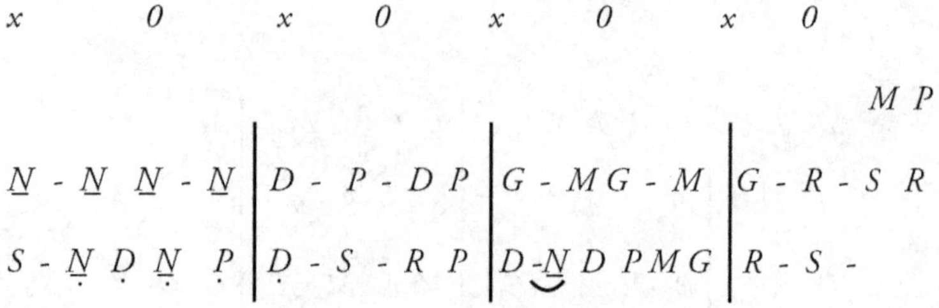

x 0	*x 0*	*x 0*	*x 0*
			M P
N̲ - N̲ N̲ - N̲	*D - P - D P*	*G - M G - M*	*G - R - S R*
S - N̲̣ Ḍ N̲̣ P̣	*Ḍ - S - R P*	*D - N̲ D P M G*	*R - S -*

104. *Sargam*
Rāg Kālingṛā, Tāl Tīvrā

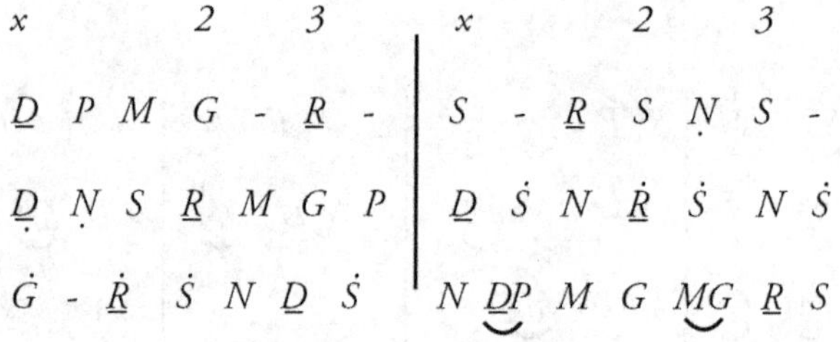

x 2 3	*x 2 3*
D̲ P M G - R̲ -	*S - R̲ S Ṇ S -*
D̲̣ Ṇ S R̲ M G P	*D̲ Ṡ N Ṙ̲ Ṡ N Ṡ*
Ġ - Ṙ̲ Ṡ N D̲ Ṡ	*N D̲P M G MG R̲ S*

105. *Sargam*
Rāg Kāfī, Tāl Cautālā

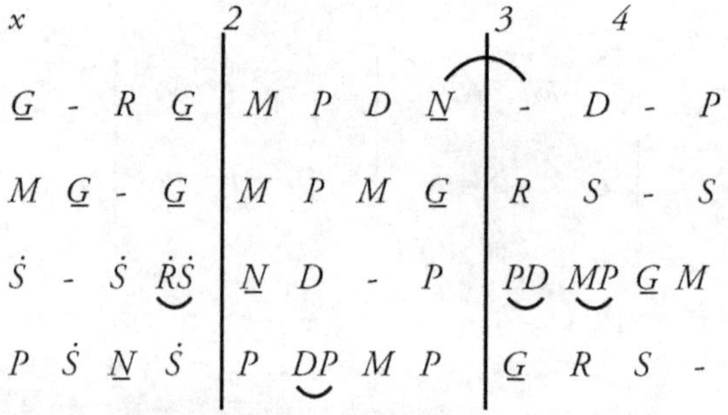

x	*2*	*3 4*
G̲ - R G̲	*M P D N̲*	*- D - P*
M G̲ - G̲	*M P M G̲*	*R S - S*
Ṡ - Ṡ ṘṠ	*N̲ D - P*	*PD MP G̲ M*
P Ṡ N̲ Ṡ	*P DP M P*	*G̲ R S -*

1 The text reads *Tetālā*, clearly a typographical error.

106. *Sargam*
Rāg Bhairavīn, Tāl Tetālā

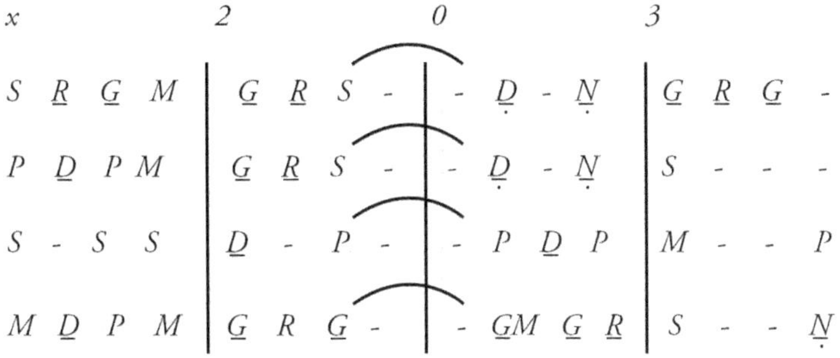

x				2				0				3			
S	R	G	M	G	R	S	-	-	D	-	N	G	R	G	-
P	D	P	M	G	R	S	-	-	D	-	N	S	-	-	-
S	-	S	S	D	-	P	-	-	P	D	P	M	-	-	P
M	D	P	M	G	R	G	-	-	GM	G	R	S	-	-	N

107. *Sargam*
Rāg Kalyān, Tāl Jhaptālā

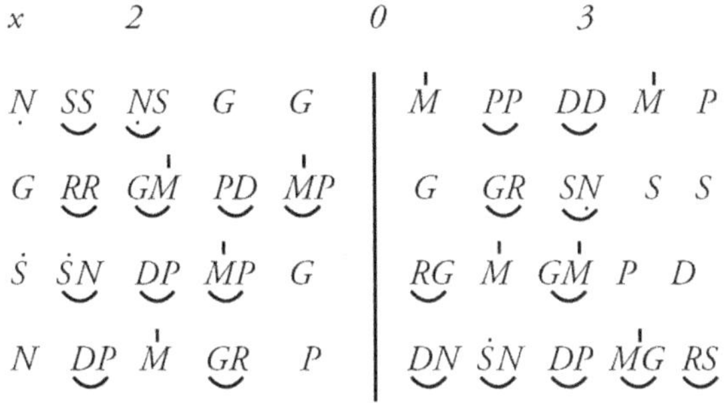

x		2			0		3		
N	SS	NS	G	G	M	PP	DD	M	P
G	RR	GM	PD	MP	G	GR	SN	S	S
S	SN	DP	MP	G	RG	M	GM	P	D
N	DP	M	GR	P	DN	SN	DP	MG	RS

108. *Sargam*
Rāg Toṛī, Tāl Bilandī[1]

x			*2*				*0*			*3*			
G̲	R̲	-	S	-	R̲	-	Ṅ	Ṇ	-	S	R̲	G̲	-
M̍	M̍	-	P	-	D̲	-	P	-	-	P	-	M̍	-
G̲	R̲	-	S	-	-	-	Ḍ̲	-	-	Ḍ̲	-	Ṇ	-
Ṡ	Ṙ̲	-	Ṡ	Ṇ	Ṡ	-	Ḍ̲	D̲	-	N	-	Ṙ̲	-
Ṡ	Ṇ	Ṡ	D̲	-	P	-	G̲	G̲	-	M̍	D̲	N	-
Ṡ	N	D̲	P	M̍	G̲	R̲	G̲	N	D̲	P	M̍	G̲	D̲
P	M̍	G̲	R̲	S	Ṇ	D̲	Ḍ̲	Ṇ	S	R̲	S	R̲	M̍

سرگم

راگ کلیان۔ تال جھپ تالا

مولا [illegible] نی سا ری سا نی سا گا گا | ما پا پا دھا دھا ما ما پا | گا رے رے گا

ما پا دھا ما ما پا | گا گا رے سا نی سا سا | سا سا نی دھا پا پا ما ما پا گا | رے گا ما گا ما

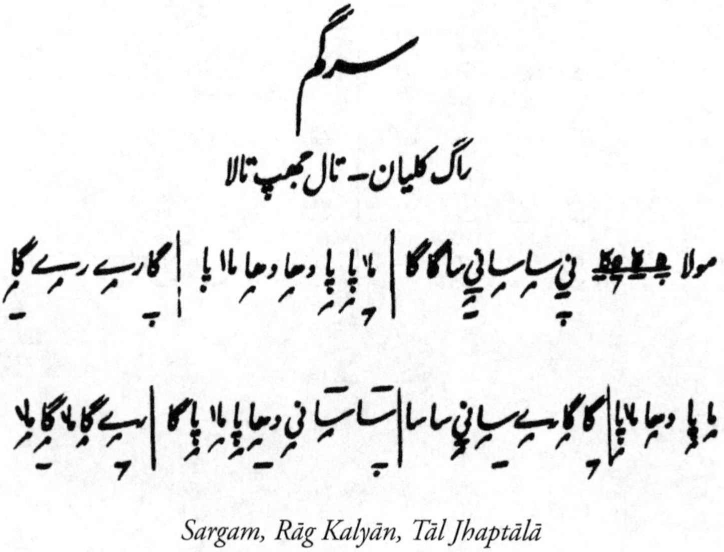

Sargam, Rāg Kalyān, Tāl Jhaptālā
(Khan, Inayat R. 1912, 266-7)

---

1 The octaves seem eccentric in this *sargam* but may be intentionally so for the purpose of practice.

Chapter Six
Rules for Playing the *tabla*

Sitting Position for *tabla* Playing

The *tabla* is used in every part of India. The beauty of vocal and instrumental music cannot be appreciated without it because *tabla* adds color to the music. In this chapter the positions of the hands for playing the syllables (*bol*) are given along with a few common *ṭhekas*.

Drawing of the *tabla*

There are three places on the *tabla* for producing the sound: the *chānṭ,* the *lav,* and the *thāp*. The *chānṭ* is on the edge of the *tabla*. The place between the *chānṭ* and the *syāhī* (black spot) is the *lav*, and the *thāp* is sounded on the *syāhī*. On the *bāyān*, sound is produced using four fingers of the left hand on the *syāhī*. To the side of the *syāhī* where there is an empty space, a sound is also produced on the *bāyān* with the left fingers cupped.

The Syllables of *tabla*

Syllables *(bol)* including the following are played on the *tabla*: *kā, kī, gā, gī, ghe, ghī, ghe, nā, nān, ṭā, ṭī, ṛā, tā, ttā, tī, tin, dī, dhā, dhī, dhū, mā, rī.*

kā, kī. This *bol* is produced by pressing the fingers of the left hand together and striking on the *syāhī* of the *bāyān*.

gā, gī, ge, ghī. Half bending the fingers of the left hand strike the *bāyān* on the empty space to the far side of the *syāhī*. If you then immediately lift the fingers, these sounds are produced.

nā, nān. These *bols* are produced on the *chānṭ* of the *tabla* by striking it with the first finger of the right hand.

ṭā. This is produced by striking the *syāhī* of the *tabla* with the first finger of the right hand and immmediately lifting it.

ṭī. This is produced by striking the *lav* with the first finger of the right hand and immediately lifting it.

ṛā. This *bol* is produced by striking the *syāhī* of the *tabla* softly with the second, third and fourth fingers of the right hand which are pressed together and slightly curved.

tā. This is produced by striking the *chānṭ* of the *tabla* with the first finger of the right hand.

tī. This *bol* is played with the second, third, and fourth fingers of the right hand joined together and striking on the *syāhī*, but only when the *bols rī* or *ṭā* occur next. An example is *tiraki-ṭataka*. If *tī* occurs with other *bols* or when one plays it by itself, the third finger of the right hand is placed on the *syāhī* of the *tabla* while the first finger strikes on the *syāhī*, as in the example *dhin tiṭa dhinnā.*

tin, tū. This *bol* is played on the *syāhī* of the *tabla* with the second, third, and fourth fingers of the right hand pressed tightly together.

dī, mā. This is often used on the *pakhāvaj*. It is played on the *syāhī* with all five fingers of the right hand pressed together and a little curved and with the palm of the hand open. On the *tabla* this *bol* is played like *tī*.

dhā. This is produced on the *tabla* and *bāyān* simultaneously. The first finger of the right hand strikes the *chānṭ* of the *tabla* while the curved four fingers of the left hand strike on the far side of the *syāhī* of the *bāyān*. The *bol* should be produced with both hands at the same time so that it does not seem to be separate sounds.

dhī. This sound is produced on the *tabla* and the *bāyān* simultaneously. The third finger of the right hand is placed on the *syāhī* of the *tabla* while the first finger strikes the *syāhī* and then is immediately lifted. The second and fourth fingers remain up. At the same time, all four fingers of the left hand strike the empty space on the far side of the *syāhī* of the *bāyān* such that the *bols* of both hands are sounded together. When *dhī* is to be followed by *rī*, the second, third and fourth fingers of the right hand are pressed together and strike the *syāhī* of the *tabla*, and at the same time, the four fingers of the left hand, which are pressed together and curved, strike the empty place on the other side of the *syāhī* of the *bāyān* so that one *bol* sounds from both hands.

dhū. This *bol* is often played on the *pakhāvaj*. All four fingers of the left hand are pressed together and strike the *bāyān* together with a half of the palm.

rī. This *bol* is produced with the first finger of the right hand on the *tabla*.

Method for Playing the *bols* of *Cautālā*

dhā. This *bol* is produced on the *tabla* and *bāyān* as it is on the *pakhāvaj*, with two hands simultaneously. The right hand from the fourth finger to the other side of the palm strikes as though from the edge on the *syāhī* of the *tabla* so that a resonance is produced. At the same time all the fingers of the left hand are pressed together, strike the *bāyān* and immediately lift away so that only half of the left hand palm remains on the *bāyān* while the rest is raised. Thus this *bol* is produced with both hands.

kī. This *bol* is produced on the *syāhī* of the *tabla* with the second, third, and fourth fingers of the right hand pressed together.

ttā. This is produced by striking with the first finger of the right hand on the *syāhī* of the *tabla*.

tā. Strike the *syāhī* of the *bāyān* with all four fingers of the left hand pressed together and do not lift them until the next *bol* sounds.

ttā, rā, kā, kkā. These *bols* are produced with the right hand on the *tabla* in a way similar to *dhā*. The special feature is that a resonance should be produced without the left hand.

gī. This is produced on the *bāyān* with all four fingers of the left hand pressed together, but half of the left palm should remain touching the drum.

dhī, dhī, nā. All these *bols* are played like the above-mentioned *dī*.

dhū. Play this like *gī*.

mā Play this like *dī*.

dhin Play this like *dhū*.

Tabla ṭhekās for Common *tāls*[1]

109. *Catūsra Jātī Tetālā,* sixteen *mātrās*

l l l l (4 4 4 4)[2]

x | | | | *2* | | | | *0* | | | | *2* | | |
---|---|---|---|---|---|---|---|---|---|---|---|---|---|---|---
nā | *dhī* | *dhī* | *nā* \| | *nā* | *dhī* | *dhī* | *nā* \| | *nā* | *tī* | *tī* | *nā* \| | *nā* | *dhī* | *dhī* | *nā*

1 There are a number of inconsistencies in this section and many rhythmic details are missing. I have made interpretations as seem most logical, largely based on the *Tāl Paddhati* (Kippen).

2 *Laghu, drut, drut viram (l, d, dv)* are "time divisions" consisting of the number of beats, added here in parentheses. *x, 0,* and numbers are translations of the Maula Bakhsh notations for hand actions. See Part One, Chapter Five and Introduction for more explanation.

110. *Jhūmrā,* fourteen *mātrās*
dv l dv l (3 4 3 4)

x 2 0 3
dhī dhī trikā | dhin dhin dhāge trikā | tin tā trikā | dhin dhin dhāge trikā

111. *Dādrā,* six *mātrās*
dv dv (3 3)

x 0
dhin dhin dhā | dhā tū nā

112. *Catūsra Jātī Cautālā,* twelve *mātrās*
l l d d (4 4 2 2)[1]

x 2
dhā dhā dhin tā | ka dhā dhin tā | kīṭā tākā gādī gīnā

113. *Tevrā,* seven *mātrās*
dv d d (3 2 2)

x 2 3
dhin trikā dhin | dhā trikā | tī nā

114. *Catūsra Jātī Āṛā Cautālā,* fourteen *mātrās*
d l l l (2 4 4 4)

x 2 3 4
dhin dhin | dhā trikā tī nā | kā tā dhī ddhī | nā dhī dhī nā

---

1 Some of the hand actions are missing in this notation.

115. *Sūlfāqta,* ten *mātrās*

l d l (4 2 4)

x   *2*   *3*

dhin trikā dhin nā | tin trikā | dhin nā tin nā

116. *Savārī,* sixteen *mātrās*

l dv l l l (4 3 4 4 4) [1]

x   *2*

dhin nā dhin nā | kāttā trikādhin- nādhī dhīnā |

0   *3*

tin--kā tīnā tā-trikā tīnā | kāttā trikādhīnā gīnādhāgī nādhātrikā

تال چتوسر ذاتی - تے تالا ماترے سولہ

نا دھی دھی نا | نا تی تی نا | نا دھی دھی نا | نا دھی دھی نا

Catūsra Jātī Tetālā
(Khan, Inayat R. 1912, 272)

117. *Ṭappa,* sixteen *mātrās*

x   *2*   *0*   *3*

nā dhī -kā dhin | nā dhī -kā dhin | nā tī -kā tin | nā dhī -kā dhin

1 The *dv* is likely an error. Thanks to James Kippen for the interpretation of this *ṭhekā* (private communication; see Kippen).

118. *Bilandī (Cāncar)*, fourteen *mātrās*

dv l dv l (3 4 3 4)

x *2* *0* *3*

dhā dhin - | dhā dhā tin - | tā tin - | dhā dhā dhin -

119. *Tīlvāṛā*, sixteen *mātrās*

l l l l (4 4 4 4)

x *2* *0* *3*

dhā trikā dhin dhin | nā nā tin tin | tā trikā dhin dhin | nā nā dhin dhin

120. *Qavālī*, eight *mātrās*

d d d d (2 2 2 2)

x *0*

trikā dhī ddhī nā | dhī ddhī dhin nā

121. *Farodast*, thirteen *mātrās*

d d dv l (2 2 3 4) [1]

x *2* *3* *4*

dhin nā | dhin nā | kātā tri-kāṛā | dhindhā ge dhin dhā ge |

tin tin tā tri-kāṛā

122. *Jhaptālā*, ten *mātrās*

d dv d dv (2 3 2 3)

x *2* *0* *3*

dhin nā | dhī dhī nā | tin nā | dhī dhī nā

---

1 The configuration should likely be *d d d dv l.* Th interpretation of this *ṭhekā* is based on the *Tāl Paddhati* (Kippen, 42).

123. *Panjābī*, sixteen *mātrās*
l l l l (4 4 4 4)

x *2* *0* *3*

dhā- -tin -kā dhā- | dhā- -tin -kā tā- | tā- -tin -kā dhā- | dhā- -tin -kā dhā-

124. *Ghazal*, seven *mātrās*
l l l l (4 4 4 4)[1]

dhin - - dhā - dhā - | tin - - - - - tākā

125. *Savārī*, fifteen *mātrās*
d l l l (2 4 4 4)[2]

dhindhā - ṛ dhin - dhā - - ṛ | dhā - dhā - dhin - tā - |

dhindhin tā-trikā | tūnā kiṛātāgā | kāttā dhindhin nādhin dhinnā

126. *Ektālā*, twelve *mātrās*
l (4)[3]

x *x* *x*

dhin dhin dhā trikā | tū nā kā tā | dhin trikā dhin tā

---

1 This configuration of sixteen *mātrās* with four clapped hand actions clearly does not fit the notation. The *ṭhekā* covers fourteen *mātrās,* making it equivalent to a slow speed seven. It is nearly identical to that in the *Tāl Paddhati* (Kippen, 42).

2 This configuration is also faulty. It indicates fourteen *mātrās* and four clapped hand actions, which are not shown in the notation. Thanks to James Kippen for the interpretation of the *ṭhekā.*

3 The configuration is of Karnatak *ekatāla* but the *ṭhekā* is Hindustani *ektāl.*

Chapter Seven
Dance

Drawing of a dancer

The basics of vocal and instrumental music have been covered in accordance with the system of *sangīt*. A discussion of dance now follows. Dance is a natural activity, which no individual lacks. Consider animals: you will see them dancing when they are in a state of excitement. Notice how birds show enthrallment in their joy and happiness. As some poet has rightly said:

The tour of eternal love passes through all things
Otherwise, whence–alas!–the poor nightingale's plaint for
the blooming rose?

The noble human being is wondrous, blessed, and endowed with all kinds of graces, indeed, a manifestation of all creation. In his every hair are joy, delight, and enthusiasm. In truth, *rāg* is the call, and dance is the enactment of that call. To the same extent that sound gives pleasure, performance enhances its beauty. Sound and performance are a single being with two bodies, so in this spirit, performance and the musical art are enthusiastic seekers.

In Nepal and Bhutan I saw the inhabitants dancing while they sang and played music, and they became so entranced while doing it that they achieved a state of rapture. Similarly in Africa and Arabia, in war and in musical gatherings, people become aroused and begin to dance. In Europe this is done with great enthusiasm, and there are even special schools for it. People reap the benefits of physical exercise and spiritual renewal from the art. Everyone, rich and poor, participates in dances called "balls," in which men and women dance together, and they take so much pleasure in it that they are freed of all their worries.

O Saki, arise and redden the cup.
Throw dust on the head of the sorrows of our days.

In India dance has existed from earliest times. The Hindu deity Mahadevji invented it and taught it to the sage Tandav. The well-known legend is that he in turn trained the celestial beings (*devas* or *gandharvas*) and the fairies (*apsaras*) in what is called *tāṇḍav nrit*. This is a masculine style of dance. Then Mahadevji demonstrated amorous play and coquetry in his eternal world, and the new creation was called *lās nrit*. This dance is feminine. A type that was created by Kanhaiyaji is called *tribhangī*. He danced it while standing on the serpent's head. Kanhaiyaji also invented a dance type called *sukumār*.

Tāṇḍav

Tāṇḍav nrit is mostly practiced in south India, and the people there still dance in accordance with its tradition. *Tāṇḍav* is danced by one woman or together by two women who look alike. They are adorned with jewelry from head to foot. They wear a blouse and the upper part of a *sāṛī* which has an embroidered border, and they drape the end of the *sāṛī* in front. The moves of this dance are masculine, but are done with the lovely actions of a beloved. And some of the gestures for the hands, neck, eyebrows, forehead, and eyes are not commonly seen. In this dance there are plenty of athletic moves such as leaps and jumps and getting up and down with speed and agility. Therefore only a strong woman can do it. *Tāṇḍav* dance uses one *pakhāvaj* drummer and two men who play the *manjīrā* (cymbals) and sing. There is a bagpipe *(mashk)* to keep the tone. The same syllables that are sung are played on the *pakhāvaj*, and these are also produced by the dancer with her feet, which is called *avghaṭ*. These days, English instruments such as the clarinet or fiddle are sometimes used in the dance ensemble.

Lās

This type of dance is current in most parts of India, but it is most prevalent in the north. Delhi and Lucknow are its treasure-houses. This dance is feminine and performed with a great deal of softness and delicacy. Women and men both perform this dance and there are a number of recognized masters *(ustād)* of it in India. *Lās* is accompanied by two *sārangī* players and a *tablā*, and sometimes a *manjīra*. It is danced by one woman, or by two together. In Hyderabad city one sometimes sees the dance in a line made up of seven or eight women. For this type of dance the performer wears a full complement of jewelry and drapes a brocade scarf on her upper body.

Sukumār

As many girls as possible come together as though playing in the Holi festival, and this is called *sukumār*, "delicate," dance.

Paristān kā nāc

Besides those above, a type of dance was invented during the time of Akbar which is called the "dance of the fairies" *(parī)*. This is not current in its entirety, but several movements *(gat)*, for example the *gat* of the fairies, still make up a part of *lās* dance. One should also note that Emperor Akbar had several dances created on the basis of the gaits of his wives. These are still found in the practices of the *kathaks*. Other types of female and male dances that were developed then are not in use anymore. The sources of their invention were the beautiful ways of walking, sweet mannerisms, and exquisite bodies of the women in Akbar's palaces. One among the women might have a sort of lilt and move like a bounding deer. Another would move slowly in a languid manner. So a *gat* was composed according to the movement and the body of each woman. This was called the *zanānā nrit* (women's dance). The dance moves that were invented on the basis of the gaits of the Emperor's boys were named *mardāni nrit* (mens' dance). Even during the period when Akbar's dances were famous, not everyone knew of this one because it was more difficult than the others.

Dance has three principles: *nrit, nrittam*, and *nātyā*. In *nrit* the rhythmic syllables of dance are performed with movements of the hands, feet and body. In *nrittam* the meanings of the song are acted out through expressions *(bhāv)*. In *nātyā,* meanings are created by the dancer. That is, if one wishes to convey sadness one makes a pained face, and if laughter is the intended meaning one makes a smiling face. In this way one can practice facial expressions such as surprise, despondency, separation, union and the like in the mirror and perform them.

The Syllables of Dance

Syllables (*bol*) that are both spoken and performed with the feet in a dance are called *parmalū*. They are *ta, tā, tat, thayī, thalāng, than, tak, dag, jag, jagat, kokat, dadhī, ghan, tag, tanjī, tarāng, talāng, dhaṭ, kaṭ, takaṭ, dhakaṭ, tādū, thangā, thangā, thang*. These syllables are set to every *tāl*, and short compositions called *toṛā* are also made from them.

"Limbs" *(ang)* of Dance

Urīn. To jump up from the floor and move in one direction to finish the phrase is *urīn*.

Sulap. Playful and flirtatious moves done with tenderness are called *sulap*.

Urap. To suddenly jump up and move forward, then move back displaying all sorts of expressions, is *urap*.

Tarap. This is almost the same as the previous.

Sidha mudra. To dance while holding a finger with the other hand or putting a finger to the forehead or to the chest is called *sidha mudra*.

Lāg. To mingle two styles together well is called *lāg*.

Dānṭ. When the styles are performed nicely with nimbleness and cleverness they are called *dānṭ*.

These are the *angs* that are the most in use. There are others as well.

"Filling the Movements" *(gat bharnā)*

Upon entering the gathering at the start of the performance, the dancer would lift her veil, present salutations, and strew flowers in the four directions. This was the practice in the old days but it is no longer current. To dance to the accompaniment of spoken syllables *(parmalū)* in any *tāl* is called *gat bharnā*. It is of many types, a few of which are given below.

Māthe kī gat is to fill out the movement with a hand placed on the head.

Salāmī kī gat is to move with the four fingers of the hand held in front of the forehead.

Mukuṭ kī gat is to move while making the shape of a crown with both hands.

Parband kī gat is to move with the hands placed near the shoulders.

Bānsurī kī gat is to hold the end of the *sāṛī* to the left side like a flute and put the right foot on top of the left.

Mukuṭ kī gat is used in *tribhangī* dance.

Jānshīn kī gat is done at the beginning of a dance.

Ādhe ghunghaṭ kī gat is to move with the veil half lifted.

Pūre ghunghaṭ kī gat is to move with the the veil entirely lifted.

Raqs tāūs kī gat, "the dance of the peacock," is done while lifting the ends of the dance dress with both hands.

Besides these there are other *gats*, such as that of the "fan-tail pigeon" *(laqqa kabūtar)*, "open hand" *(dast kushādagī)*, "scorn" *(angushtnumā)*, "chest" *(chātī)*, and "dress" *(peshvāz)*.

First begin the dance in single rhythm, then fill out the *gats* as described and vary them with different syllables. After that, increase the speed and use different syllables to act out expressions *(abhinay)* with tenderness.

Bhāv

Bhāv means to draw out the meaning of the song. *Bhāv* is dependent on the skill of the dancer. There are several types of it and the most current are given below.

Nayan bhāv is to act out the meaning of the song with glances, using movements of the eyebrows and eyes.

Bol bhāv is to act out the words of the song in various ways.

Arth bhāv is to act out the meaning of the song exactly as the words denote, in other words to become the puppet for the meaning of the song and to display its meaning in different ways. One makes a smiling face for a funny meaning and a displeased face to express anger. For astonishment one makes a face displaying astonishment. Likewise, expressions such as cunning, smartness, languor, and laziness should be acted out to charm everyone in the gathering. This should be done in such a way that each person thinks "this dancer is speaking to me" and feel that "her attention is on me."

Nrit bhāv is to dance and act at the same time.

Gīt arth bhāv is to dance, sing, and act all at the same time.

Ang bhāv is to portray the meaning of the song with the body and fill out the *gat* in various new ways.

The Structure of a Dance

First, the dancer should put on the special dress *(peshvāz)*, drape a scarf *(dupaṭa)* over her and tie a knot in it, and tie bells *(ghunguru)* to her ankles. She should produce the syllables with the correct feet and timing just as they are composed. As she continues to do this and with the fingers closed and hands held together at the wrists, she should bend them at each syllable. But at each round when the *sam* comes, she should open both hands, "fill the *gat*" on the downbeat, move forward a bit and pause. Then from there she should turn and at an angle move backward, pausing on each step until she returns to the place where she started then stand there not averting her face from the front. The *tabla* player keeps the *ṭhekā* along with the dance. The *manjīrā* player plays the syllables on the *manjīrā*, and the *sārangī* player keeps a *lahara* repeating tune in a *rāginī* suited to the time of the performance.

Descriptions of *gats*

Mukuṭ kī gat

The features of this *gat* are as follows. Hold the hands with the palms open above the head in the shape of a crown *(mukuṭ)*, place one foot at an angle on top of the other, and dance this *gat*. Take a round of the entire gathering, moving the body in the various ways. This *gat* is also done in a fast tempo. One should note that this *gat* comes from the *tribhangī* and *naṭvar* types of dance, which were inspired by Kanhaiyaji.

Parband kī gat

The features of this *gat* are that one should spread the arms out to the sides like wings *(par)*. Gesture with the hands like wings and dance with playfulness and flirtatiousness. Move the eyes and eyebrows and the head about; keep bending at the waist as well, and send bewitching glances. One should do this *gat* as fast as the wind. This is a dance of the fairy quarters *(paristān)*.

Mukuṭ kī gat

Make the hands like a crown *(mukuṭ)*, that is, hold the open hands above the head with the fingers straight, and hold them on the head as you dance. This *gat* comes from the *tribhangī* and *naṭvar* dances which were created by Kanhaiyaji. There are several styles of doing this *gat*, but this style is the most correct and well known.

Jhurmaṭ kī gat

Pull the edge of the scarf to the part of the hair and hold it there with the left hand fingers. With the right hand , the edge *(jhurmaṭ)* of the scarf to the eyebrows. Holding it there firmly, dance the *gat* with boldness *(nāz)*. Circle in all directions, meet each person's eyes, and tease everyone with your amorous glances and winks. In this *gat*, one should move and sway the body.

Kamar kī gat

Place the open fingers of the right hand firmly on the waist, extend the other hand and dance. Every part should be moved about—the fingers of the right hand on the waist, those of the left hand which are extended, the forearm, the elbow, the upper arm, the waist, the wrist, and the chest. One should find quickness and nimbleness in this *gat* and do it in such a way that the onlookers and audience become thoroughly entranced.

Donon Chapton kī gat

Place the hands to both breasts and dance with playfulness and flirtatiousness. The moves are as described above in other *gats*. When the dancer links the fingers of both hands and rests them on the chest this will be called the *sīne kī gat* (*gat* of the chest). In a similar way several *gats* can be made from any one by varying it in different ways, as in the *mukuṭ* and *kamar kī gat*.

Kamar kī gat

The right hand is held on the waist and the left hand is extended. There are two ways of doing this *gat.* One way is that the inside of the right hand thumb is placed on the waist and the other way is that the fingers of the right hand are placed on the waist while the other hand is extended. One should flex the waist in this *gat.*

Angusht Pacīda kī gat

Link the thumbs of both hands, that is, intertwine the fingers, and hold them at the head. Jut out the body and the chest while you dance, shoot glances in each person's direction and move about in all the various ways. One should perform this dance in such a way that the onlookers are infatuated and seduced at every footstep.

Chātī kī gat

The right hand is held to the chest *(chātī)* and the left hand is extended straight out like an arrow. One should sway the breast and smile while dancing. The chest is puffed out and the eyes shoot glances toward the front. Each onlooker should feel "she knows me and is speaking to me." While dancing, one should move the wrists and belly, the face, the eyes, and the eyebrows. The eyes should be filled with intoxication and should gaze at each person.

Jānshīn kī gat

The right hand is a hand's width from the head, and it touches the earlobe. The left hand is straight like an arrow. The chest should be swelled out, and no limb should be bent. Glances should be shot to the front and the eyes should not turn away from anyone, but remain on each person. The fingers and the wrists of both hands should move with each rhythmic syllable and at the syllables *tat* and *tā* the palms should open up.

Mukuṭ Bānsurī kī gat

Make the left hand into the shape of a crown and hold it to the head; hold the right hand as though it were playing an imaginary flute *(bānsurī)*. Dance while circling the entire gathering. Continue to move the limbs about as already described and shoot glances such that each and every audience member feels wounded by love's arrows. This dance is from that of the *naṭvars* and originated with Kanhaiyaji.

Bānsurī kī gat

This *gat* should convey the impression that someone is playing the flute while dancing. With both hands, hold an imaginary flute to the right. The face is to the left and one foot is diagonally across the other. In this dance it is appropriate to bend slightly. The wrists, waist, eyes and eyebrows move continually while one circles the entire gathering. This *gat* is also from the tribhangī and *naṭvar* traditions which originated with Kanhaiyaji.

Thālī kī gat

Fill a plate *(thālī)* with water. Grip the edges with the toes of both feet. Hold both hands at the navel and dance making a loud sound on the floor. All the moves of the dance should be completed with not one drop of water jumping from the plate and falling onto the floor. In other words, one should dance with extreme skill. This *gat* is adapted from the dances of the *kathaks*.

Ghūngaṭ kī gat

Drape the veil *(ghūngaṭ)* of the scarf over the face, then lift the dress with both hands and revolve around to do this dance. First revolve to the right then to the left. If you dance in the same way but without the veil and with the dress raised up to the shoulders, this becomes the *gat* of the peacock dance *(raqs tāūs kī gat)*.

Angushtnumā kī gat

Extend the arms out like a bird, make fists and extend one finger on each hand upright and dance. The wrists and the waist should keep moving. The breasts and the eyes and the eyebrows should also continually move. This *gat* should be danced so that the audience and onlookers feel every move along with the dancer.

Thālī Kaṭore kī gat

Hold glass cups filled with water in both hands. Grasping the edge of a plate with the toes, dance this *gat*. No water should spill out of the glass and the plate should not slip from the feet. It should seem that the dance is being done in all four directions as the limbs are moved about in the described ways. This *gat* is more difficult than all the others. It is one of the dances done by the *kathaks*.

Thoṛī kī gat

Hold the right hand to or above the shoulder to the ear ornament *(thoṛī)* and extend the left hand widely out. Move the limbs in the described ways. This *gat* is danced in single speed, and variations will also be done the same way.

Mardānī gat

This *gat* is masculine *(mardānī)*. The method and technique comes from the dances of the minstrels *(bhāṭṭ)*. Rhythmic syllables are often composed for this sort of dance. And they are danced with the feet while holding the hands clasped in front. The ankle bells accompany the syllables as they are played on the *pakhāvaj*. This is a technique of the *kathaks*.

Raqs Tāūs kī gat

The method for this *gat* is such that playfulness and flirtatiousness extend to the whole gathering. Grab both ends of the skirt with both hands and dance like a peacock, circling to the right and the left. One should lift the skirt and dance so that it looks exactly like a peacock dancing with its tail spread.

Toṛās for Dance[1]

127. *Toṛā*

x	2	0	3
ek - do -	*tīn - cār -*	*pānc - ek -*	*do - tīn -*
ek do ek do	*tīn - ek do*	*do tīn ek -*	*do ek do tīn*

128. *Toṛā*

x	2	0	3
ek - - -	*do - - -*	*ek - do -*	*ek - do -*
tīn - ek -	*do - ek -*	*do - tīn -*	*ek - - -*
do - - -	*ek - - -*	*do - - -*	*tīn - - -*
ek do tīn			

1 The *toṛās* and *parmalūs* notated here come directly from the *Sarmāya-i ishrat* (Khan, Sadiq,1869, 163-4). Inayat Khan's readings do not precisely reflect the rhythmic settings given there. See Appendix D.

129. *Toṛā*

x	2	0	3
tā dhā kiṭa taka	*dhā kiṭa taka the'ī*	*nā kiṭa taka the'ī*	*tī dhā kiṭa taka*
the'i tā dhā kiṭa	*taka the'ī tī dhā*	*kiṭa taka the'ī tī*	*dhā kiṭa taka the'i*

130. *Toṛā*

x	2	0	3
ṭā kī ṭā dhī	*kī ṭā tā kā*	*tā kā tā kā*	*dhī dhī kā ṭā*
dhā - - -	*nā - kā tā*	*kā - tā kā*	*dhī dhī kā ṭā*
thun - gā thun	*- gā ta kā*	*dhī dhī kā ṭā*	*dhī dhī kā ṭā*

131. *Parmalū*

x	2	0	3
tā - the'ī -	*tat - the'ī -*	*tat - the'ī -*	*the'ī - tā -*
the'ī the'ī tā the'ī	*the'ī tā the'ī tā*	*the'ī tā tad dhā*	*tā tā tat the'ī*

132. *Parmalū*

x	2
tākā tīrān -gā tākā	*tākā tākā dhīdhī kīṭā*
0	**3**
dhīdhī dhīdhī kīṭā dhīlā	*-nga tā kā thū*

x	2
tīkī ṭādhī kīṭā tākā	*tākā tākā tākā tākā*
0	**3**
tat tīlā -nga thū	*tākā dādhī genā the'ī*

133. *Parmalū*

x				2			
tun	*jī*	*kī*	*tan*	*jī*	*kī*	*tun*	*jī*
0				3			
dhīgā	*tanjī*	*tā*	*kā*	*dīgā*	*dīgā*	*dīgā*	*tun*
x				2			
jī	*dīgā*	*tun*	*jī*	*jāgā*	*kokā*	*tākā*	*thūnā*
0				3			
thānā	*tākā*	*dīgā*	*dīgā*	*jāgā*	*jāgā*	*thulā*	*-nga*
x				2			
jāgā	*jāgā*	*thūla*	*-nga*	*thūlā*	*-nga*	*thūlā*	*-nga*
0				3			
tā	*kā*	*dā*	*dhī*	*ke*	*nā*	*the'ī*	-

134. *Parmalū*

x				2				0				3			
tā	*tī*	*tā*	*dhī*	*ṭī*	*tī*	*tā*	*dhī*	*tī*	*tī*	*tākā*	*tīgā*	*tānī*	*gānī*	*-gā*	*the'ī*

135. *Parmalū*

x				2			
tā	*da*	*thun*	*gā*	*kī*	*kīṭa*	*thun*	*gā*
0				3			
tī	*kīṭa*	*kā*	*dhī*	*kīṭa*	*tāgā*	*thūn*	-
x				2			
tīkī	*ṭādhī*	*kīṭā*	*tākā*	*dhī*	*dhī*	*dhī*	*dhī*
0				3			
kā	*ṭā*	*thun*	*ga*	*thunga*	*tākā*	*thunga*	*tākā*
x				2			
dādī	*kenā*	*tā*	--	*dī*	*gā*	*dī*	*gā*
0				3			
tā	*kā*	*dī*	*gā*	*tā*	*tādhī*	*kenā*	*the'ī*

In accompaniment to dance there is the practice of playing the *manjīrā* as support for the strokes of the *ghunguru* ankle bells. The *manjīrā* consists of a pair of cymbals. One is heavy and one light, and they call them the "male" and "female" *(nar, mādah).* On the *manjīrā* the sounds *kaṭ tān* are set and played in every *tāl.*

Commonly Used Patterns for the *manjīrā*[1]

136. *Tetālā*

x	2	0	3
tā nā tā nā	*kī ṭā tā nā*	*kī ṭā tā nā*	*kī ṭā tā nā*

137. *Ektālā*

x	x	x
tā nā tā nā	*kī ṭā tā nā*	*kī ṭā kī ṭā*

138. *Dādrā*

x	0
tā nā tā	*nā kīṭā kīṭā*

139. *Sulfāqta*

x	2	3
tā nā tā nā	*kī ṭā*	*kī ṭā tā nā*

1 The notations are based on a section in the *Sarmāya-i ishrat* (Khan, Sadiq,1869, 151). Sadiq Ali writes the sounds as *kaṭ* and *tān.* Inayat Khan has notated them as above.

Final Verse set of the Book with the Date by the Author

Inayat, whether every tune *(tān)* falters or not the melody *(sur)* of Surayya Sahana will resound until the Day of Resurrection.

What form is it that is more beautiful than ours? Still, with all our delicate beauty, we mingle with dust in the end.

The star and the peacock have so many dance steps *(gat)*, but all of these moves are just ringings of the Truth.

When a pen comes to the hand of a wanderer this soul's very vagrancy is its authority.

If the glance falls on the essence of a heart moved by divine passion, for an instant everything becomes the Truth.

Inayat, if you too have some aspiration, whatever you may have is grace *('ināyat)* from God.

O God, my gratitude ought not be half-hearted, for the work I have begun is today finished.

In my assignment dwells Your Truth; in my humility dwells Your Power.

A book is a memorial, they say. Thus the author lives on until the Day of Resurrection.

But author and book, these are so merely in name. O God, everything is the product of Your Power.

Existence belongs to You, this whole place is Yours
Your name alone endures, O noble Lord.

When you ennobled a bit of dust, the angels all fell in
awe of it.

Prophecy, sainthood, holy wonders and blessings,
these are all winks in the amorous play of Your Power.

O God, when your bounty surges forth the fortune
of those You favor blossoms.

The stamp of travel in the gardens of the Deccan was
inscribed in my fate by the divine bounty,

O God, keep safe the Deccan and its King until the
next world comes, with all its miracles.

How can I sufficiently praise the Deccan? It is the
refuge of the world, the sanctuary of prosperity.

Each artist's assembly is superb; it is a place of peace,
a nocturnal abode of mercy.

How could the great king of this land not be excellent?
He is Mahbub Ali Khan, auspicious in his majesty.

Pure king, with an always well-intentioned heart, the
patron of the poor, the security of his subjects.

In his largesse, whatever he gives is a cloud of generosity.
His munificence is renowned the world over.

If he gave something, he gave it, and will keep on giving.
His hand does not tire when it is time for munificence.

In this way too is he honored, that in the eye of
the world his image is seen glittering in the pupil.

It was with him in mind that I have written this book:
one who meets with his approval deserves respect.

He who is the great and eminent Prime Minister of this land, may God keep him happy *(shād)* until the Day of Resurrection.

Firm yet dexterous, honored savant, devoted to the service of the king of pure essence.

The king of pure essence's premier grandee, peerless in his mastery of every art and craft.

Inayat, what you have boldly laid out in these pages is all by the felicity of this premier grandee of the king.

These are the sweet winks of the possessors of felicity, but still more sublime is the Holy Grace.

O God, keep prosperous this Deccan which in the whole world is the happiest expanse.

When this lowly one's book reached its conclusion I prostrated in submission with gratitude for what I have received.

Inayat, with the date in mind my heart said, on the year of completion, "It is the music of the soul" *(naghmah-i rūh hai)*[1]

1324 Hijri (1906 CE)

Verse Set Pertaining to Date

When Inayat received a bequest from David, people said his voice could work wonders.

He wrote a fine book about song; all who saw it deemed it a tray of perfumes.

1 Chronogram in the *abjad* system: N/50+Gh/1000+M/40+H/5+R/200+U/6+H/8+H/5+Y/10=1324

Your well-wishing supporter rendered the year of its completion as "the cry from the beak of the *mūsīqār* bird" (*shūrī-i minqār-i mūsīqār*).[2]

1324 Hijri

2 Chronogram in the *abjad* system:: Sh/300+U/6+R/200+Y/10+M/40+N/50+Q/100+A/1+R/200+M/40+U/6+S/60+Y/10+Q/100+A/1+R/200=1324

What "gift" *('ināyat)* is there in Inayat's book?—it's all magic! By way of persuasion, you display your qualities through the words.

Authority is song in this quarter of the world.
The policy of emotion is the beauty of the composition.

If you hurry after the pure ones in abundance of goodness, you'll be drunken and elated by intoxication from their cup.

When his rare and inspiring book was finished,
the day ended with the author's wish for honor.

With great care, I composed in the Hashimi system the year of its completion: "A mirror of the canon of song."

تدوین عنایت چه عنایت همه جادو   در جلب درونهای خلایق ز کلامش
دستور سرود است برین صفحهٔ عالم   آئینِ طرب هست همه حسنِ نظامش
ارباب صفا گر دوی از غایتِ خوبی   سرمست مسرّت ز پیِ مستیِ جامش
چون ختم شد آن نغز کتابش طرب انگیز   آمد سرِ تاریخ بتوقیر مرامش
کردیم رقم هاشمی از راه تأمل
آئینهٔ قانون غنا سال تمامش

Appendix A
List of Ragas
notated by Hidayat Inayat-Khan

List of Ragas

" From the book called "Minka-i-Musikar"

by

Prof. Inayat Khan of Baroda

KAMIKI 14 Balks

1
2
3
4
5
6
7
8
9
10
11
12
13
14
15
16
17
18
19
20
21
22
23
24
25
26
27
28
KAMIKI 14 Balks

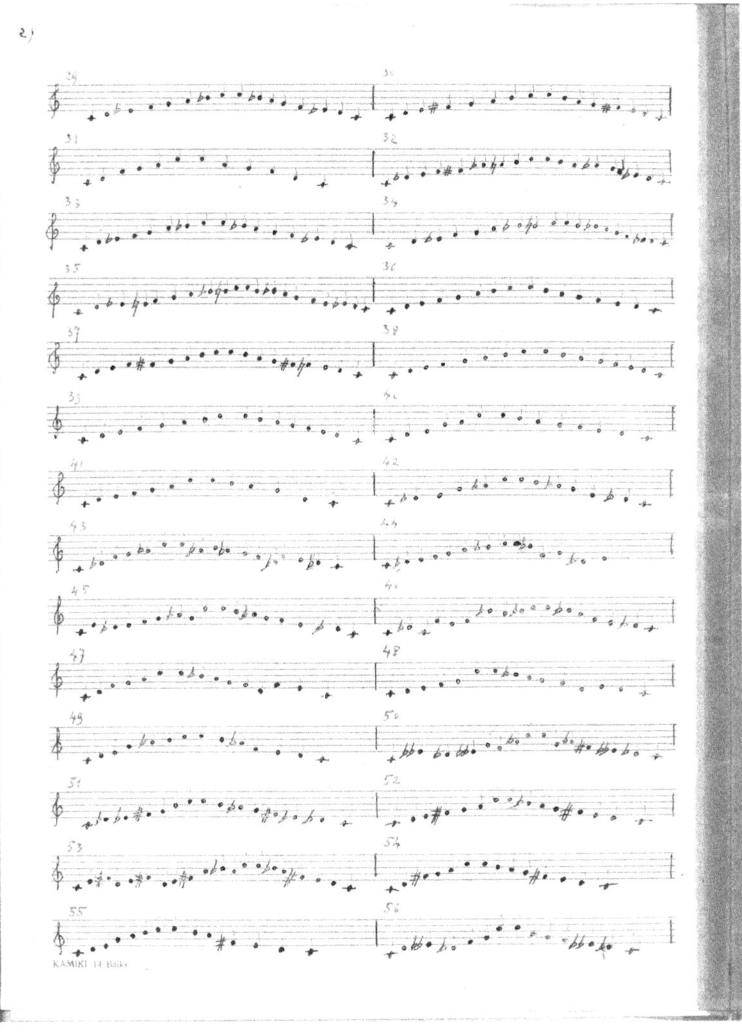
31
32
33
34
35
36
37
38
41
42
45
47
48
51
52
53
54
55
56

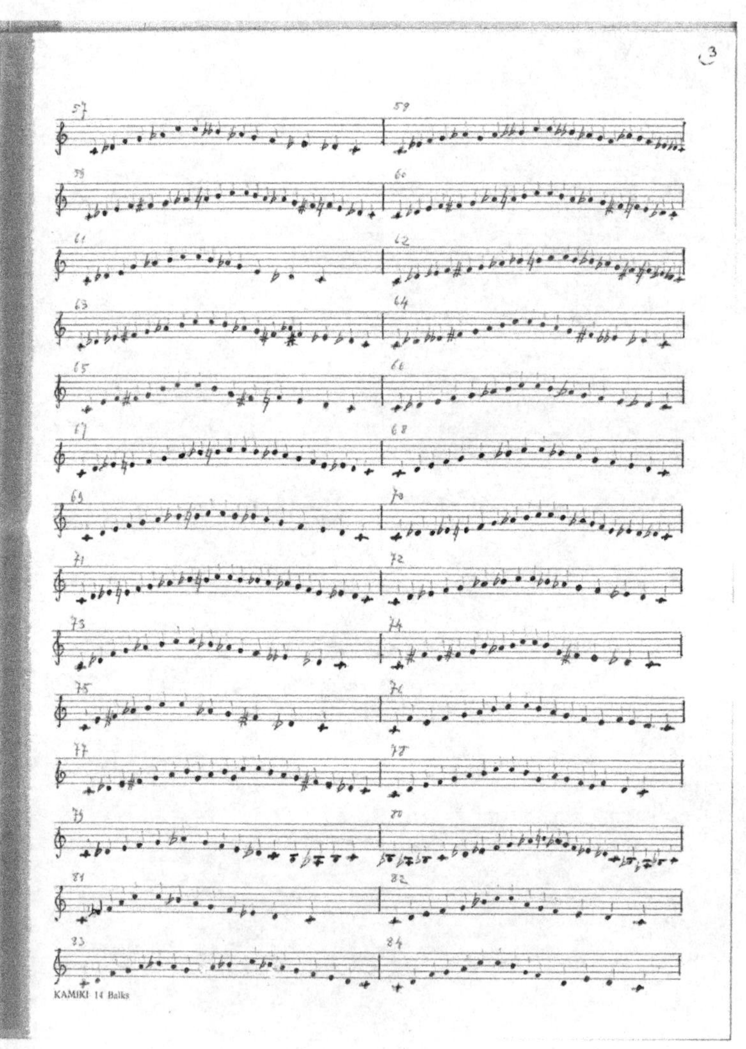
3
57
58
59
60
61
62
63
64
65
66
67
68
69
70
71
72
73
74
75
76
77
78
79
80
81
82
83
84
KAMIKI 14 Balks

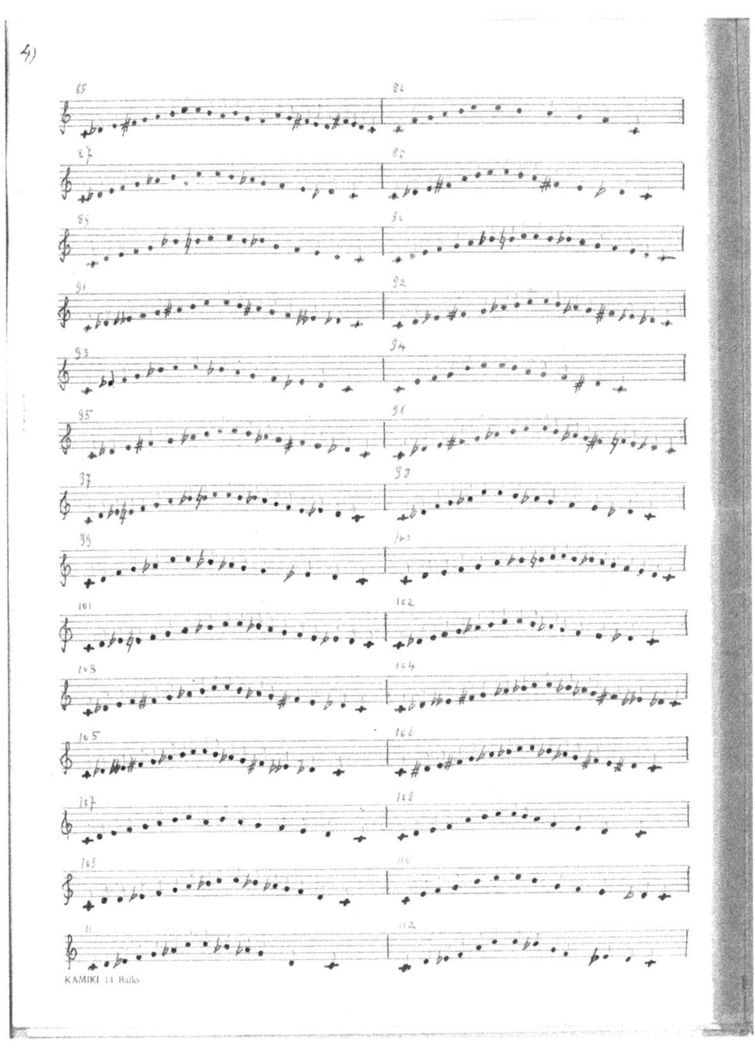

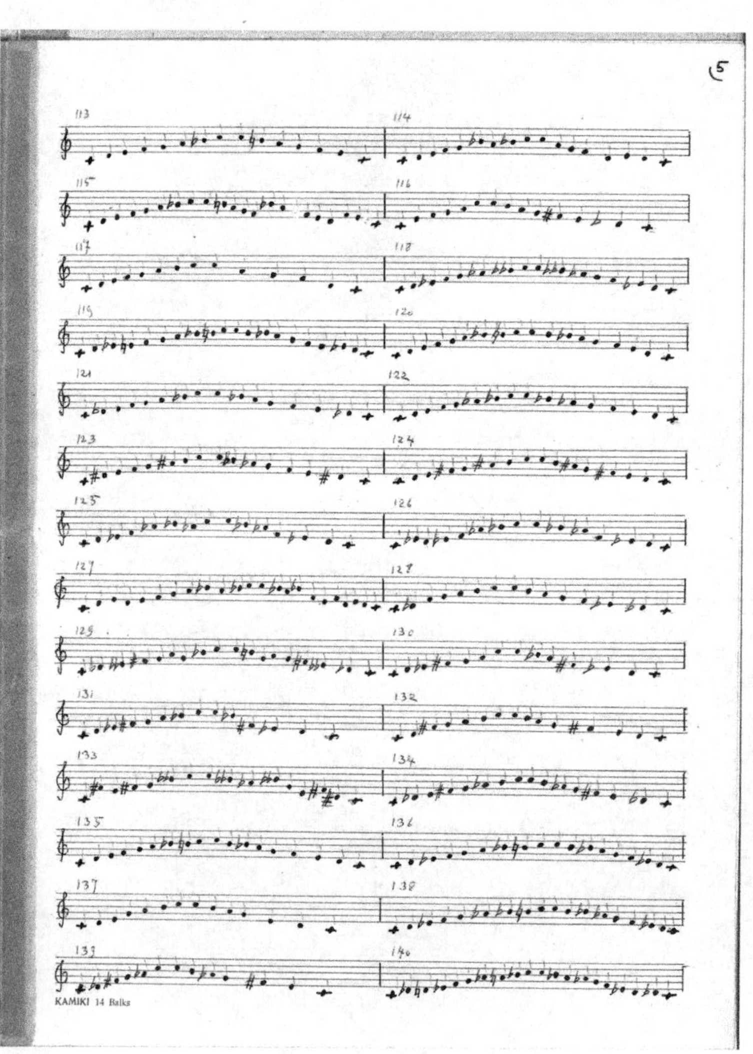
15
113
114
115
116
117
118
119
120
121
122
123
124
125
126
127
128
129
130
131
132
133
134
135
136
137
138
139
140
KAMIKI 14 Balks

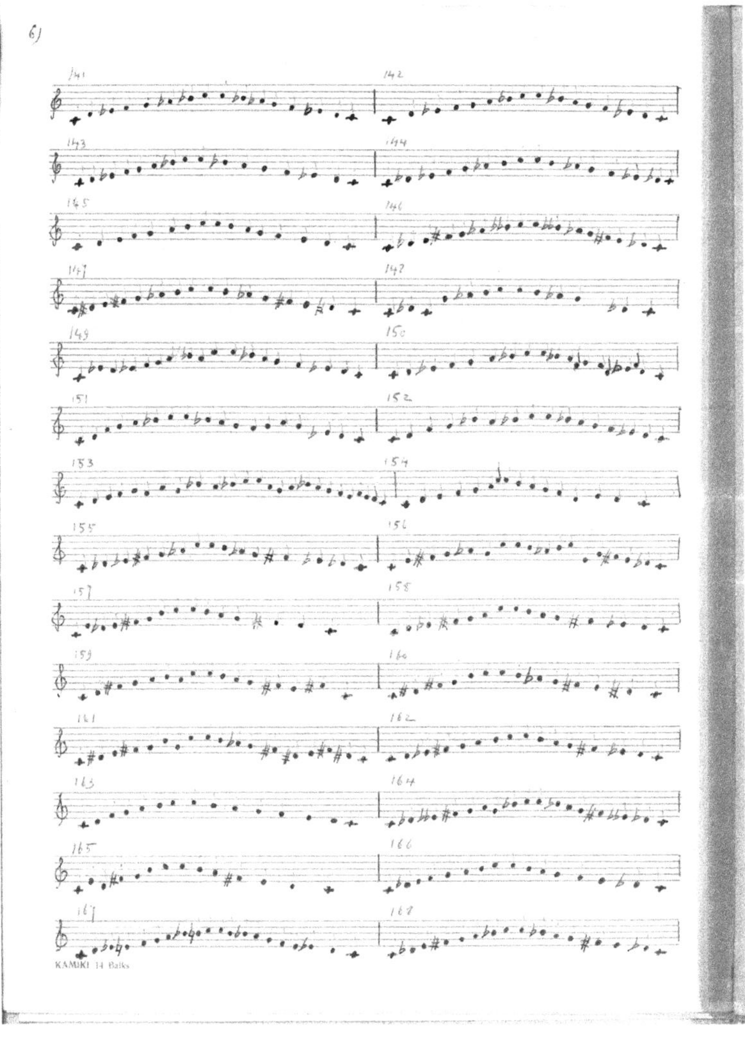

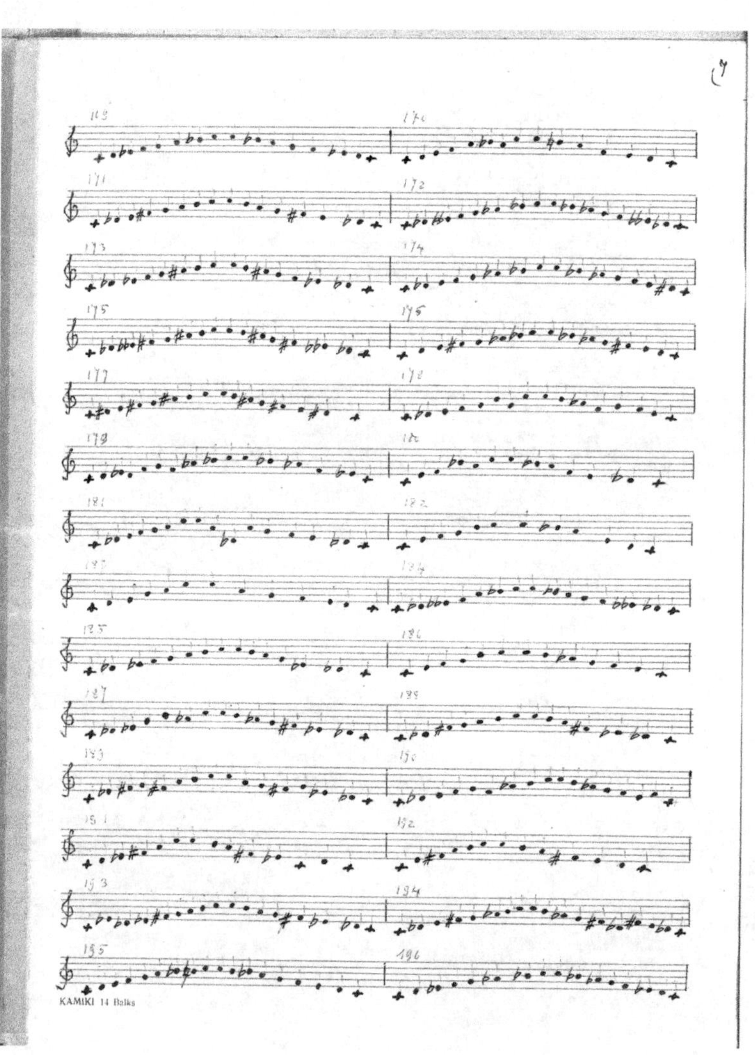
KAMIKI 14 Balks

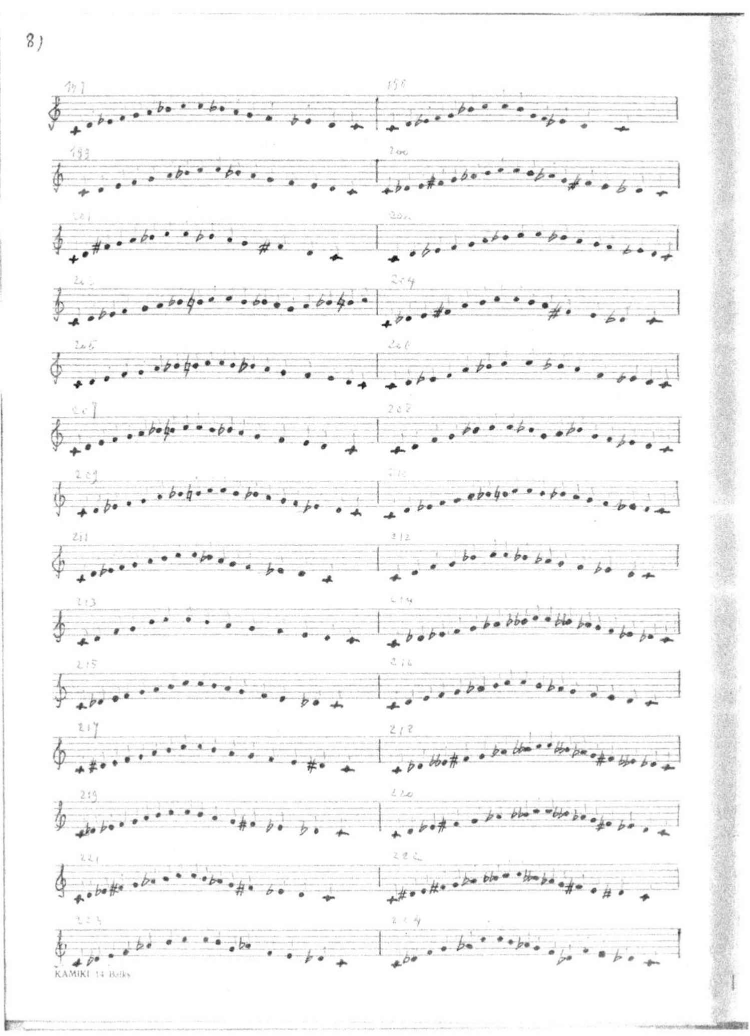

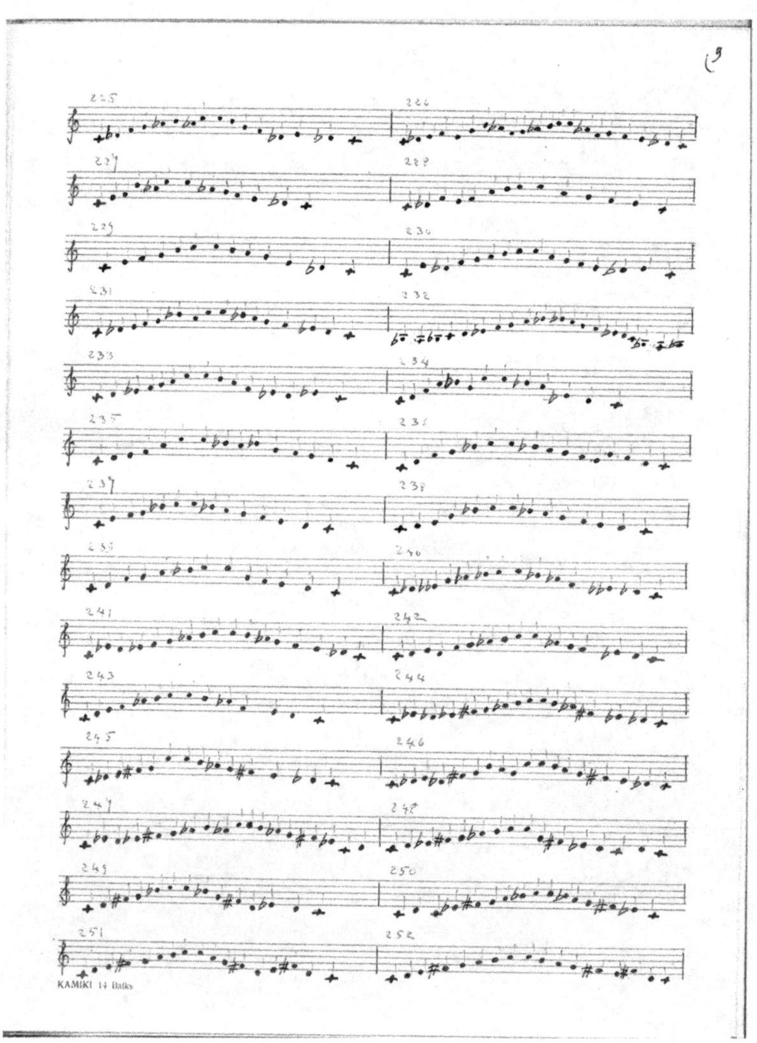

225
226
227
228
229
230
231
232
233
234
235
236
237
238
239
240
241
242
243
244
245
246
247
248
249
250
251
252
KAMIKI 14 Balks

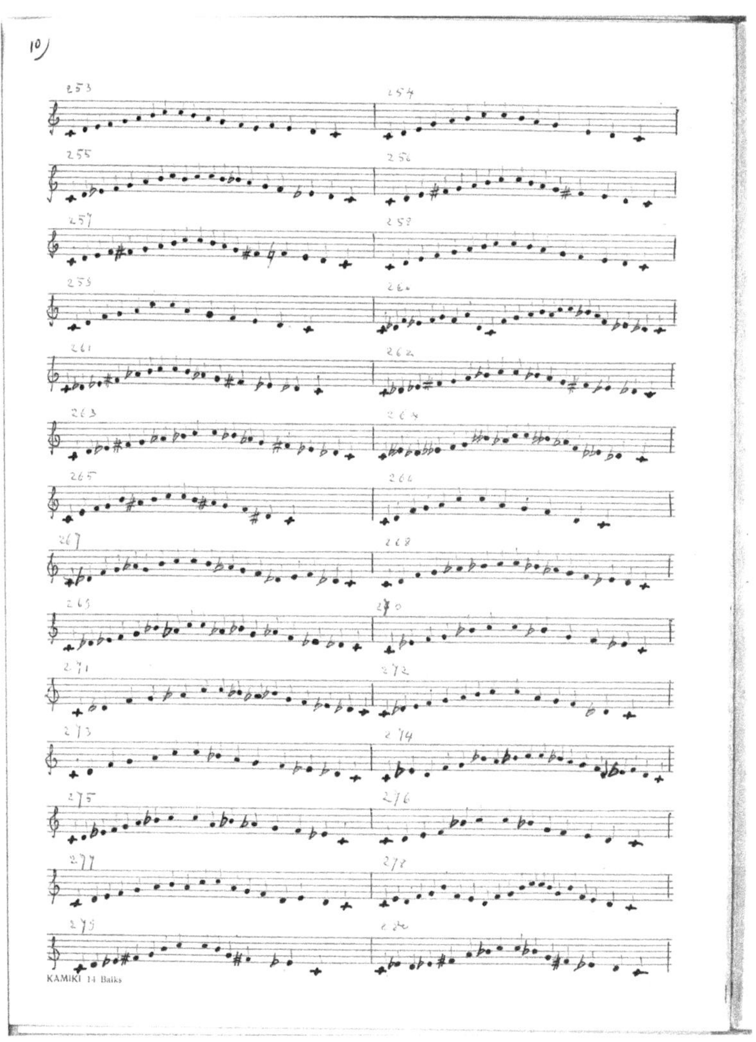
10)
253
254
255
256
257
258
259
260
261
262
263
264
265
266
267
268
269
270
271
272
273
274
275
276
277
278
279
280
KAMIKI 14 Baiks

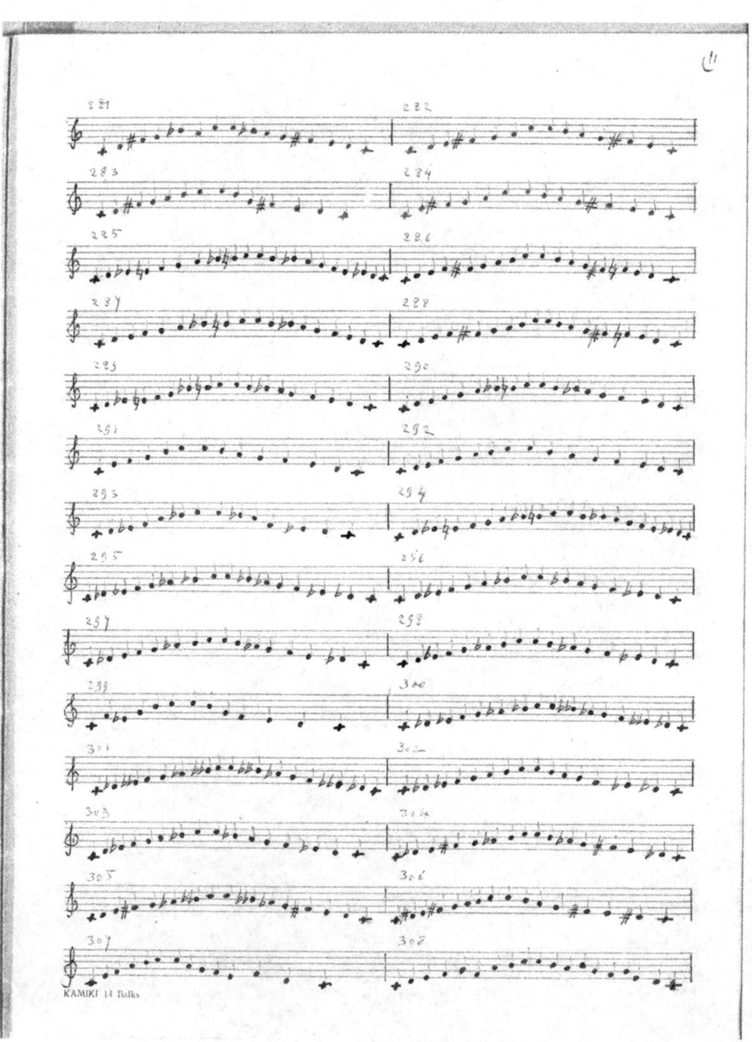
281
282
283
284
285
286
287
288
289
290
291
292
293
294
295
296
297
298
299
300
301
302
303
304
305
306
307
308
KAMIKI 14 Balks

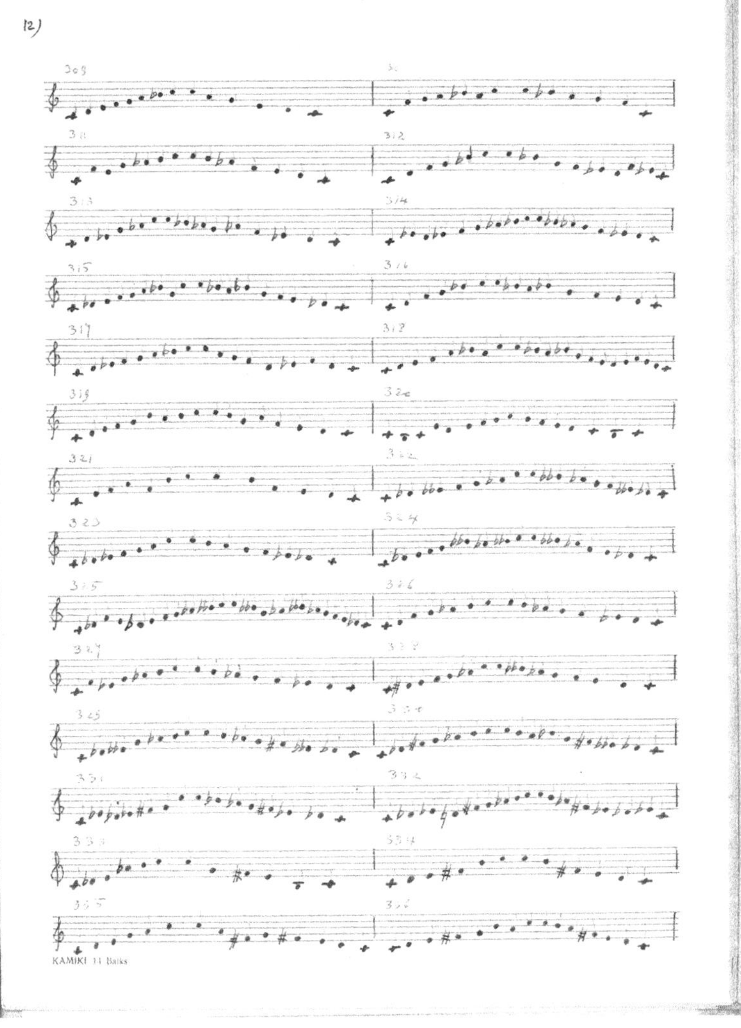

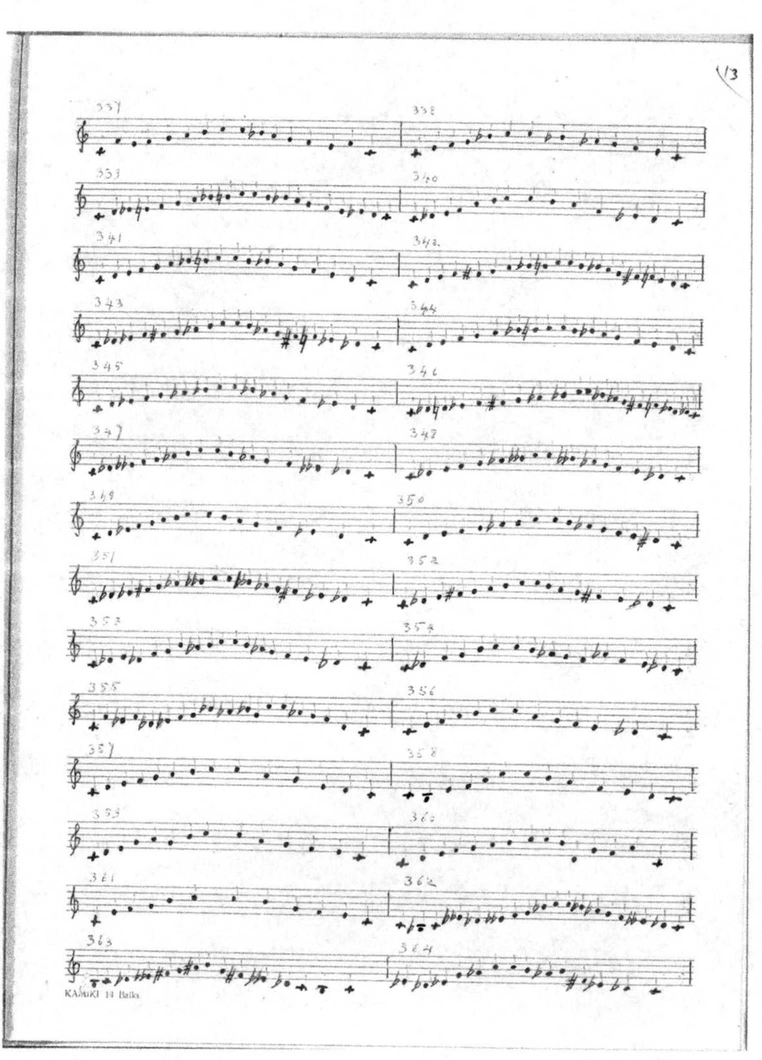
13
337
338
339
340
341
342
343
344
345
346
347
348
349
350
351
352
353
354
355
356
357
358
359
360
361
362
363
364

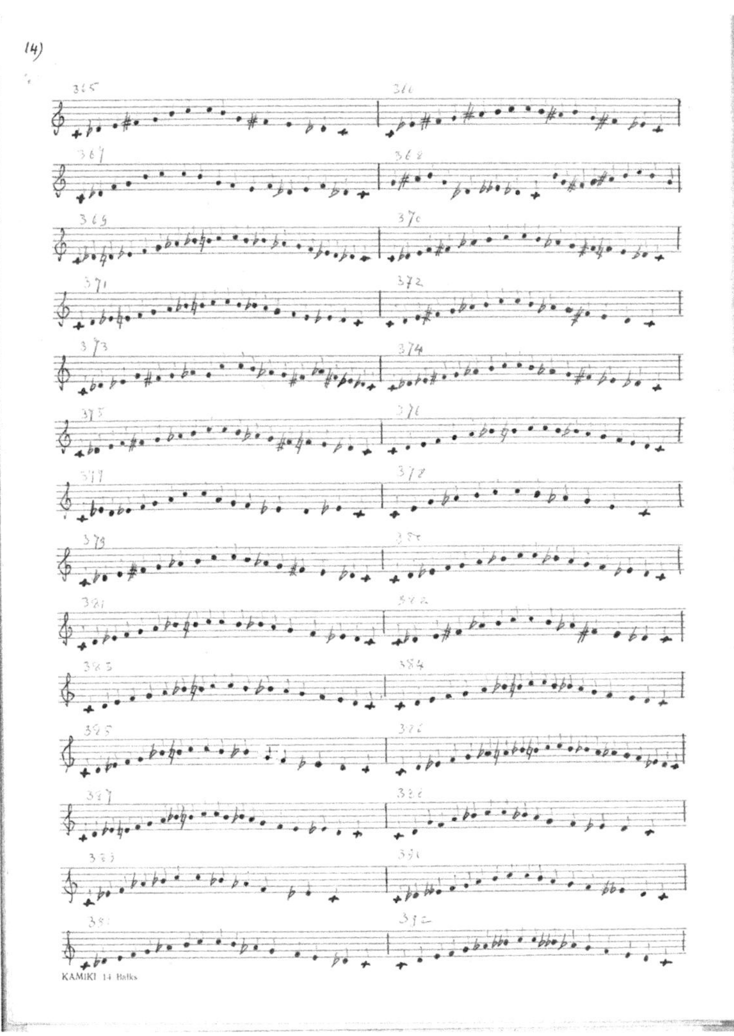
14)
KAMIKI 14 Balks

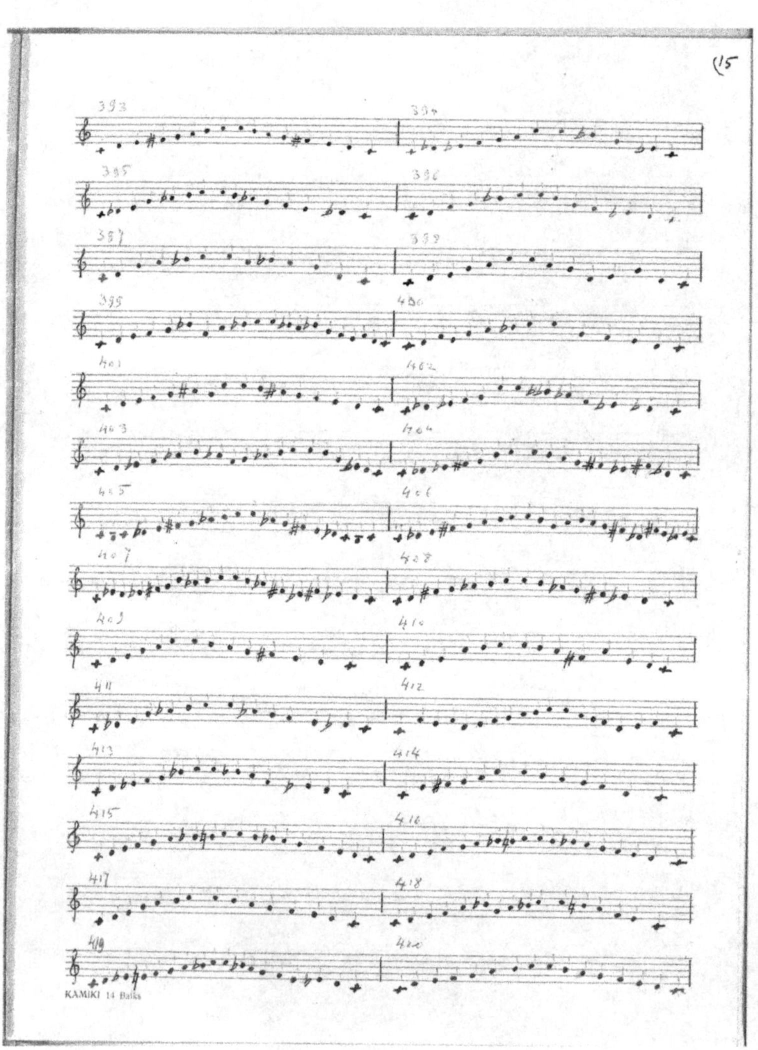
15
393
394
395
396
397
398
399
400
401
402
403
404
405
406
407
408
409
410
411
412
413
414
415
416
417
418
419
420
KAMIKI 14 Balks

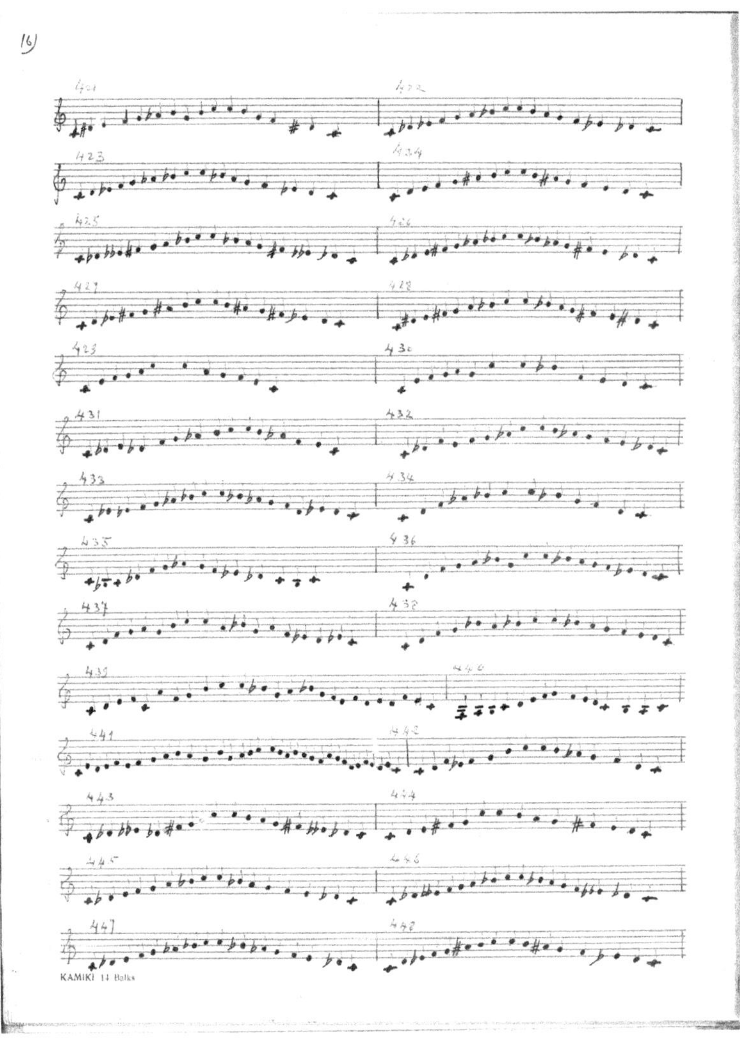
KAMIKI 14 Balks

17
449
450
451
452
453
454
455
456
457
458
459
460
461
462
463
464
465
466
467
468
469
470
471
472
473
474
475
476
KAMIKI 14 Balks

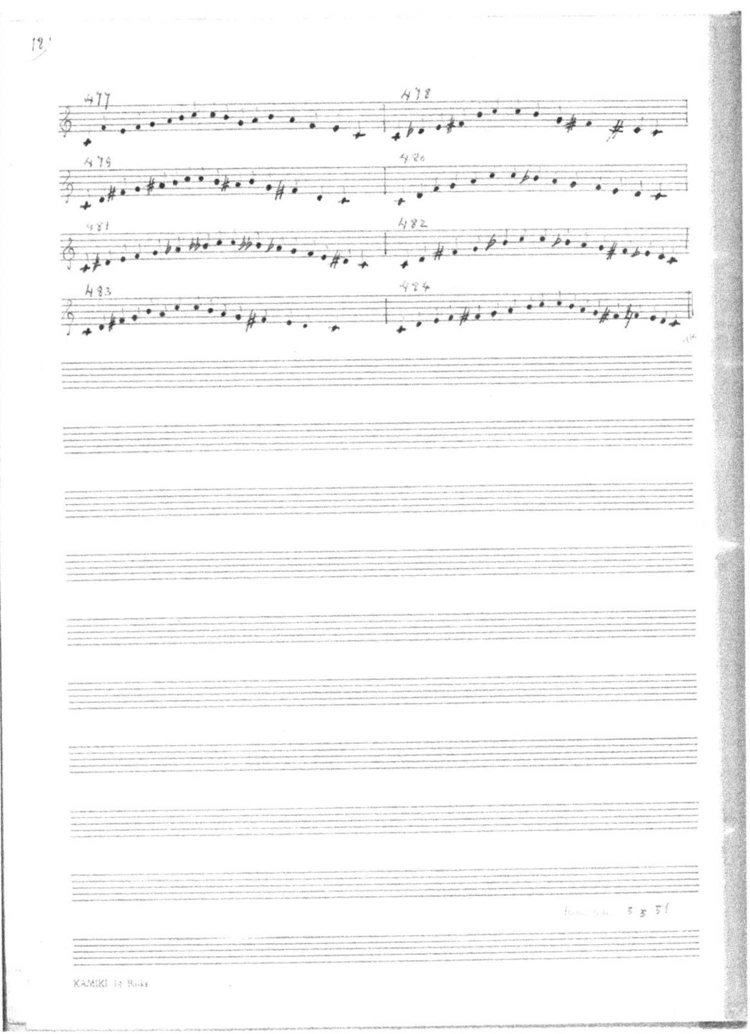
12
477
478
479
480
481
482
483
484

Appendix B
List of Tabla Rhythms
notated by Hidayat Inayat-Khan

List of Tabla Rythms

"From the book called "Minka-i-Musikar"

by

prof. Inayat Khan of Baroda

KAMIKI 14 Bilks

accents
> fort
· faible

KAMIKI 14 Balks

KAMIKI 14 Balks

KAMIKI 14 Bolks

Appendix C

Poets in the *Minqār-i Musiqar*

Akhtar (Urdu) Nawab Wajid Ali Shah 1822–87

'Āli (Persian)

Amir (Urdu) Amir Minai 1828–1900

Ashna (Urdu)

Asif (Urdu) Mir Mahbub Ali Khan, 1866–1911

Bedil (Persian) Abdul Qadir, 1642–1720

Dagh (Urdu) Nawab Mirza Khan, 1831–1905

Faiz (Urdu)

Hafiz (Persian) Khwaja Shams-ud-Din Muhammad Hafez-e Shirazi, d.1389

Hasan (Persian) Hasan Ghaznavi, twelfth century

Hashimi (Persian))

Hazin (Persian) Hazin Lahji, 1692–1766

Inayat (Urdu) Inayat Khan, 1882–1927)

Iqbal (Urdu) Sir Muhammad Iqbal, 1877–1938

Iraqi (Persian) Fakhr al-Din Ibrahim 'Iraqi, 1213–89

Ishrati (Persian) Aqa Ali 'Ishrati, seventeenth century (?)

Jami (Persian) Nur ad-Din Abd ar-Rahman Jami, 1414–92

Jura't (Urdu) Qalandar Bakhsh Jura't, 1748–1809

Kaifi (Urdu)

Khusrau (Persian) Amir Khusrau, 1253–1325

Maghribi (Persian) Muhammad Shirin Maghrebi, d. 1406.

Mahmud (Persian) Mahmud Shabestari 1288–1340

Momin (Urdu) Momin Khan Momin, 1800–51

Muhi (Persian)

Munir (Persian) Abul Barakat, Molla Monir Lahuri, d. 1644

Nasikh (Urdu) Bakhsh Nasikh, 1771–1838

Nasim (Urdu) Daya Shankar Kaul, 1811–45

Nawab (Urdu)

Niyaz (Urdu) Niaz Fatehpuri, 1884–1966

Nizami (Persian) Ilyas ibn Yusuf, d. 1209

Qudsi (Persian) Qudsi Mashadi, seventeenth century

Qutb (Persian) Qutb al-din Shirazi, 1236–1311

Rasikh (Urdu) Ghulam Ali of Patna, b. 1749 (?)

Sa'di (Persian) Musharrif al-Din ibn Muslih al-Din, 1213–91

Saib (Persian) Saib Tabrizi, 1601–77

Sauda (Urdu) Mirza Muhammad Rafi, 1713–81

Shad (Persian, Urdu) Maharaja Sir Kishen Pershad, 1864–1940

Shadan (Urdu) Sayyid Aulad Husain Shadan Bilgrami, 1869–1948

Shams (Persian) Shams-i Tabrizi, 1185-1248. Spiritual mentor of Jalal ad-Din Rumi. Rumi often used "Shams" as a pen name in his own poetry.

Shamshad (Urdu) Shamshad Muhammad Abdul Ahad Firangi Mahal, d. 1915

Sharaf (Persian) Abdulla of Shiraz, 7th century (?) Sharaf

Jahan, 10th century (?)

Sharif (Persian) Muhammad Sharif Nasafi, d.1620 (?)

Siraj (Urdu) Siraj Aurangabadi, 1712–63

Turki (Persian)

Zafar (Urdu) Abu Zafar Sirajuddin Muhammad Bahadur Shah, 1775–1862

Zahir (Urdu), in the circle of the Hyderabad Nizam (Khan and Westbrook, 1996, 8)

Zamin (Urdu)

Appendix D

Toṛās and *Parmalūs* from the *Sarmāya-i ishrat* used as the basis for the *Minqār-i Mūsīqār* notations 127-35[1]

First *Toṛā*

x	2	0	3
ek do tīn chār	*pānc ek do ekdo*	*ekdo tīn ek do*	*tīn ekdo ekdo tīn*

Second *Toṛā*

x				2				0				3			
ek	-	-	-	*do*	-	-	-	*ek*	-	*do*	-	*ek*	*do*	*tin*	-
ek	-	*do*	-	*ek*	*do*	*tin*	-	*ek*	-	*do*	-	*ek*	*do*	*tin*	-
ek	*do*	*tin*	-	*ek*	*do*	*tin*	-	then the entire pattern twice again (?)							

Third *Toṛā*

x				2			
tā	-	*dhā*	-	*kiṭa*	*taka*	*tā*	-
0				3			
dhā	*kiṭa*	*taka*	*te*	*tā*	*kiṭa*	*taka*	*the'ī*
x				2			
tī	-	*dhā*	-	*kiṭa*	*taka*	*the'ī*	-
0				3			
tīdhā	*kiṭataka*	*the'ī*	*tīdhā*	*kiṭataka*	*the'ī*	*tīdhā*	*kiṭataka*
x							
the'ī							

1 The author of the *Sarmāya-i ishrat* does not use chart notation but indicates *tāl* divisions and rough directions above the syllables ("single speed," "fast" etc) (Khan, Sadiq,1869, 163-4).The *toṛās* contain sufficient directions but the *parmalūs* show few indications of rhythm. The settings here are my interpretations. I have left some without settings.

Fourth *Toṛā*

x	*2*	*0*	*3*
ṭa ka ṭa	*dha ka ṭa*	*ta kā ta kā*	*dha ṛa ka ṭa*
dhā - - -	*ta - kā -*	*ta kā ta kā*	*dha ṛa ka ṭa*
thang - - -	*thang - ta kā*	*dha ṛa ka ṭa*	*dha ṛa ka ṭa*
dhā			

Parmalūs, which are performed in dance after *toṛās*

First *Parmalū* of *the'ī*

x	*2*
tā the'ī tat the'ī	*tat the'ī the'ī tā*
0	*3*
the'ī the'ī tā the'ī the'ī tā the'ī tā	*the'ī tā taddhā tāt ta tata*

x

the'ī tītū the'ī the'ī ta – "begin like this and continue to present *bols* with the hands and feet to come to *sam*"

Second *Parmalū* of *the'ī*

x

Taka tarā -nga takā takā takā ḍhaṛa kaṭa
ḍhaṛa ḍhaṛa kiṭa dhalā -nga taka thūṭa kaṭa
dhaka ṭa ta kā ta kā ta kā ta kā ta kā - ta ta
talā -nga dhalān -nga taka dadi ghana the'ī

Third *Parmalū* of *thapei* (?)

Tanje ke tanje taka dhaga tanje taka daga daga daga tanje diga tanje jagata kūka taka thun thun taka diga diga jaga jaga thulā-nga jaga jaga thulā-nga thulā-nga thulā-nga taka dadi ghana the'ī sam

Fourth *Parmalū* of *titāla*

tī te'i dhī tītī | te'i tadhī tītī tiga | niga tā tiga tiga | tā tiga dhā the'ī
sam

Toṛā of the *Parmalū*, *tāl titāla*

Tā 'ū thungā ṭikaṭa thungā ṭikaṭa ṭaka dhikaṭa tiga thū ṭikaṭa taka dhikaṭa taka ḍhiṛa ḍhiṛakiṭa thunga taka thunga taka dadaghana tā diga diga taka dada ghana sam

Glossary of Names and Terms[1]

Abu Hashim Madani: the author's Sufi master.

acal ṭhāṭ : immoveable fret system in *sitār.*

ālāp: section of a *dhrupad.*

Alauddin Khan Pathan: the author's brother.

alg͟hoza: wind instrument.

anādrut: a time division.

ang (in dance) "limb," typical moves.

ang (in *tāl*): "limb," sections or patterns.

antarā: section of a *dhrupad.*

anūvādī (Sskt *anuvādi*): prominent note in a *rāg.*

āṛ kī lay : a complex rhythm.

ārohī, avarohī: ascent, descent.

ashṭapadī: a song genre.

āstāī (*k͟hayāl*): a song genre.

āstāī (Sskt, H: *sthāī*): section of a *dhrupad.*

auṛav: a *rāg* category.

āvāz: sound in general.

bānī: *dhrupad* styles.

bansī: a wind instrument.

bānsurī: a wind instrument.

bāyān: left hand drum of *tabla* pair.

bhajan: a song genre.

bhāv: expression.

bherī: a wind instrument.

bhog (Sskt, H: *ābhog*): section of a *dhrupad.*

bīn (Sskt: *vīṇā*): a string instrument.

1 Entries include notes of variant spellings in Sanskrit (Sskt), Hindi (H) and Persian/Urdu (P/U). *Rāg* and *tāl* names are not included in the Glossary.

bisrām (Sskt: *viśrāma*): rhythmic rest.
bol (in dance): spoken syllable.
bol (in *manjīra*): syllable, stroke.
bol (in *sitār*): stroke.
bol (in *tabla*): spoken syllable, stroke.
brahm bīn: a string instrument.
budhbudī: a skin-covered instrument.
cal ṭhāṭ: moveable fret system in *sitār*.
cang: a solid instrument.
caturang: a song genre.
catūsra jāt (Sskt: *catuśra jāti*): a rhythmic setting.
cautālā (Sskt cautāla; H *cautāl*): a twelve-beat *tāl*.
chan (Sskt, H: *kṣaṇ)*: time division.
chaugun kī lay: quadruple time.
cikārā: a string instrument.
dādrā: a song genre; a six-beat *tāl*.
daf: a skin-covered instrument.
Dāgar bānī: a *dhrupad* style.
ḍamaru: a skin-covered instrument.
ḍanka: a skin-covered instrument.
desī: an archaic *rāg* category.
ḍhak: a drum.
dhamār: song genre; a *tāl*.
ḍhapṛā: a skin covered instrument.
ḍhol: a skin-covered instrument.
ḍholak: a skin-covered instrument.
ḍholkī: a skin-covered instrument.
dhrupad: a song genre.
dhuvā: an archaic song genre.
dilrubā: a string instrument.
ḍorū: a skin-covered instrument.
drut: a time division.

drut: fast tempo.

dugḍugī: a skin-covered instrument.

dugun lay: double tempo.

dundubhī: a skin-covered instrument.

dvīguru (Sskt *dviguru*): a time division.

ektārā (H: *ektār*): a string instrument.

fiqrā: extemporization on *sitār*.

Fīrozkhvānī (H: *Firozkhānī*): a *sitār* composition style.

gamak (Sskt: *gamaka*): techniques; ornaments.

garbā: a dance.

gat (in dance): movement, position.

gat (in *sitār*): composition.

gāyan, vādan, nart : instrumental music, song, dance.

ghan: solid instruments category.

ghanṭa: a solid instrument.

ghanṭī: a solid instrument.

ghaṛā: a solid instrument.

g͟hazal: a song genre.

ghunguru: a solid instrument.

Goharmārī bānī: a *dhrupad* style.

grah (Sskt: *graha*): place in the *tāl* cycle where the song begins.

grām (Sskt: *grāma*): an ancient scale category.

guru: a time division.

Hakim Abu Ali Sina (Avicenna) (d.1037): Persian scholar, scientist, physician, author.

harmonium: a keyboard instrument.

horī: a song genre.

Hyderabad: Indian city, princely state.

isrār: a string instrument.

jaltarang: a solid instrument.

jāt, tāl jāt (Sskt: *jāti*): "class;" internal count of a *tāl*)

jāvalī: a solid instrument.

jhānjar: a solid instrument.
jhānjh: a solid instrument.
jhunjhūnā: a solid instrument.
kā'iṛkā: a skin-covered instrument.
kachap bīn: a string instrument.
kāfi: a song genre; a *rāg*.
kāgpad: a time division.
kaharva: a song genre; a *tāl*.
kāl: "time" slow, medium, fast.
kamānca: a string instrument.
kandahārī bānī: a style of *dhrupad*.
kaṛā: a solid instrument.
karnāh or *qurnā*: a wind instrument.
kaṛtāl or *caṭka*: a solid instrument.
k͟hālī: non-clapped section of a *tāl*.
k͟hayāl (H *khya̱l*): a song genre, aslo called *āsthāī*.
khanḍ jāt (Sskt: *khaṇḍa jāti*): a rhythmic category.
khanjarī: a skin-covered instrument.
khaṭkā: an ornament.
kinnar bīn or *kinarī*: a string instrument.
kirtan: a song genre.
Kishen Pershad: Prime Minister of Hyderabad 1901–1912 and 1926–1937.
komal: flat note.
kuāṛ kī lay: a complex rhythm.
laghu (U: also *laghū*): a time division.
lās: a dance category.
lāvanī: a dance.
made kāl: middle tempo.
madh saptak: middle octave.
Mahbub Ali Khan: Nizam of Hyderabad, ruled 1869–1911.
mandra saptak: lower octave.

manjīrā: a solid instrument.

mārg: archaic *rāg* category.

mashk or *surtī apang*: a wind instrument.

māṭhā: an archaic song genre.

mātrā: beat.

Maula Bakhsh (1833–96): the author's grandfather.

mridang (Sskt: *mṛdanga*): a skin-covered instrument.

mridang yatī: a notational sign, ornament.

Imam Muhammad Ghazali (1058–1111): Persian theologian, mystic.

mukh bīn: a wind instrument.

mūrchanā: archaic scale types.

murlī: a wind instrument.

Musīdkhvānī (H: *Masītkhānī*): a style of *sitār* composition.

mūsīqār: magical bird.

na'e: a wind instrument.

nafirī: a wind instrument.

nāg sur: a wind instrument.

naghāra: a skin-covered instrument.

naqāra: a skin-covered instrument.

nārad bīn: a string instrument.

nastarang: a wind instrument.

naubat: a skin-covered instrument.

Nauhārbānī: a style of *dhrupad*.

nrit, nrittam, nāṭyā: dance, expressional dance, theater.

pad: a song genre.

pakhāvaj: a skin-covered instrument.

pallavī: a song genre.

paran: a drum composition.

paristān: a type of dance.

parmalū: a type of syllabic dance composition.

pāvā: a wind instrument.

plut: a time division.

pungī: a wind instrument.

qānūn: a string instrument.

qavālī: a song genre.

qurnā: a wind instrument.

rabāb: a string instrument.

rāg: classical melody.

rāginī, putra, bhārjā: old *rāg* categories of females, sons, and wives.

Rahmat Khan (1843-1910): the author's father.

rudra bīn: a string instrument.

sam: first beat of a *tāl* cycle.

sama': Sufi ritual music.

sangīt (Sskt: *saṅgīta*): Indian classical music.

Saṅgītaratnākara: thirteenth-century Sanskrit musicological text.

sankha: a wind instrument.

saptak: octave.

sārangī: a string instrument.

sarasvatī bīn or *vīnā*: a string instrument.

sargam: the Hindustani scale tones *Sā Re, Ga Ma Pa Dha Nī*; practice pieces using the scale tones.

sārinda: string instrument.

sarod: a string instrument.

shahnā'ī: a wind instrument.

sharab bīn or *sharbat*: a string instrument.

sharnā'ī: a wind instrument.

Shīvmat, Kishanmat, Bharatmat Hanumatmat: *rāga-rāginī* systems.

shudh (Sskt: *shuddha;* H: *shuddh:* U: *shudh* or *shud):* natural note.

sīng: a wind instrument.

sitār, sehtār, sitārī or *sundarī*: a string instrument.

sruti (Sskt: *śruti*): microtones.

sur (Sskt *svara*; H: *svar*): musical sound, note, or tone.

sur: a wind instrument.

surbīn: a string instrument.

surmaṇḍal: a string instrument.
sursanghār: a string instrument.
sursoṭā: a string instrument.
surūp: structure of a *tāl*.
sūshir (Sskt: *suṣira*): wind instruments.
tabla (P/U: *ṭabla*): two-piece drum
tāl (Sskt *tāla*): classical rhythmic cycles.
tāli: clap.
ṭanbūrā or *ṭanbūrī* (H: *tamburā, tānpurā*): a drone string.
tāṇḍav: a category of dance.
Tansen: Miyan Tansen (d.1589); legendary composer, musican.
ṭappa: a song genre.
tār saptak: high octave.
tarāna: a song genre.
tārtar saptak: highest octave.
tāsh or *tāsha*: a skin-covered instrument.
tat: string instruments.
ṭāus: a string instrument.
ṭhāṭ: fret configuration on *sitār*.
ṭhekā: strokes, syllables of a *tāl*.
ṭhumrī: a song genre.
tigun kī lay: triple speed.
tirvaṭ: a song genre.
tīsra jāt (Sskt: *tisra jāti*): a rhythmic category.
tīvra: sharp note.
toṛā (in dance): a type of composition or variation.
toṛā (in *sitār*): a variation on a composition.
trivaṛī: a time division.
tumburu bīn: a string instrument.
tura'ī: a wind instrument.
tūtārī: a wind instrument.
urs: "wedding,"anniversary of the death of a Sufi saint.

ustād: master, expert.
vādī—vivādī sur: two prominent notes of a *rāg*.
varnam: a song genre.
vīlamb (H: *vilambit*): slow tempo.
vitat: skin-covered instruments.
yatī (Sskt: *yati*): slur or ornament.

Bibliography

Ahmed, Zahir. *Life's Yesterdays: Glimpses of Sir Nizamat Jung and His Times.* Bombay: Thacker & Co,. Ltd. 1945. http://krishikosh.egranth.ac.in/bitstream/1/2025593/1/G7123.pdf

Bakhle, Janaki. *Two Men and Music: nationalism in the making of an Indian classical tradition.* Oxford, New York: Oxford University Press, 2005.

Bakhsh, Maula, Professor, Ghise Khan. *Saṅgītanubhav.* Vol. 1 Mumbai and Baroda 1888. http://www.ibiblio.org/guruguha/MusicResearchLibrary/Books-Guj/BkGuj-MaulaBaksh-sangItAnubhava-1888-0002.pdf (accessed 4/18/16).

Bhatkhande, Vishnu Narayan. *Saṅgīta-paddhati kramika pustaka-mālikā.* 6 vols. Edited and translated from Marathi into Hindi by Lakshminaryan Garg. Hathras U.P. Sangita karyalaya, 1954-68.

Biography of Pir-O-Murshid Inayat Khan. London and The Hague: East-West Publications, 1979.

Bloch, Regina Miriam. *The Confessions of Inayat Khan.* London: The Sufi Publication Society, 1915.

Bor, Joep and Jane Harvey. CD Booklet. Katwijk, Holland: Panta Rhei Publishers. In *Inayat Khan: The Complete Recordings of 1909: 31 Classical Indian songs from the legendary Sufi musician Hazrat Inayat Khan.* Discography by Michael S. Kinnear. CD NF 50129-30 (Stereo) Double CD Set. EMI and The Gramophone Company of India, 1994.

Brockschmidt, S.K. 2003. *The Harmonium Handbook: Owning, Playing , and Maintaining the Devotional Instrument of India.* Nevada City, CA: Crystal Clarity, 2003.

Brown, Katherine Butler, "The Ṭhāṭ System of Seventeenth-Century North Indian Rāgas: A Preliminary Report on the Treatises of Kāmilkhānī" In *Asian Music* Vol. 35, No. 1 (Autumn, 2003–Winter, 2004), pp. 1–13. http://www.jstor.org/stable/4098470 (accessed 4/15/16).

Buyers, Christopher J. "India" http//www.4dw.net/royalark/India/hyder.htm.

Das, Sisir Kumar. *History of Indian Literature 1800-1910* vol 1. https://books.google.com/books?id=sHklK65TKQ0C&pg=PA494&lpg=PA494&dq=Urdu+poet+Shamshad&source=bl&ots=sRDR4jVxS9&sig=j84wbEt6Yu0KVb6l1aaN5iDvpbQ&hl=en&sa=X&ved=0ahUKEwiM1-rn57nKAhXCdx4KHUW-C_kQ6AEIVDAN#v=onepage&q=Urdu%20poet%20Shamshad&f=false (accessed 6/15/16).

Du Perron, Lalita. *Hindi Poetry in a Musical Genre: Thumri Lyrics*. London; New York: Routledge, 2007.

Ebeling, Klaus. *Ragamala Painting*. Basel, Paris, New Delhi: Ravi Kumar ©1973.

Gangoli, O.C. *Ragas and Raginis: a pictorial and iconographical study of Indian musical modes based on original sources.* Bombay: Nalanda Publications, 1948.

Hastings, Charles S. and Beach, Frederick E. *A Text-book of General Physics: for the use of Colleges and Scientific Schools.* Boston: Ginn & Co. 1899, 514-98. https://ia600301.us.archive.org/2/items/atextbookgenera00beacgoog/atextbookgenera00beacgoog.pdf (accessed 4/3/16).

Hindustani Music: Thirteenth to Twentieth Centuries. Edited by Joep Bor, Francoise 'Nalini' Delvoye, Jane Harvey, Emmie te Nijenhuis. New Delhi: Codarts and Manohar. 2010.

Inayat Khan: The Complete Recordings of 1909: 31 Classical Indian songs from the legendary Sufi musician Hazrat Inayat Khan. Discography by Michael S. Kinnear. CD NF 50129-30 (Stereo)

Double CD Set. EMI and The Gramophone Company of India, 1994.

Inayat-Khan, Hidayat. Appendix A. “List of Ragas.” Handwritten transcription of the *rāga* list in Part One, Chapter Four of the *Minqār-i Mūsīqār.* Provided by International Headquarters of the Sufi Movement, The Netherlands.

Inayat-Khan, Hidayat. Appendix B, “List of Tabla Rhythms.” Handwritten transcription of the *tāla* list in Part One, Chapter Five of the *Minqār-i Mūsīqār*. Provided by International Headquarters of the Sufi Movement, The Netherlands.

Inayat-Khan, Zia. "The ‘Silsila-i Sufian’: From Khwāja Mu’īn al Dīn Chishtī to Sayyid Abū Hāshim Madanī.” In *A Pearl in Wine: Essays on the Life, Music and Sufism of Hazrat Inayat Khan.* Edited by Pir Zia Inayat-Khan. New Lebanon, NY: Omega Publications, 2001, 267–321.

Khan, Inayat and Jessie Duncan Westbrook. *Songs of India: Rendered from the Urdu, Hindi, and Persian by Inayat Khan and Jessie Duncan Westbrook.* London: The Sufi Publishing Society Ltd, 1915. http://babel.hathitrust.org/cgi/pt?id=hvd.32044051106656;view=1up;seq=9 (accessed 1/20/16).

Khan, Inayat R. Pathan, Professor. *Minqār-i Mūsīqār.* Allahabad: Indian Press, 1912.

Khan, Inayat and Jessie Duncan Westbrook. *Hindustani Lyrics: Rendered from the Urdu by Inayat Khan and Jessie Duncan Westbrook.* Delhi: Motilal Banarsidass. First Indian Edition 1996. 1st edition London: The Sufi Publishing Society Ltd. 1919. https://wahiduddin.net/hik/hik_lyrics.htm (accessed 1/20/16).

Khan, Inayatkhan Rahematkhan Pathan, Professor. *Ināyat Gīt Ratnāvalī.* Baroda: 1903a.

Khan, Inayatkhan Rahematkhan Pathan, Professor. *Ināyat Hārmoniam Śikṣak.* Pustak Pahala. Baroda: 1903b.

Khan, Muhammad Mardan 'Ali. *Ghuncha-i rāg.* Lucknow: Naval Kishore, 1863. Lucknow: Naval Kishore, 1879.

Khan, Sadiq 'Ali. *Sarmāya-i ishrat* or *Qānūn-i mūsīqī.* Delhi: Matba'-i Faiz 'ām, 1869. Delhi: Narayan Das Jangli Mal, 1874–5. Delhi: Munshi Muhammad Ibrahim, 1884.

Khan, Shaikh al-Mashaik Mahmood. "Hazrat Inayat Khan: A Biographical Perspective," "The Mawlābakhsh Dynastic Lineage, 1833-1972." In *A Pearl in Wine: Essays on the Life, Music and Sufism of Hazrat Inayat Khan.* Edited by Pir Zia Inayat-Khan. New Lebanon, NY: Omega Publications, 2001, 3–64, 65–126.

Kippen, James, "The Tal Paddhati of 1888: An Early Source for Tabla." In *Journal of the Indian Musicological Society*, 38, 2007, pp.151–239.

The Koran. University of Michigan Digital Library, 2000. http://quod.lib.umich.edu/k/koran/ Electronic version of The Holy Qur'an, translated by M.H. Shakir and published by Tahrike Tarsile Qur'an, Inc., 1983. Text provided by Online Book Initiative

Library of Congress. "ALA-LC Romanization Tables" https://www.loc.gov/catdir/cpso/roman.html (accessed 6/15/16).

Luther, Narendra. "Kishen Pershad—a multifaceted noble." http://narendralutherarchives.blogspot.com/2006/12/kishen-pershad-multifaceted-noble.html. (accessed 4/20/16).

Lynton, Harriet Ronken and Mohini Rajan. *The Days of the Beloved.* Berkeley, Los Angeles, London: University of California Press, 1974.

Manuel, Peter. *Thumri in Historical and Stylistic Perspectives.* Delhi : Motilal Banarasidass, 1990.

Martin, H. Newell. *The Human Body; a text-book of anatomy, physiology and hygiene, with practical exercises.* 5th ed., rev. New York, H. Holt, 1899. 288-93. http://babel.hathitrust.org/cgi/

pt?id=coo1.ark:/13960/t3fx7tv0r;view=1up;seq=327 (accessed 4/3/16).

Mehta, R.C. *Indian Classical Music and Gharana Tradition.* New Delhi Readworthy Publications 2008.

Miner, Allyn. "Raga in the early sixteenth century." In *Tellings and Texts: Music, Literature and Performance in North India.* Edited by Francesca Orsini and Katherine Schofield. Open Book Publishers, 2015, 385-406. http://www.openbookpublishers.com/product/311/tellings-and-texts—music—literature-and-performance-in-north-india (accessed 4/20/16)

Miner, Allyn. "The Minqar-i musiqar and Inayat Khan's Early Career in Music." In *A Pearl in Wine: Essays on the Life, Music and Sufism of Hazrat Inayat Khan.* Edited by Pir Zia Inayat-Khan. New Lebanon, NY: Omega Publications, 2001, 177-205.

Miner, Allyn. *Sitar and Sarod in the Eighteenth and Nineteenth Centuries.* International Institute for Traditional Music, Berlin. Florian Noetzel, Heinrichshofen-Bücher, Wilhelmshaven, 1993. Indian Edition. New Delhi: Motilal Banarsidass, 1997.

Neuman, Daniel. "The Social Organization of a Music Tradition: Hereditary Specialists in North India". In *Ethnomusicology.* Vol. 21, No. 2. (May, 1977), pp.233-245. https://www.academia.edu/1333894/The_Social_Organization_of_a_Music_Tradition_Hereditary_Specialists_in_North_India (accessed 4/4/16)

Pacholczyk, Józef M. *Sūfyāna mūsīqī: the classical music of Kashmir. Intercultural music studies 9.* Berlin: VWB-Verlag fur Wissenschaft und Bildung, c1996.

Pershad, Maharaja Kishan. *Guldasta-e-Shād.* AP Urdu Academy, Hyderabad. http://syedakbarindia.blogspot.com/2010/07/book-review-maharaja-kishan-pershan.html

Pritchett, Frances. "Some Useful Sources on Hindi/Urdu Language and Literature." Website: http://www.columbia.edu/itc/mealac/pritchett/00urduhindilinks/index.html (accessed 4/20/16)

Rahaim, Matt. "That Ban(e) of Indian Music: Hearing Politics in The Harmonium." In *The Journal of Asian Studies.* Vol. 70, No. 3 (August 2011), pp. 657-682
Stable URL: http://www.jstor.org/stable/41302388

Rosse, Michael David. "The Movement for the Revitalization of 'Hindu' Music in Northern India, 1860–1930: the role of associations and institutions." Ph.D. dissertation, University of Pennsylvania, 1995.

Sangīta-Ratnākara of Śārngadeva. Text and Translation, Vol. 1. Translated by R.K. Shringy. Delhi, Varanasi, Patna: Motilal Banarsidass 1978.

Sanyal, Ritwik and Richard Widdess. *Dhrupad: Tradition and Performance in Indian Music.* SOAS Musicology Series. Aldershot: Ashgate 2004.

Subramanian , Lakshmi. *From the Tanjore Court to the Madras Music Academy: a social history of music in south India.* New Delhi: Oxford University Press, 2006.

Tagore, Sourindro Mohun. *Hindu Music from Various Authors.* Chowkhamba Sanskrit studies, vol. 49. Varanasi: Chowkhamba Sanskrit Series Office,1965.

Wade, Bonnie. Khyal: *Creativity within North India's Classical Music Tradition* (Cambridge Studies in Ethnomusicology) 1985.

Wahiduddin's Web. Texts, photos, resources on Hazrat Inayat Khan. https://wahiduddin.net (accessed 4/18/16).

Walker, Margaret E. "The 'Nautch' Reclaimed: Women's Performance Practice in Nineteenth-Century North India." In

South Asia: Journal of South Asian Studies, 2014/ http://dx.doi.org/10.1080/00856401.2014.938714

Woodfield, Ian. *Music of the Raj: a social and economic history of music in late eighteenth-century Anglo-Indian society.* New York: Oxford University Press, 2000.

Allyn Miner is a Lecturer in the Department of South Asia Studies at the University of Pennsylvania. Her research and publications relate to the history of North Indian music and its literature in Sanskrit, Hindi, and Urdu.

Allyn received her B.A. in South Asian studies from the University of Wisconsin. Between 1971 and 1982 she lived and studied in Varanasi, India, first on the Wisconsin Year in India Program and later with the support of Fulbright and Rockefeller grants. She studied sitar performance with Thakur Raj Bhan Singh and musicology with Professor Prem Lata Sharma at Banaras Hindu University. She received a Ph.D. in 1982 from the Department of Musicology, B.H.U., for her dissertation "Sitar and Sarod in the Eighteenth and Nineteenth Centuries."

After returning to the U.S. she began performance training under Ustad Ali Akbar Khan and became his formal disciple in 1990. Allyn began teaching at the University of Pennsylvania in 1988 and received a Ph.D. in Sanskrit in 1994 for her work on the Sanskrit musicological text, *Saṅgītopaniṣatsāroddhāra*.

She continues to teach, perform, and pursue research and lives with her husband in Havertown PA.

Other publications by Allyn Miner include:

Sitar and Sarod in the Eighteenth and Nineteenth Centuries. International Institute for Traditional Music, Berlin. Florian Noetzel, Heinrichshofen-Bucher, Wilhelmshaven, 1993. Reprint,New Delhi: Motilal Banarsidass, Performing Arts Series 7, 1997.

The Saṅgītopaniṣatsāroddhāra: a fourteenth-century text onmusic from western India. Indira Gandhi National Centre for the Arts (IGNCA) Kalamulasastra Series 28, 1998.

"Raga in the Early Sixteenth Century." In *Tellings and Texts: Music, Literature and Performance in North India*. Edited by Francesca Orsini, Katherine Butler Schofield. Open Book Publishers, 2015 385-406, 2015

Pir Zia Inayat-Khan is a scholar and teacher of Sufism in the lineage of his grandfather, Hazrat Inayat Khan. He received his B.A. (Hons) in Persian Literature from the London School of Oriental and African Studies, and his M.A. and Ph.D. in Religion from Duke University. Pir Zia is president of The Inayati Order and founder of Suluk Academy, a school of contemplative study with branches in the United States and Europe. He is also founder of the interspiritual institute Seven Pillars House of Wisdom.

Since 2004 Pir Zia has served as Head of the Inayati Order, guiding Sufi communities in the North America, South America, Europe, the Middle East, Asia, and the South Pacific.

Outside the Sufi sphere, Pir Zia has taken part in numerous interreligious and interdisciplinary gatherings. Pir Zia is also a Fellow of the Lindisfarne Association, and an Advisor to the Contemplative Alliance.

Pir Zia is editor of *A Pearl in Wine: Essays on the Life, Music and Sufism of Hazrat Inayat Khan* (Omega, 2001) and *Caravan of Souls: An Introduction to the Sufi Path of Hazrat Inayat Khan* (Suluk Press, 2013), and author of *Saracen Chivalry: Counsels on Volar, Generosity and the Mystical Quest* (Suluk Press, 2012).

He lives with his wife and children in the United States and at Fazal Manzil in Suresnes, France.

Index

A

Abd al-Jalil 127
absorption in God 19
acal ṭhāṭ 311, 409
addiction 131
Afghanistan 301, 303
Africa 349
Akbar, Emperor 351
Akhtar, Wajid Ali Shah 220, 403
ālāp 15, 27, 131, 134, 302, 409
Alauddin Khan xxii, 20, 409
alg͟hoza 306, 409
Allah 11, 16, 20–23, 28, 160, 185, 212, 224, 263, 284, 307. *See also* beloved, God.
Amir Khusrau 181–182, 229, 403
Amir Minai xl, 190, 199, 256, 277, 289, 303, 403
anādrut xxxiii, xxxv, 81–83, 111–112, 409
anatomy xxx, 421
ang 83–84, 87, 352, 409
ankle bells 363, 367
antarā 132, 409
anūvādī 44, 409
apsaras 349. *See also* fairies.
Arab(ic) xxix, xxx, 16, 28, 126, 283, 299, 305; Quranic Arabic 81. *See also* Arabia.
Arabia 125, 301, 349. *See also* Arab.
arbāb-i nishāṭ 125
āṛ kī lay 409
ārohī xvii, xxxi, 35–36, 409. *See also* ascent.
art xxviii–xxix, xxx, 11, 4–5, 19, 196, 286, 371; art of music xxvii, 3–6, 22–23, 25, 28–29, 43, 78, 81, 103, 108–109, 119, 125–126, 129–131, 286, 349,
ārtī 135
ascent xxxi, 35, 77, 409: ascending scale xxxii, 35, 45. *See also* *ārohī*, descent.
Ashna 292, 403
ashṭapadī 135, 409
Asif xi, xxix, 22, 123, 193, 205, 241, 271, 280, 403. *See also* Mahbub Ali Khan Bahadur.
āstāī, 128, 132–133, 409
atīkomal 41
atītīvra 41
Aurangzeb 127
auṛav xxxi, 409; *auṛav rāg* 45
avarohī xxxi, 35–36, 409
āvāz 30–34, 409

B

bānī xxxvi, 128, 409–413
bansī 306, 409
bānsurī 301, 306, 409; *bānsurī kī gat* 353, 360
Baroda (Vadodara) xii, xxi, xxiii, xxv, xxviii–xxix, xxxvii, xliii, 4–5, 7, 20, 108, 417, 419–420
battle music 28, 79, 126, 305. *See also* military band.
bāyān xliv, 305, 340–343, 409
Bedil, Abdul Qadir 202–203, 403
beloved (Beloved) xl, 16–17, 21–22, 27, 141, 160, 169, 179, 184, 209, 211, 224, 248, 251, 259, 269, 278, 283–284, 298, 350. *See also* Allah, God.
Bengal 304
Bhairavī rāg xli, 47, 210, 249, 282, 294, 301

Bhairavīn rāg 45, 175–176, 323, 329, 334, 337
bhajan xxxiii, 78, 135, 304, 308, 409
Bharat 46
Bharatmat 46, 415
bhārjā xxxi, 46–50, 52, 54, 57, 60, 64–65, 69–71, 76, 414
Bhatkhande, V.N. xxiii, xxxiv–xxxv, xlii, 417
bhāv 351, 353–354, 409
bherī 301, 409
bhog 132, 409
Bhutan 349
Bībhās rāg 45, 47
Bihāg rāg xli, 51, 160–161, 176–177, 231, 270
Bihārī rāg xli, 48, 165–166, 225, 234
bīn xlii, 301–303, 410, 412–415
bisrām xxxv, 81, 112, 410. *See also* rest.
bol xxxiii, xliv–xlv, 80, 106, 133, 312, 339–343, 351, 353, 410: *brahm bīn* 410
budhbudī 306, 410

C

Calcutta (Kolkata) xxi, xxv–xxvii, 4–5
cal ṭhāṭ 311, 410
cang 93, 308, 410
caste xxx, xliv; hereditary caste musician caste xxxvi
caṛhī 40
caturang 134, 410
catūsra jāt xxxiii, 85–86, 343–345, 410
Cautālā 92, 132–133, 139, 142, 145, 336, 342, 344, 410
celestial beings. *See apsaras, devas,* fairies, *ghandarvas.*
chan xxxiii, 83, 410; *chan chan* 305
chaugun kī lay 410
Christianity xxx; Christian 28, 278
chromatic scale xxxviii, 46
cikārā 303, 410
clapping xxxiv, xxxviii, 78–80, 104, 105, 114, 347, 412, 415. *See also tāli.*
College of Music xxix, 20
consonant xxxi, 44
Cordoba (Qurtuba) 125
cuckoo 131, 169
cymbals 305–306, 308, 350, 367. *See also manjīrā.*

D

dādrā *See tāl dādrā.*
daf 28, 132, 301, 305, 410
Dagh, Nawab Mirza Khan xl, 214, 403
ḍamaru 306, 410
dance xxvii, xxix, xxxvi, xliv–xlv, 25–26, 129, 133–134, 136, 227, 305, 307–308, 348–367, 406, 409–413, 415; dance of the fairies 351; dance of the peacock 133, 353; dancers xxiv, xlv, 119. *See also ang, gat, nrit.*
ḍanka 305, 410
Darbārī Kānarā rāg 44, 153–155, 171–172
Da'ud (David) 25, 126, 371
Day of Resurrection 190, 212, 369, 371
Deccan 11, 21–22, 123, 370–371
Delhi xv, 128, 350, 418–422, 425–426
descent v, xxviii, 21, 35, 45, 77, 283, 284, 409. *See also* ascent, *avarohī.*
desī rāgs xxxi, 46–47, 410

devas 349
ḍhak 305, 410
dhamār 85, 128, 133, 410; *horī dhamār* xxxix, 171–172
ḍhapṛā 305–306, 410
ḍhol xxxiii, 30, 301, 305, 308, 410
ḍholak 305, 410
ḍholkī 305, 410
dhrupad xxxvi, xix, 128, 132, 133–135, 302, 305, 312, 409–411
dhuvā 128, 410
dilrubā 304, 410
discipline xxxix, xlii, 19, 302
dissonant xxxi, 44
ḍorū 306, 410
drone xx, 306–307, 415. *See also tambura.*
drum xxxiii, xliv, 28, 133, 176, 305–306, 343, 409–410, 413, 415; drummer xx, 350
drut xxxiii–xxxv, 81–82, 84–85, 104–105, 111– 114, 343, 410–411
dugun lay xxxiv, 104, 411
dundubhī 305, 411
dvīguru 81–82, 411

E

ear xxx 16, 27, 30–34, 77, 129, 157, 212, 215, 272, 359; ear ornament 363
East(erner) 127, 278. *See also* individual countries and areas by name.
ecstasy xxviii, xxx, xl, 19, 78, 182, 218, 242, 247, 253; ecstatic dancers xlv; ecstatic trance 306. *See also* intoxication.
Egypt 127, 301
ektārā 132, 135, 304, 411
England (English) xii, xxiii, xvii, xxviil–xxviii, xxx–xxxi, 5, 7, 20, 26, 31–36, 39, 41, 46, 81, 135; English instruments 350; English music 5, 46; English notation 35, 82. *See also* London.
ensemble xx, 79, 306; dance ensemble 350
Europe(an) xxi, xxiii, xxviii, xli–xlii, xlv, 4– 6, 126, 129, 131, 301, 349, 427

F

fairies 226, 349; dance of the fairies 351, 355. *See also apsaras, paristān.*
Faiz 268, 403, 419
fan-i haqīqī 28
female. *See* women.
fiqrā xli, 312, 411. *See also* variations.
Fīrozkhvānī 312, 411
flat note xxxv, xxxviii, 15, 41, 45, 109, 311, 412; double flat 41

G

Gaekwar of Baroda xxi, 20
gamak xliii, 312, 314–316, 411
gandharvas 349
garbā 134–135, 411
gat xlii–xliii, xlv, 108, 303, 311–312, 317–325, 351–364; *gat bharnā*, 352. *See also* dance, movement.
gāyan 25, 128–136, 411
Gayanshala xxii–xxiii, xliv
ghan xli, 301, 351, 411
ghanṭa 308, 411
ghanṭi 308, 411
ghaṛā 301, 411

Ghasit Khan xxi
Gauṛ Sārang rāg 45
ghazal xxxix–xl, 78, 103, 128, 134, 181– 360, 411
Ghuncha-i rāg xxvii, xxix, xxxi–xxxii, 419
ghunguru 308, 354, 367, 411
God xxvii–xxviii, xxxvi, xl, xlv, 11, 17, 19–22, 25, 28, 81, 117, 119, 123, 125–126, 128, 131, 167, 187, 193, 197, 202, 208, 215, 220, 224, 227, 233, 239, 256, 271–272, 283, 292, 307, 369–371; absorption in God 19; deity, xxx, 349; gods 301. *See also* Allah, beloved, goddess.
goddess 302; Mother Goddess 306. *See also* Allah, beloved, God.
Goharmārī bānī 128, 411
gourd 302–304, 307, 312
grace 11, 19–22, 25, 119, 131, 224, 242, 254, 298, 349, 369, 371
grah xxxiv, 105, 131, 411
grām xxxi, 43, 411
Gujarat xxi, xxxv, 134–135, 304
guru xxxiii, 81–85, 112–114, 150, 412

H

Hafiz: Khwaja Shams ad-Din Muhammad Hafiz Shirazi xi, 29, 182, 206, 227, 251, 290, 293, 403
Hakim Abu Ali Sina (Avicenna) 127
half tone 40–41
Hanuman 46, 306
Hanumatmat 46, 414
harmonium xx, xxiii, xxxvi, xliii, 30, 32, 132, 326–338, 417, 422
Hasan Ghaznavi 272, 403
Hashimi xi, 214, 283, 403
Hazin Lahji 242, 403
Hindi xvii, xxxv, xxxix, xliii, 6, 105, 133, 306, 327, 409, 417–419, 422, 425
Hindu xxiii, 4, 6, 78–79, 134–135, 194, 275, 422, 425; Hindu deity 349; Hindu goddess 302; Hindu gods 301. *See also* individual Hindu gods and godesses by name.
Hindustan(i) xix, xx, xxii–xxxiv, xxxix, 4–6, 127, 347, 415, 418–419, 426. *See also* India.
Holi 171, 173, 305, 350
horī xxxix, 128, 133, 171–174, 305, 412. *See also dhamār.*
household xxi–xxii, xxxvii, 129. *See also* lineage.
Hyderabad ii, xi, xxiii–xxv, xxviii–xxix, xxxix, xl, xliv–xv, 3, 6, 22, 350, 411, 422
hymn 135. *See also ārtī, bhajan.*

I

improvisation xix–xx, xli, 307
India(n) xii, xv, xviii–xix, xxi, xix, xxi, xxxiii–xliv, 3–7, 9, 20, 22, 42, 78–79, 103, 108, 129, 133–135, 202, 301–307, 311, 326, 339, 349–350, 414, 417–423, 425–426; east India 133, 135, 312; north India xvii–xviii, xxxi–xxxii, xxxv, xxxvii, xxxix, xlii–xliv, 42, 135, 302, 311, 350, 425; south India xix, xxi–xxii, xxv, xxvii–xxxviii, 6, 42, 103, 135, 302–303, 305,

307, 350; western India xxii. *See also* Hindustan, Sanskrit, South Asia, Urdu, individual places by name.
instrument(al) xxvii, xxix–xx, xxxiii, xxxvii, xxxix, xli–xliii, 3, 109, 119, 125, 128–129, 132, 301–309, 409–416; instrumentalists xiii, xx, xxiv, xxvii, xxix–xx, 15, 25–26, 30, 38, 79, 81, 105. *See also* stringed instruments, wind instruments, individual instruments by name.
intoxication 15, 27, 78, 197, 204, 306, 359, 373; intoxicant 131. *See also* ecstasy.
Iqbal, Sir Muhammad 262, 295, 403
Iraqi: Fakhr al-Din Ibrahim Iraqi 200, 218, 403
Ishrati: Aqa Ali Ishrati 236, 403
Islam xxviii, xxx, 6, 22, 28, 127. *See also* Ka'ba, muezzin, Muhammad, mullah, Muslim, Qur'an.
isrār 304, 411

J

Jaidev Kavi 135
jaltarang 3, 6–7, 301, 308, 411
Jami: Nur ad-Din ʿAbd ar-Rahman Jami xi, 260, 263, 403
jāt xxiii, xli, 85–86, 410–412, 415. *See also tāl.*
Jalal ad-Din Rumi xi. *See also* Shams.
jhānjar 308, 412
jhānjh xxxiii, 78, 301, 412
Jhinjhoṭī xli, 186, 201, 288, 314, 333, 336
jhunjhūnā 308, 412
Jur'at: Qalandar Bakhsh Jurat 250, 403

K

Ka'ba xl, 200, 224, 241, 250, 272, 295, 299.
kachap bīn 303, 412
Kāfī rāg xli, 66, 135, 167–168, 207, 222, 239–240, 285, 297, 314, 319, 329, 334, 336, 412
kāgpad xxxiii, 81–82, 84, 111–112, 412
kaharva 133, 412
Kaifi 244, 403
kā'īṛkā 306, 412
kāl xxxiv, 104–105, 412–413, 416. *See also* tempo.
kamānca 303, 412
kandahārī bānī 412
Kanhaiyaji 349, 355–356, 360
kanwālī xxiii
karnāh 307, 412
Karnatak xix, xxvii, xxxii–xxxiv, xli, xliii, 5, 135–136, 332, 347
kaṛtāl 301, 308, 412
kathak xliv, 351, 361
Kathiavar 134, 304
Kaunsī Kānharā rāg 45, 157–158
k͟hālī xxxiii–xxxiv, xxxviii, 79–80, 85, 114, 412
Khamāj rāg xli, 66., 163–164
khanjarī 305, 412
k͟hayāl xxxvii, xxxix, 128, 132–134, 409, 412
Khusrau. *See* Amir Khusrau
kinnar bīn (kinarī) 303, 413
kirtan xxxiii, 78, 135, 412
Kishanmat 46, 414
Kishen Pershad, Maharaj Sir Kishen Pershad Bahadur xxiv, xxviii, xxxvi, xli, 3, 21, 122–123, 412, 420, 422. *See also* Shad.

Kolkata *See* Calcutta.
komal xxiii, 28, 40–42, 45, 109–110, 145, 147, 210, 311, 412
Krishna xxv, 46, 306
kuāṛ kī lay xxxiv, 105, 412

L

laghu xxxiii, xxxv, 81–82, 111–114, 412
lās xlv, 349–351, 412
lāvanī 135, 306, 412
lay 104–108, 409–411, 413, 415. *See also* tempo.
lineage xv, xx–xxi, xxx, 28, 145, 284, 420, 427; non-lineage xxii. *See also* household.
London xxii, xxix, 20
Lucknow 350

M

Madani: Sayyid Muhammad Abu Hashim Madani Chisht xi, xxv, xxviii, 2, 17, 298, 409
Madar Khan 128
made kāl xxxiv, 104–105, 412
madh saptak 38, 412
Madras (Chennai) xxii–xxiii, 4–6, 422
Maghribi: Muhammad Shirin Mahghrebi 194, 221, 403
Mahadev 301, 349. *See also* Shiva.
Mahbub Ali Khan Bahadur xi, xxkv, xxviii, xxix, 10–11, 21–22, 205, 370, 412. *See also* Asif.
Mahmud Shabestari 287, 403
Malabar 5, 306
male xxxi–xxxii, xxxvii, 46, 367; male voice xxxvii, 33, 131; manly 28, 185, 241; masculine dance xlv, 349–351, 363
mandra saptak 38, 109–110, 311, 412
manjīrā 308, 350, 354, 367, 413
Marathi 135, 306, 417
mārg xxxi, 45, 128, 413
Marvar(is) 304–305
mashk 307, 350, 413
master (of music) 3, 23, 43, 109, 127–130, 167, 283, 350, 416; mastery xxvii, 6, 129, 131, 371. *See also ustād.*
mātrā 28, 81, 83, 111–112, 114, 413
Maula Bakhsh xv, xvii, xxi–xxii, xxiv, xxvii, xxix, xxxi, xxxiv–xxxix, xli, xliii–xiv, 4, 6–7, 20, 108, 118–119,125, 343, 413
melody xix, xli,15–16, 20, 25, 26, 81, 106, 119, 135, 145, 181, 215, 254, 276, 297, 369, 414. *See also rāg*, song.
micro-intervals xxviii; microtones 415. *See also sruti.*
military band 301; military instruments 307. *See also* battle music.
Miyan Shori 133
Momin Khan Momin 211, 403
mood xx, xliii, 194
Moses (Musa) 25, 191, 221, 256, 298
movements xlv, 23, 27, 32–33, 77, 79, 103–104, 130, 131, 351, 353; motion 34, 130–131. *See also* dance, *gat.*
mridang xxxiii, 78, 106, 113, 132, 301, 305, 413; *mridang yatī* 106, 413
muezzin 126
Muhammad, The Prophet xi,

xxxix, xl, 16, 272, 298. *See also* Islam, Muslim, Qur'an.
Muhammad Ghazali: Abu Hamid Muhammad ibn Muhammad al-Ghazali 126, 413
Muhi 185, 403
mullah 28
Munir: Abul Barakat, Molla Monir Lahuri 299, 404
mūrchanā xxxi, 42, 413
murlī 306, 413
musician xx–xxiv, xxx, xxxvi–xxxviii, 3, 6–7, 103, 125, 129, 301, 417, 419; Divine Musician 15
Musīdkhvānī 312, 413
mūsīqār 25, 372, 413
Muslim xxxvi, xi, 22, 125–127, 211, 236, 278, 301; Muslim rule 127, 301. *See also* Islam.
Myanmar xxviii
Mysore xxi–xxii, 3–7

N

na'e 306, 413
nafīrī 307, 413
naghāra 305, 413
Nanak, Guru 78
naqāra xxiii, 28, 30, 79, 134, 305, 413
Narada 302
nārad bīn 302, 413
nart 25, 128, 411
Nasim Daya Shankar Kaul 202, 404
nastarang 308, 413
nāṭyā xlv, 351, 413
naubat xxiii, 79, 305–306, 413
Nauhārbānī 413
Navab 208
Nasir Ahmad 128
Nepal xxii, xlv, 349
Niaz Fatehpuri 247, 404
Nizam al-Din 127
Nizami, Ilyas ibn Yusuf xi, 269, 405
notation xiii, xxixv, xvii, xxi–xxv, xxvii, xxix, xxxi, xxxiii, 5, 20, 35–36, 38–41, 80–84, 108–117, 137, 343, 413. *See also* Bhatkhande, Maula Bakhsh.
note, musical xxxiv, xxxviii, 5, 16, 35– 38, 40–45, 77, 86, 105–107, 109–110, 113, 116–117, 128–129, 131–134, 307–308, 311, 314, 327, 409, 412, 414–416. *See also* flat note, *saptak*, *sargam*, sharp note, *shudh*.
nrit xlv, 349–351, 354, 413; *nrittam* xlv, 351, 413. *See also* dance.

O

octave xxxi, xxxv, xxxviii, 33, 39, 110, 130, 180, 311, 412, 414–415. *See also saptak*.
ornament, musical 107, 412–413, 416. *See also gamak*, *khaṭkā*, *yatī*.

P

pad 135, 413
pakhāvaj xxxiii, 79, 132, 176, 305, 341–342, 350, 363, 413
pallavī 136, 413
Panjab(i) xxxix, 133
paran 108, 413
paristān 355, 413; *Paristān kā nāc* xlv, 351. *See also* fairies.
parmalū xlv, 351–352, 364–366, 405–407, 414

Pashto 89, 306; *tāl Pashto* 210, 216, 234, 255, 264, 276, 282, 297, 306
pāvā 306, 413
peacock 157, 169, 182, 303–304, 361, 364, 369; peacock dance (*Raqs tāūs kī gat) 9,* 353, 361
Persia(n) xi, xv, xix, xxvii–xxviii, xxx, xxxvi, xxxix, xl–xli, 134, 176, 181, 227, 301, 303, 403–404, 411, 413, 419, 427. *See* individual Persians by name.
physics xxx, 418
Pīlū rāg xli, 53, 213, 258, 314, 322–323
pitch xxxvii–xxxviii, xix, xxx–xxxi, 33
plectrum 303–304
plut 85, 107, 413
poetry xii, xix–xxi, xxxix–xl, 28, 81, 131, 248. *See also ghazal.*
Prakrit 135, 306
Prophet, The *See* Muhammad.
pungī 301, 307, 414
putra xxxi–xxxii, 46–47, 414
Pythagoras 25

Q

qānūn 303, 414
qavālī 78, 346, 414; *mehfil-i qavālī* xxxiii, 128. *See also sama'*, Sufism.
Qudsi Mashadi 245, 284, 296, 404
Qur'an 126, 224; Quranic Arabic 81. *See also* Islam, Muhammad, Muslim.
qurnā 301, 307, 412, 414
Qutb al-din Shirazi 248, 404

R

rabāb 303–304, 414
rāg xv, xix–xx, xxiv, xxvi–xxvii, xxxi–xxxiii, xxxviii, xli–xliii, 16, 19, 25, 26, 28–29, 41, 45–77, 86, 104, 109, 128–129, 131–134, 311–312, 349, 409–410, 412–414, 416, 420. *See also rāgs* by name, melody, *rāginī*
rāg-rāginī xxxii, 414
rāginī xxxi–xxxii, 49–50, 53–54, 57–58, 62, 65–66, 68, 70–71, 73, 354, 414–415
Rahmat Khan xxi–xxii, xlii, 313, 414
Rajput 307
Rangoon (Yangon)) xxv
Rasikh Ghulam Ali of Patna 217, 232, 404
recitation xlv, 126
rest xix, 81–82, 112. *See also bisrām.*
rhythm *See tāl.*
rhythmic cycles xix, 415
rudra bīn 302, 414
Rumi. *See* Jalal ad-Din Rumi, Shams-i Tabrizi.

S

Sa'di of Shiraz: Musharrif al-Din ibn Muslih al-Din xi, 281, 404
Saqi 182, 259, 274, 290, 293, 296
Saib Tabrizi 209, 404
sam xxxiv, 79–80, 85, 105–106, 114, 131–132, 354, 406–407, 414
sama' xxxii, 78, 126, 414. *See also qavālī*, Sufism, *urs.*
sampūrn rāg xxxi, 45
sangīt xxix, 26, 37, 78, 83, 85, 348,

414
Sangītanubhav xxxi–xxxii
Sangītaratnākara 414
sankīrn rāg 45
Sanskrit xvii, xix, xxix, xxx–xxxii, xxxiv, xliii, 25–26, 135, 305–306, 409, 415, 422, 425
saptak xxx, 33–34, 38–39, 107, 109–110, 311, 412, 414–415. *See also* octave.
sārangī xviii, 132, 301, 350, 354, 415
Sarasvati 302
sarasvatī bīn 302, 415
sargam xxxviii, xliii, 117, 129, 134, 136–137, 327–338, 414. *See also* scale, syllable.
sārinda 304, 414
Sarmāya-i ishrat xxxii, xlii, xlv, 364, 367, 405, 419
sarod 303, 414, 421, 425
Sauda, Mirza Muhammad Rafi xi, 184, 404
Sayyid Ghulam Nabi 127
scale xix, xxvii, xxx–xxxii, xxxv, xxxviii, xli–xliv, 45–46, 413–414; major scale xxxviii, 46; minor scale 46. *See also* ascent, chromatic scale, descent, *sargam*.
scarf 350, 354, 356, 361. *See also* veil.
science xxix, 18. *See also* physics.
science of music xxi, xxvii–xxviii, 3–6, 19–21, 23, 25–26, 126–127, 129
sehtār 303, 414. *See also sitār.*
Shad xxix, 123, 191, 196, 224, 404. *See also* Kishen Pershad.
Shadan, Sayyid Aulad Husain Shadan Bilgrami 259, 404
Shahab Khan of Delhi 128
Shahāna xli
shahnā'ī 301, 305–306, 414
Shams: Shams-i Tabrizi 197, 278, 404. *See also* Jalal ad-Din Rumi.
Shamshad: Shamshad Muhammad Abdul Ahad Firangi Mahal 235, 286, 404
sharab bīn 303, 414
Sharaf Abdulla of Shiraz 212, 404
shāṛav rāg 45
sharbat 303, 414
Sharif: Muhammad Sharif Nasafi 254, 404
sharnā'ī 301, 305–306, 414
sharp note xxxv, xxxix, 15, 41, 45, 109, 311, 415; double sharp 41. *See also tīvra.*
Shiva 46, 141; Shivji 302. *See also* Mahadev, *Shīvmat.*
Shīvmat 46, 414.
shudh 40–44, 311, 414
Sindh 135
Sindhūra rāg xli, 47, 60, 62, 147–149, 173–175, 322
sīng 307, 414
singer xxiv, xxxvii–xxxviii, 33, 81, 105, 108, 129–130, 135, 227, 251, 293, 304, 308. *See also* song, vocalist, voice.
Siraj Aurangabadi 253, 404
sitār xxxvi–xxxvii, xlii–xliii, 132, 301, 303–304, 310–313, 317, 409–411, 413, 414–415; *sitārī* 303, 414
slides xix, xxxviii, 106, 302–304, 311
slur xxxiv, 416. *See also yatī.*
snake charmers 307
song xvii, xix–xx, xxiii, xxvii, xxix, xxxvi–xl, xliii, 7, 20, 50–51, 54–55, 57, (*cont. overleaf*)

song (*cont.*) 60, 64–66, 68, 76–77, 79, 81, 108, 116–117, 119, 125, 131–137, 150, 163, 167, 173, 176, 211, 235, 251, 276, 351, 353–354, 371, 373, 409–414, 416–419, *See also* melody, singer, vocalist, voice. individual song genres by name..
South Asia(n) xv, xvii, xxxix, 423, 425. *See also* India.
speed of sound xxx, 31. *See also* vibration, waves of sound.
spirit xxx, 19, 153, 215, 238, 260, 274–275, 349; soul of the soul 19. *See also* spirituality.
spirituality xi, xxii xxv, xxviii–xxix, 17–10, 25, 29, 349. *See also* spirit.
sruti xxxi, 42–43, 414
structure (musical) xxxix, 19, 83–86, 113, 415; structure of dance 354. *See also surūp.*
Sufi xi, xxi, xxv, xl, 26–27, 224, 409, 427. *See also* Sufism, individual Sufis by name.
Sufism xxv, xxiv, xxx, xxxiii, 6, 414, 420, 421, 427. *See also qavālī, sama'*, Sufis, *urs*.
sukumār 350
Sulaiman (Solomon) 25
sundarī 303, 414
sur xxx, 26–27, 31, 35, 37, 40–44, 77–79, 81–83, 104, 106, 108–110, 112, 117, 126–127, 129–130, 132, 141, 305–306, 369, 414– 416
surbīn 303, 415
surmanḍal 303, 415
sursanghār 304, 415
sursoṭā 304, 415
surtī apang 307, 413
surūp xxxiii, 83–86, 113, 415
sūshir 301, 415
syllable xxxiv–xxxv, xxxviii, xliv–xlv, 35, 80, 106–107, 113, 134, 137, 176, 307, 339–341, 350–354, 359, 363, 405, 410, 415. *See also sargam*.
sympathetic strings 303–304

T

tabla xx, xvii, xxxiii, xxxiv, xxxvi, xliv, 79–80, 132, 134, 339–343, 354, 395–402, 409, 410, 415, 419–420; *tabla ṭhekās* 343–347
Tagore, Sourindro Mohun xxi–xxii, 422
tāl xv, xix, xxvii, xxxiii–xxxv, xxxviii, xli–xliv, 26–28, 35, 78–81, 83–87, 105, 109, 112– 114, 126, 129–130, 132–135, 139, 304–305, 308, 317–322, 323–325, 327–338, 352, 367, 405, 407, 409–412, 414, 415
tāl ang xxiii, 83–84
tāl dādrā 133, 285, 300, 410
tāli 415. *See also* clapping.
tāl jāt xxxiii, 85–86, 411
Tāl Paddhati xxvii, xliv, 343, 346–347
ṭanbūrā (ṭanbūrī) 302, 415
tāṇḍav 349–350, 415
Tansen: Mian Tansen 128, 415: Tansen az-Zaman xi
*taqsīm-i avaqā*t 81
tarāna 15, 128, 134, 415
Turki 188, 404
tār saptak xxxv, 38, 109–110, 311, 415

tārtar saptak 38, 110, 415
tāsh(a) 308, 415
tat xli, 351, 359, 415
Telangana 306
temple xix, xl, 27, 78, 135, 196, 200, 224, 268, 296, 305–307
tempo xxxiv, xl, 26, 104–107, 319, 355, 411, 412, 416. *See also dugun lay, kāl, lay,* time divisions.
Tetālā xxxiii, xli, 85, 90, 132–133, 156–157, 159–160, 162, 167, 169, 177–178, 317, 318–325, 327–328, 330–331, 333–337, 343, 345, 367. *See also Tīntāl.*
ṭhāṭ 314, 415
ṭhekā 343–347, 354, 415
throat xxx, 26, 33, 133–134, 308
ṭhumrī xxxvii, xxxix, 128, 133, 415
tigun kī lay xxxiv, 104, 415
time division 83–84, 409–413, 415; timing xxxiii–xxxiv, 79, 81–82, 104, 354. *See also* tempo.
Tīntāl xxxiii, xli. *See also Tetālā*
Tipu Sultan xxi
tirvaṭ xxxix, 134, 176, 178–179, 415
tisra jāt xxxii, 85, 415
tīvra xxxv, xxxviii, 28, 40–42, 45, 109–110, 311, 415. *See also* sharp note.
tone xix, xxx–xxxi, xxxv, xxxviii–xxix, 16, 33, 40–41, 137, 305, 307, 350, 414. *See also sargam.*
toṛā xlv, 311–312, 352, 364–365, 405–407, 415. *See also* variations.
trivaṛī xxxiii, 415
Tukaram, Guru 78
tumburu 302, 415
tumburu bīn 302, 415
tura'ī 307, 415
tūtārī 301, 307, 415

U

United States xxv, 427
Urdu xi, xv, xvii,xix, xxvii–xxix, xxxii–xxxiii, xxxvi, xxxix, xl–xliii, 134, 181, 209, 306, 409, 419, 421–422; Urdu poetry xxxvii
urs xxv, 78, 415
ustād xxix, 23, 35, 129, 133, 136, 350, 416: *See also* master.
ūtarī 40

V

vādan 25, 128, 301, 411
vādī vi, 43–44; *vādī—vivādī* 416
Vadodara. *See* Baroda.
vakra sampūrn rāg xxxi, 45
variations xx, xlii, xliv, 6, 311–312, 416. *See also fiqrā, toṛā.*
varnam xxxix, 135–136, 179–180, 416
veil xl, 29, 185, 239, 352–353, 361; unveiling 188, 262. *See also* scarf.
vibration xxx, 30. *See also* waves of sound.
vīlamb kāl 104–105, 416
vīnā 302–303, 415. *See also bīn.*
vitat xxxli, 301, 416
vivādī sur xxxi, 43–44, 416
vocalist xi, xx, 130–131. *See also* singer, voice.
voice xxx, xxxvii, xli, 4–6, 16, 20, 31, 33, 37–38, (*cont. overleaf*)

voice (*cont.*) 106–107, 126, 130–133, 136, 202, 301, 371; animal voice 37, 103, 131. *See also* singer, throat, vocalist.

W

waves of sound xxx, 30–31, 33–34. *See also* speed of sound.
waves of the hand xxxv, xxxviii, 80, 130. *See also* *kh̲ālī.*
wedding 28, 79, 305–306, 415
West(ern) xx, xxix, xxxi– xxxiii, xxxv–xxxvi, 36, 39, 41–42, 44, 81, 83, 103; Western notation xxix, xxxi– xxxiii, 39. *See also* England, Europe.
wind instrument 409, 412–415
women xxxvii, 33, 127, 131, 134–135, 150, 156, 305, 349–351, 422; female xxxi–xxxii, 46, 304, 351, 367; female singers 304; female voice 33, 131; feminine xxxvii, xlv, 131, 349– 350. *See also* goddess.
See also female.

Y

yatī xxxiv–xxxv, xxxviii, 106–107, 113, 416. *See also* slur.

Z

Zafar: Mirza Abu Zafar Sirajuddin Muhammad Bahadur Shah Zafar 238–239, 265, 274, 404
Zahir 226, 404
Zamin 187, 404
Ẕila' xxxli, 162

The Inayati Order is an international organization dedicated to spreading the Sufi Message of Hazrat Inayat Khan, who introduced Sufism to the Western world in 1910. Its objective is to realize and spread the knowledge of unity, the religion of love and wisdom, so that the human heart may overflow with love, and all animosity caused by distinctions and differences may be rooted out.

For more information, please contact:
The Inayati Order
www.inayatiorder.org
112 East Cary Street
Richmond Virginia 23219

CPSIA information can be obtained
at www.ICGtesting.com
Printed in the USA
BVHW041601080620
581024BV00006B/367